X AMAZING X-MEN

ONCE AND FUTURE JUGGERNAUT

JAMES
TYNION IV
WRITER

JORGE
JIMÉNEZ
PENCILER

RACHELLE
ROSENBERG
COLORIST

COVER ART: **NICK BRADSHAW & RACHELLE ROSENBERG**

ISSUE #13

CHRISTOPHER
YOST
WRITER

CARLO
BARBERI & COELLO
PENCILERS

IBAN

WALDEN
WONG & COELLO
INKERS

IBAN

RACHELLE
ROSENBERG
COLORIST

COVER ART: **KRIS ANKA**

ISSUE #14

CHRISTOPHER
YOST
WRITER

JORGE
FORNÉS
ARTIST

RACHELLE
ROSENBERG
COLORIST

COVER ART: **KRIS ANKA (#15-16)**
AND **JORGE FORNÉS & RACHELLE ROSENBERG (#17-19)**

ISSUES #15-19

"GODDESS"
WRITER: **MONTY NERO**
PENCILER: **SALVADOR LARROCA**
COLORIST: **SONIA OBACK**

"ART HISTORY"
WRITER: **MARGUERITE BENNETT**
PENCILER: **JUAN DOE**

COVER ART: **SALVADOR LARROCA**

ANNUAL #1

LETTERER: **JOE CARAMAGNA** WITH TRAVIS LANHAM (#14)
EDITOR: **XANDER JAROWEY**
X-MEN GROUP EDITOR: **MIKE MARTS**

X-MEN CREATED BY STAN LEE & JACK KIRBY

COLLECTION EDITOR: **JENNIFER GRÜNWALD** ASSISTANT EDITOR: **SARAH BRUNSTAD**
ASSOCIATE MANAGING EDITOR: **ALEX STARBUCK** EDITOR, SPECIAL PROJECTS: **MARK D. BEAZLEY**
SENIOR EDITOR, SPECIAL PROJECTS: **JEFF YOUNGQUIST** SVP PRINT, SALES & MARKETING: **DAVID GABRIEL**

EDITOR IN CHIEF: **AXEL ALONSO** CHIEF CREATIVE OFFICER: **JOE QUESADA**
PUBLISHER: **DAN BUCKLEY** EXECUTIVE PRODUCER: **ALAN FINE**

AMAZING X-MEN VOL. 3: ONCE AND FUTURE JUGGERNAUT. Contains material originally published in magazine form as AMAZING X-MEN #13-19 and ANNUAL #1. First printing 2015. ISBN# 978-0-7851-9248-0. Published by MARVEL WORLDWIDE, INC., a subsidiary of MARVEL ENTERTAINMENT, LLC. OFFICE OF PUBLICATION: 135 West 50th Street, New York, NY 10020. Copyright © 2015 MARVEL No similarity between any of the names, characters, persons, and/or institutions in this magazine with those of any living or dead person or institution is intended, and any such similarity which may exist is purely coincidental. Printed in the U.S.A. ALAN FINE, President, Marvel Entertainment; DAN BUCKLEY, President, TV, Publishing and Brand Management; JOE QUESADA, Chief Creative Officer; TOM BREVOORT, SVP of Publishing; DAVID BOGART, SVP of Operations & Procurement, Publishing; C.B. CEBULSKI, VP of International Development & Brand Management; DAVID GABRIEL, SVP Print, Sales & Marketing; JIM O'KEEFE, VP of Operations & Logistics; DAN CARR, Executive Director of Publishing Technology; SUSAN CRESPI, Editorial Operations Manager; ALEX MORALES, Publishing Operations Manager; STAN LEE, Chairman Emeritus. For information regarding advertising in Marvel Comics or on Marvel.com, please contact Jonathan Rheingold, VP of Custom Solutions & Ad Sales, at jrheingold@marvel.com. For Marvel subscription inquiries, please call 800-217-9158. Manufactured between 4/24/2015 and 6/1/2015 by R.R. DONNELLEY, INC., SALEM, VA, USA.

10 9 8 7 6 5 4 3 2 1

PREVIOUSLY

Born with genetic mutations that give them abilities beyond those of normal humans, mutants are the next stage in evolution. As such, they are feared and hated by humanity. But a group of mutants known as the X-Men fight for peaceful coexistence between humans and mutants.

At the Jean Grey School for Higher Learning, young mutants are taught to use and control their unusual abilities. Their teachers, being mutants themselves, know all too well how cruel the world can be to their kind, especially for those mutants who are unable to hide their mutations. Despite doing their best to help their young charges cope with a world that rejects them, for some students it can feel like a burden too heavy to bear. When all you want is to be a normal teenager, even superpowers can feel like a poor consolation prize.

Recently, the Red Skull utilized the stolen psychic power of the deceased mutant Charles Xavier to round up and execute mutants. Trying to put an end to his evil, Doctor Strange, the Scarlet Witch and Doctor Doom cast an immensely powerful spell. Though the spell seemed to defeat the threat of the Skull, those who were present for its casting seem to have somehow been affected. Among their number is Kurt Wagner, known as Nightcrawler. Gifted with a mutation he was unable to conceal, Nightcrawler was abandoned by his mother, Mystique, shortly following his birth. In his time with the X-Men, he has come in contact with his mother many times, but has always managed to rise above the hatred. However, sometimes the purest souls are the ones most easily tainted.

With the recent deaths of Charles Xavier and Wolverine, the Jean Grey School has been left in chaos. The X-Men are splintered and broken, and with the future of mutantkind hanging in the balance, ideological differences have set lifelong friends against each other. In the wake of the schism, many of the X-Men have found themselves lost and searching for purpose. One of these X-Men is Piotr Rasputin, known as Colossus. He has seen his family torn apart, even having his sister captured by the demon Belasco and infected by the dark magic of his realm Limbo. He watched as the women he loved were kidnapped, lost and killed. He has died and been resurrected. And he has had his mind possessed and perverted by beings such as the Phoenix and Cyttorak. A man who once stood as a shining, metal example of good has seen his soul tainted by his choices and the blood of those he's killed. Despite all this, he was given a chance at redemption by Wolverine, rejoining the X-Men at the Jean Grey School. However, facing his demons will take more than just some free room and board.

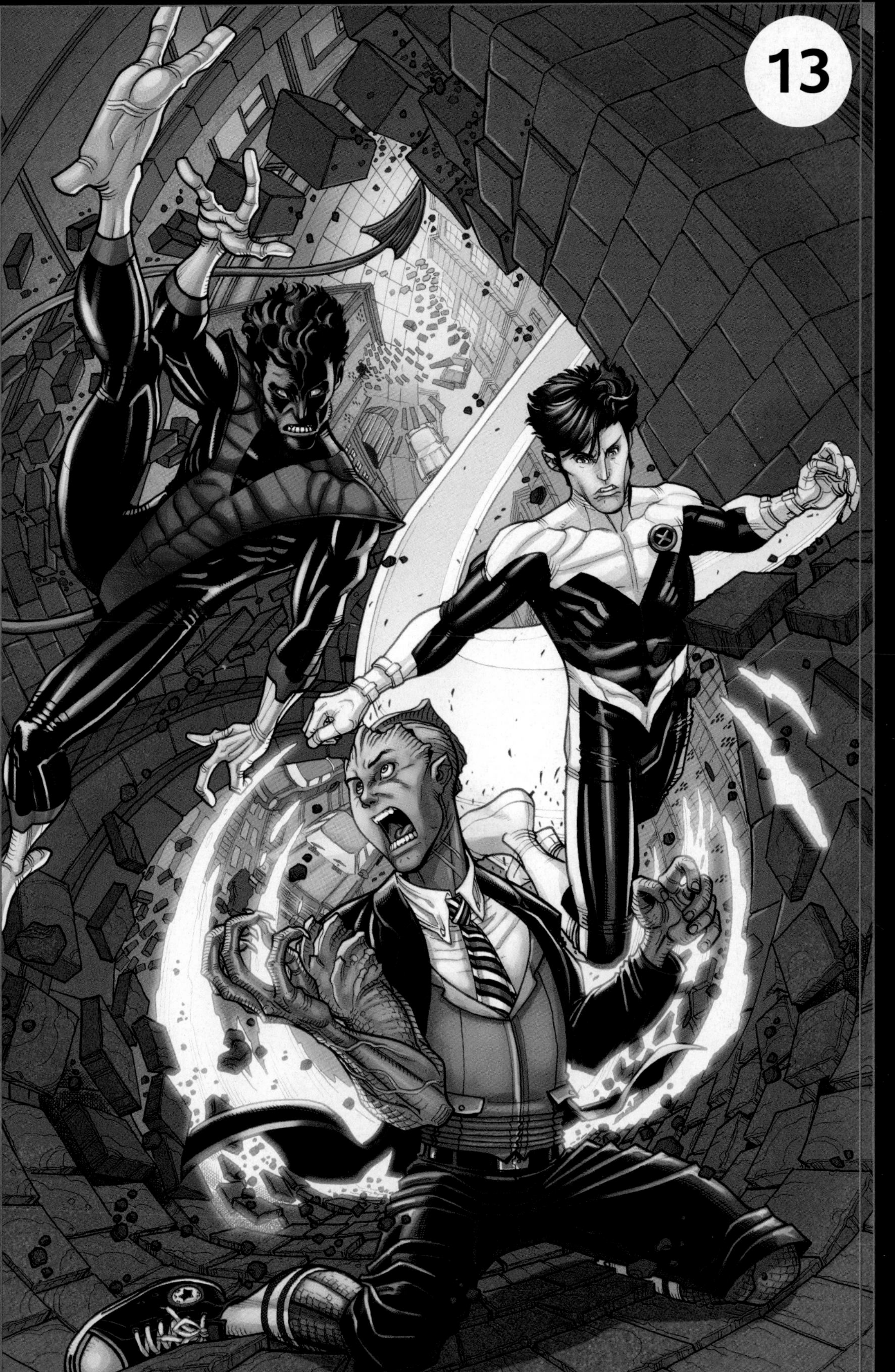
13

CHARM SCHOOL

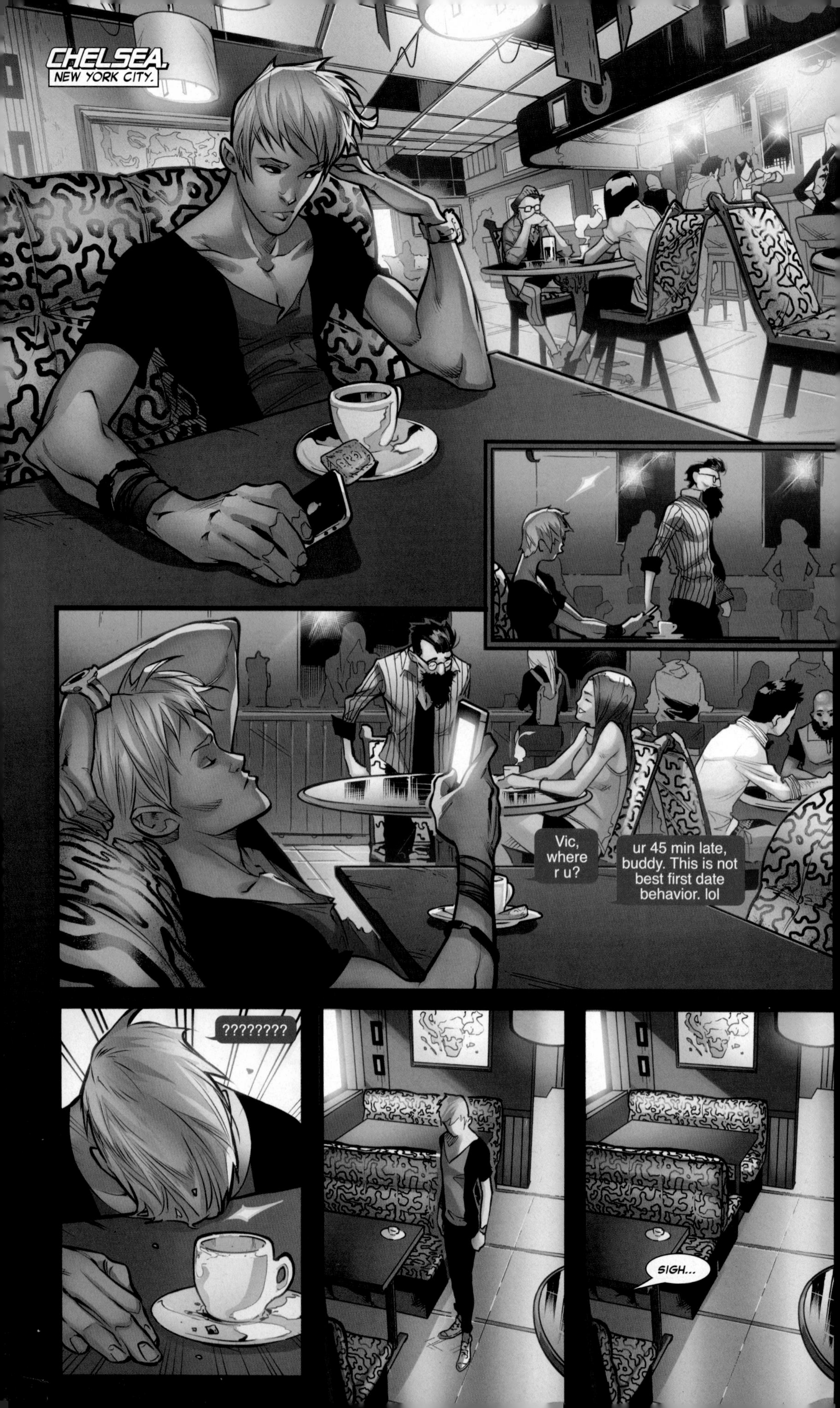

CHELSEA.
NEW YORK CITY.
Vic, where r u?
ur 45 min late, buddy. This is not best first date behavior. lol
????????
SIGH...

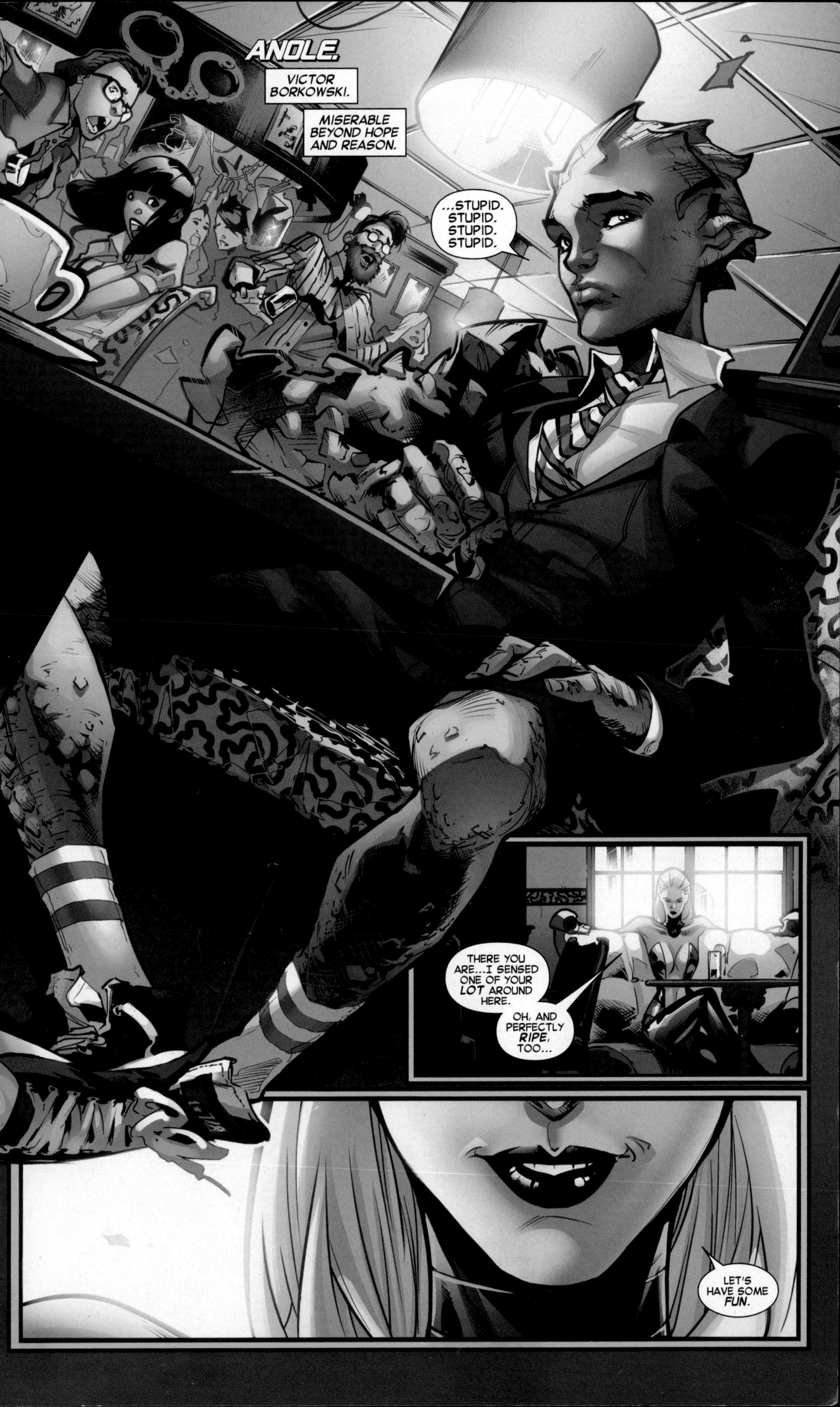

ANOLE.
VICTOR BORKOWSKI.
MISERABLE BEYOND HOPE AND REASON.
...STUPID. STUPID. STUPID. STUPID.
THERE YOU ARE...I SENSED ONE OF YOUR LOT AROUND HERE.
OH, AND PERFECTLY RIPE, TOO...
LET'S HAVE SOME FUN.

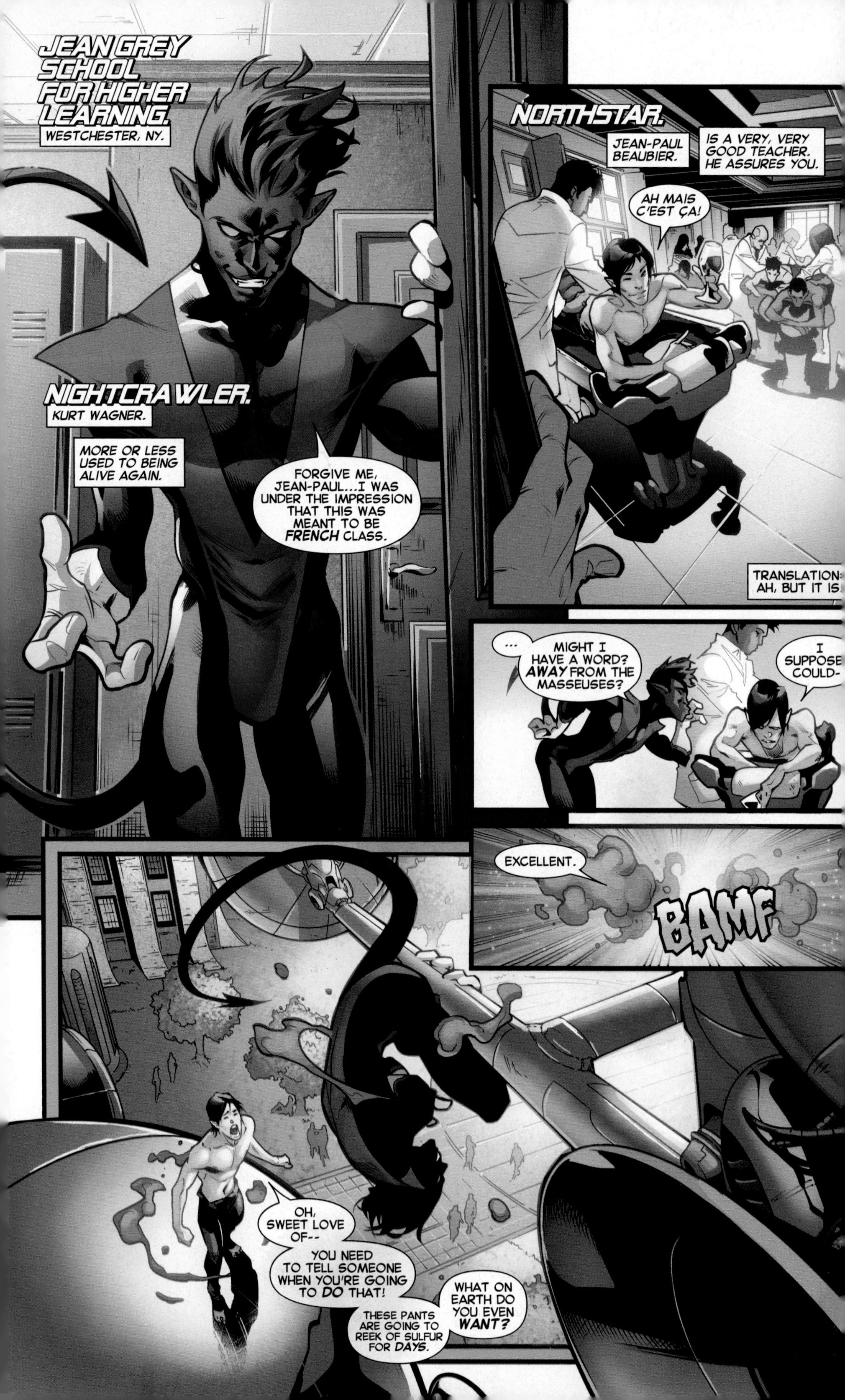
JEAN GREY SCHOOL FOR HIGHER LEARNING.
WESTCHESTER, NY.
NIGHTCRAWLER.
KURT WAGNER.
MORE OR LESS USED TO BEING ALIVE AGAIN.
FORGIVE ME, JEAN-PAUL...I WAS UNDER THE IMPRESSION THAT THIS WAS MEANT TO BE FRENCH CLASS.
NORTHSTAR.
JEAN-PAUL BEAUBIER.
IS A VERY, VERY GOOD TEACHER. HE ASSURES YOU.
AH MAIS C'EST ÇA!
TRANSLATION: AH, BUT IT IS.
...
MIGHT I HAVE A WORD? AWAY FROM THE MASSEUSES?
I SUPPOSE I COULD-
EXCELLENT.
BAMF
OH, SWEET LOVE OF--
YOU NEED TO TELL SOMEONE WHEN YOU'RE GOING TO DO THAT!
THESE PANTS ARE GOING TO REEK OF SULFUR FOR DAYS.
WHAT ON EARTH DO YOU EVEN WANT?

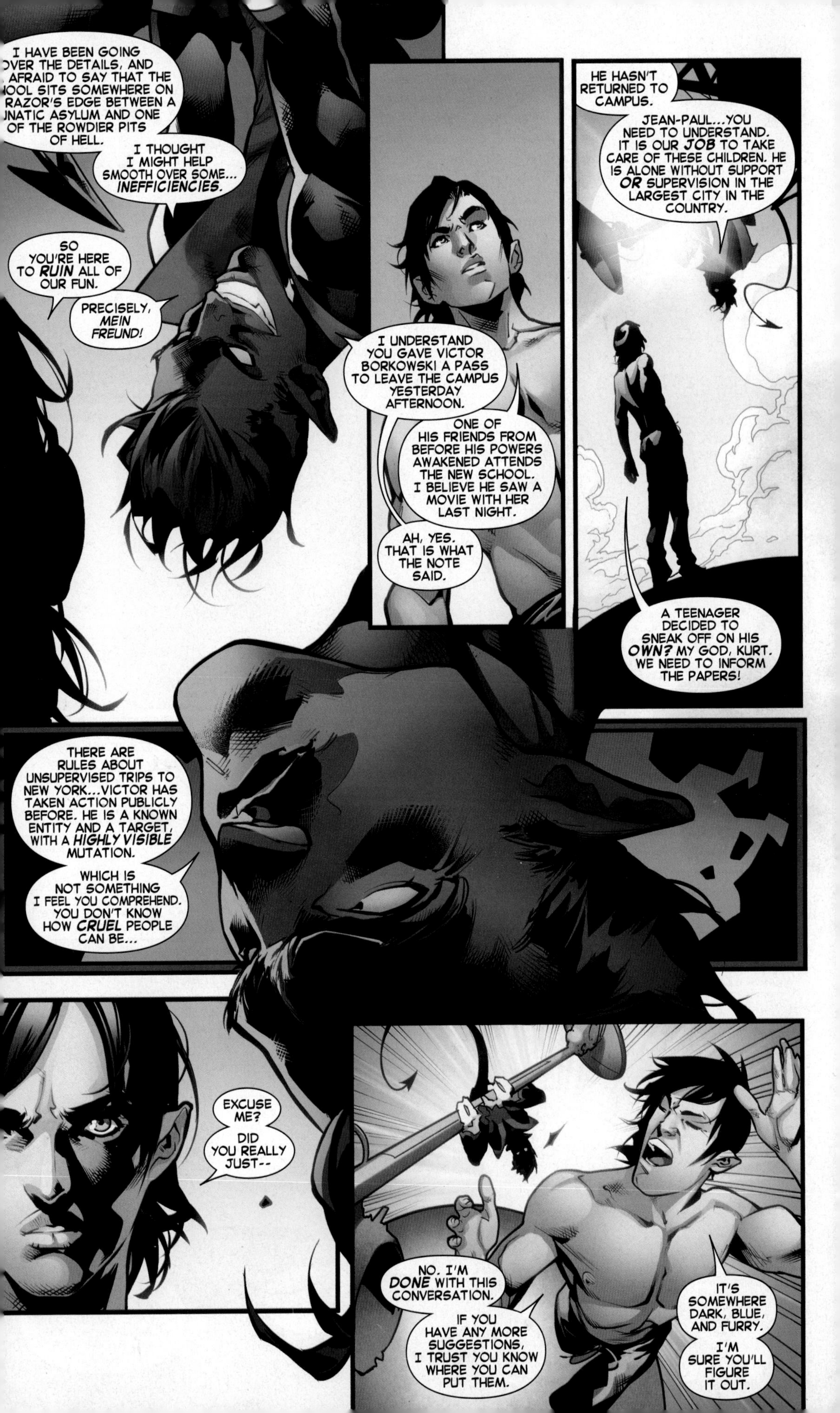
I HAVE BEEN GOING OVER THE DETAILS, AND AFRAID TO SAY THAT THE HOOL SITS SOMEWHERE ON RAZOR'S EDGE BETWEEN A UNATIC ASYLUM AND ONE OF THE ROWDIER PITS OF HELL.
I THOUGHT I MIGHT HELP SMOOTH OVER SOME... INEFFICIENCIES.
SO YOU'RE HERE TO RUIN ALL OF OUR FUN.
PRECISELY, MEIN FREUND!
I UNDERSTAND YOU GAVE VICTOR BORKOWSKI A PASS TO LEAVE THE CAMPUS YESTERDAY AFTERNOON.
ONE OF HIS FRIENDS FROM BEFORE HIS POWERS AWAKENED ATTENDS THE NEW SCHOOL. I BELIEVE HE SAW A MOVIE WITH HER LAST NIGHT.
AH, YES. THAT IS WHAT THE NOTE SAID.
HE HASN'T RETURNED TO CAMPUS.
JEAN-PAUL...YOU NEED TO UNDERSTAND. IT IS OUR JOB TO TAKE CARE OF THESE CHILDREN. HE IS ALONE WITHOUT SUPPORT OR SUPERVISION IN THE LARGEST CITY IN THE COUNTRY.
A TEENAGER DECIDED TO SNEAK OFF ON HIS OWN? MY GOD, KURT. WE NEED TO INFORM THE PAPERS!
THERE ARE RULES ABOUT UNSUPERVISED TRIPS TO NEW YORK...VICTOR HAS TAKEN ACTION PUBLICLY BEFORE. HE IS A KNOWN ENTITY AND A TARGET, WITH A HIGHLY VISIBLE MUTATION.
WHICH IS NOT SOMETHING I FEEL YOU COMPREHEND. YOU DON'T KNOW HOW CRUEL PEOPLE CAN BE...
EXCUSE ME? DID YOU REALLY JUST--
NO. I'M DONE WITH THIS CONVERSATION.
IF YOU HAVE ANY MORE SUGGESTIONS, I TRUST YOU KNOW WHERE YOU CAN PUT THEM.
IT'S SOMEWHERE DARK, BLUE, AND FURRY.
I'M SURE YOU'LL FIGURE IT OUT.

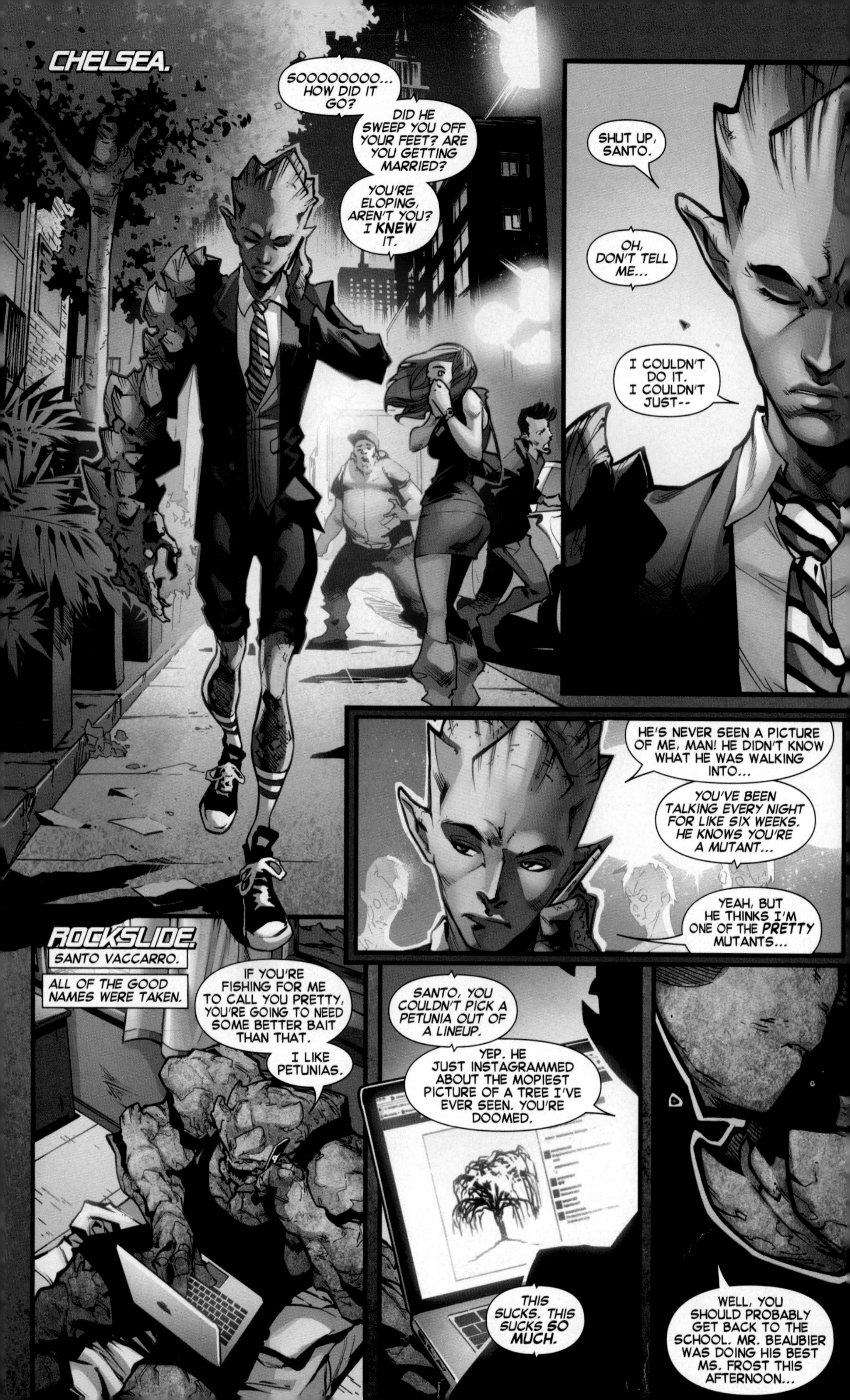
CHELSEA.
SOOOOOOOO... HOW DID IT GO?
DID HE SWEEP YOU OFF YOUR FEET? ARE YOU GETTING MARRIED?
YOU'RE ELOPING, AREN'T YOU? I KNEW IT.
SHUT UP, SANTO.
OH, DON'T TELL ME...
I COULDN'T DO IT. I COULDN'T JUST--
HE'S NEVER SEEN A PICTURE OF ME, MAN! HE DIDN'T KNOW WHAT HE WAS WALKING INTO...
YOU'VE BEEN TALKING EVERY NIGHT FOR LIKE SIX WEEKS. HE KNOWS YOU'RE A MUTANT...
YEAH, BUT HE THINKS I'M ONE OF THE PRETTY MUTANTS...
ROCKSLIDE.
SANTO VACCARRO.
ALL OF THE GOOD NAMES WERE TAKEN.
IF YOU'RE FISHING FOR ME TO CALL YOU PRETTY, YOU'RE GOING TO NEED SOME BETTER BAIT THAN THAT.
I LIKE PETUNIAS.
SANTO, YOU COULDN'T PICK A PETUNIA OUT OF A LINEUP.
YEP. HE JUST INSTAGRAMMED ABOUT THE MOPIEST PICTURE OF A TREE I'VE EVER SEEN. YOU'RE DOOMED.
THIS SUCKS. THIS SUCKS SO MUCH.
WELL, YOU SHOULD PROBABLY GET BACK TO THE SCHOOL. MR. BEAUBIER WAS DOING HIS BEST MS. FROST THIS AFTERNOON...

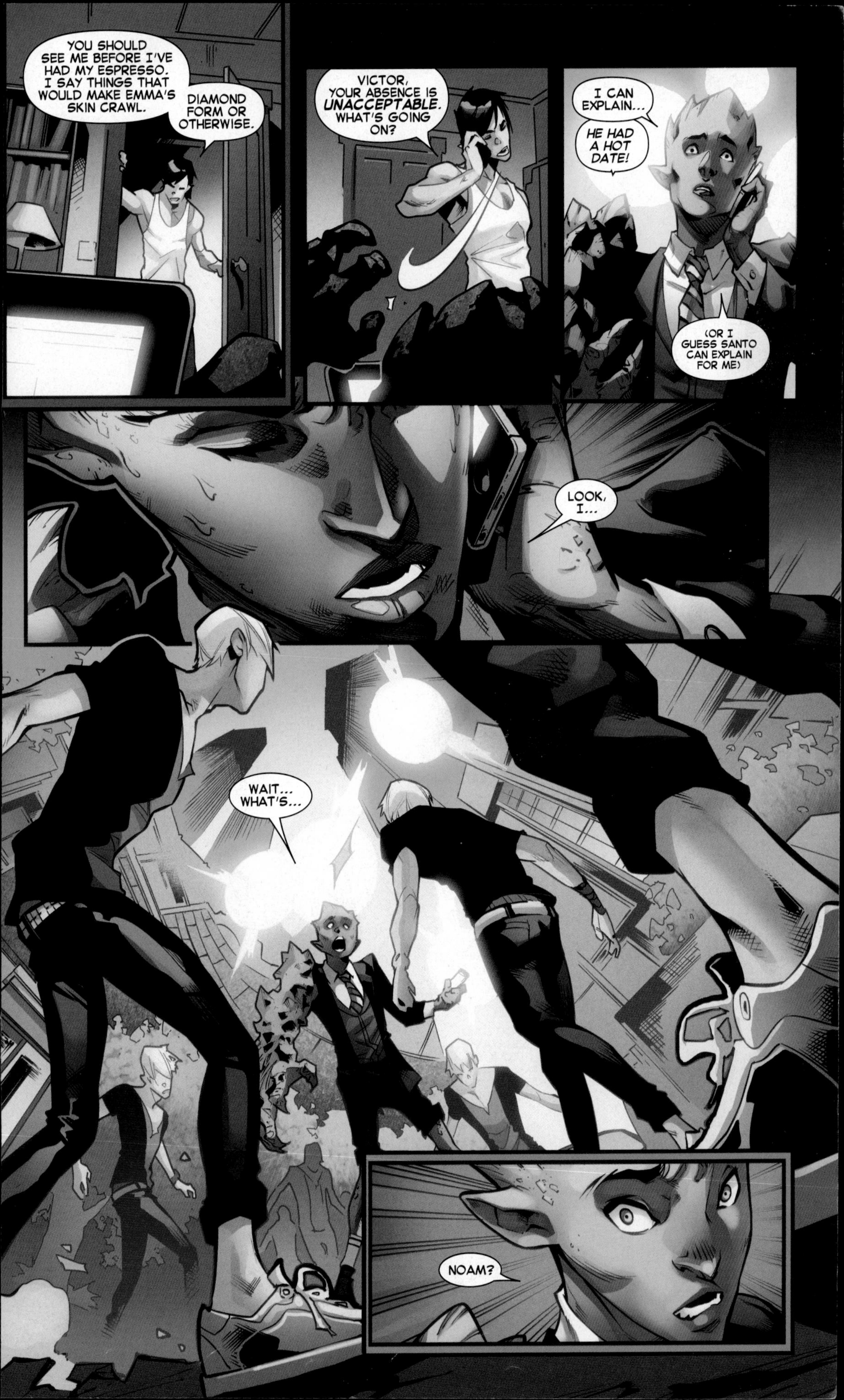
YOU SHOULD SEE ME BEFORE I'VE HAD MY ESPRESSO. I SAY THINGS THAT WOULD MAKE EMMA'S SKIN CRAWL.
DIAMOND FORM OR OTHERWISE.
VICTOR, YOUR ABSENCE IS UNACCEPTABLE. WHAT'S GOING ON?
I CAN EXPLAIN...
HE HAD A HOT DATE!
(OR I GUESS SANTO CAN EXPLAIN FOR ME)
LOOK, I...
WAIT... WHAT'S...
NOAM?

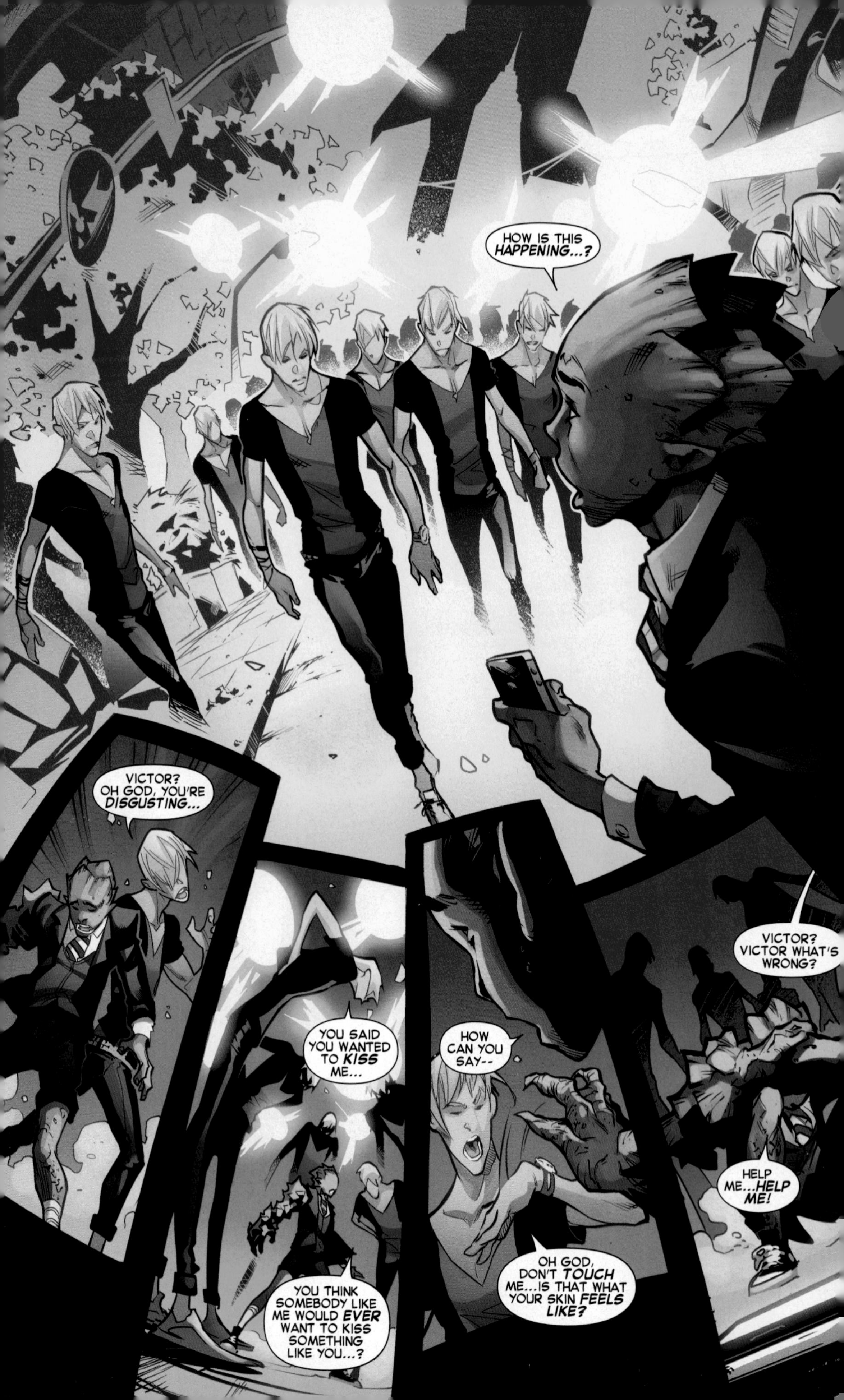
HOW IS THIS HAPPENING...?
VICTOR? OH GOD, YOU'RE DISGUSTING...
YOU SAID YOU WANTED TO KISS ME...
YOU THINK SOMEBODY LIKE ME WOULD EVER WANT TO KISS SOMETHING LIKE YOU...?
HOW CAN YOU SAY--
OH GOD, DON'T TOUCH ME...IS THAT WHAT YOUR SKIN FEELS LIKE?
VICTOR? VICTOR WHAT'S WRONG?
HELP ME...HELP ME!

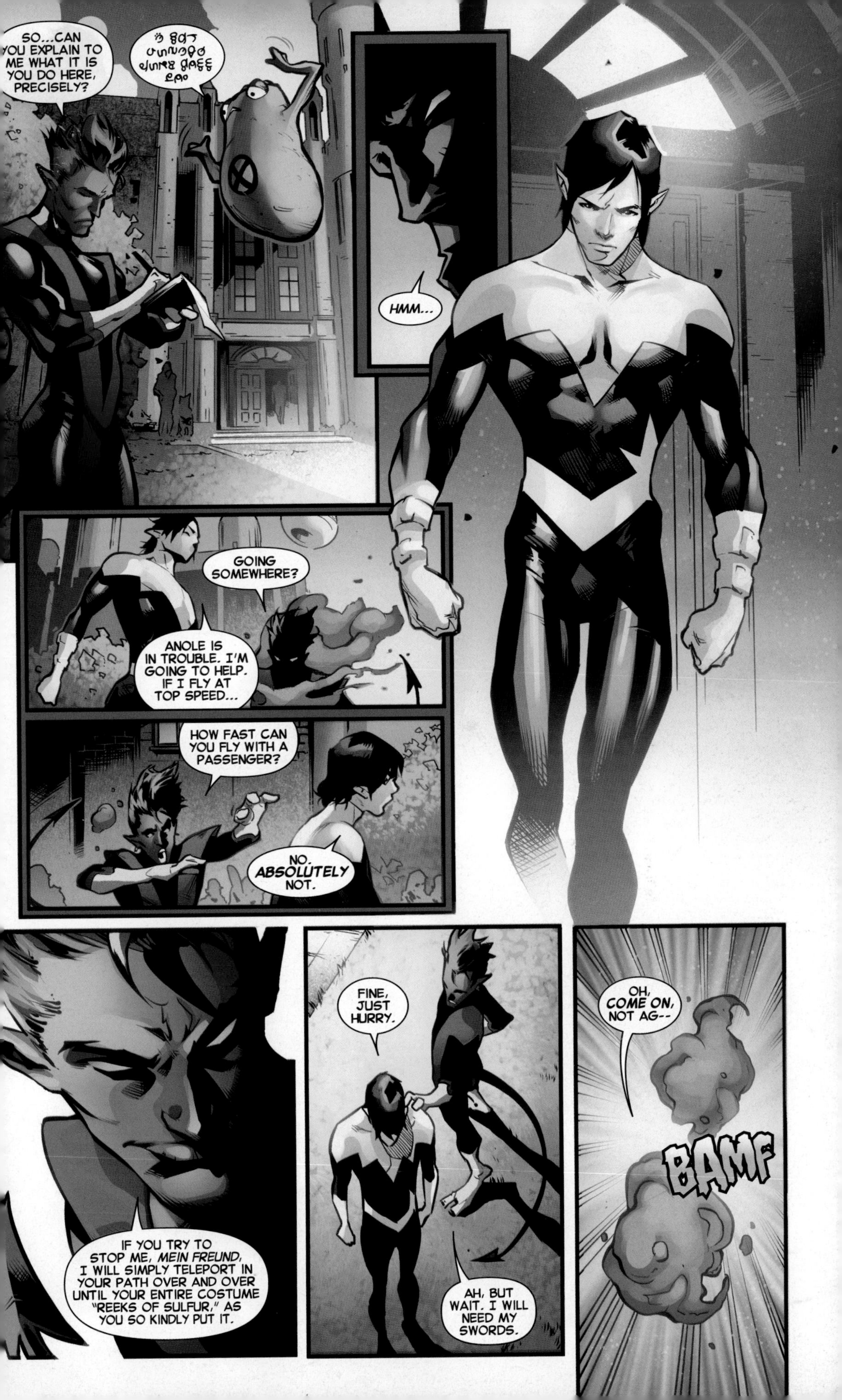

SO...CAN YOU EXPLAIN TO ME WHAT IT IS YOU DO HERE, PRECISELY?
HMM...
GOING SOMEWHERE?
ANOLE IS IN TROUBLE. I'M GOING TO HELP. IF I FLY AT TOP SPEED...
HOW FAST CAN YOU FLY WITH A PASSENGER?
NO. ABSOLUTELY NOT.
IF YOU TRY TO STOP ME, MEIN FREUND, I WILL SIMPLY TELEPORT IN YOUR PATH OVER AND OVER UNTIL YOUR ENTIRE COSTUME "REEKS OF SULFUR," AS YOU SO KINDLY PUT IT.
FINE, JUST HURRY.
AH, BUT WAIT. I WILL NEED MY SWORDS.
OH, COME ON, NOT AG--
BAMF

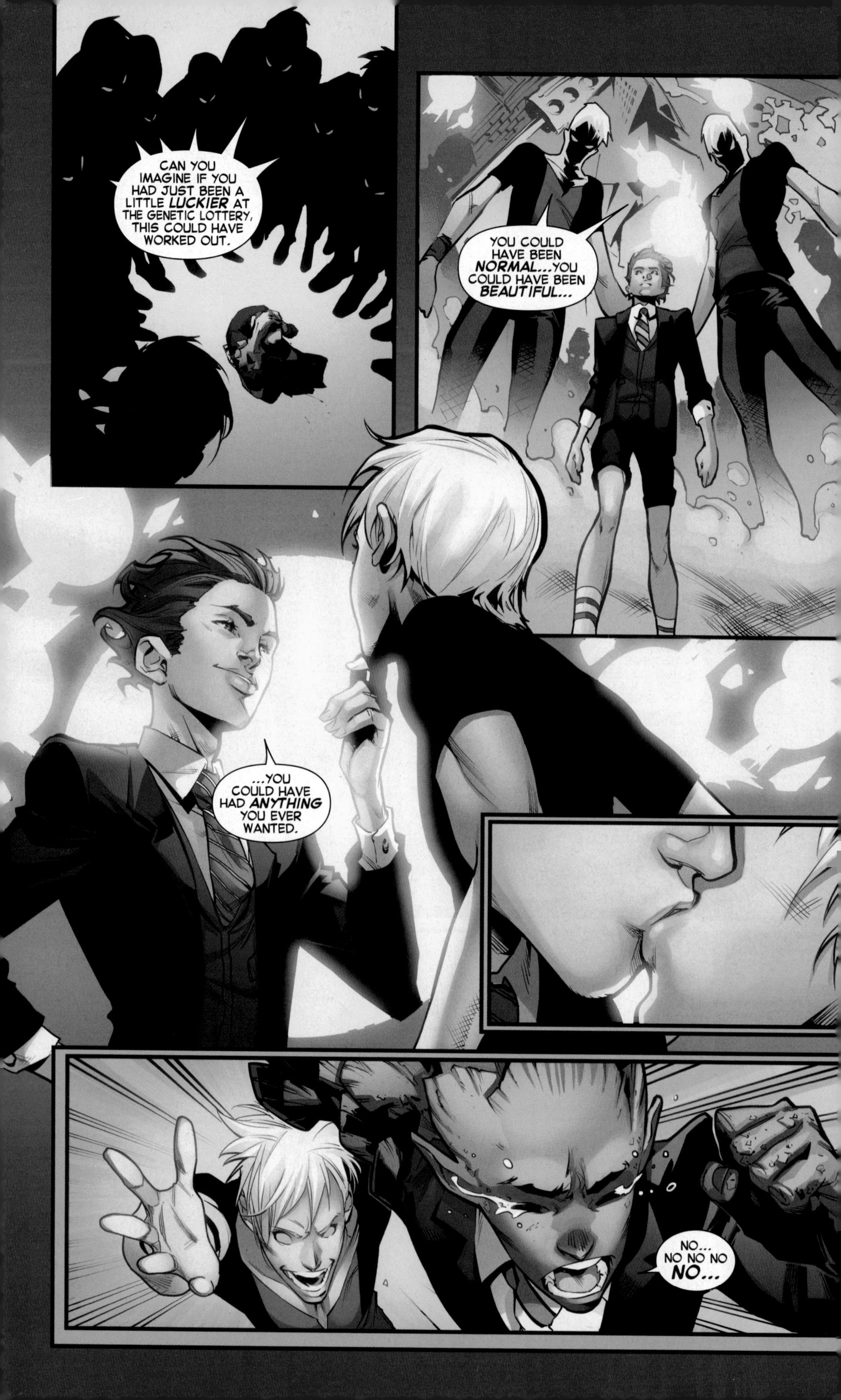
CAN YOU IMAGINE IF YOU HAD JUST BEEN A LITTLE LUCKIER AT THE GENETIC LOTTERY, THIS COULD HAVE WORKED OUT.
YOU COULD HAVE BEEN NORMAL...YOU COULD HAVE BEEN BEAUTIFUL...
...YOU COULD HAVE HAD ANYTHING YOU EVER WANTED.
NO... NO NO NO NO...

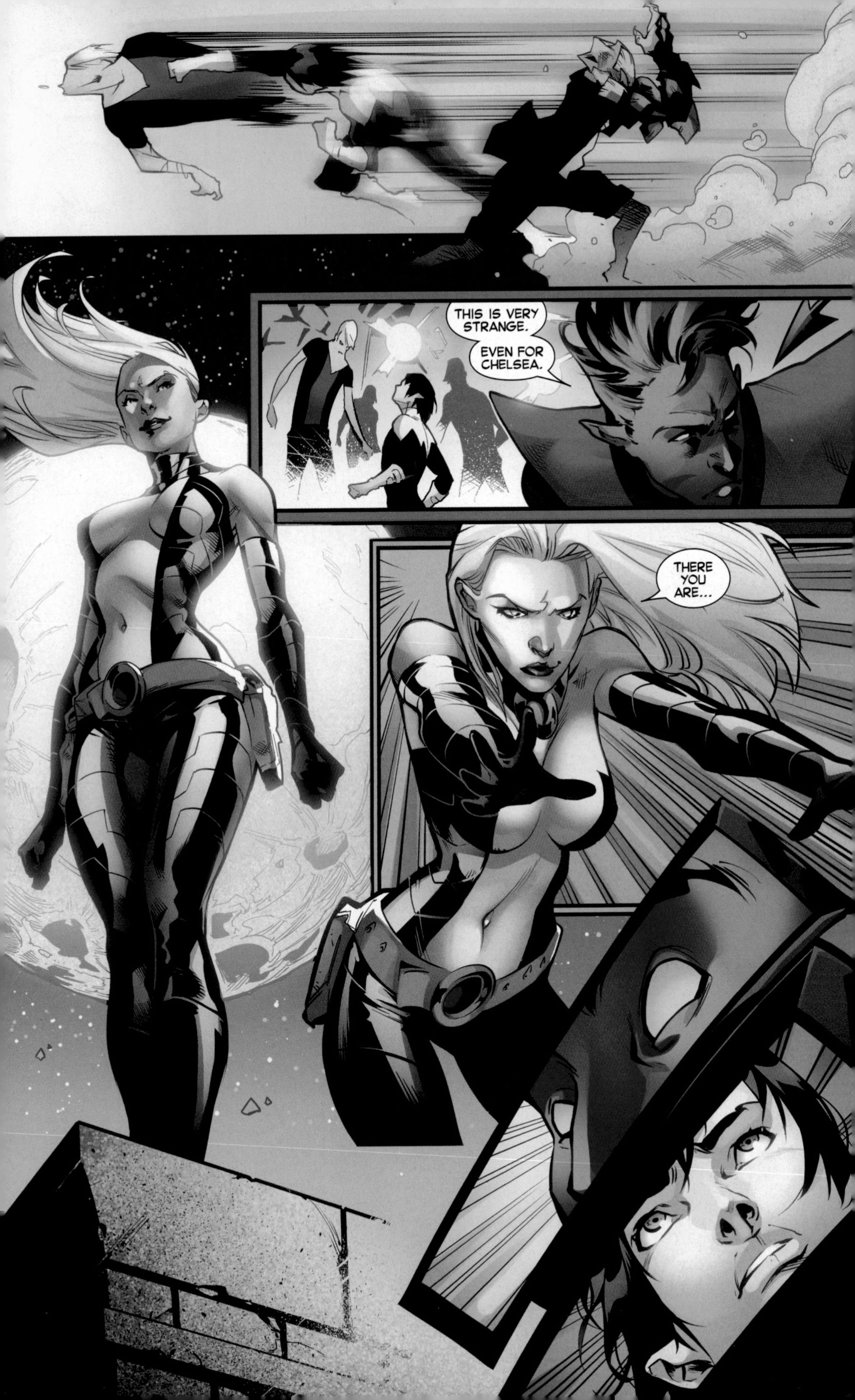
THIS IS VERY STRANGE.
EVEN FOR CHELSEA.
THERE YOU ARE...

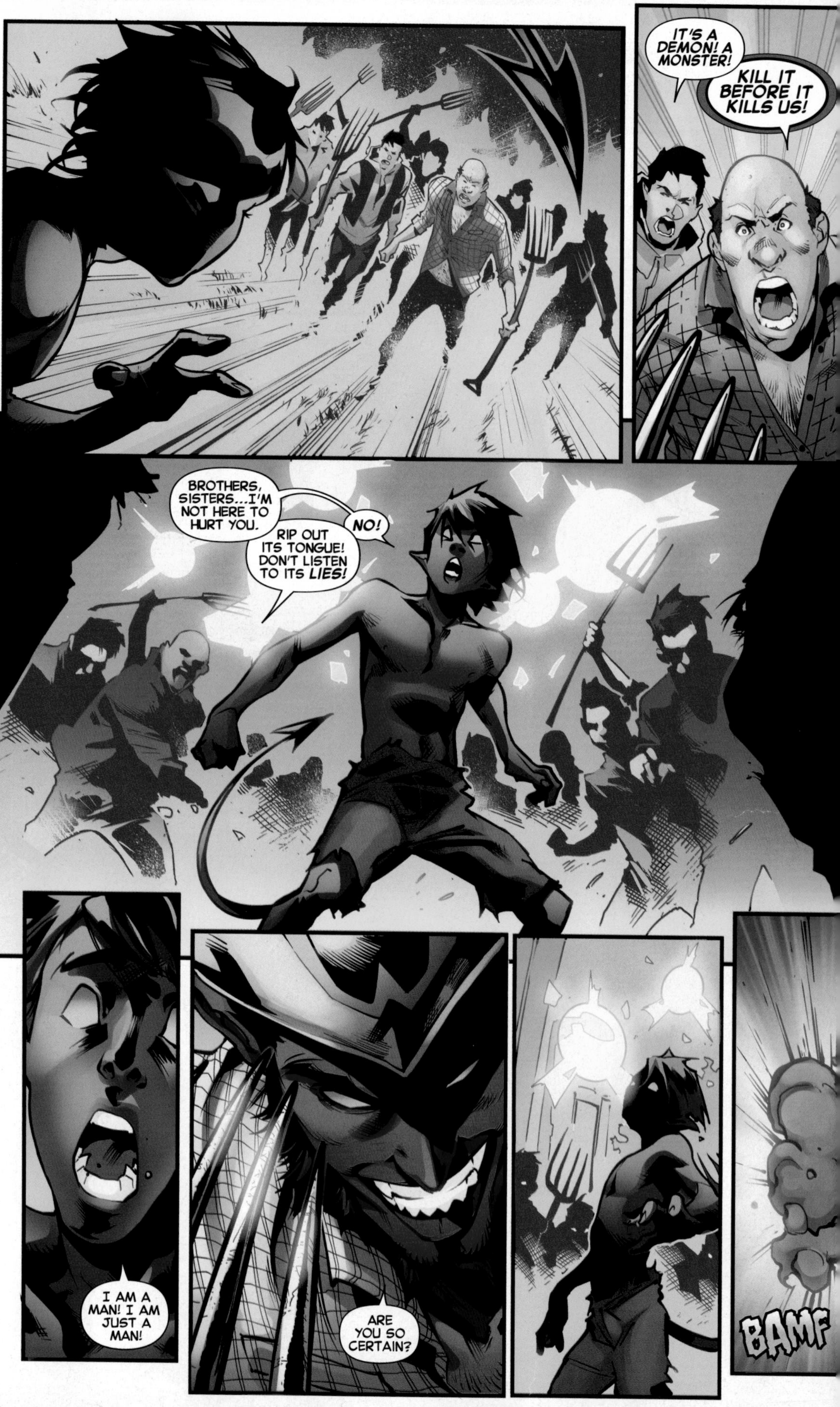
IT'S A DEMON! A MONSTER!
KILL IT BEFORE IT KILLS US!
BROTHERS, SISTERS...I'M NOT HERE TO HURT YOU.
NO!
RIP OUT ITS TONGUE! DON'T LISTEN TO ITS LIES!
I AM A MAN! I AM JUST A MAN!
ARE YOU SO CERTAIN?
BAMF

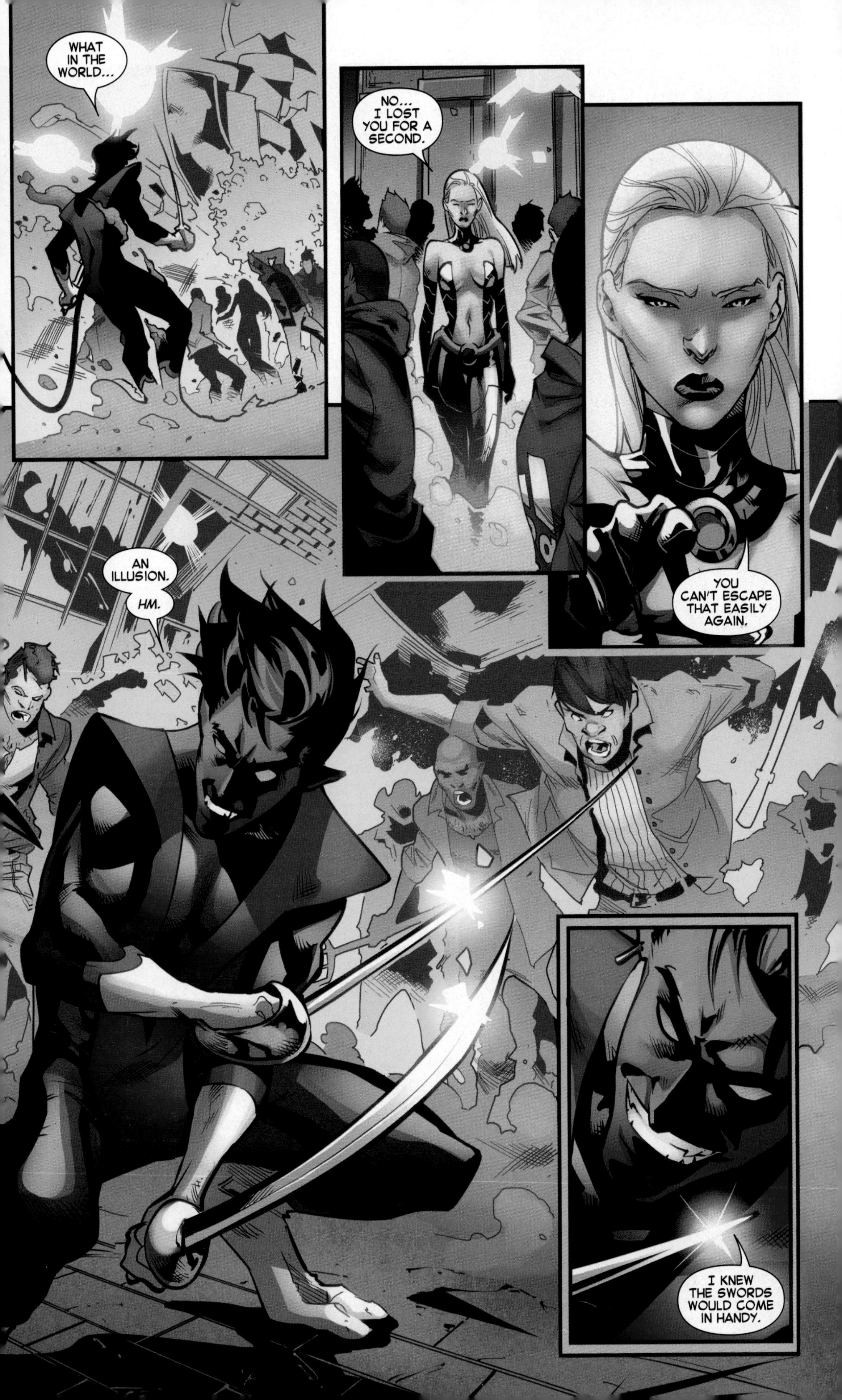
WHAT IN THE WORLD...
NO... I LOST YOU FOR A SECOND.
YOU CAN'T ESCAPE THAT EASILY AGAIN.
AN ILLUSION.
HM.
I KNEW THE SWORDS WOULD COME IN HANDY.

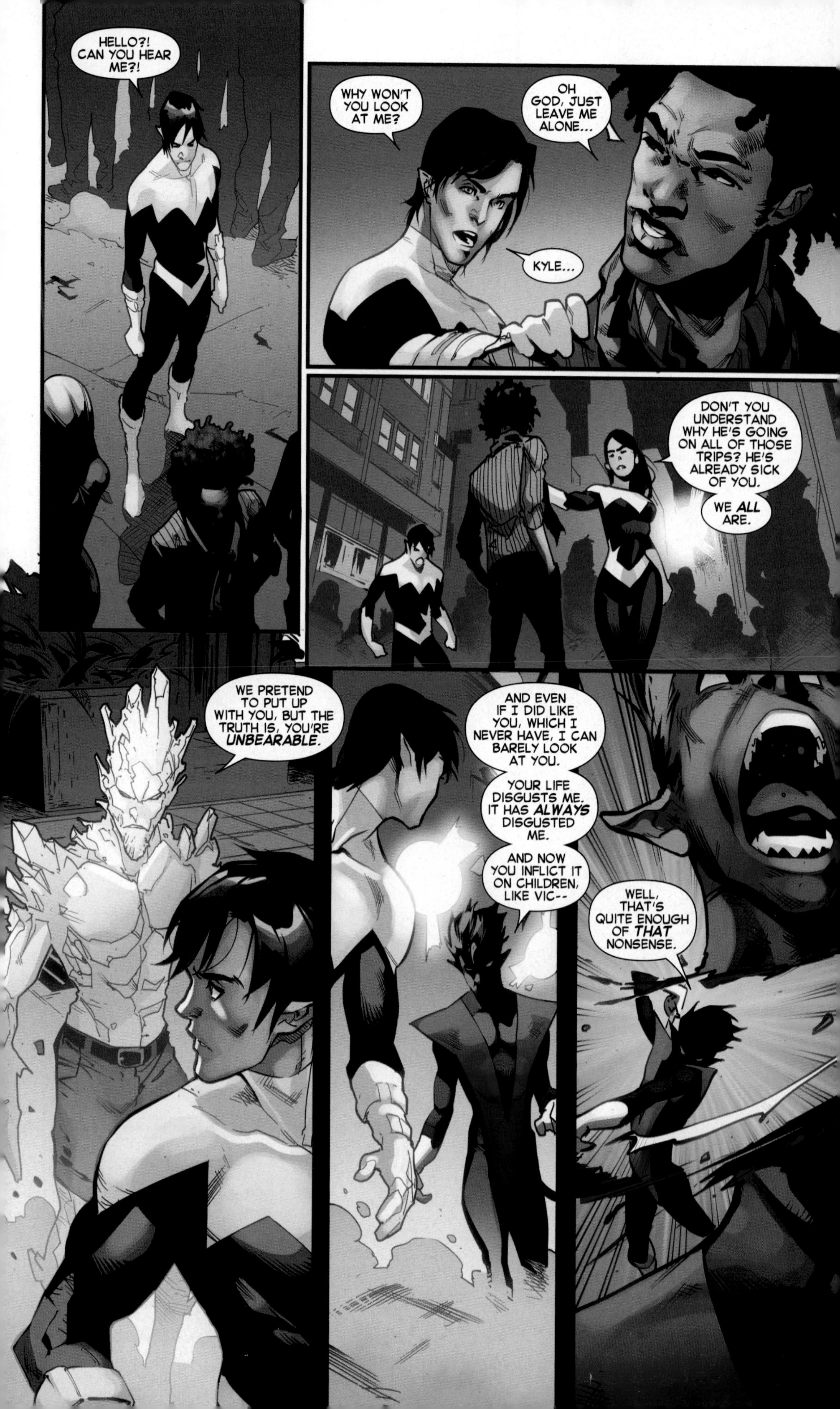
HELLO?! CAN YOU HEAR ME?!
WHY WON'T YOU LOOK AT ME?
OH GOD, JUST LEAVE ME ALONE...
KYLE...
DON'T YOU UNDERSTAND WHY HE'S GOING ON ALL OF THOSE TRIPS? HE'S ALREADY SICK OF YOU.
WE *ALL* ARE.
WE PRETEND TO PUT UP WITH YOU, BUT THE TRUTH IS, YOU'RE *UNBEARABLE*.
AND EVEN IF I DID LIKE YOU, WHICH I NEVER HAVE, I CAN BARELY LOOK AT YOU.
YOUR LIFE DISGUSTS ME. IT HAS *ALWAYS* DISGUSTED ME.
AND NOW YOU INFLICT IT ON CHILDREN, LIKE VIC--
WELL, THAT'S QUITE ENOUGH OF *THAT* NONSENSE.

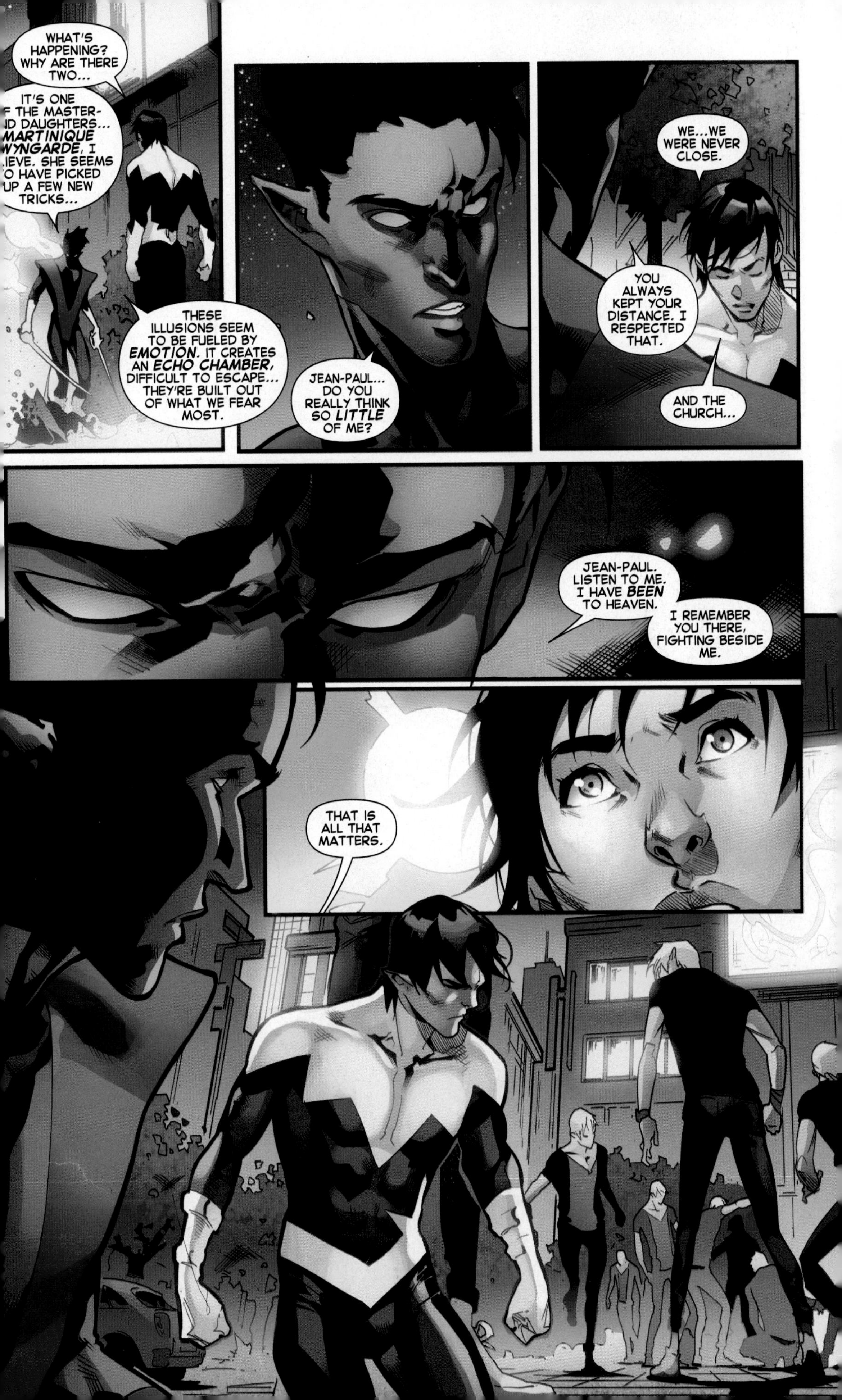

WHAT'S HAPPENING? WHY ARE THERE TWO...
IT'S ONE F THE MASTER-ND DAUGHTERS... MARTINIQUE WYNGARDE, I LIEVE. SHE SEEMS O HAVE PICKED UP A FEW NEW TRICKS...
THESE ILLUSIONS SEEM TO BE FUELED BY EMOTION. IT CREATES AN ECHO CHAMBER, DIFFICULT TO ESCAPE... THEY'RE BUILT OUT OF WHAT WE FEAR MOST.
JEAN-PAUL... DO YOU REALLY THINK SO LITTLE OF ME?
WE...WE WERE NEVER CLOSE.
YOU ALWAYS KEPT YOUR DISTANCE. I RESPECTED THAT.
AND THE CHURCH...
JEAN-PAUL. LISTEN TO ME. I HAVE BEEN TO HEAVEN.
I REMEMBER YOU THERE, FIGHTING BESIDE ME.
THAT IS ALL THAT MATTERS.

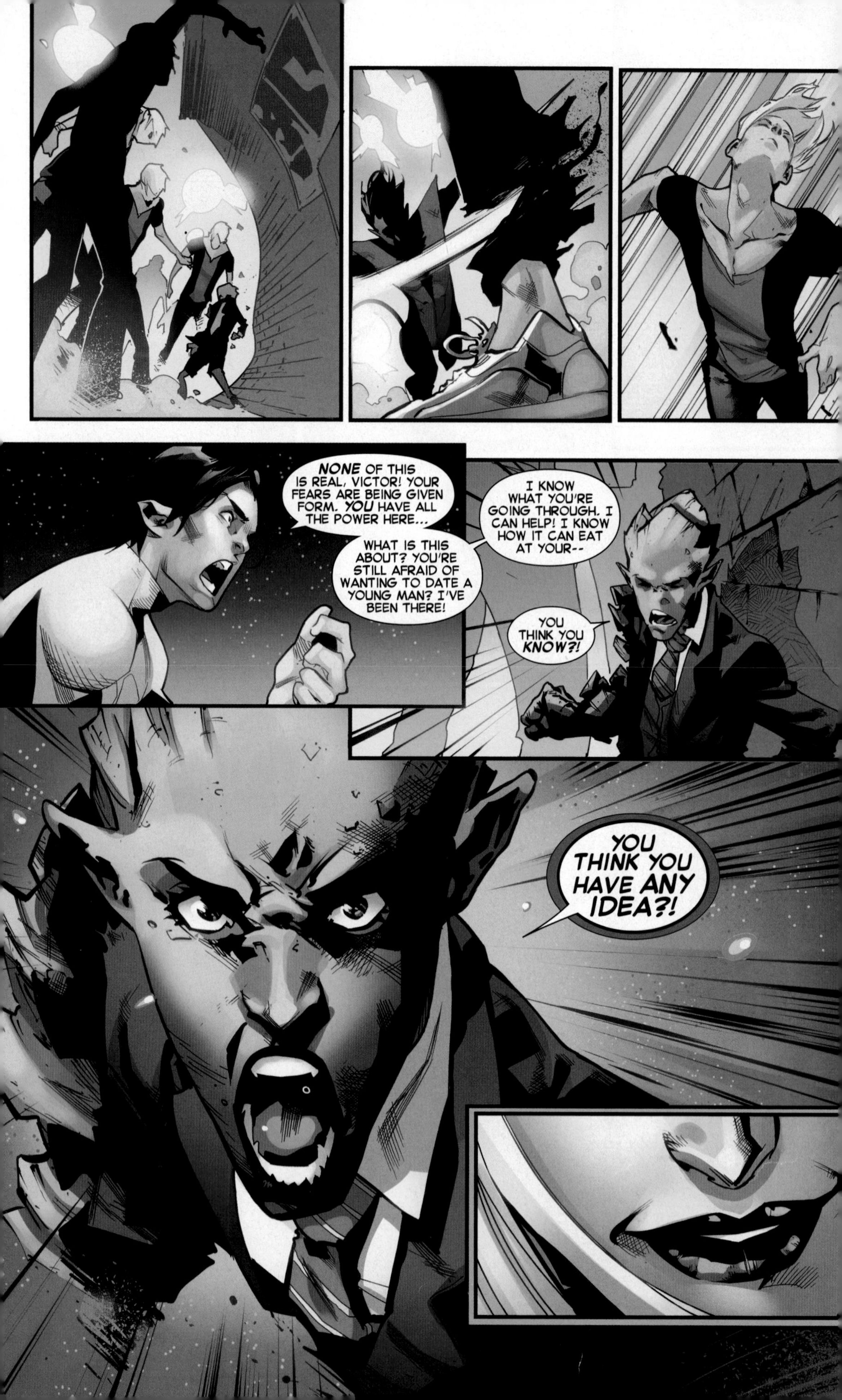
NONE OF THIS IS REAL, VICTOR! YOUR FEARS ARE BEING GIVEN FORM. YOU HAVE ALL THE POWER HERE...
WHAT IS THIS ABOUT? YOU'RE STILL AFRAID OF WANTING TO DATE A YOUNG MAN? I'VE BEEN THERE!
I KNOW WHAT YOU'RE GOING THROUGH. I CAN HELP! I KNOW HOW IT CAN EAT AT YOUR--
YOU THINK YOU KNOW?!
YOU THINK YOU HAVE ANY IDEA?!

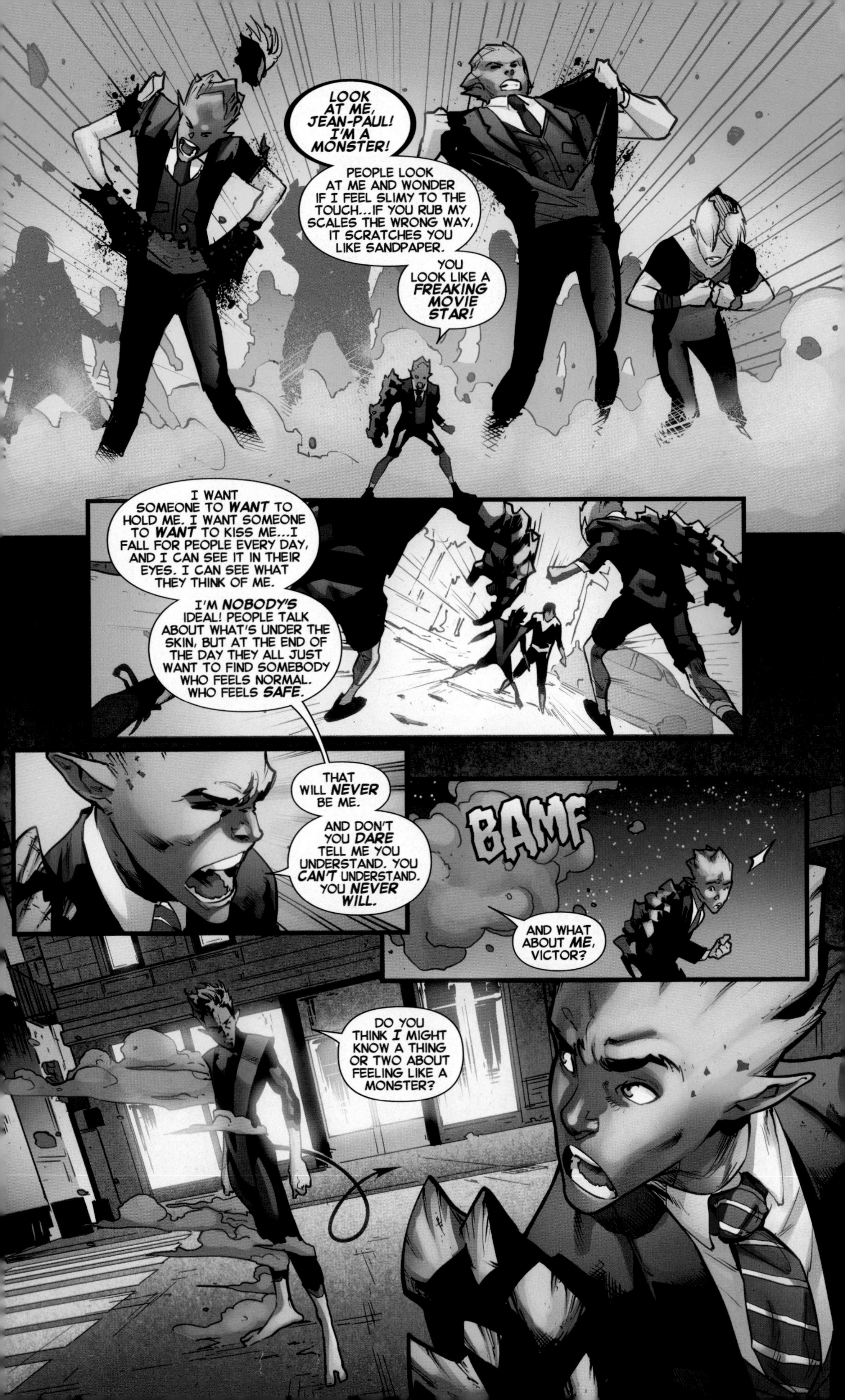
LOOK AT ME, JEAN-PAUL! I'M A MONSTER!
PEOPLE LOOK AT ME AND WONDER IF I FEEL SLIMY TO THE TOUCH...IF YOU RUB MY SCALES THE WRONG WAY, IT SCRATCHES YOU LIKE SANDPAPER.
YOU LOOK LIKE A FREAKING MOVIE STAR!
I WANT SOMEONE TO WANT TO HOLD ME. I WANT SOMEONE TO WANT TO KISS ME...I FALL FOR PEOPLE EVERY DAY, AND I CAN SEE IT IN THEIR EYES. I CAN SEE WHAT THEY THINK OF ME.
I'M NOBODY'S IDEAL! PEOPLE TALK ABOUT WHAT'S UNDER THE SKIN, BUT AT THE END OF THE DAY THEY ALL JUST WANT TO FIND SOMEBODY WHO FEELS NORMAL. WHO FEELS SAFE.
THAT WILL NEVER BE ME.
AND DON'T YOU DARE TELL ME YOU UNDERSTAND. YOU CAN'T UNDERSTAND. YOU NEVER WILL.
BAMF
AND WHAT ABOUT ME, VICTOR?
DO YOU THINK I MIGHT KNOW A THING OR TWO ABOUT FEELING LIKE A MONSTER?

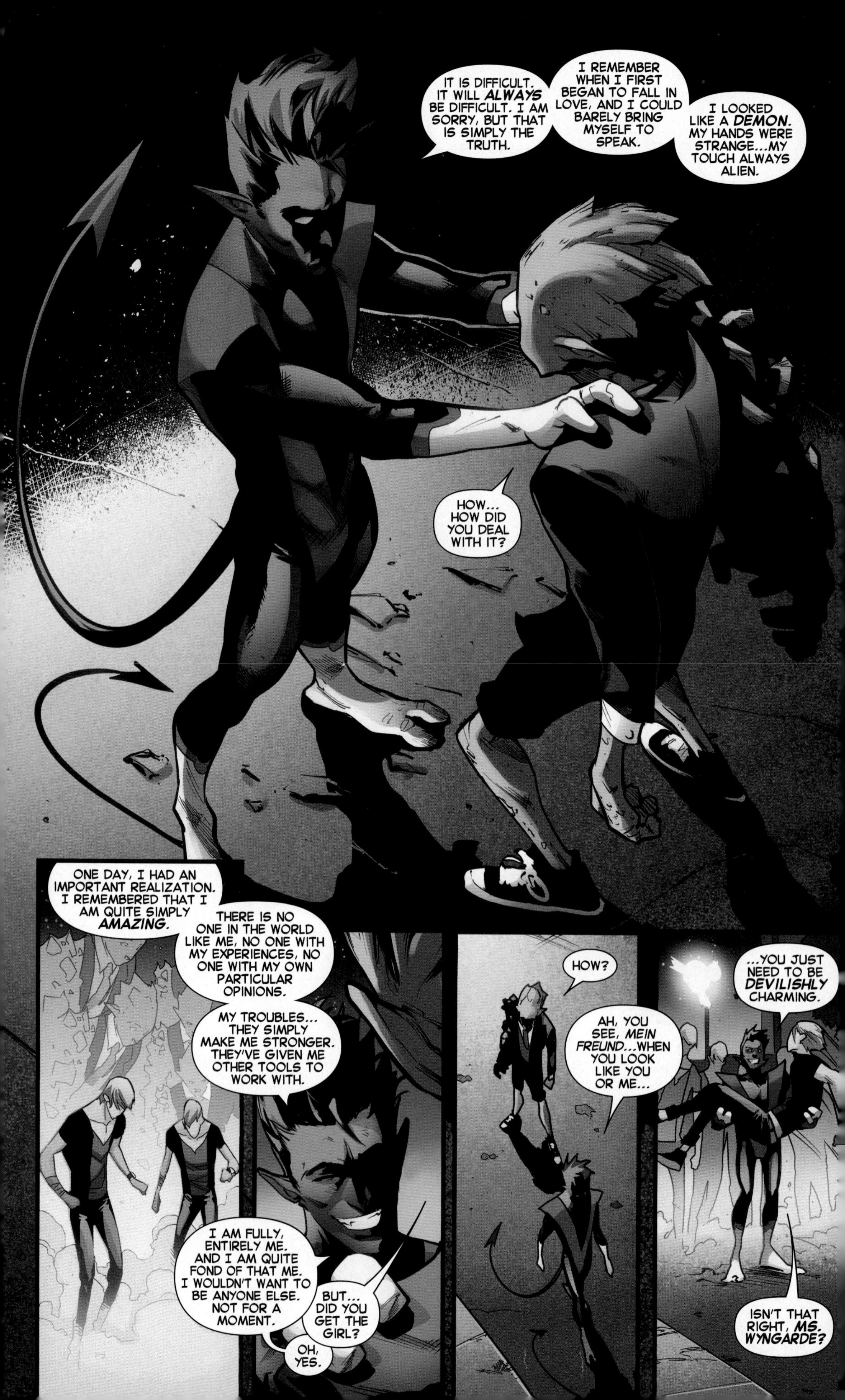

IT IS DIFFICULT. IT WILL ALWAYS BE DIFFICULT. I AM SORRY, BUT THAT IS SIMPLY THE TRUTH.
I REMEMBER WHEN I FIRST BEGAN TO FALL IN LOVE, AND I COULD BARELY BRING MYSELF TO SPEAK.
I LOOKED LIKE A DEMON. MY HANDS WERE STRANGE... MY TOUCH ALWAYS ALIEN.
HOW... HOW DID YOU DEAL WITH IT?
ONE DAY, I HAD AN IMPORTANT REALIZATION. I REMEMBERED THAT I AM QUITE SIMPLY AMAZING.
THERE IS NO ONE IN THE WORLD LIKE ME, NO ONE WITH MY EXPERIENCES, NO ONE WITH MY OWN PARTICULAR OPINIONS.
MY TROUBLES... THEY SIMPLY MAKE ME STRONGER. THEY'VE GIVEN ME OTHER TOOLS TO WORK WITH.
I AM FULLY, ENTIRELY ME. AND I AM QUITE FOND OF THAT ME. I WOULDN'T WANT TO BE ANYONE ELSE. NOT FOR A MOMENT.
BUT... DID YOU GET THE GIRL?
OH, YES.
HOW?
AH, YOU SEE, MEIN FREUND... WHEN YOU LOOK LIKE YOU OR ME...
...YOU JUST NEED TO BE DEVILISHLY CHARMING.
ISN'T THAT RIGHT, MS. WYNGARDE?

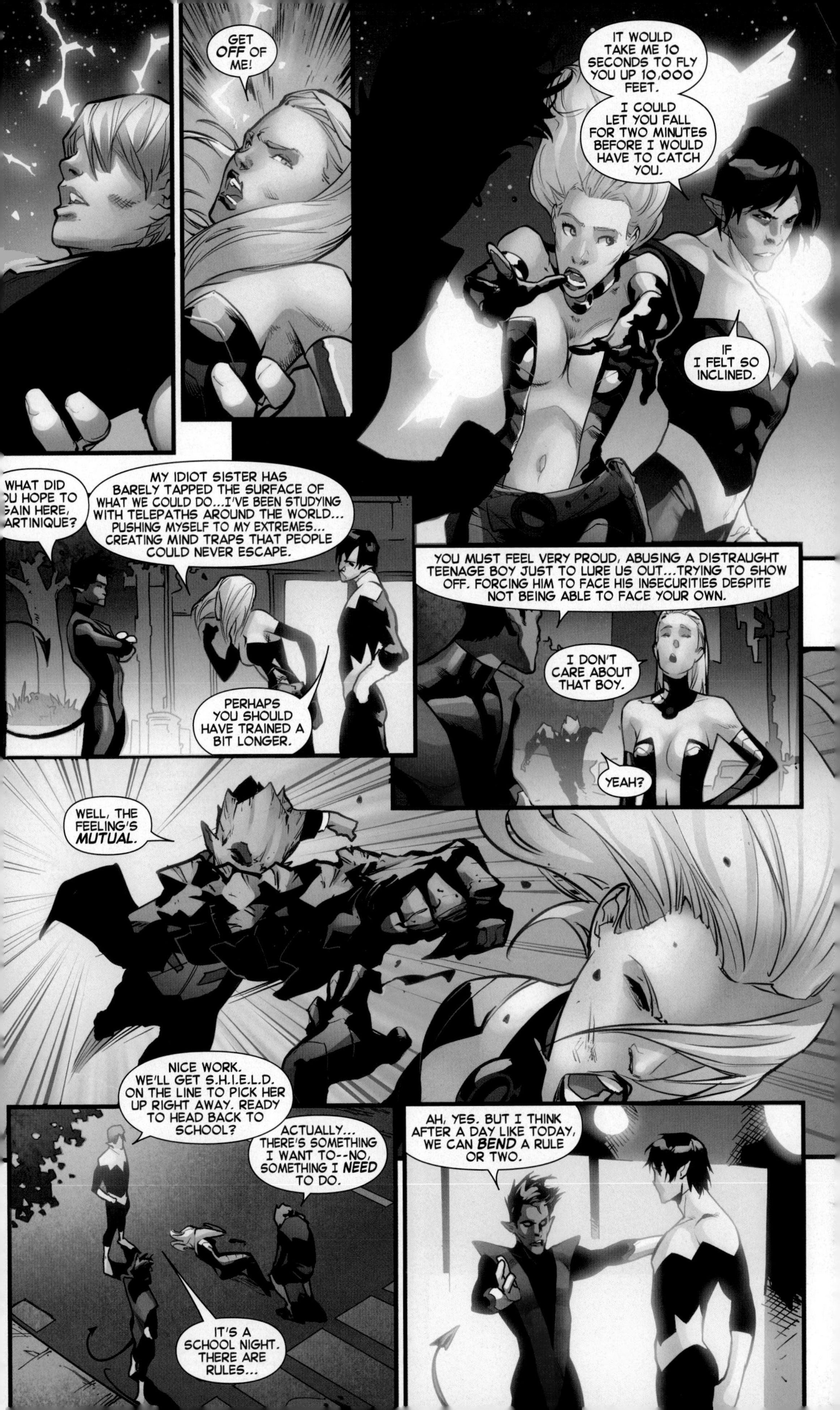
GET OFF OF ME!
IT WOULD TAKE ME 10 SECONDS TO FLY YOU UP 10,000 FEET.
I COULD LET YOU FALL FOR TWO MINUTES BEFORE I WOULD HAVE TO CATCH YOU.
IF I FELT SO INCLINED.
WHAT DID OU HOPE TO GAIN HERE, ARTINIQUE?
MY IDIOT SISTER HAS BARELY TAPPED THE SURFACE OF WHAT WE COULD DO...I'VE BEEN STUDYING WITH TELEPATHS AROUND THE WORLD... PUSHING MYSELF TO MY EXTREMES... CREATING MIND TRAPS THAT PEOPLE COULD NEVER ESCAPE.
PERHAPS YOU SHOULD HAVE TRAINED A BIT LONGER.
YOU MUST FEEL VERY PROUD, ABUSING A DISTRAUGHT TEENAGE BOY JUST TO LURE US OUT...TRYING TO SHOW OFF. FORCING HIM TO FACE HIS INSECURITIES DESPITE NOT BEING ABLE TO FACE YOUR OWN.
I DON'T CARE ABOUT THAT BOY.
YEAH?
WELL, THE FEELING'S MUTUAL.
NICE WORK. WE'LL GET S.H.I.E.L.D. ON THE LINE TO PICK HER UP RIGHT AWAY. READY TO HEAD BACK TO SCHOOL?
ACTUALLY... THERE'S SOMETHING I WANT TO--NO, SOMETHING I NEED TO DO.
IT'S A SCHOOL NIGHT. THERE ARE RULES...
AH, YES. BUT I THINK AFTER A DAY LIKE TODAY, WE CAN BEND A RULE OR TWO.

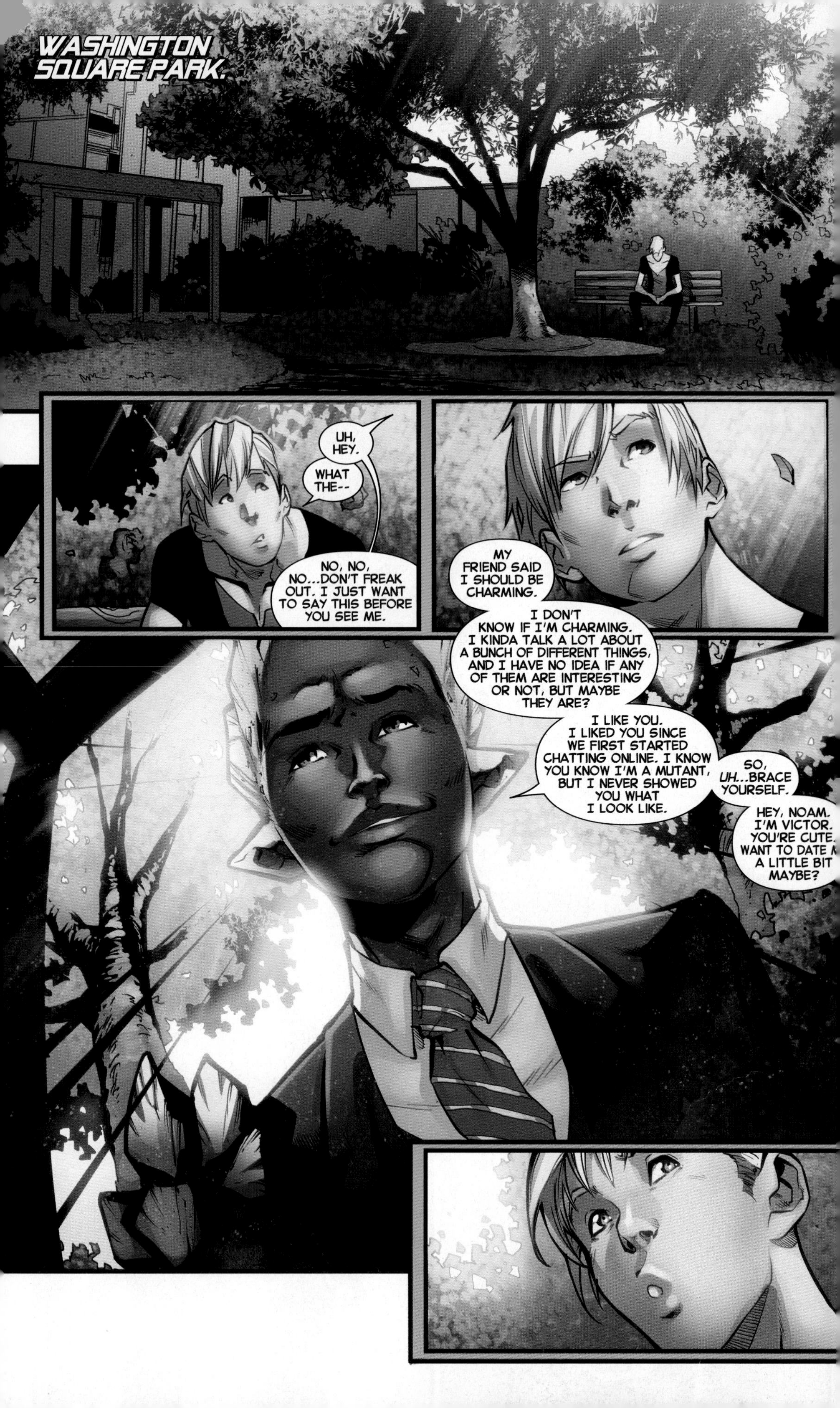

WASHINGTON SQUARE PARK.
UH, HEY.
WHAT THE--
NO, NO, NO...DON'T FREAK OUT. I JUST WANT TO SAY THIS BEFORE YOU SEE ME.
MY FRIEND SAID I SHOULD BE CHARMING.
I DON'T KNOW IF I'M CHARMING. I KINDA TALK A LOT ABOUT A BUNCH OF DIFFERENT THINGS, AND I HAVE NO IDEA IF ANY OF THEM ARE INTERESTING OR NOT, BUT MAYBE THEY ARE?
I LIKE YOU. I LIKED YOU SINCE WE FIRST STARTED CHATTING ONLINE. I KNOW YOU KNOW I'M A MUTANT, BUT I NEVER SHOWED YOU WHAT I LOOK LIKE.
SO, UH...BRACE YOURSELF.
HEY, NOAM. I'M VICTOR. YOU'RE CUTE. WANT TO DATE A LITTLE BIT MAYBE?

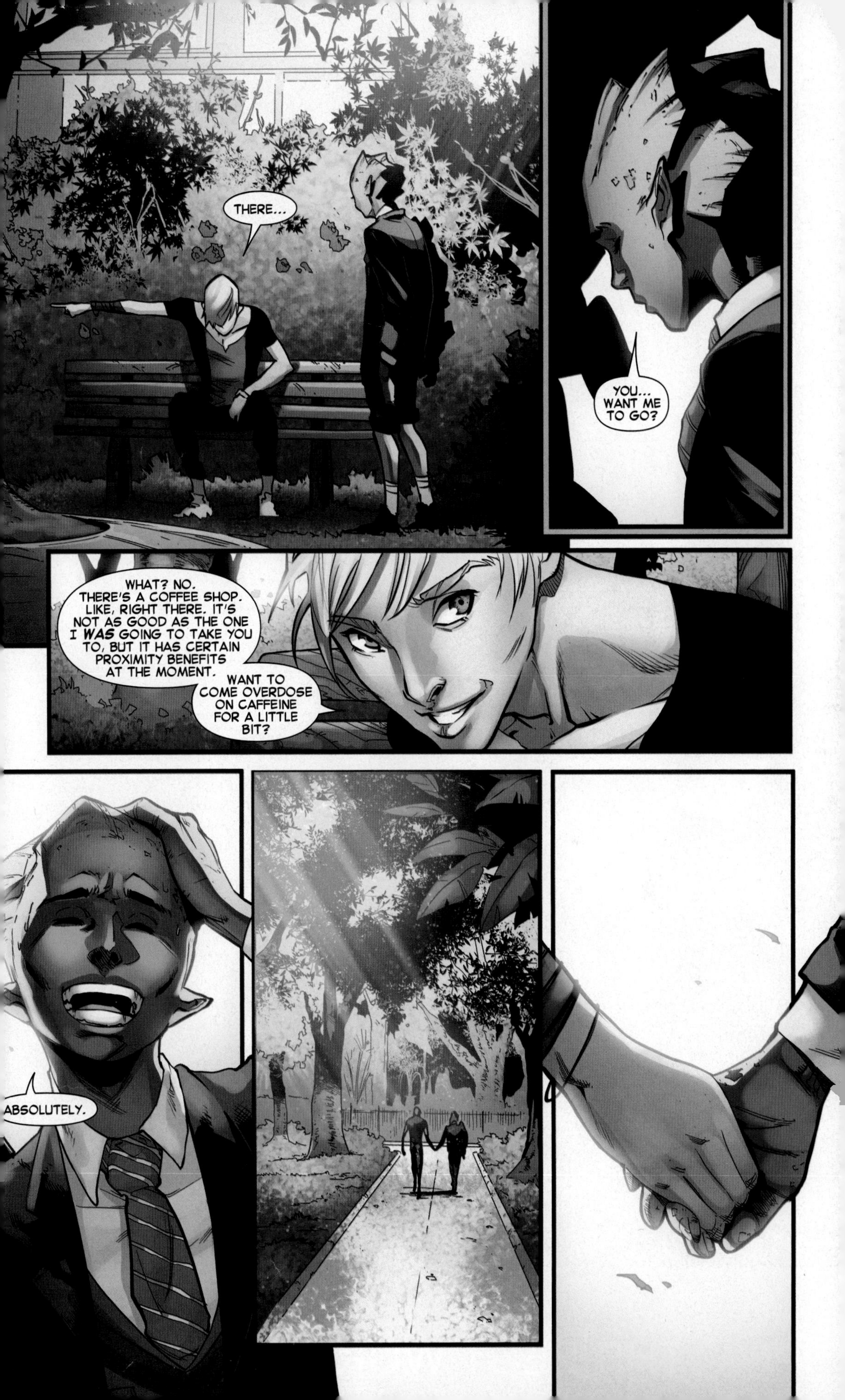
THERE...
YOU... WANT ME TO GO?
WHAT? NO. THERE'S A COFFEE SHOP. LIKE, RIGHT THERE. IT'S NOT AS GOOD AS THE ONE I *WAS* GOING TO TAKE YOU TO, BUT IT HAS CERTAIN PROXIMITY BENEFITS AT THE MOMENT.
WANT TO COME OVERDOSE ON CAFFEINE FOR A LITTLE BIT?
ABSOLUTELY.

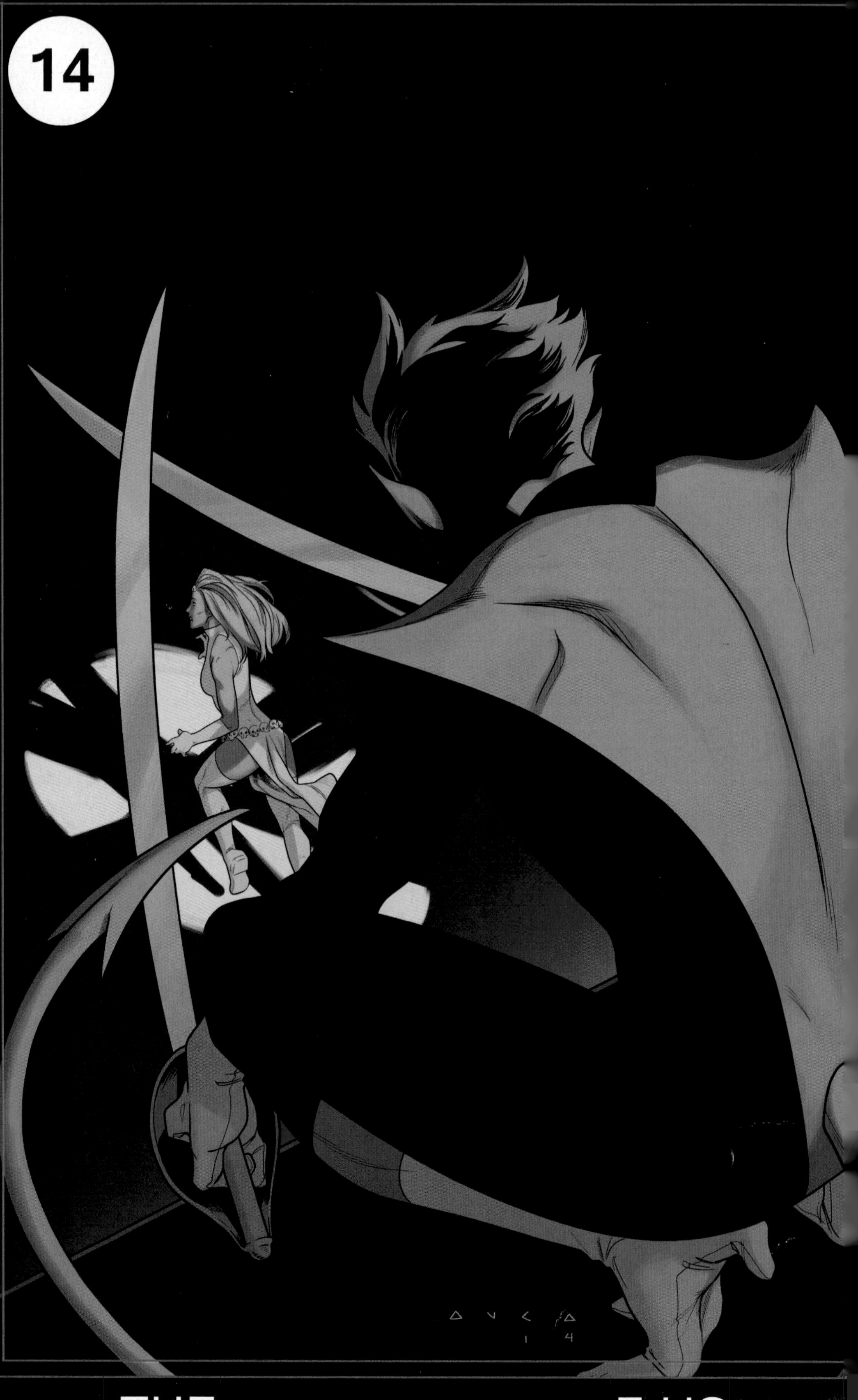
14

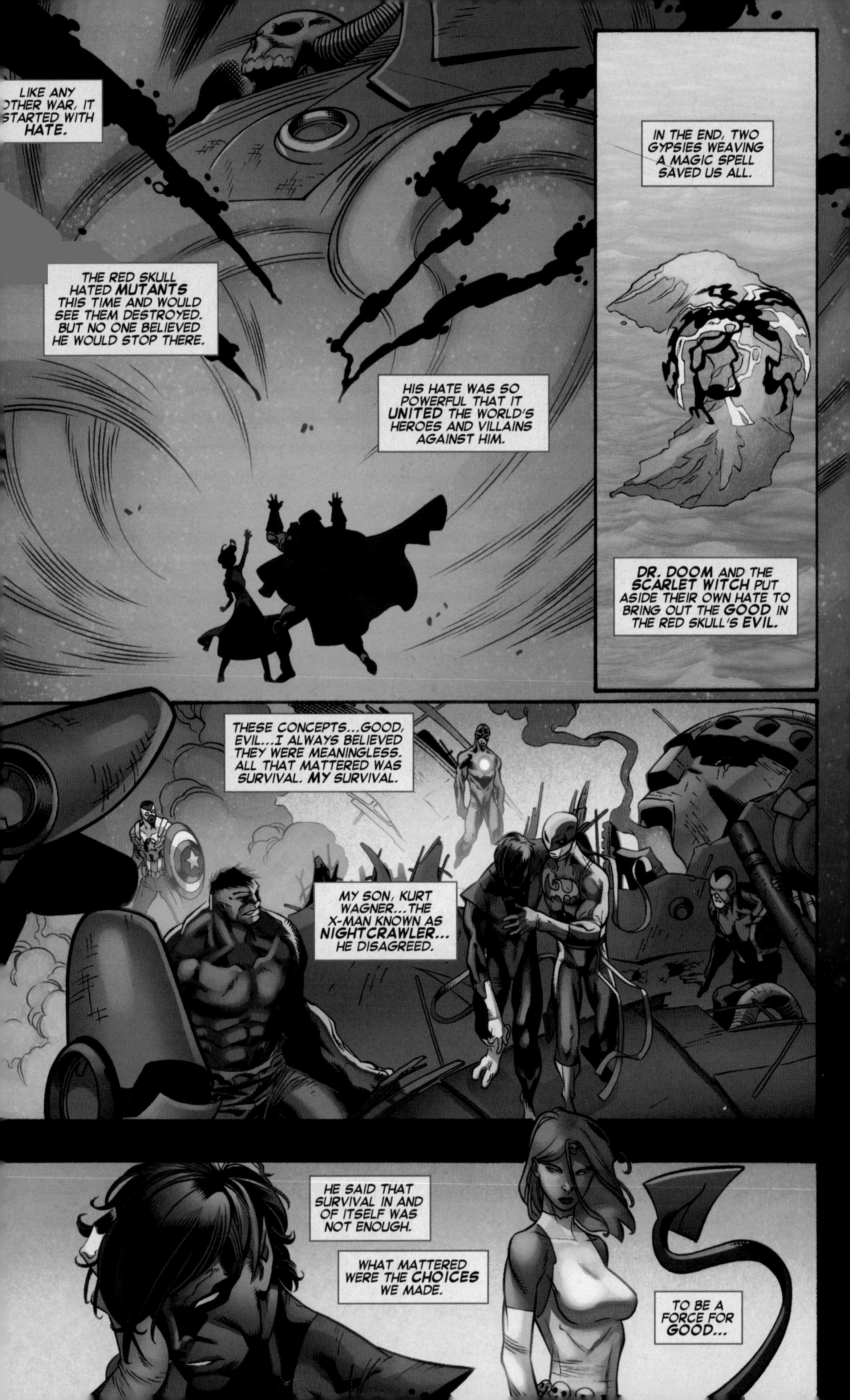
LIKE ANY OTHER WAR, IT STARTED WITH HATE.
THE RED SKULL HATED MUTANTS THIS TIME AND WOULD SEE THEM DESTROYED. BUT NO ONE BELIEVED HE WOULD STOP THERE.
HIS HATE WAS SO POWERFUL THAT IT UNITED THE WORLD'S HEROES AND VILLAINS AGAINST HIM.
IN THE END, TWO GYPSIES WEAVING A MAGIC SPELL SAVED US ALL.
DR. DOOM AND THE SCARLET WITCH PUT ASIDE THEIR OWN HATE TO BRING OUT THE GOOD IN THE RED SKULL'S EVIL.
THESE CONCEPTS...GOOD, EVIL...I ALWAYS BELIEVED THEY WERE MEANINGLESS. ALL THAT MATTERED WAS SURVIVAL. MY SURVIVAL.
MY SON, KURT WAGNER...THE X-MAN KNOWN AS NIGHTCRAWLER... HE DISAGREED.
HE SAID THAT SURVIVAL IN AND OF ITSELF WAS NOT ENOUGH.
WHAT MATTERED WERE THE CHOICES WE MADE.
TO BE A FORCE FOR GOOD...

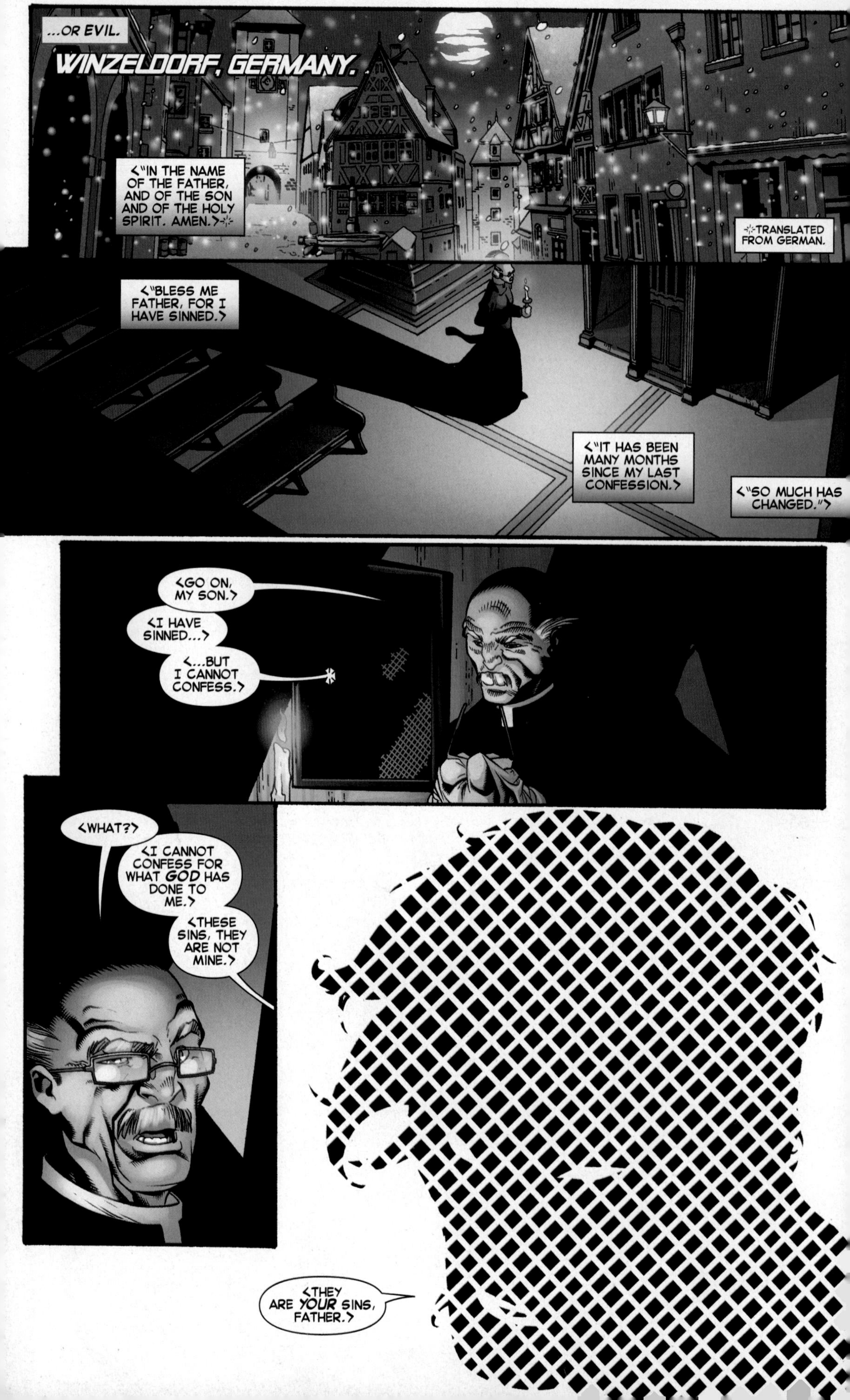

...OR EVIL.
WINZELDORF, GERMANY.
<"IN THE NAME OF THE FATHER, AND OF THE SON AND OF THE HOLY SPIRIT. AMEN.>*
*TRANSLATED FROM GERMAN.
<"BLESS ME FATHER, FOR I HAVE SINNED.>
<"IT HAS BEEN MANY MONTHS SINCE MY LAST CONFESSION.>
<"SO MUCH HAS CHANGED.">
<GO ON, MY SON.>
<I HAVE SINNED...>
<...BUT I CANNOT CONFESS.>
<WHAT?>
<I CANNOT CONFESS FOR WHAT GOD HAS DONE TO ME.>
<THESE SINS, THEY ARE NOT MINE.>
<THEY ARE YOUR SINS, FATHER.>

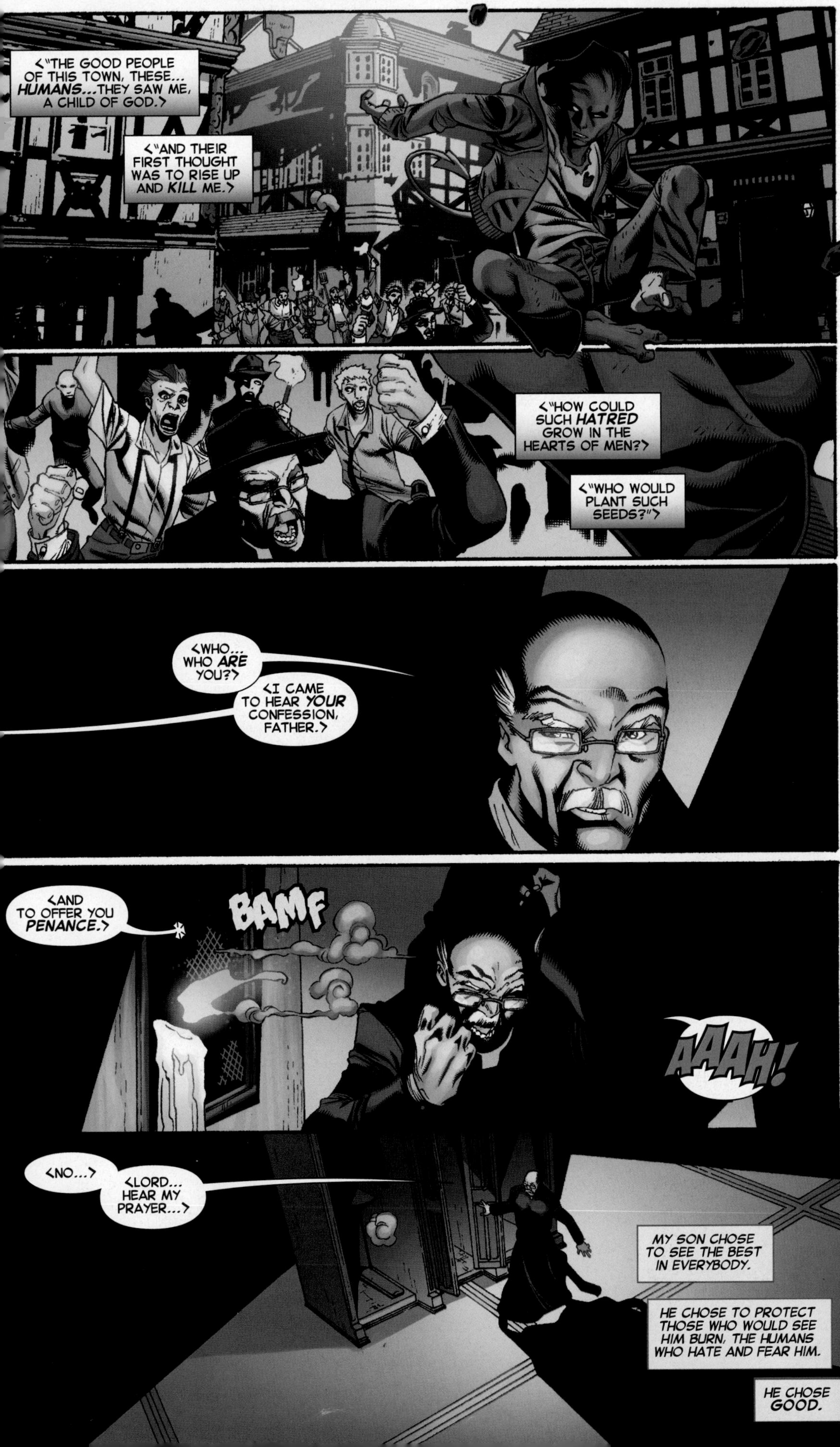
<"THE GOOD PEOPLE OF THIS TOWN, THESE... HUMANS...THEY SAW ME, A CHILD OF GOD.>
<"AND THEIR FIRST THOUGHT WAS TO RISE UP AND KILL ME.>
<"HOW COULD SUCH HATRED GROW IN THE HEARTS OF MEN?>
<"WHO WOULD PLANT SUCH SEEDS?">
<WHO... WHO ARE YOU?>
<I CAME TO HEAR YOUR CONFESSION, FATHER.>
<AND TO OFFER YOU PENANCE.>
BAMF
AAAH!
<NO...>
<LORD... HEAR MY PRAYER...>
MY SON CHOSE TO SEE THE BEST IN EVERYBODY.
HE CHOSE TO PROTECT THOSE WHO WOULD SEE HIM BURN, THE HUMANS WHO HATE AND FEAR HIM.
HE CHOSE GOOD.

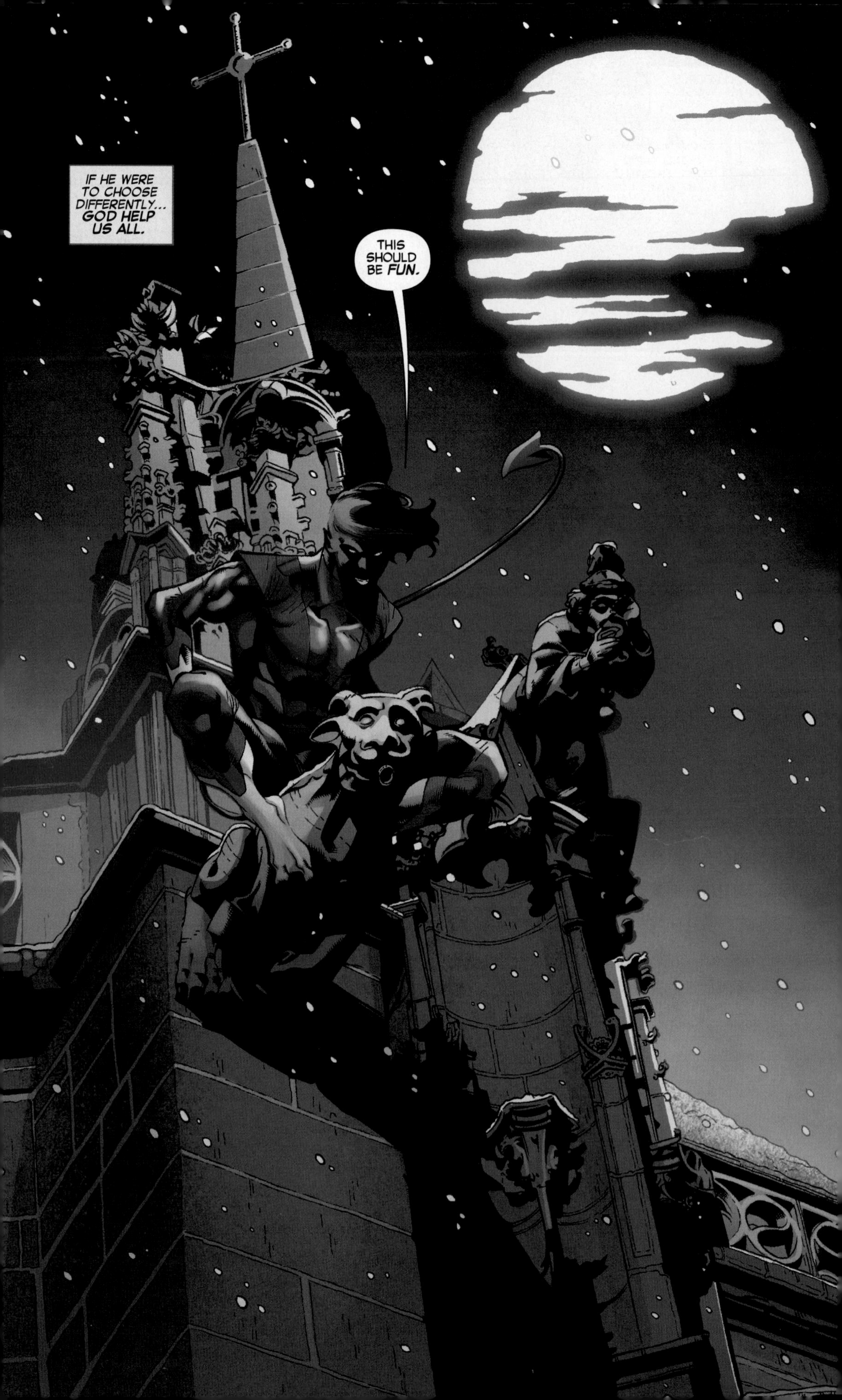
IF HE WERE TO CHOOSE DIFFERENTLY... GOD HELP US ALL.
THIS SHOULD BE FUN.

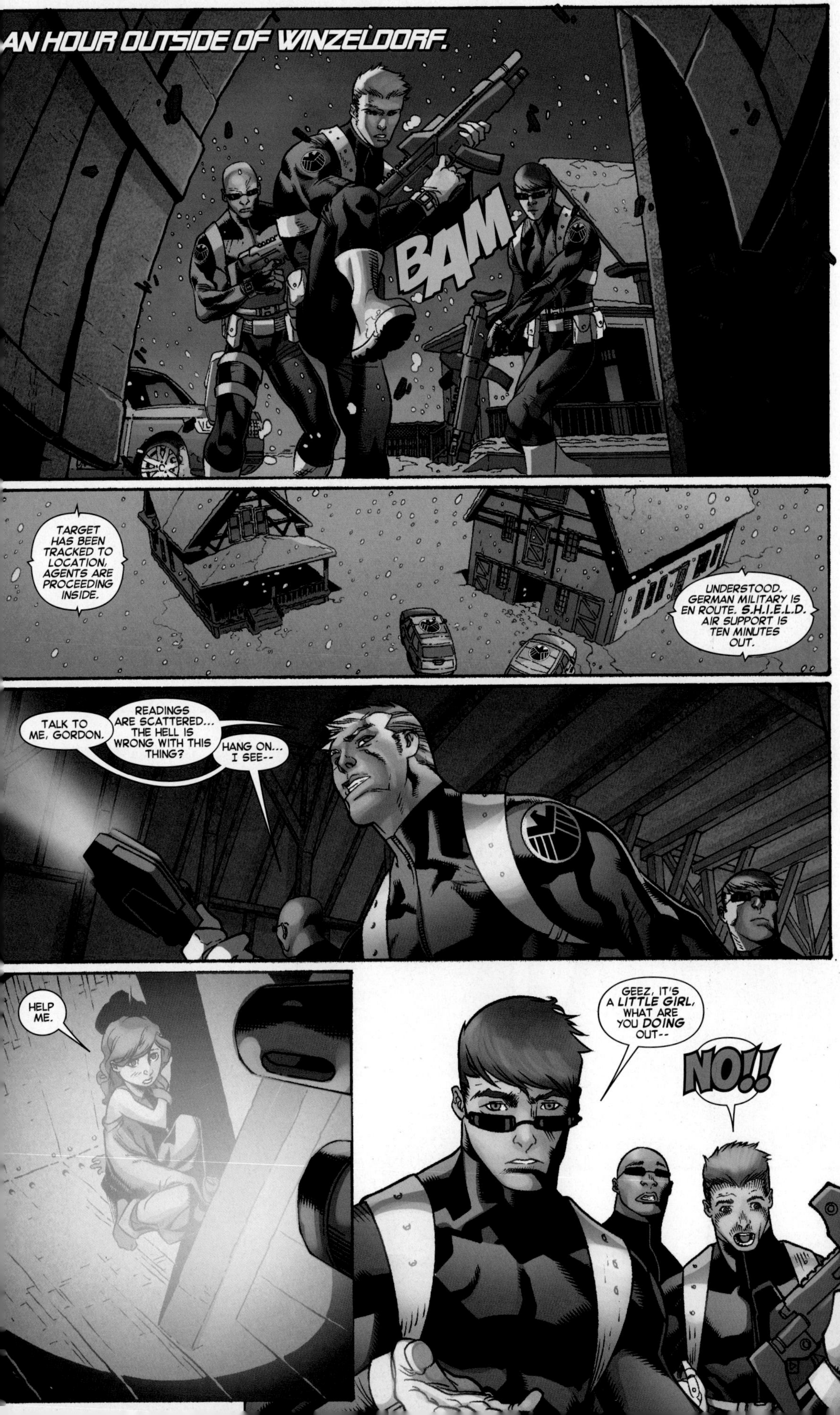

AN HOUR OUTSIDE OF WINZELDORF.
BAM
TARGET HAS BEEN TRACKED TO LOCATION, AGENTS ARE PROCEEDING INSIDE.
UNDERSTOOD. GERMAN MILITARY IS EN ROUTE. S.H.I.E.L.D. AIR SUPPORT IS TEN MINUTES OUT.
TALK TO ME, GORDON.
READINGS ARE SCATTERED... THE HELL IS WRONG WITH THIS THING?
HANG ON... I SEE--
HELP ME.
GEEZ, IT'S A LITTLE GIRL, WHAT ARE YOU DOING OUT--
NO!!

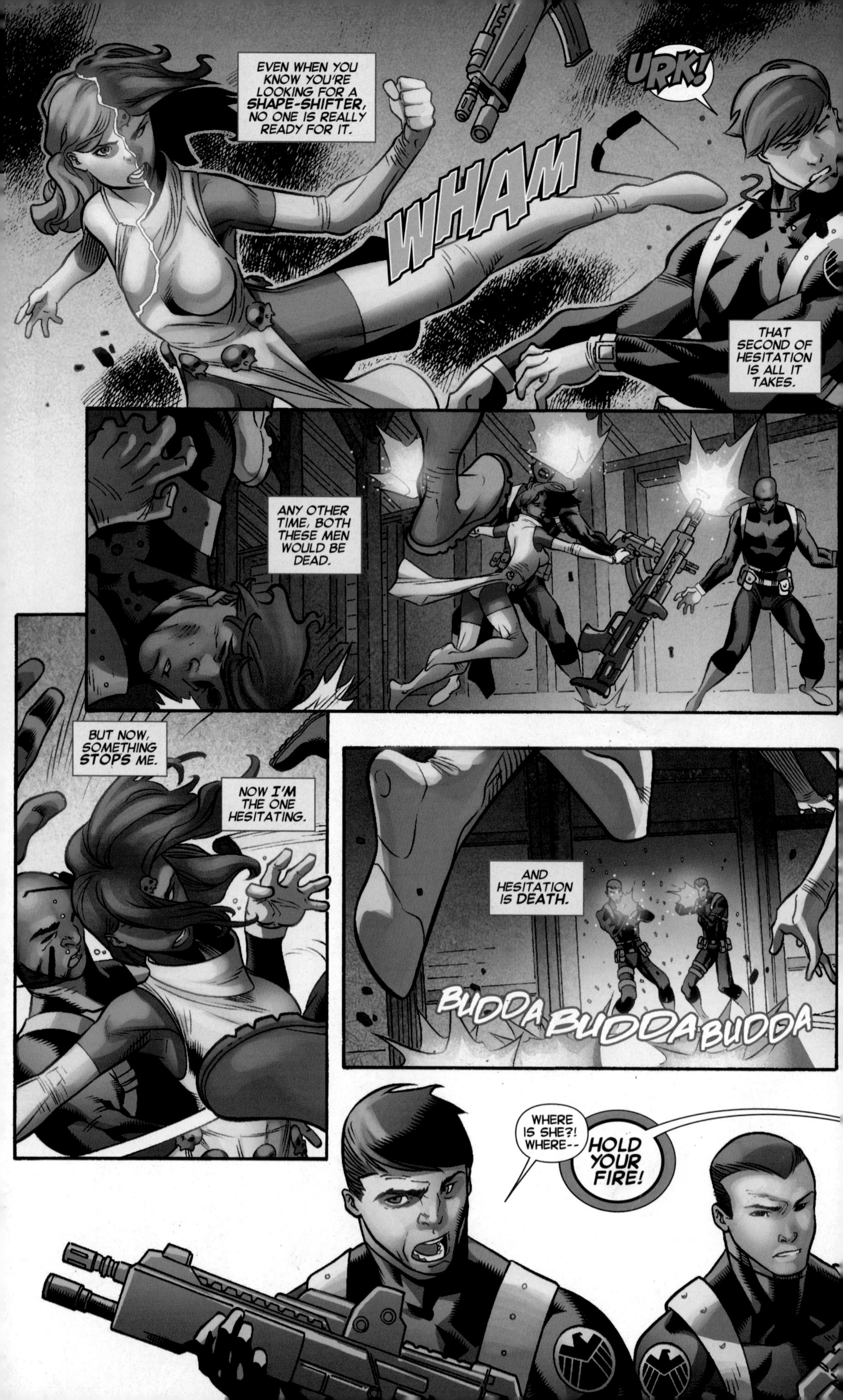

EVEN WHEN YOU KNOW YOU'RE LOOKING FOR A SHAPE-SHIFTER, NO ONE IS REALLY READY FOR IT.
URK!
WHAM
THAT SECOND OF HESITATION IS ALL IT TAKES.
ANY OTHER TIME, BOTH THESE MEN WOULD BE DEAD.
BUT NOW, SOMETHING STOPS ME.
NOW I'M THE ONE HESITATING.
AND HESITATION IS DEATH.
BUDDA BUDDA BUDDA
WHERE IS SHE?! WHERE--
HOLD YOUR FIRE!

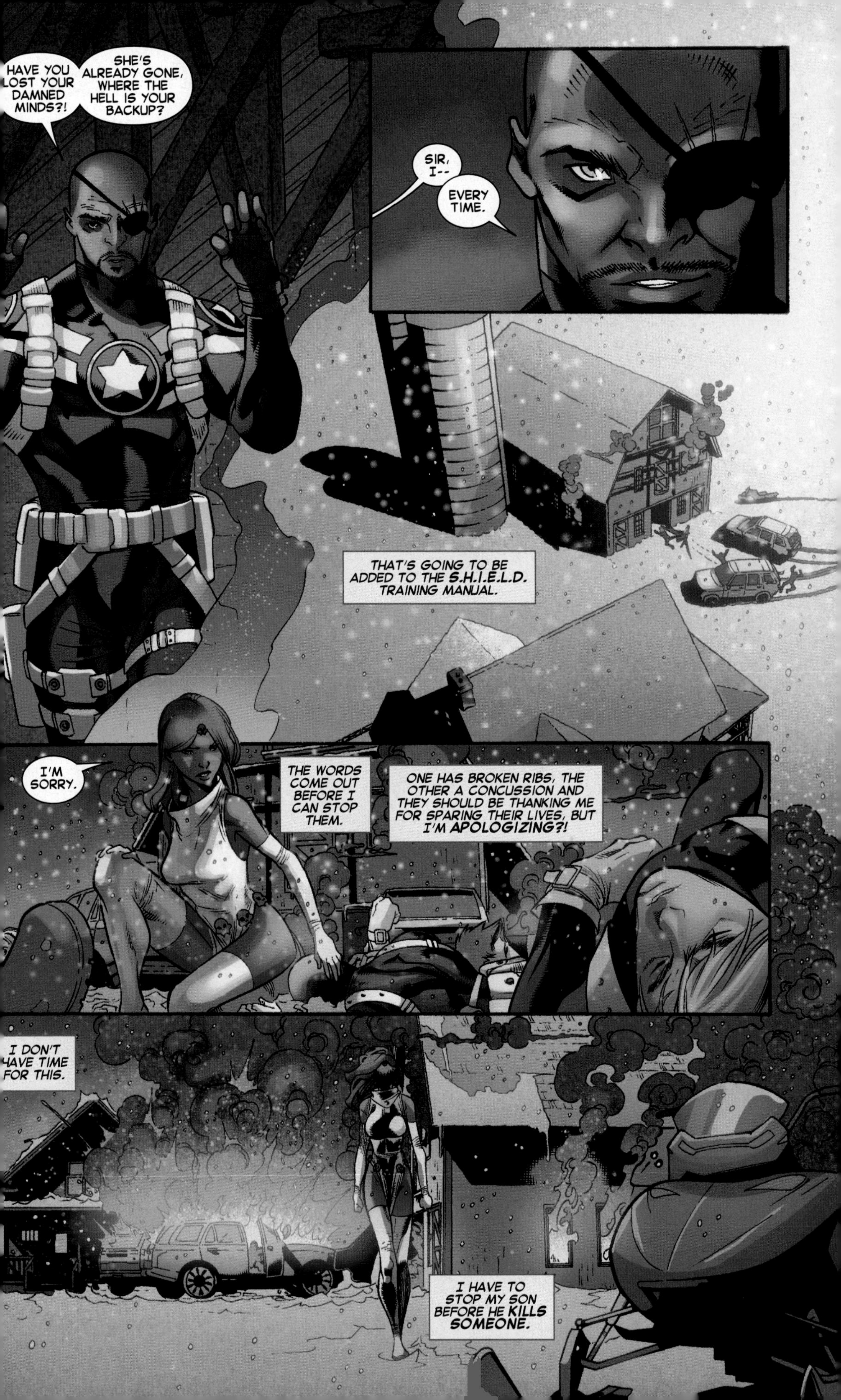
HAVE YOU LOST YOUR DAMNED MINDS?!
SHE'S ALREADY GONE, WHERE THE HELL IS YOUR BACKUP?
SIR, I--
EVERY TIME.
THAT'S GOING TO BE ADDED TO THE S.H.I.E.L.D. TRAINING MANUAL.
I'M SORRY.
THE WORDS COME OUT BEFORE I CAN STOP THEM.
ONE HAS BROKEN RIBS, THE OTHER A CONCUSSION AND THEY SHOULD BE THANKING ME FOR SPARING THEIR LIVES, BUT I'M APOLOGIZING?!
I DON'T HAVE TIME FOR THIS.
I HAVE TO STOP MY SON BEFORE HE KILLS SOMEONE.

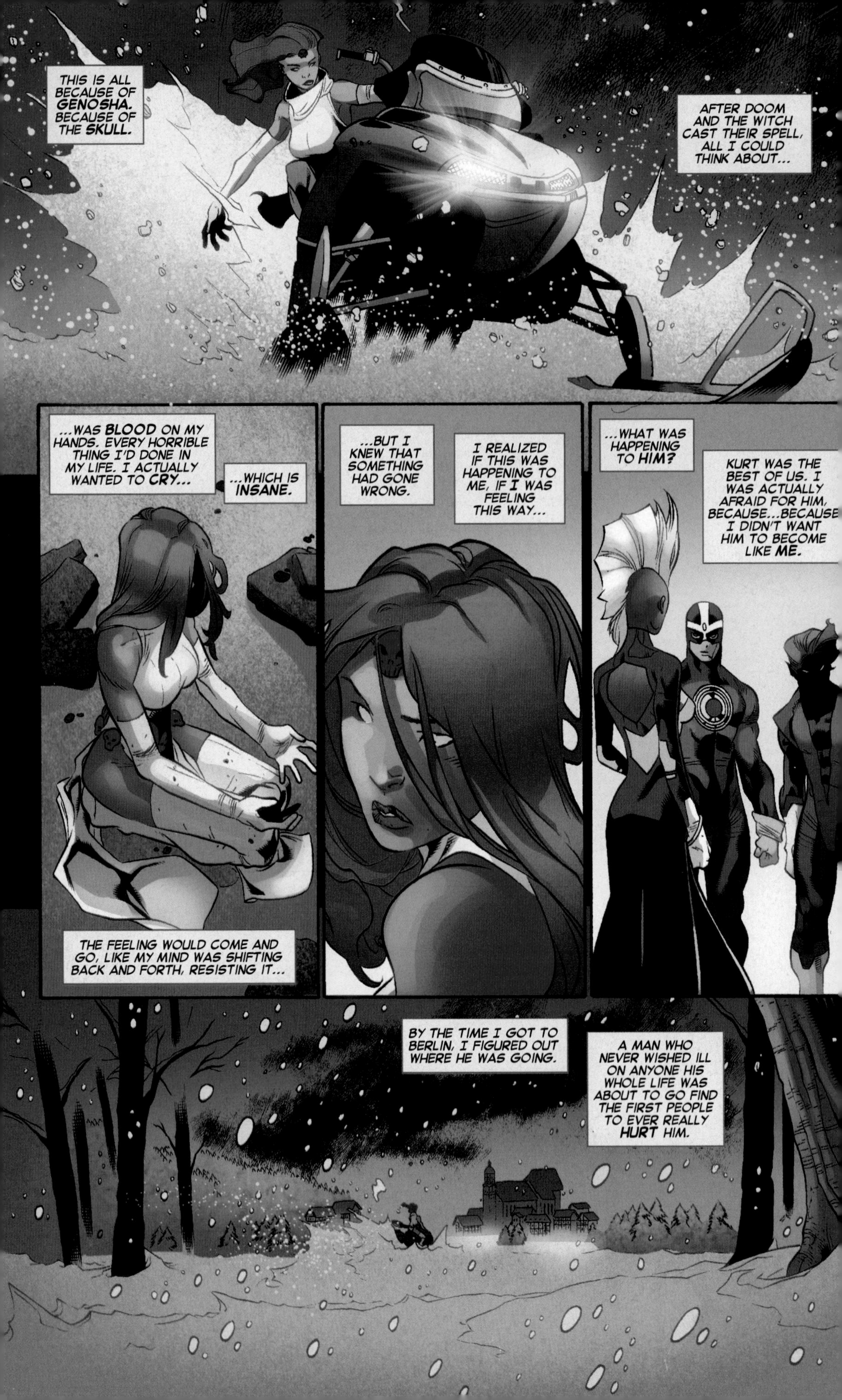

THIS IS ALL BECAUSE OF GENOSHA. BECAUSE OF THE SKULL.
AFTER DOOM AND THE WITCH CAST THEIR SPELL, ALL I COULD THINK ABOUT...
...WAS BLOOD ON MY HANDS. EVERY HORRIBLE THING I'D DONE IN MY LIFE. I ACTUALLY WANTED TO CRY...
...WHICH IS INSANE.
THE FEELING WOULD COME AND GO, LIKE MY MIND WAS SHIFTING BACK AND FORTH, RESISTING IT...
...BUT I KNEW THAT SOMETHING HAD GONE WRONG.
I REALIZED IF THIS WAS HAPPENING TO ME, IF I WAS FEELING THIS WAY...
...WHAT WAS HAPPENING TO HIM?
KURT WAS THE BEST OF US. I WAS ACTUALLY AFRAID FOR HIM, BECAUSE...BECAUSE I DIDN'T WANT HIM TO BECOME LIKE ME.
BY THE TIME I GOT TO BERLIN, I FIGURED OUT WHERE HE WAS GOING.
A MAN WHO NEVER WISHED ILL ON ANYONE HIS WHOLE LIFE WAS ABOUT TO GO FIND THE FIRST PEOPLE TO EVER REALLY HURT HIM.

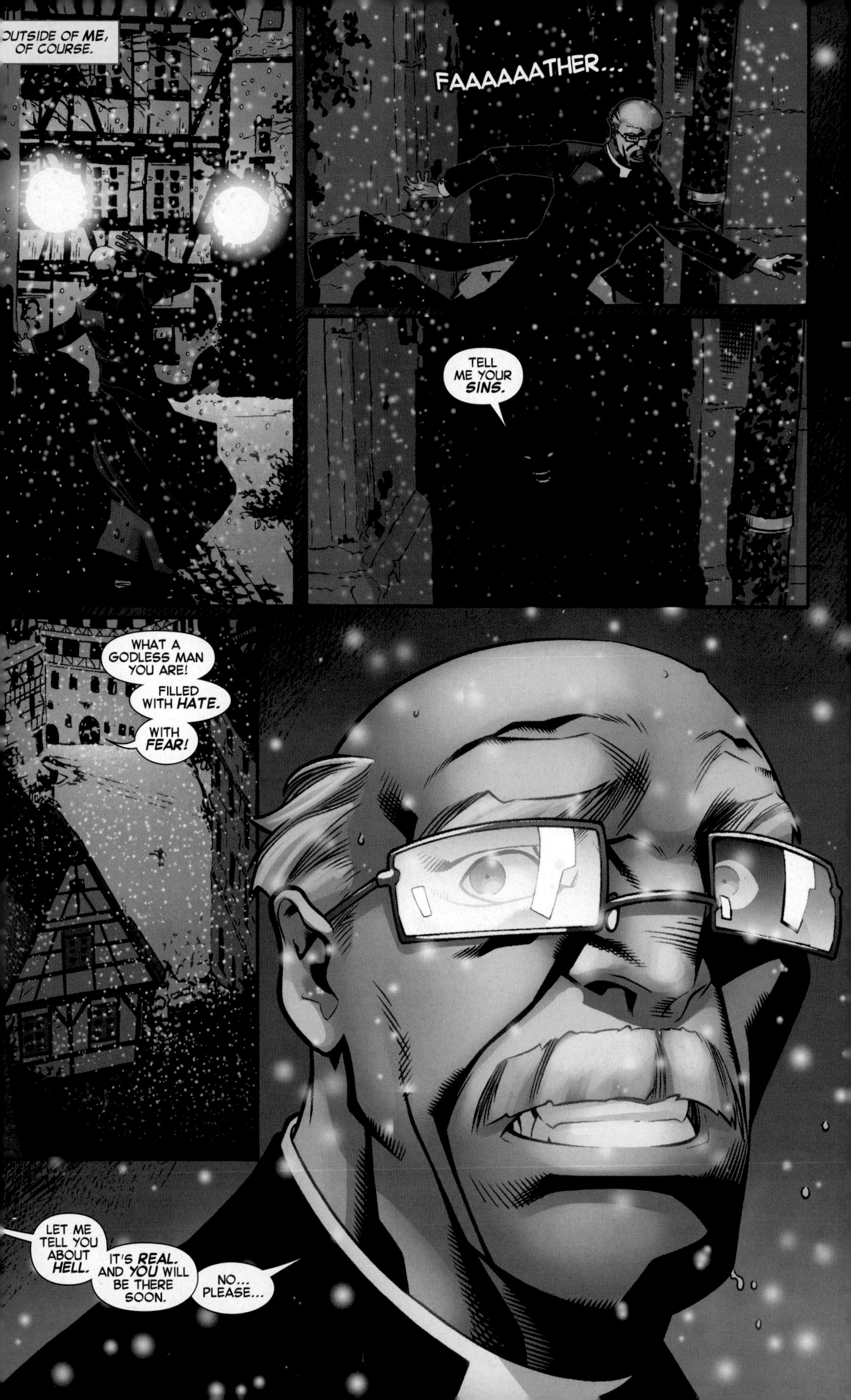
OUTSIDE OF ME, OF COURSE.
FAAAAAATHER...
TELL ME YOUR SINS.
WHAT A GODLESS MAN YOU ARE!
FILLED WITH HATE.
WITH FEAR!
LET ME TELL YOU ABOUT HELL.
IT'S REAL. AND YOU WILL BE THERE SOON.
NO... PLEASE...

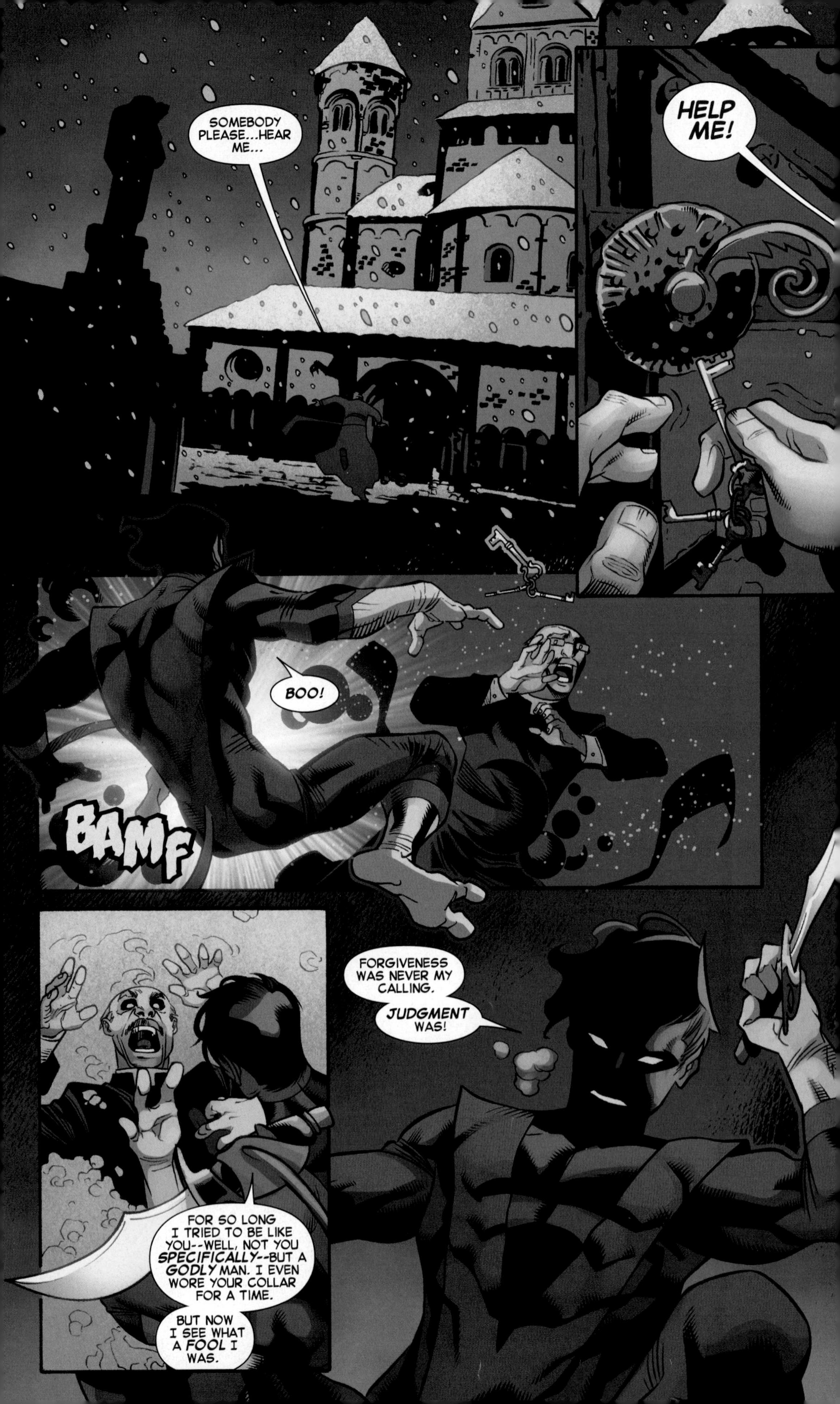

SOMEBODY PLEASE...HEAR ME...
HELP ME!
BOO!
BAMF
FORGIVENESS WAS NEVER MY CALLING.
JUDGMENT WAS!
FOR SO LONG I TRIED TO BE LIKE YOU--WELL, NOT YOU SPECIFICALLY--BUT A GODLY MAN. I EVEN WORE YOUR COLLAR FOR A TIME.
BUT NOW I SEE WHAT A FOOL I WAS.

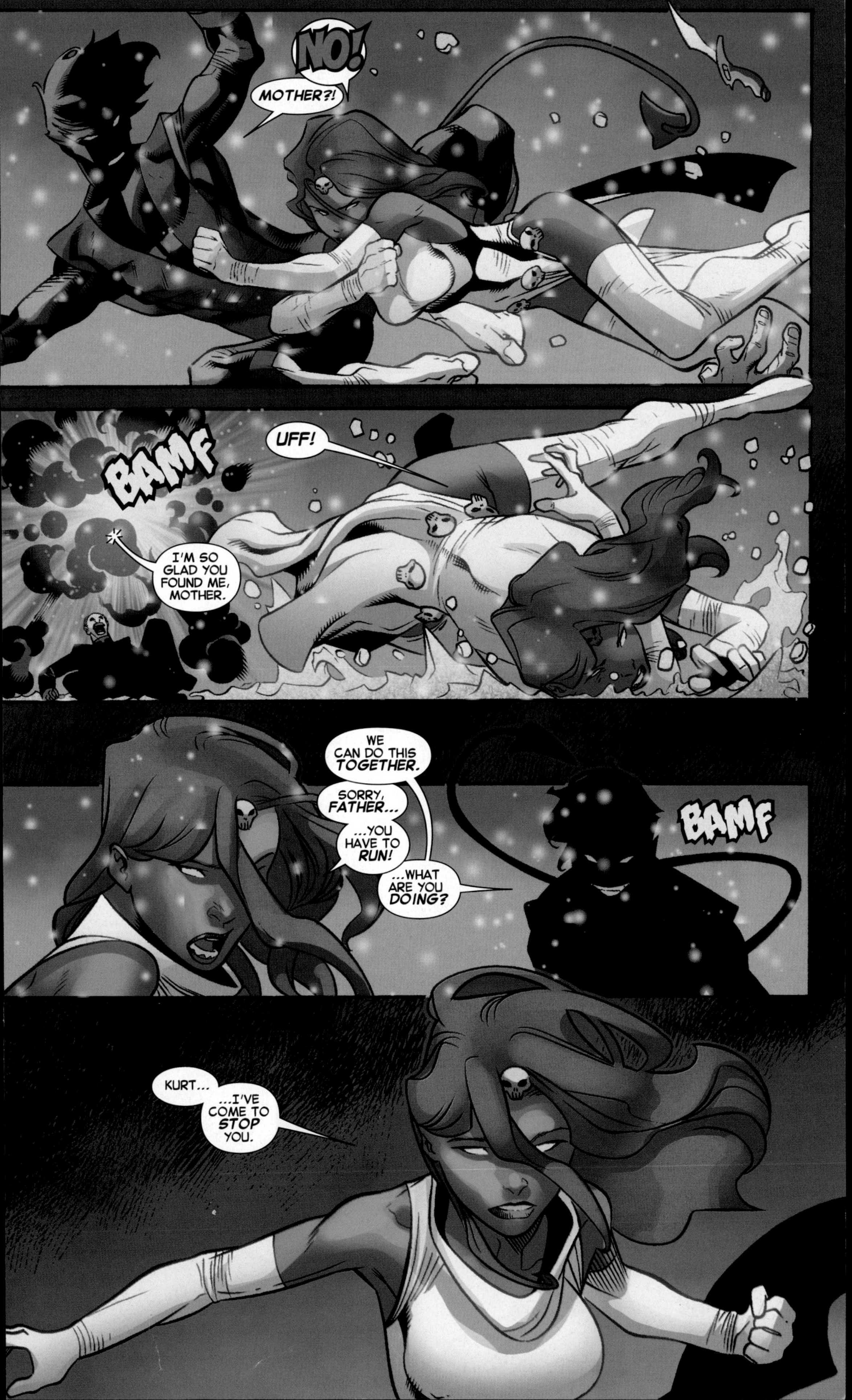
NO!
MOTHER?!
BAMF
UFF!
I'M SO GLAD YOU FOUND ME, MOTHER.
WE CAN DO THIS TOGETHER.
SORRY, FATHER...
...YOU HAVE TO RUN!
...WHAT ARE YOU DOING?
BAMF
KURT...
...I'VE COME TO STOP YOU.

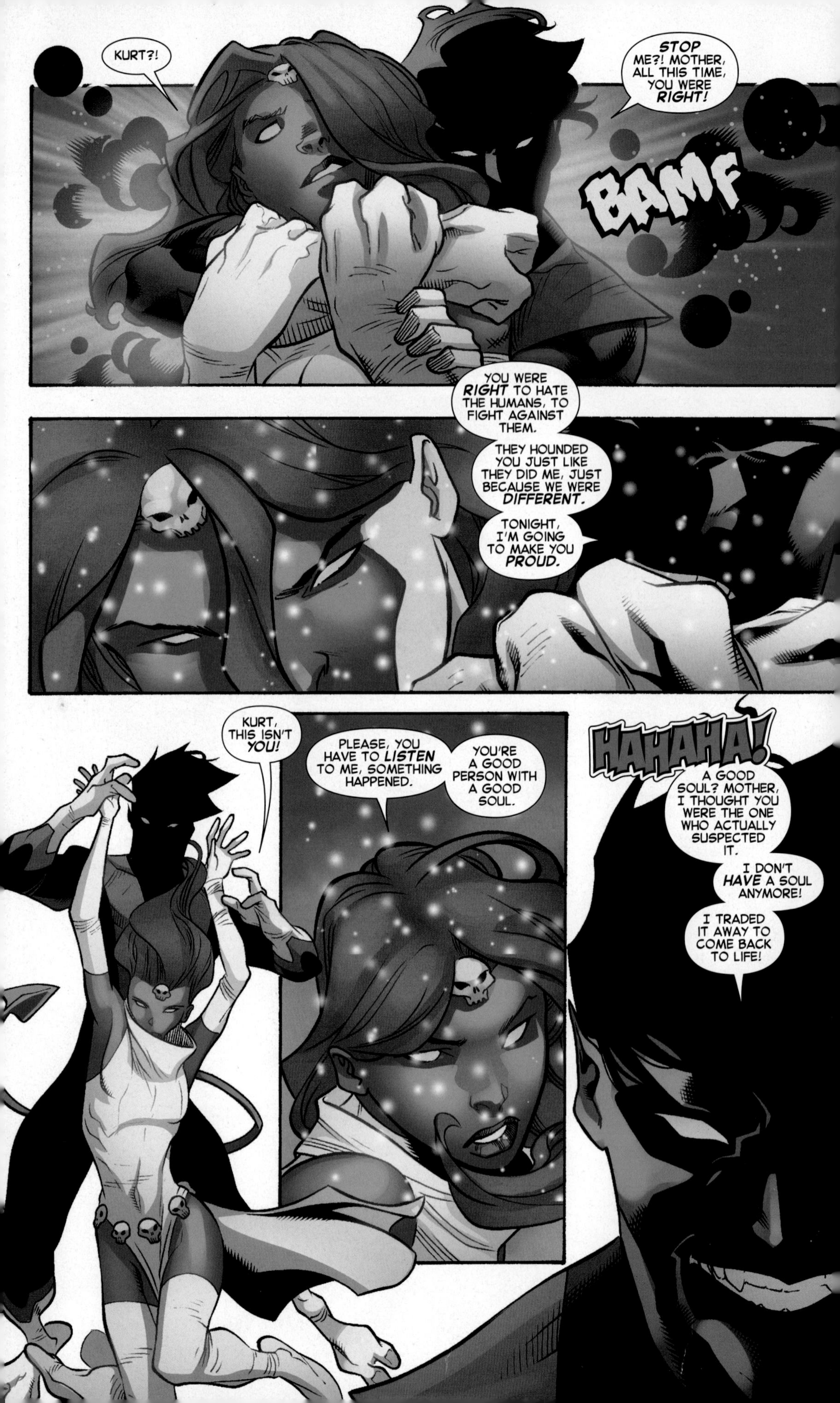
KURT?!
STOP ME?! MOTHER, ALL THIS TIME, YOU WERE RIGHT!
BAMF
YOU WERE RIGHT TO HATE THE HUMANS, TO FIGHT AGAINST THEM.
THEY HOUNDED YOU JUST LIKE THEY DID ME, JUST BECAUSE WE WERE DIFFERENT.
TONIGHT, I'M GOING TO MAKE YOU PROUD.
KURT, THIS ISN'T YOU!
PLEASE, YOU HAVE TO LISTEN TO ME, SOMETHING HAPPENED.
YOU'RE A GOOD PERSON WITH A GOOD SOUL.
HAHAHA!
A GOOD SOUL? MOTHER, I THOUGHT YOU WERE THE ONE WHO ACTUALLY SUSPECTED IT.
I DON'T HAVE A SOUL ANYMORE!
I TRADED IT AWAY TO COME BACK TO LIFE!

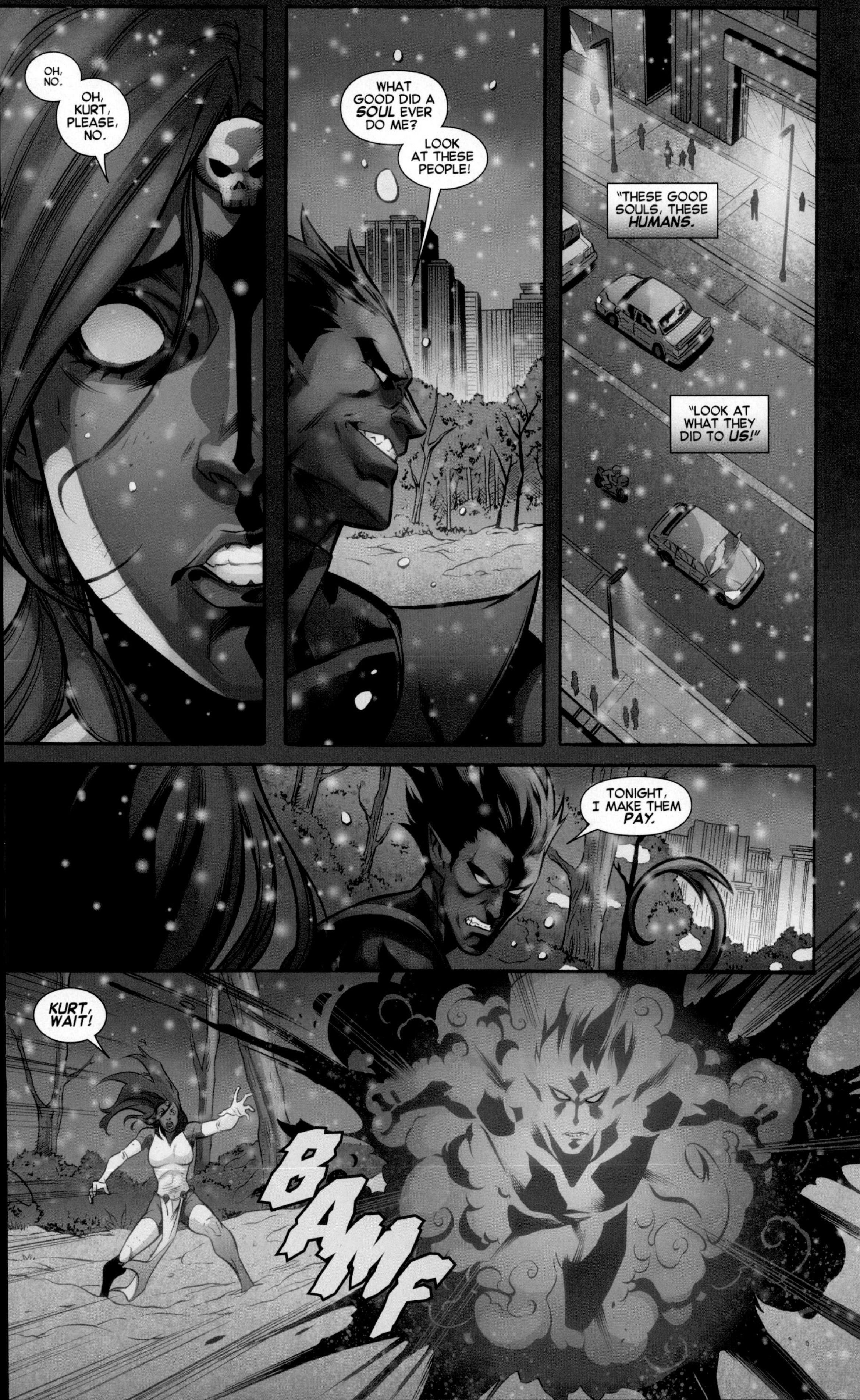
OH, NO.
OH, KURT, PLEASE, NO.
WHAT GOOD DID A SOUL EVER DO ME?
LOOK AT THESE PEOPLE!
"THESE GOOD SOULS, THESE HUMANS.
"LOOK AT WHAT THEY DID TO US!"
TONIGHT, I MAKE THEM PAY.
KURT, WAIT!
BAMF

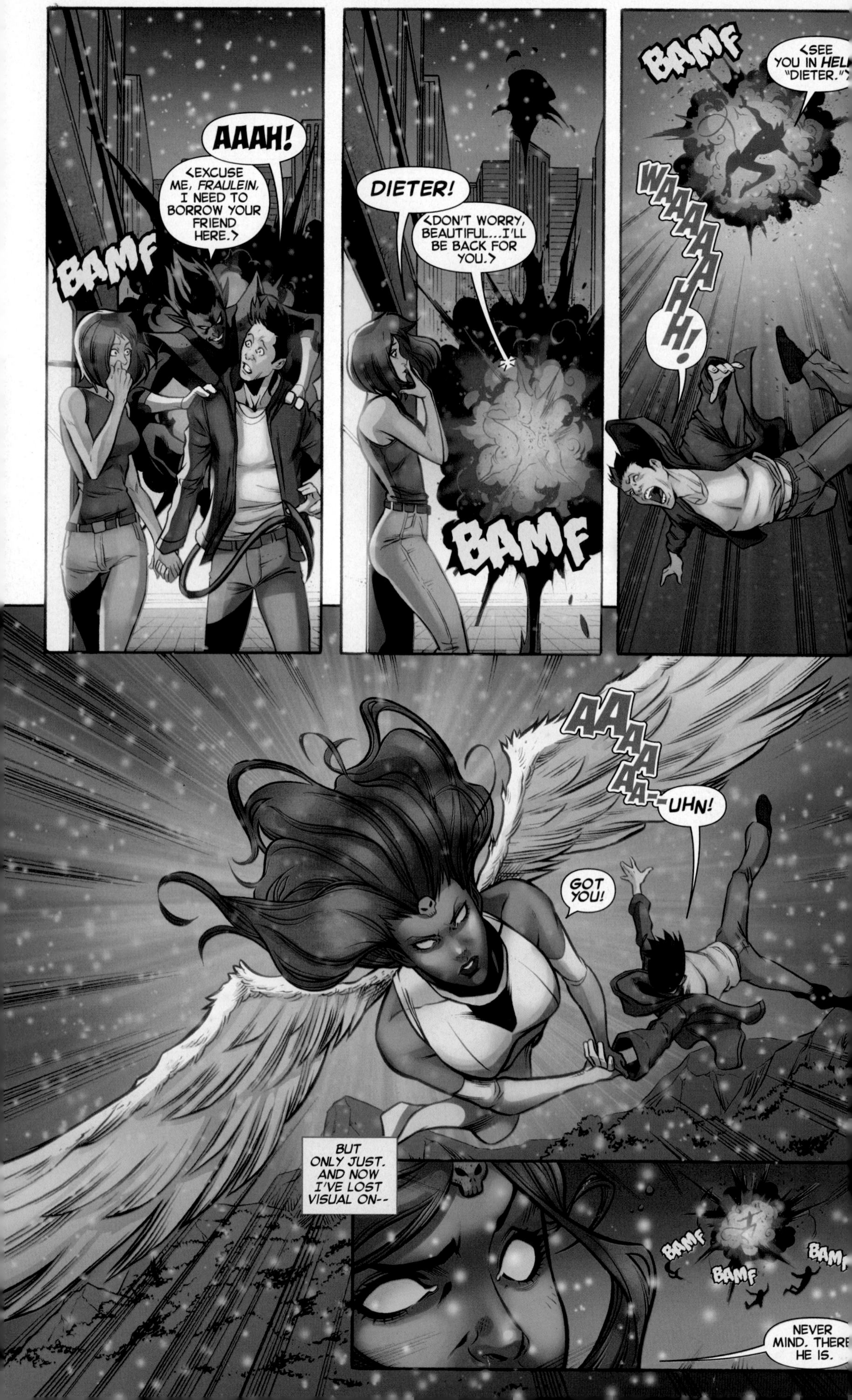
AAAH!
<EXCUSE ME, FRAULEIN, I NEED TO BORROW YOUR FRIEND HERE.>
BAMF
DIETER!
<DON'T WORRY, BEAUTIFUL...I'LL BE BACK FOR YOU.>
BAMF
BAMF
<SEE YOU IN HELL "DIETER.">
WAAAAAAHHH!
AAAAAAA--UHN!
GOT YOU!
BUT ONLY JUST. AND NOW I'VE LOST VISUAL ON--
BAMF
BAMF
BAMF
NEVER MIND. THERE HE IS.

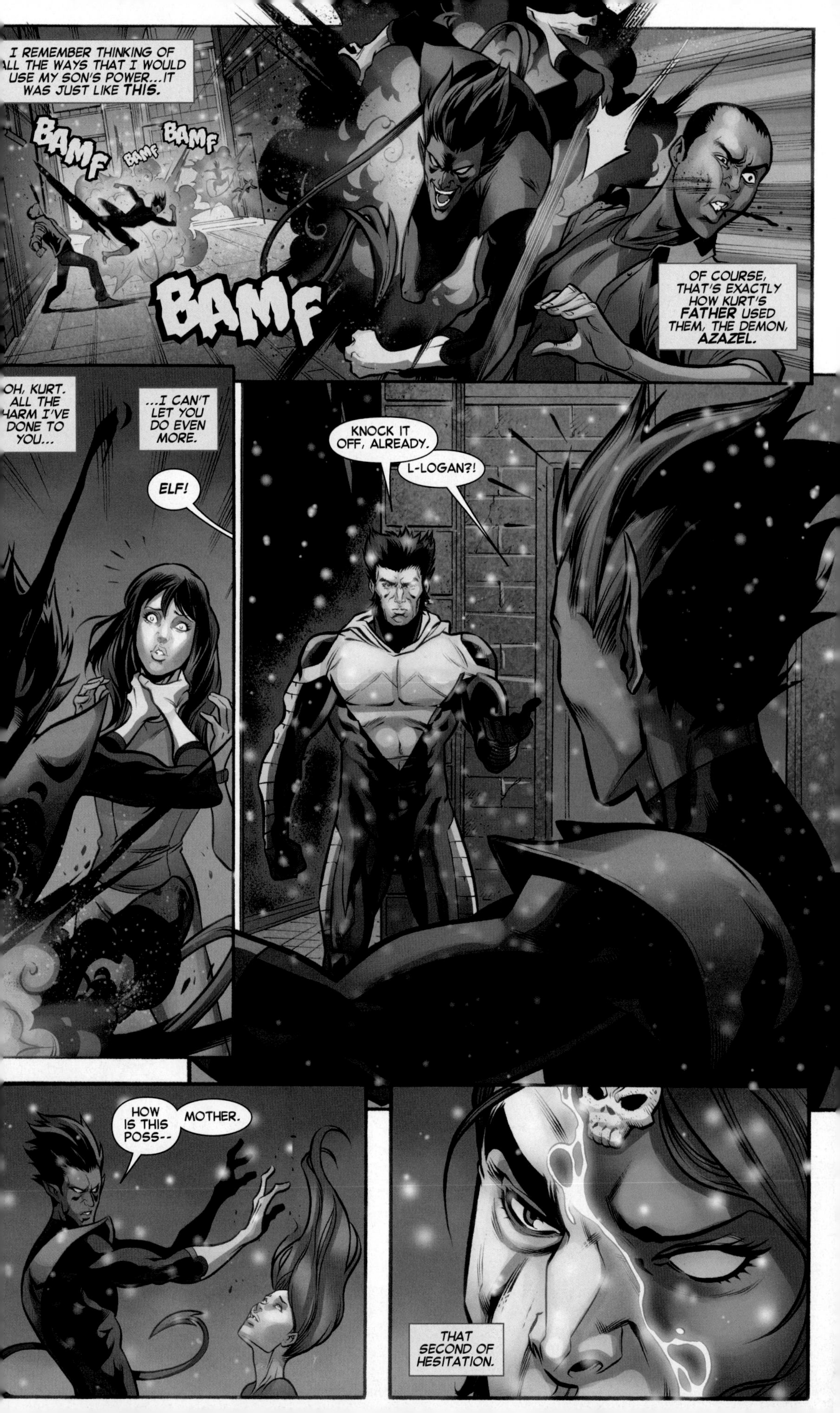
I REMEMBER THINKING OF ALL THE WAYS THAT I WOULD USE MY SON'S POWER...IT WAS JUST LIKE THIS.
BAMF
BAMF
BAMF
BAMF
OF COURSE, THAT'S EXACTLY HOW KURT'S FATHER USED THEM, THE DEMON, AZAZEL.
OH, KURT. ALL THE HARM I'VE DONE TO YOU...
...I CAN'T LET YOU DO EVEN MORE.
ELF!
KNOCK IT OFF, ALREADY.
L-LOGAN?!
HOW IS THIS POSS--
MOTHER.
THAT SECOND OF HESITATION.

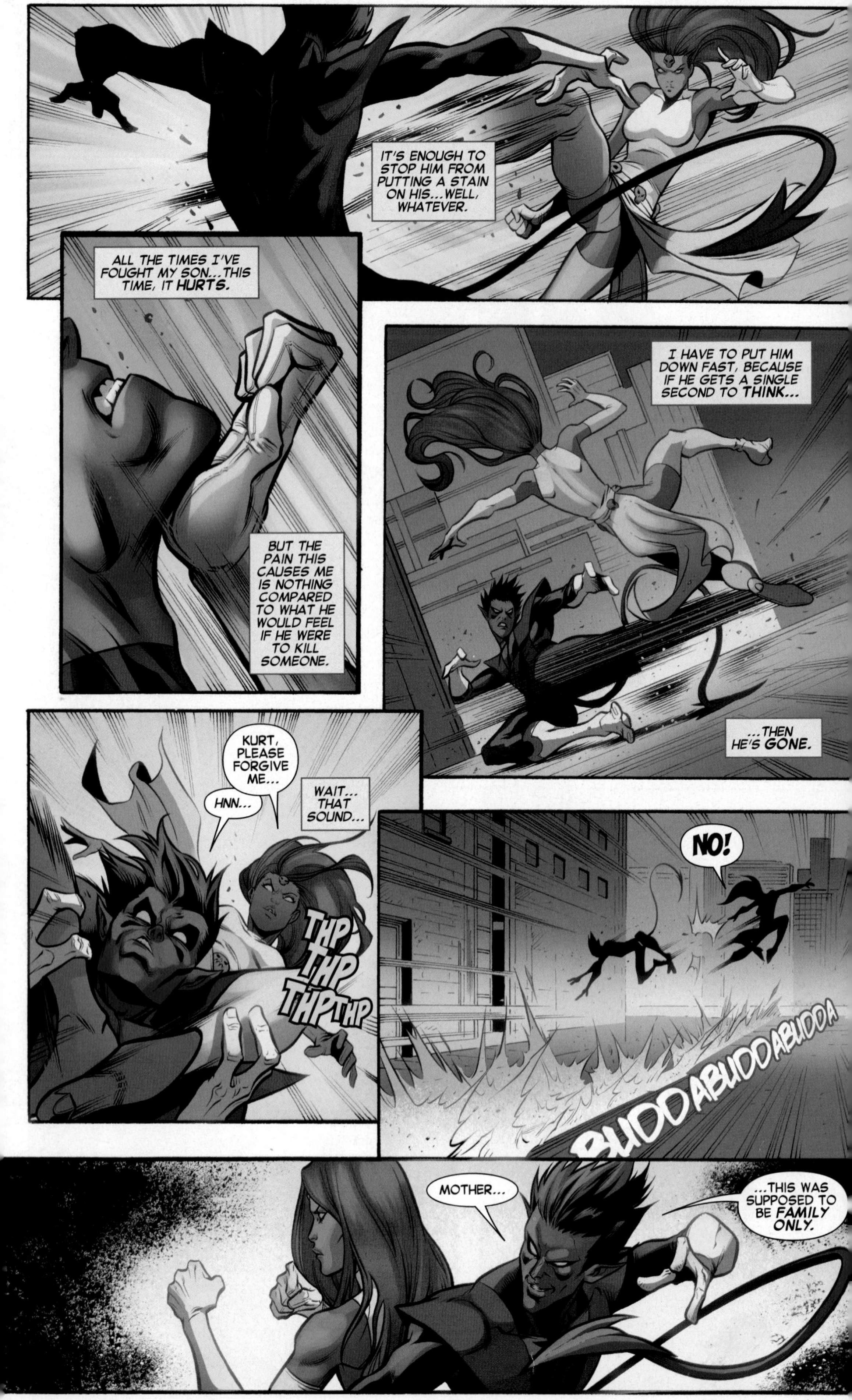
IT'S ENOUGH TO STOP HIM FROM PUTTING A STAIN ON HIS...WELL, WHATEVER.
ALL THE TIMES I'VE FOUGHT MY SON...THIS TIME, IT HURTS.
BUT THE PAIN THIS CAUSES ME IS NOTHING COMPARED TO WHAT HE WOULD FEEL IF HE WERE TO KILL SOMEONE.
I HAVE TO PUT HIM DOWN FAST, BECAUSE IF HE GETS A SINGLE SECOND TO THINK...
...THEN HE'S GONE.
KURT, PLEASE FORGIVE ME...
HNN...
WAIT... THAT SOUND...
THP THP THP THP
NO!
BUDDABUDDABUDDA
MOTHER...
...THIS WAS SUPPOSED TO BE FAMILY ONLY.

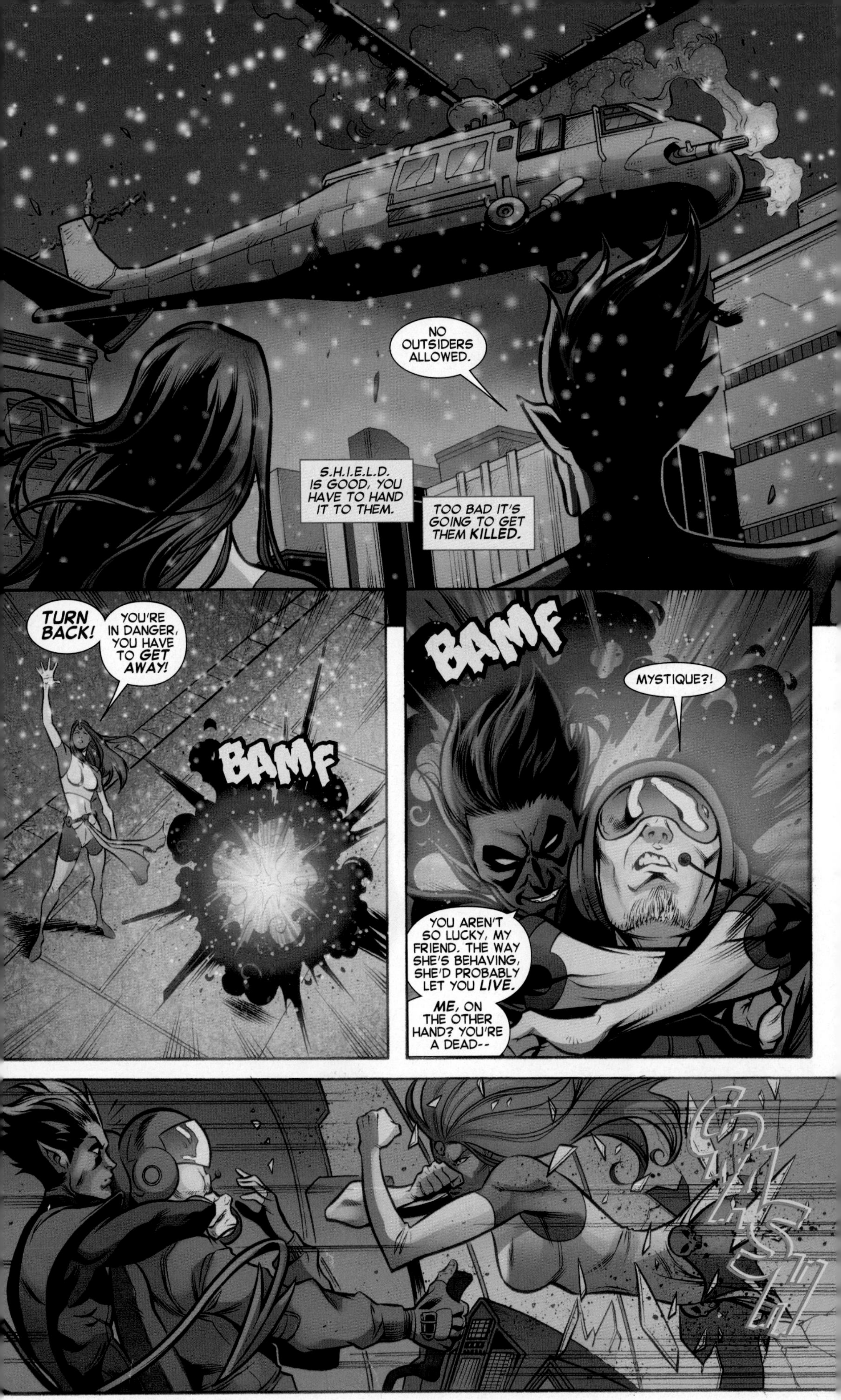
NO OUTSIDERS ALLOWED.
S.H.I.E.L.D. IS GOOD, YOU HAVE TO HAND IT TO THEM.
TOO BAD IT'S GOING TO GET THEM KILLED.
TURN BACK!
YOU'RE IN DANGER, YOU HAVE TO GET AWAY!
BAMF
BAMF
MYSTIQUE?!
YOU AREN'T SO LUCKY, MY FRIEND. THE WAY SHE'S BEHAVING, SHE'D PROBABLY LET YOU LIVE.
ME, ON THE OTHER HAND? YOU'RE A DEAD--

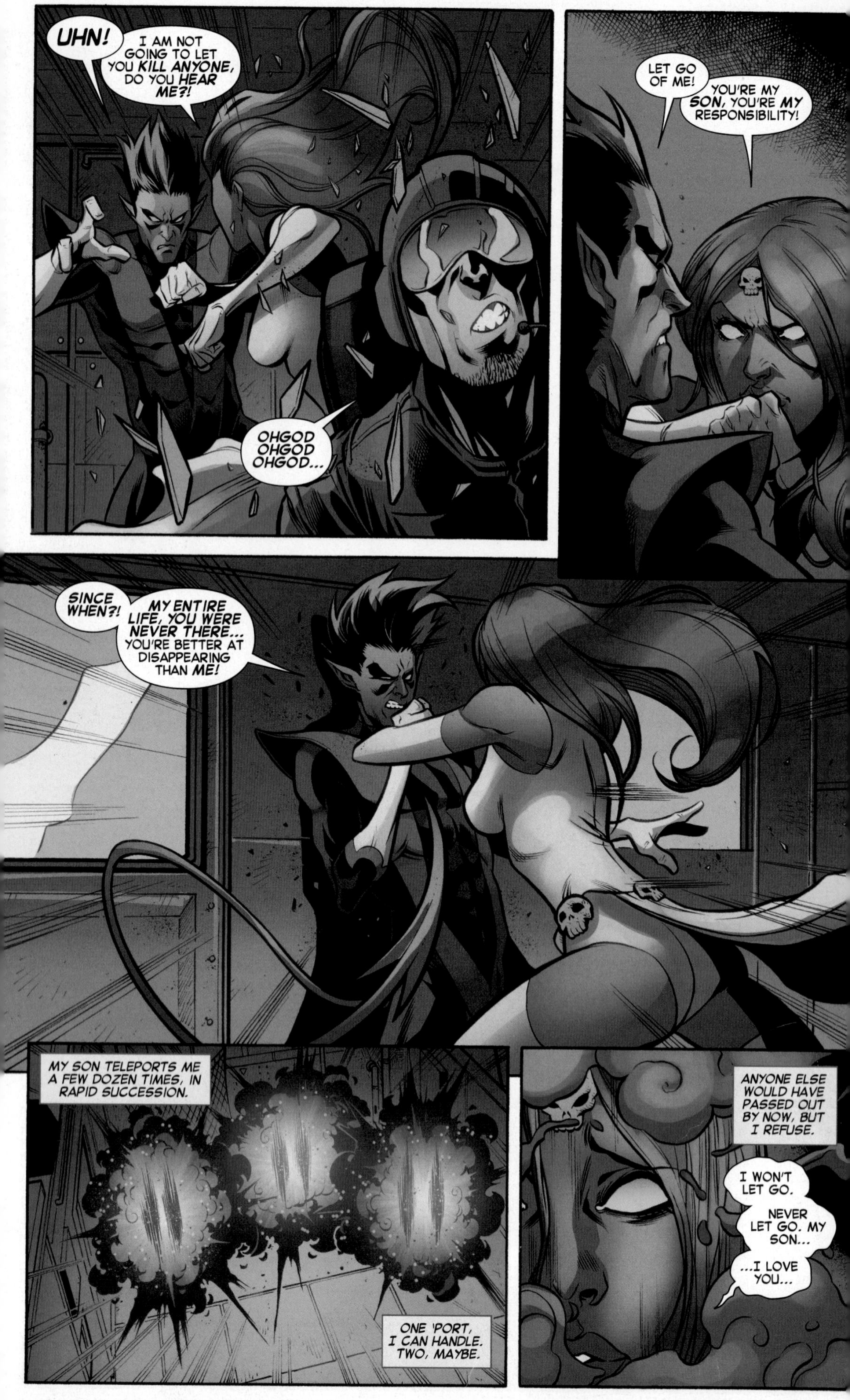
UHN!
I AM NOT GOING TO LET YOU KILL ANYONE, DO YOU HEAR ME?!
OHGOD OHGOD OHGOD...
LET GO OF ME!
YOU'RE MY SON, YOU'RE MY RESPONSIBILITY!
SINCE WHEN?!
MY ENTIRE LIFE, YOU WERE NEVER THERE... YOU'RE BETTER AT DISAPPEARING THAN ME!
MY SON TELEPORTS ME A FEW DOZEN TIMES, IN RAPID SUCCESSION.
ONE 'PORT, I CAN HANDLE. TWO, MAYBE.
ANYONE ELSE WOULD HAVE PASSED OUT BY NOW, BUT I REFUSE.
I WON'T LET GO.
NEVER LET GO. MY SON...
...I LOVE YOU...

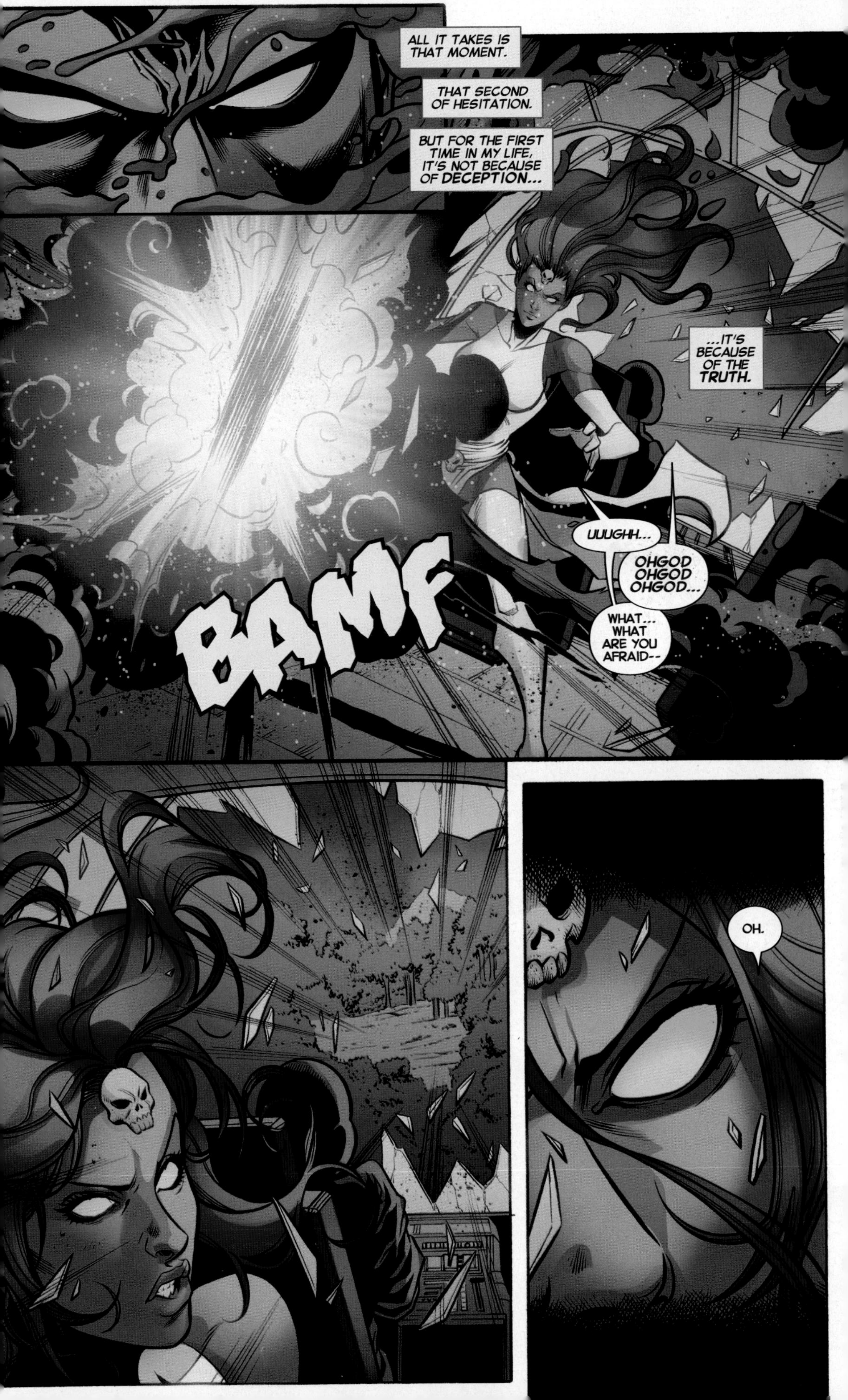
ALL IT TAKES IS THAT MOMENT.
THAT SECOND OF HESITATION.
BUT FOR THE FIRST TIME IN MY LIFE, IT'S NOT BECAUSE OF DECEPTION...
...IT'S BECAUSE OF THE TRUTH.
BAMF
UUUGHH...
OHGOD OHGOD OHGOD...
WHAT... WHAT ARE YOU AFRAID--
OH.

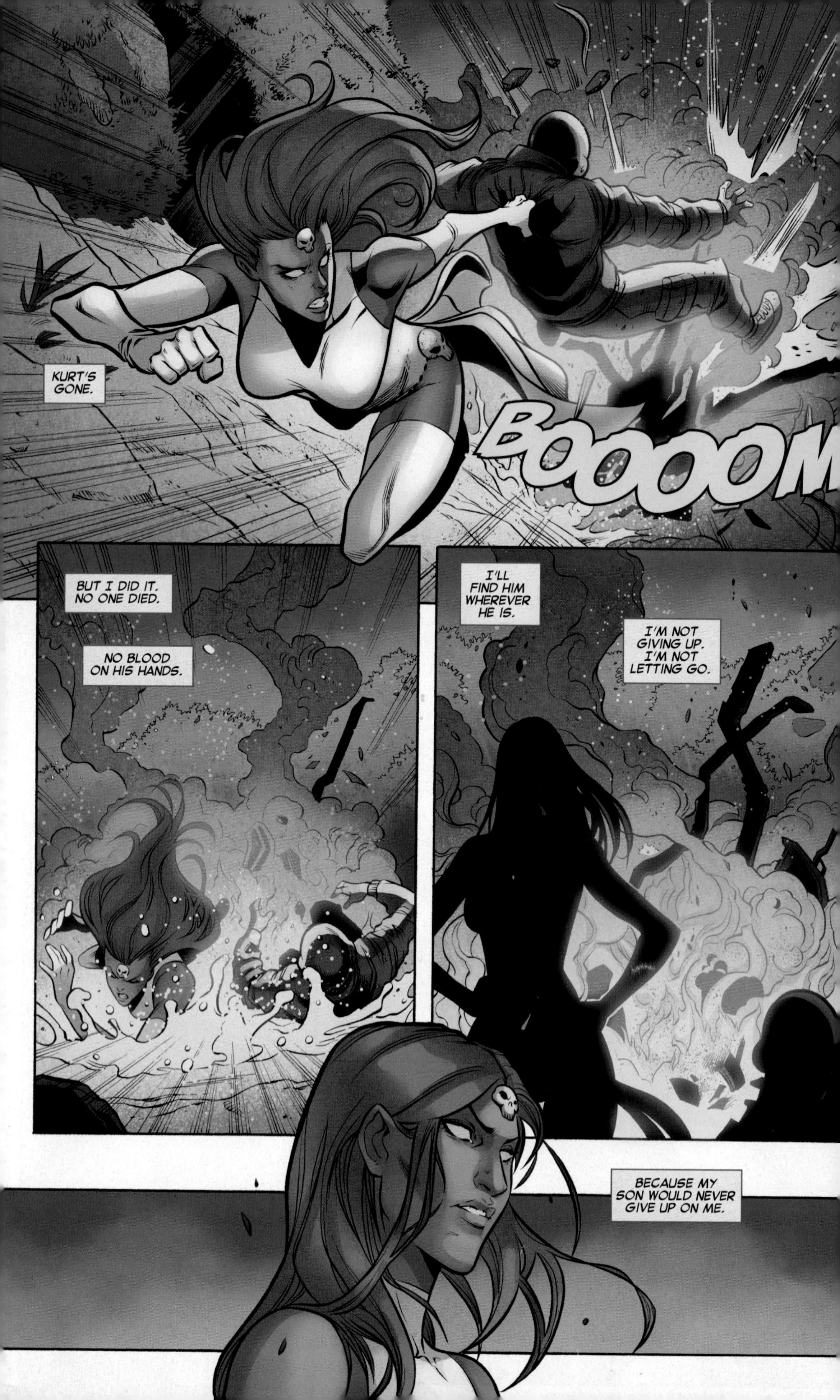

KURT'S GONE.
BOOOOOM
BUT I DID IT. NO ONE DIED.
NO BLOOD ON HIS HANDS.
I'LL FIND HIM WHEREVER HE IS.
I'M NOT GIVING UP. I'M NOT LETTING GO.
BECAUSE MY SON WOULD NEVER GIVE UP ON ME.

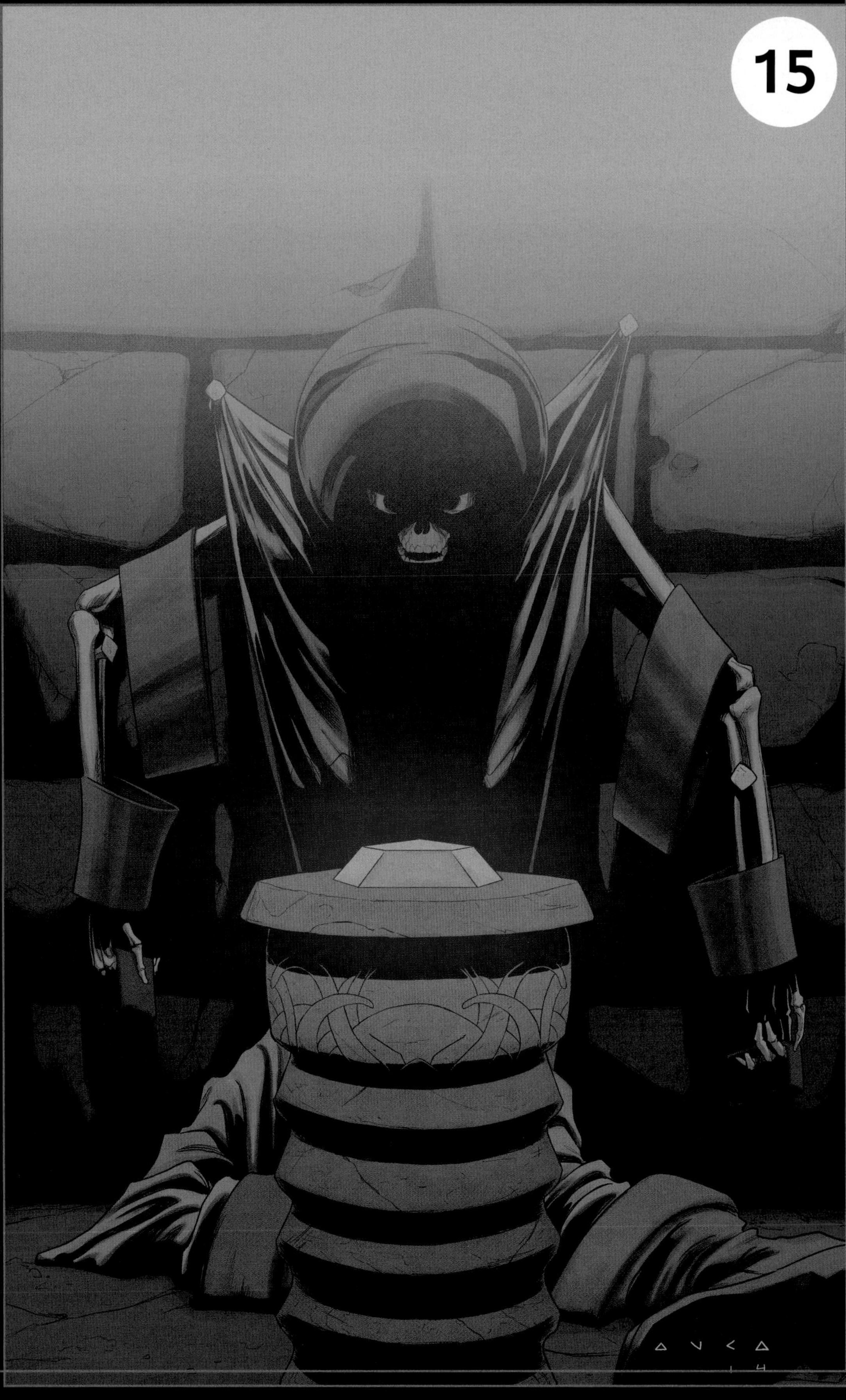
15

THE ONCE AND FUTURE JUGGERNAUT PART 1

THE YEAR 736 A.D.
AS LI PARK, THE IMMORTAL IRON FIST AND THE GREAT SORCERER XUN BATTLED THE ELDER DEMON KNOWN AS CYTTORAK, THEY ASKED THE CREATURE WHAT IT WANTED:
WORSHIP ME!

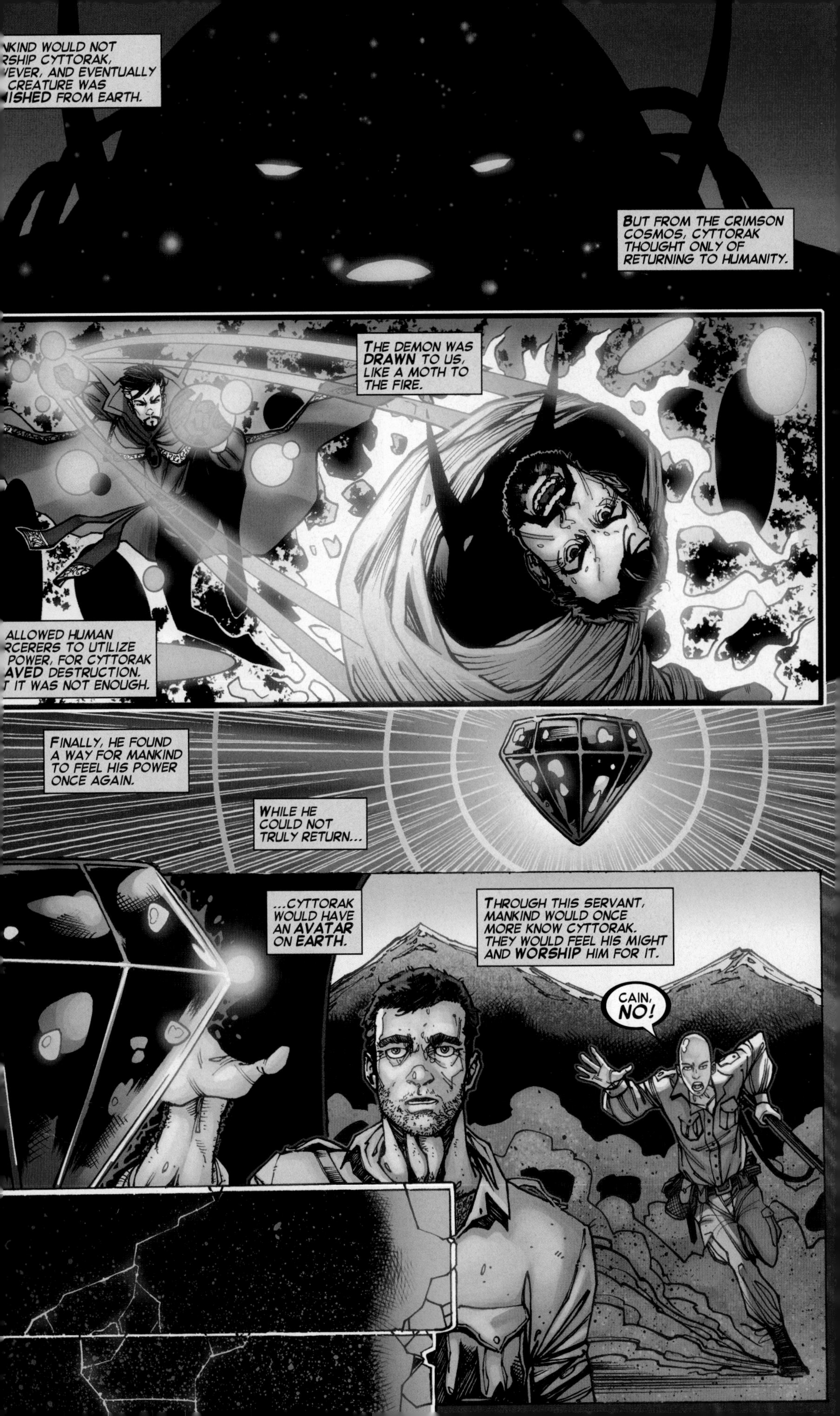
NKIND WOULD NOT
RSHIP CYTTORAK,
VEVER, AND EVENTUALLY
CREATURE WAS
IISHED FROM EARTH.
BUT FROM THE CRIMSON COSMOS, CYTTORAK THOUGHT ONLY OF RETURNING TO HUMANITY.
THE DEMON WAS DRAWN TO US, LIKE A MOTH TO THE FIRE.
ALLOWED HUMAN
RCERERS TO UTILIZE
POWER, FOR CYTTORAK
AVED DESTRUCTION.
T IT WAS NOT ENOUGH.
FINALLY, HE FOUND A WAY FOR MANKIND TO FEEL HIS POWER ONCE AGAIN.
WHILE HE COULD NOT TRULY RETURN...
...CYTTORAK WOULD HAVE AN AVATAR ON EARTH.
THROUGH THIS SERVANT, MANKIND WOULD ONCE MORE KNOW CYTTORAK. THEY WOULD FEEL HIS MIGHT AND WORSHIP HIM FOR IT.
CAIN, NO!

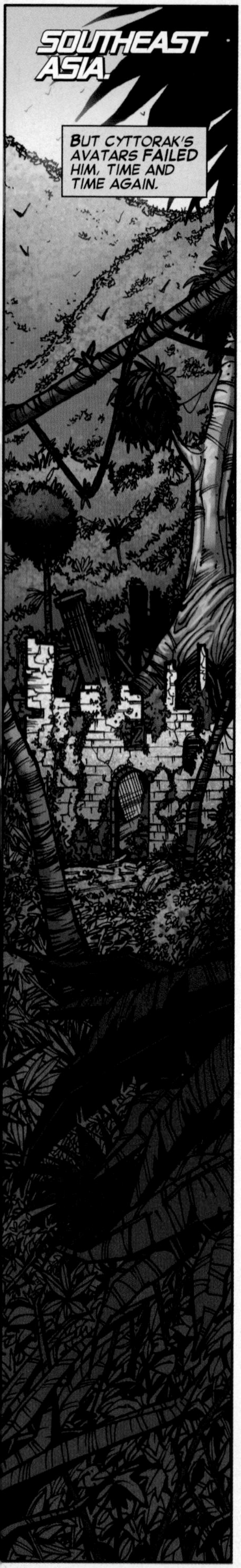
SOUTHEAST ASIA.
BUT CYTTORAK'S AVATARS FAILED HIM, TIME AND TIME AGAIN.

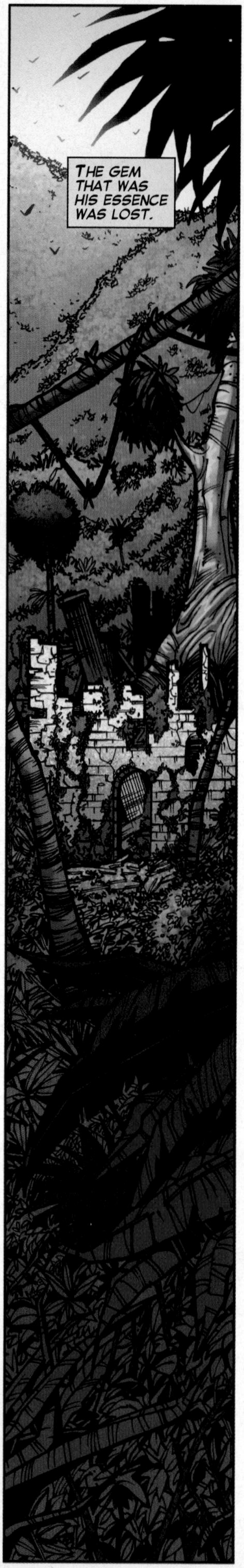
THE GEM THAT WAS HIS ESSENCE WAS LOST.

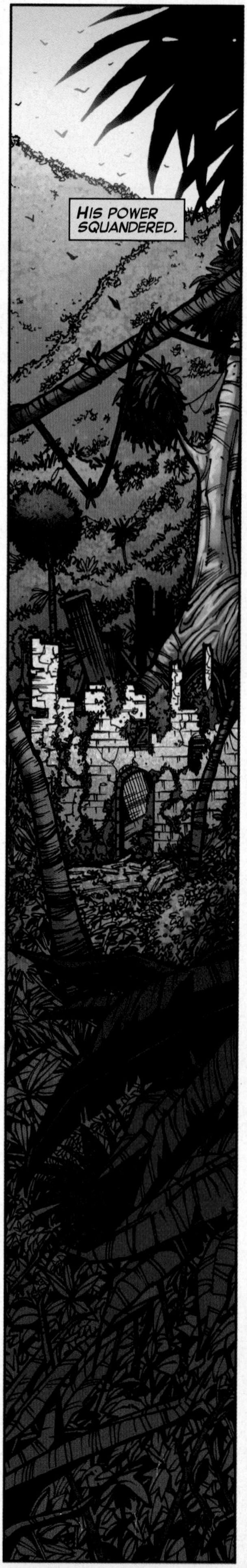
HIS POWER SQUANDERED.

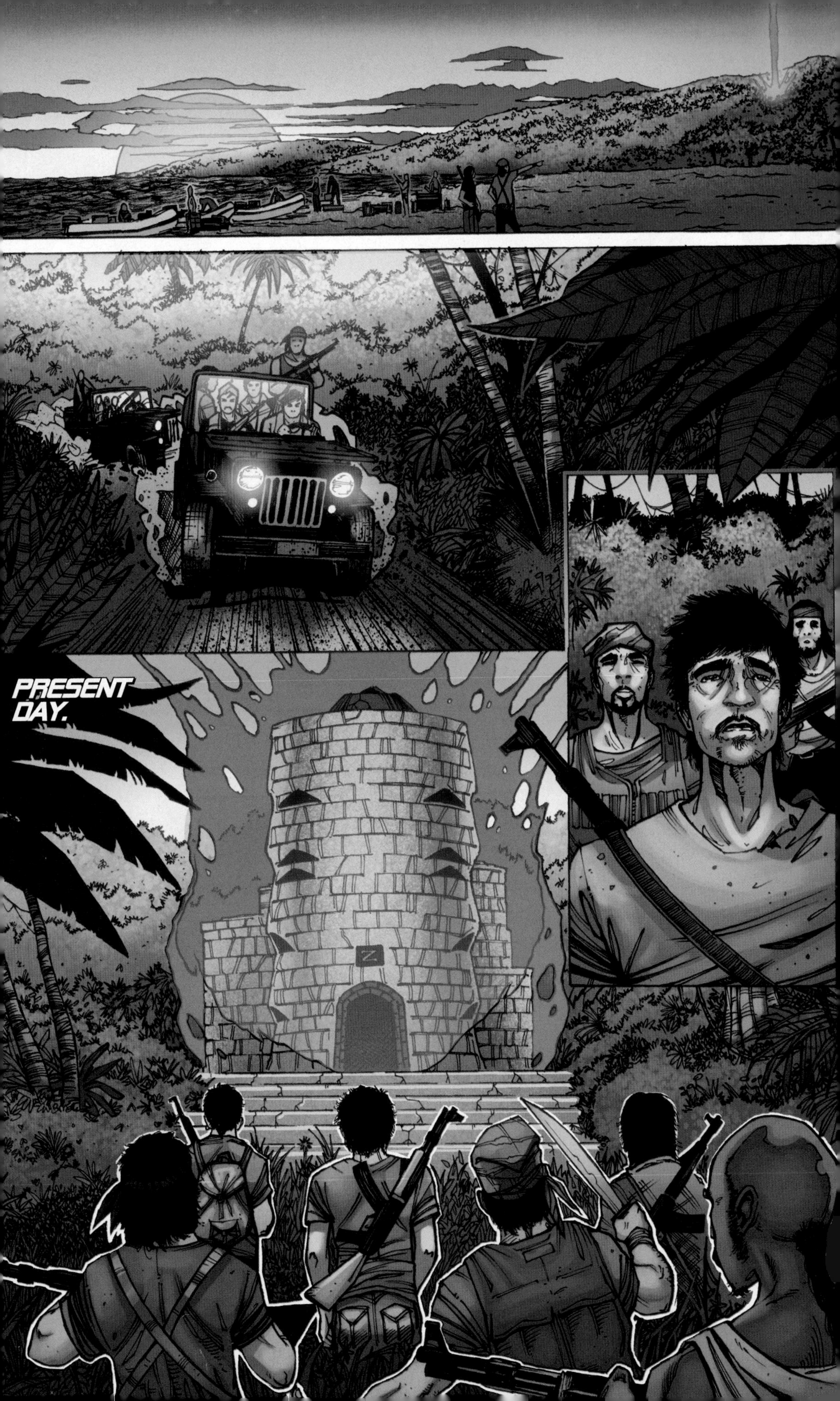
PRESENT DAY.

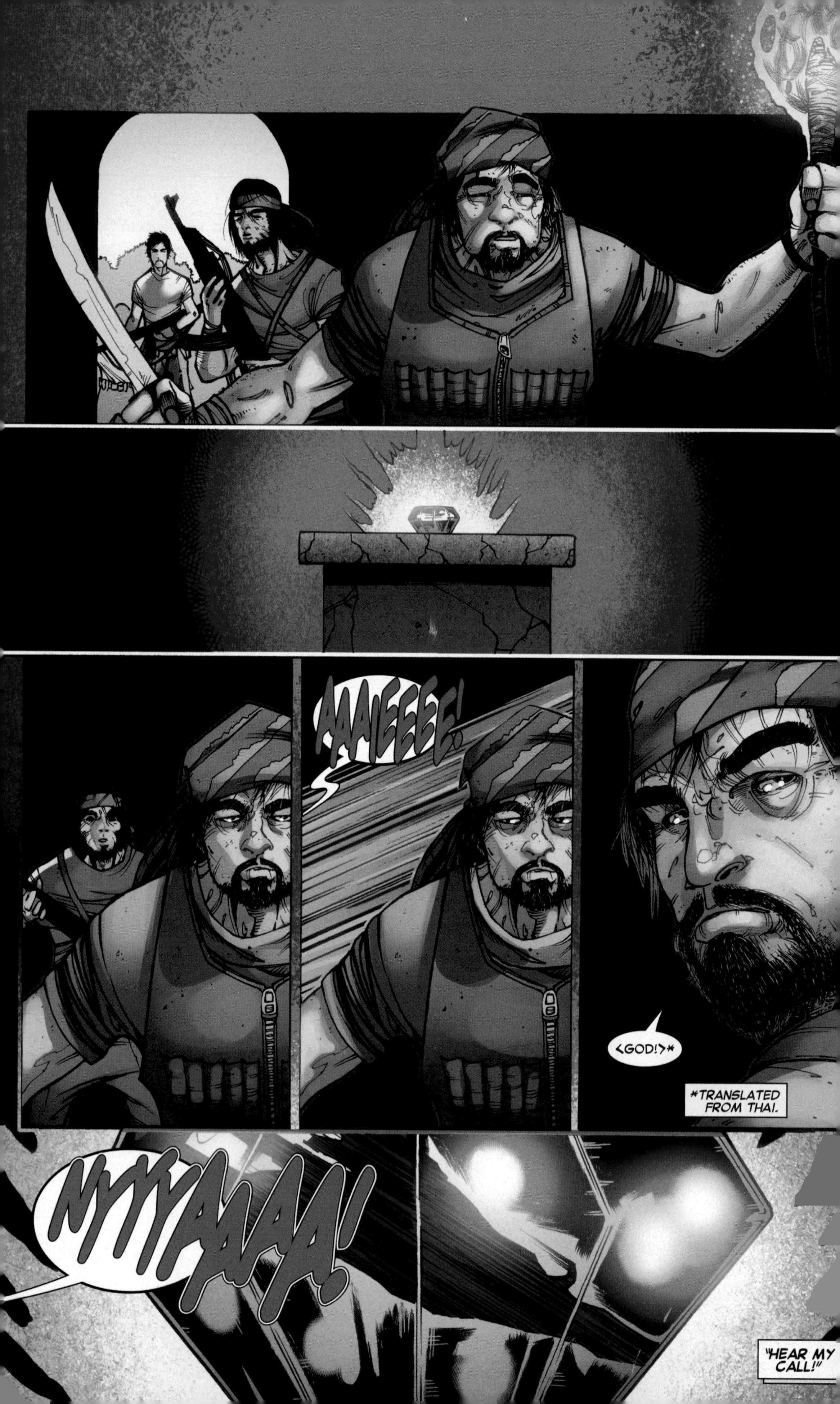
AAAIEEEE!
<GOD!>*
*TRANSLATED FROM THAI.
NYYYAAAA!
"HEAR MY CALL!"

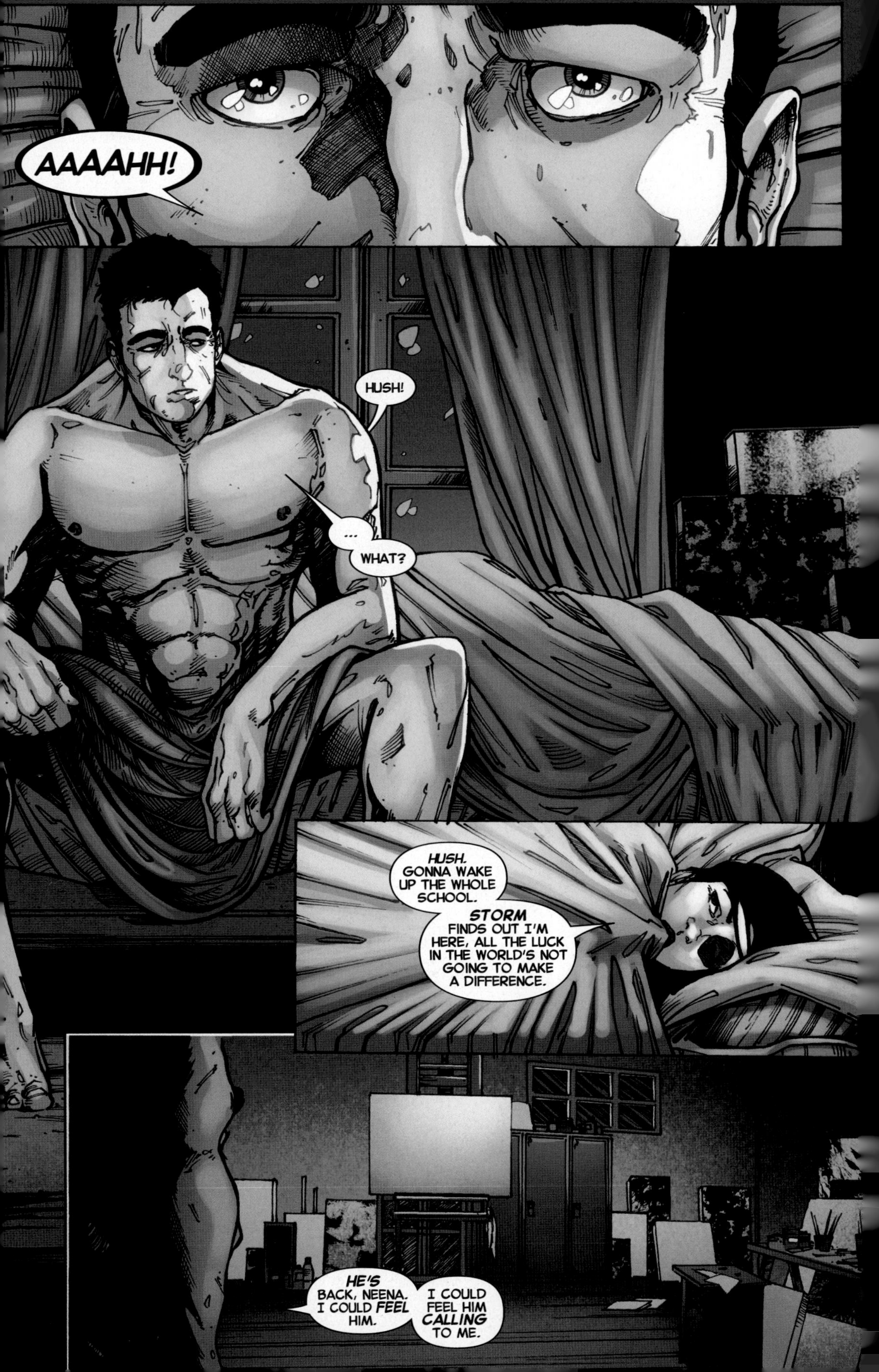
AAAAHH!
HUSH!
... WHAT?
HUSH. GONNA WAKE UP THE WHOLE SCHOOL.
STORM FINDS OUT I'M HERE, ALL THE LUCK IN THE WORLD'S NOT GOING TO MAKE A DIFFERENCE.
HE'S BACK, NEENA. I COULD FEEL HIM.
I COULD FEEL HIM CALLING TO ME.

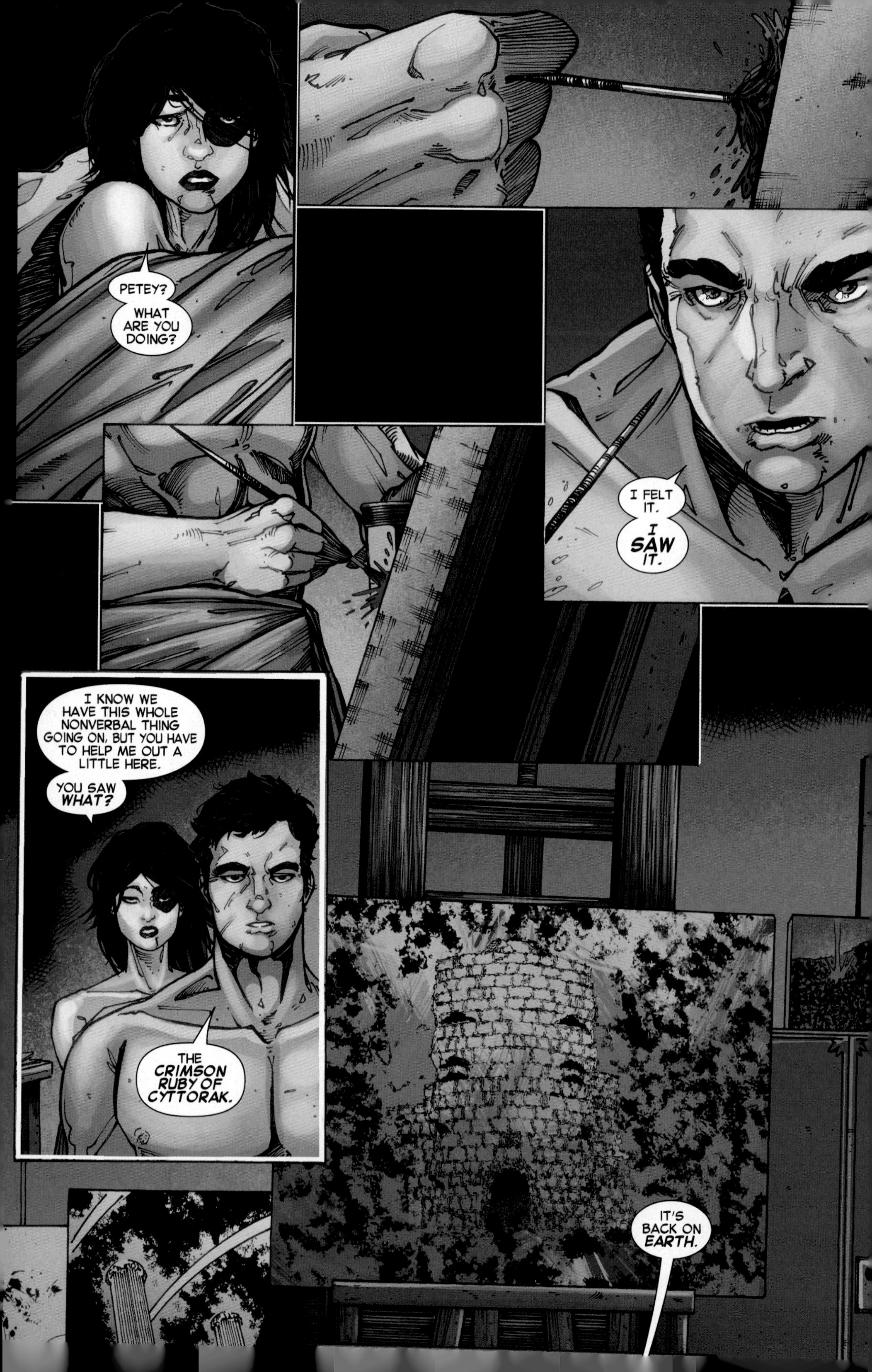
PETEY? WHAT ARE YOU DOING?
I FELT IT. I SAW IT.
I KNOW WE HAVE THIS WHOLE NONVERBAL THING GOING ON, BUT YOU HAVE TO HELP ME OUT A LITTLE HERE.
YOU SAW WHAT?
THE CRIMSON RUBY OF CYTTORAK.
IT'S BACK ON EARTH.

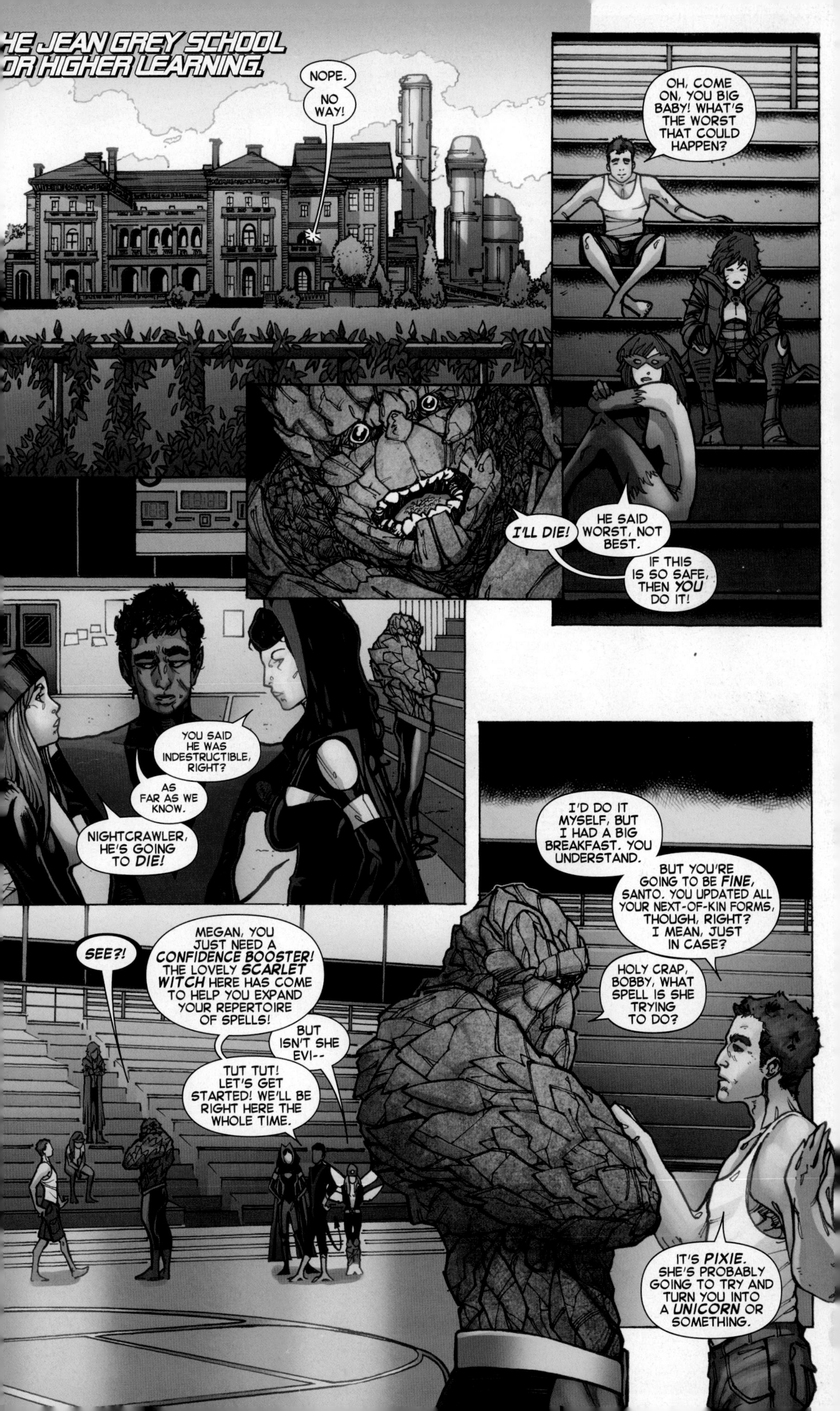
HE JEAN GREY SCHOOL
OR HIGHER LEARNING.
NOPE.
NO WAY!
OH, COME ON, YOU BIG BABY! WHAT'S THE WORST THAT COULD HAPPEN?
I'LL DIE!
HE SAID WORST, NOT BEST.
IF THIS IS SO SAFE, THEN YOU DO IT!
YOU SAID HE WAS INDESTRUCTIBLE, RIGHT?
AS FAR AS WE KNOW.
NIGHTCRAWLER, HE'S GOING TO DIE!
I'D DO IT MYSELF, BUT I HAD A BIG BREAKFAST. YOU UNDERSTAND.
BUT YOU'RE GOING TO BE FINE, SANTO. YOU UPDATED ALL YOUR NEXT-OF-KIN FORMS, THOUGH, RIGHT? I MEAN, JUST IN CASE?
SEE?!
MEGAN, YOU JUST NEED A CONFIDENCE BOOSTER! THE LOVELY SCARLET WITCH HERE HAS COME TO HELP YOU EXPAND YOUR REPERTOIRE OF SPELLS!
BUT ISN'T SHE EVI--
TUT TUT! LET'S GET STARTED! WE'LL BE RIGHT HERE THE WHOLE TIME.
HOLY CRAP, BOBBY, WHAT SPELL IS SHE TRYING TO DO?
IT'S PIXIE. SHE'S PROBABLY GOING TO TRY AND TURN YOU INTO A UNICORN OR SOMETHING.

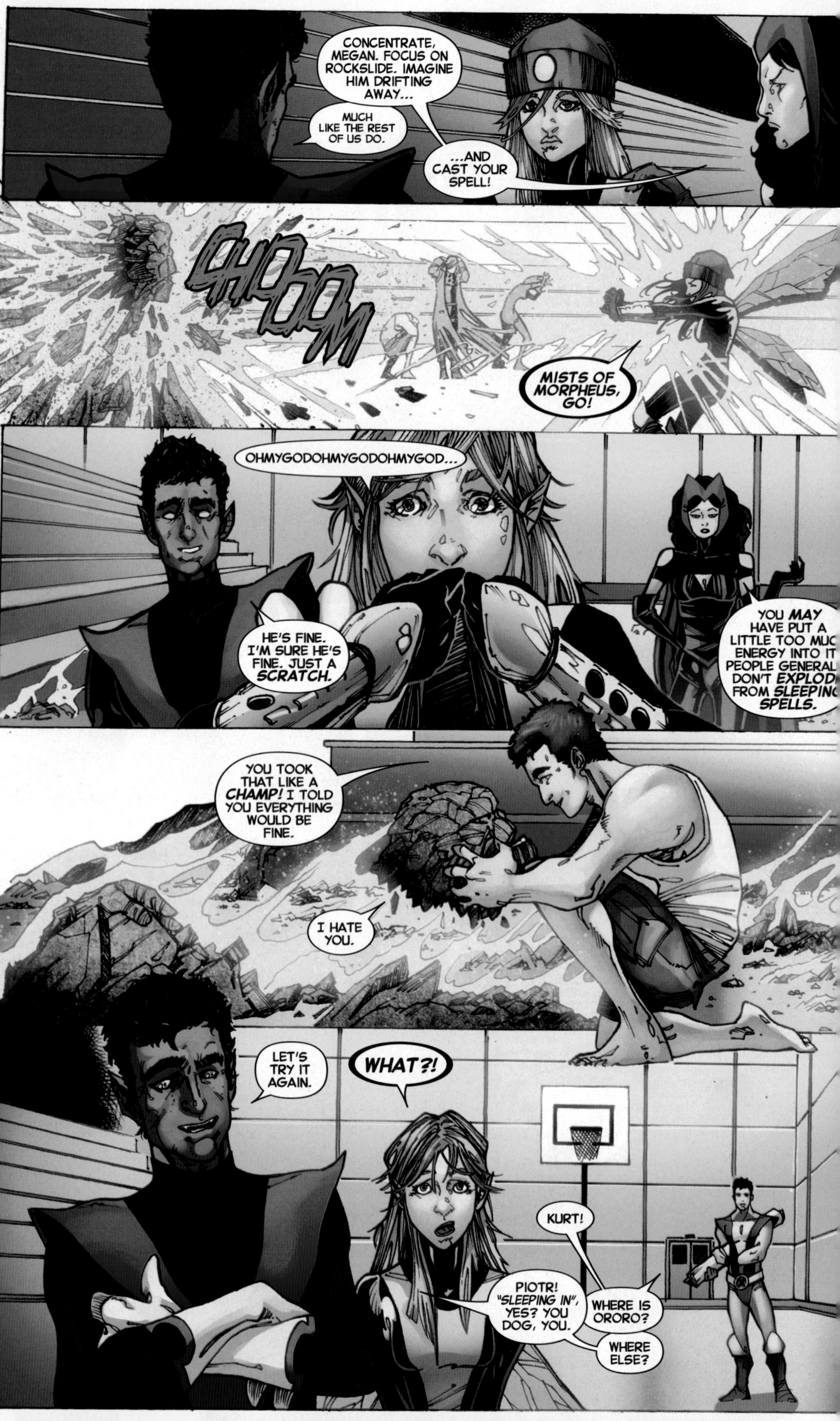
CONCENTRATE, MEGAN. FOCUS ON ROCKSLIDE. IMAGINE HIM DRIFTING AWAY...
MUCH LIKE THE REST OF US DO.
...AND CAST YOUR SPELL!
CHOOOM
MISTS OF MORPHEUS, GO!
OHMYGODOHMYGODOHMYGOD...
HE'S FINE. I'M SURE HE'S FINE. JUST A SCRATCH.
YOU MAY HAVE PUT A LITTLE TOO MUC ENERGY INTO IT PEOPLE GENERAL DON'T EXPLOD FROM SLEEPING SPELLS.
YOU TOOK THAT LIKE A CHAMP! I TOLD YOU EVERYTHING WOULD BE FINE.
I HATE YOU.
LET'S TRY IT AGAIN.
WHAT?!
KURT!
PIOTR! "SLEEPING IN", YES? YOU DOG, YOU.
WHERE IS ORORO?
WHERE ELSE?

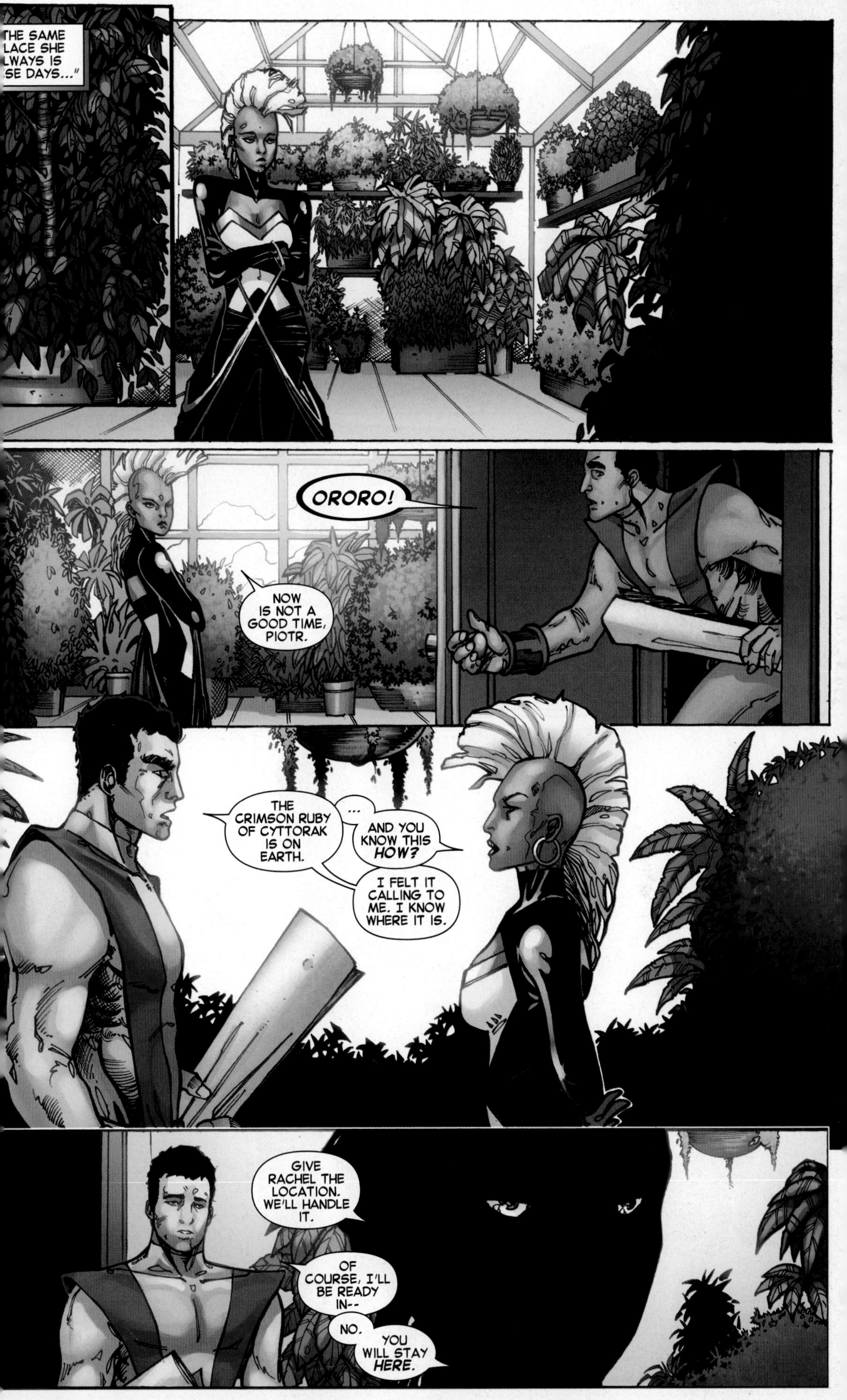
THE SAME
LACE SHE
LWAYS IS
SE DAYS..."
ORORO!
NOW IS NOT A GOOD TIME, PIOTR.
THE CRIMSON RUBY OF CYTTORAK IS ON EARTH.
...
AND YOU KNOW THIS *HOW?*
I FELT IT CALLING TO ME. I KNOW WHERE IT IS.
GIVE RACHEL THE LOCATION. WE'LL HANDLE IT.
OF COURSE, I'LL BE READY IN--
NO.
YOU WILL STAY *HERE.*

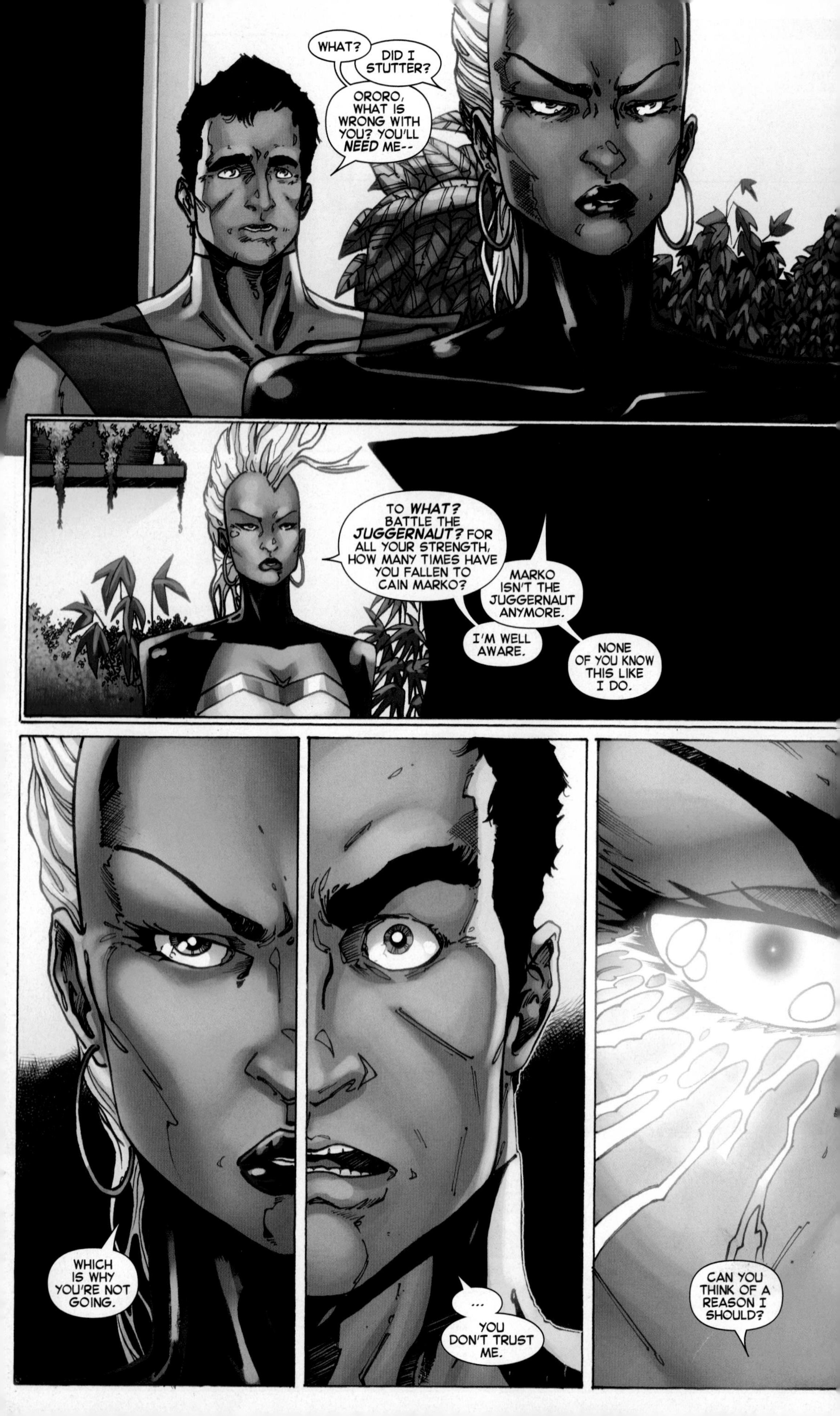

WHAT?
DID I STUTTER?
ORORO, WHAT IS WRONG WITH YOU? YOU'LL *NEED* ME--
TO *WHAT?* BATTLE THE *JUGGERNAUT?* FOR ALL YOUR STRENGTH, HOW MANY TIMES HAVE YOU FALLEN TO CAIN MARKO?
MARKO ISN'T THE JUGGERNAUT ANYMORE.
I'M WELL AWARE.
NONE OF YOU KNOW THIS LIKE I DO.
WHICH IS WHY YOU'RE NOT GOING.
...
YOU DON'T TRUST ME.
CAN YOU THINK OF A REASON I SHOULD?

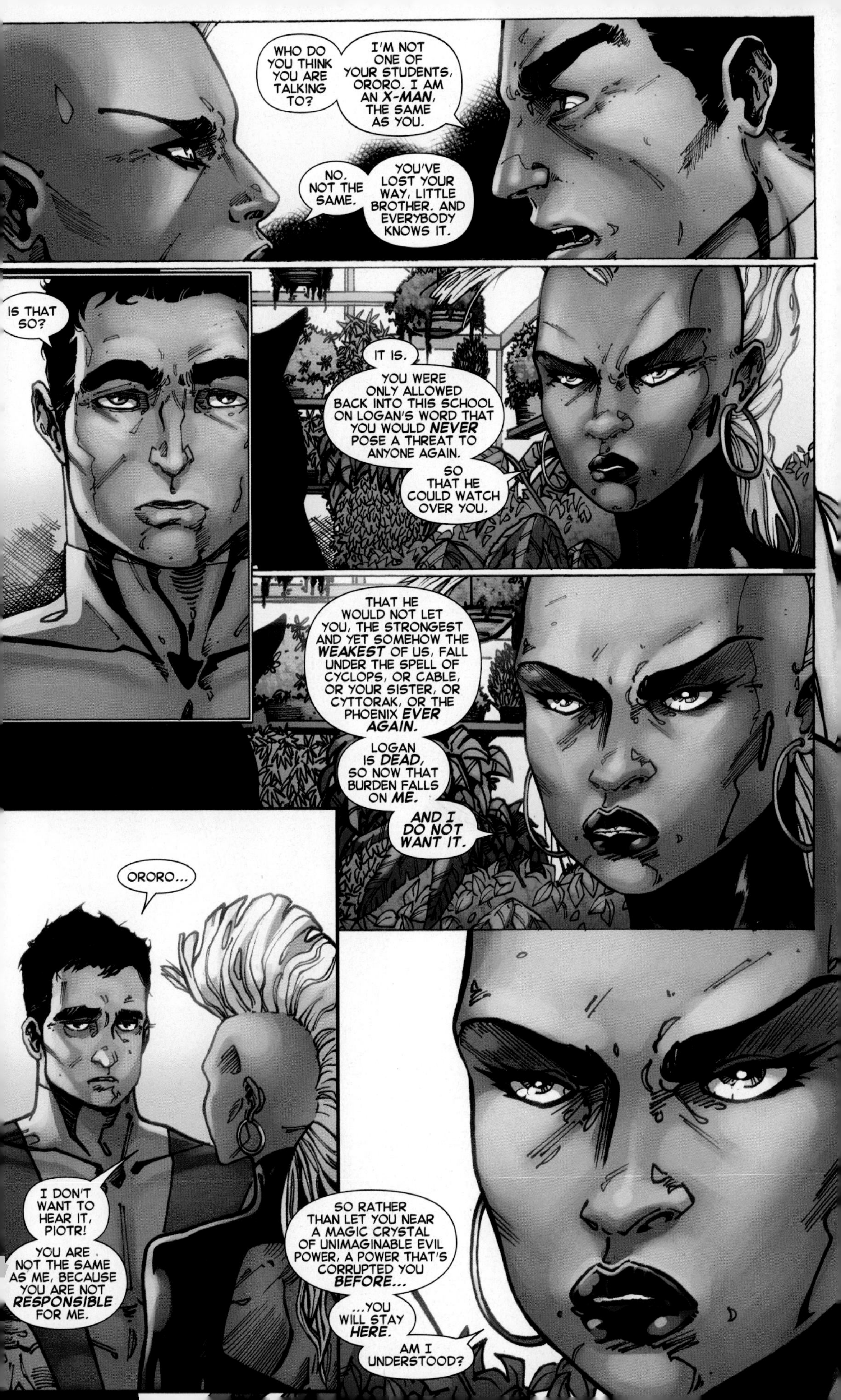
WHO DO YOU THINK YOU ARE TALKING TO?
I'M NOT ONE OF YOUR STUDENTS, ORORO. I AM AN X-MAN, THE SAME AS YOU.
NO. NOT THE SAME.
YOU'VE LOST YOUR WAY, LITTLE BROTHER. AND EVERYBODY KNOWS IT.
IS THAT SO?
IT IS.
YOU WERE ONLY ALLOWED BACK INTO THIS SCHOOL ON LOGAN'S WORD THAT YOU WOULD NEVER POSE A THREAT TO ANYONE AGAIN.
SO THAT HE COULD WATCH OVER YOU.
THAT HE WOULD NOT LET YOU, THE STRONGEST AND YET SOMEHOW THE WEAKEST OF US, FALL UNDER THE SPELL OF CYCLOPS, OR CABLE, OR YOUR SISTER, OR CYTTORAK, OR THE PHOENIX EVER AGAIN.
LOGAN IS DEAD, SO NOW THAT BURDEN FALLS ON ME.
AND I DO NOT WANT IT.
ORORO...
I DON'T WANT TO HEAR IT, PIOTR!
YOU ARE NOT THE SAME AS ME, BECAUSE YOU ARE NOT RESPONSIBLE FOR ME.
SO RATHER THAN LET YOU NEAR A MAGIC CRYSTAL OF UNIMAGINABLE EVIL POWER, A POWER THAT'S CORRUPTED YOU BEFORE...
...YOU WILL STAY HERE.
AM I UNDERSTOOD?

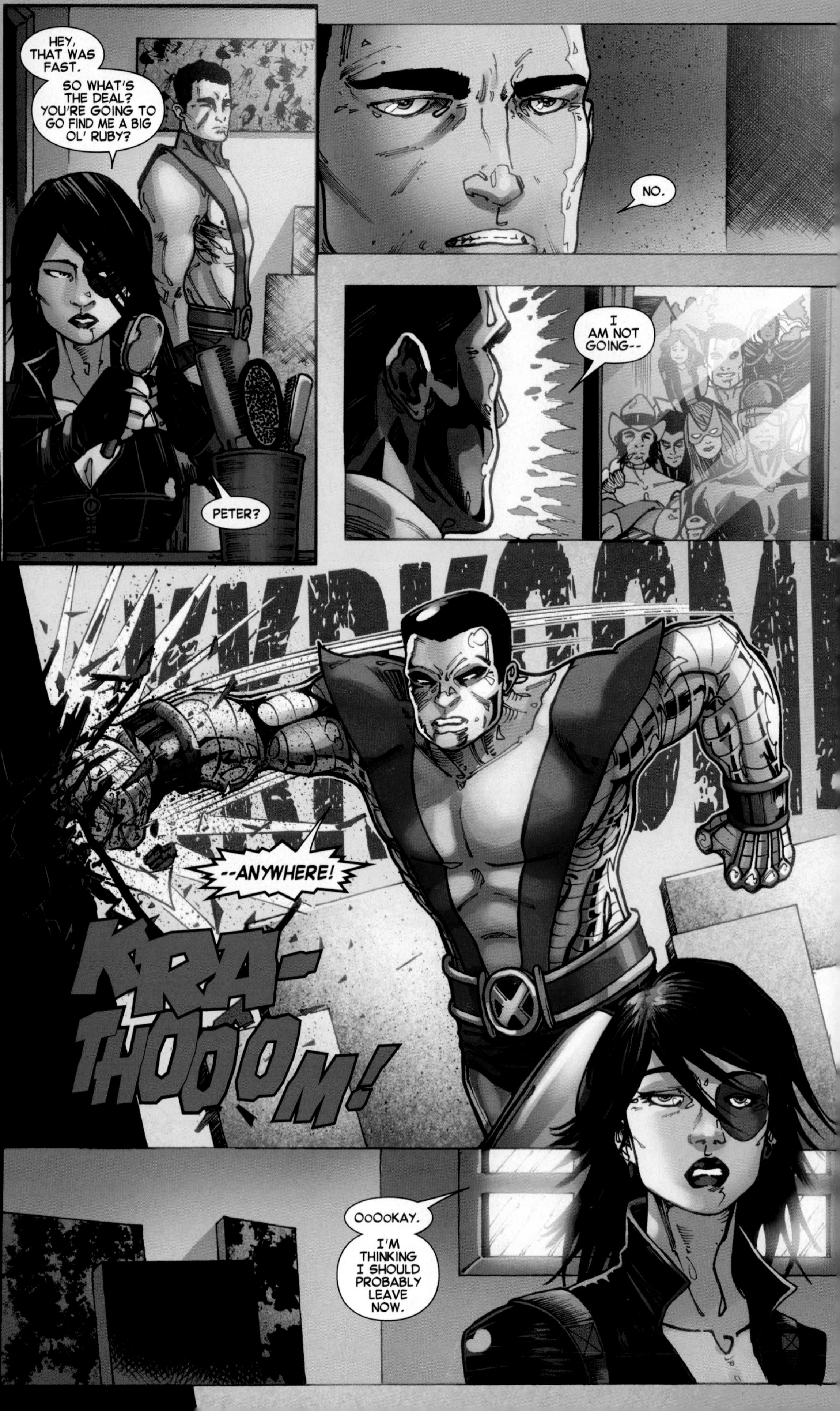

HEY, THAT WAS FAST.
SO WHAT'S THE DEAL? YOU'RE GOING TO GO FIND ME A BIG OL' RUBY?
PETER?
NO.
I AM NOT GOING--
--ANYWHERE!
KRA-THOOOOM!
OOOOKAY.
I'M THINKING I SHOULD PROBABLY LEAVE NOW.

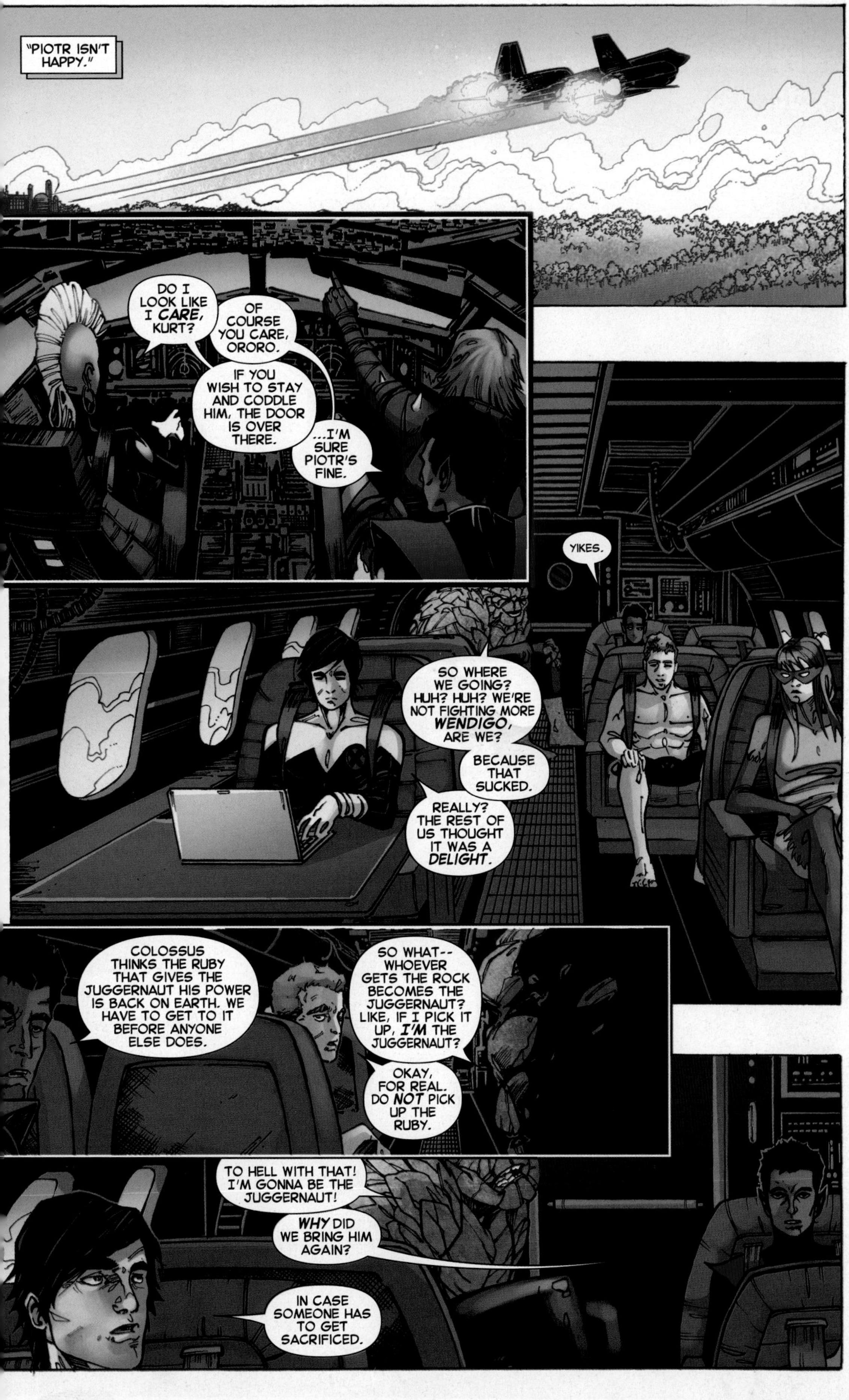
"PIOTR ISN'T HAPPY."
DO I LOOK LIKE I CARE, KURT?
OF COURSE YOU CARE, ORORO.
IF YOU WISH TO STAY AND CODDLE HIM, THE DOOR IS OVER THERE.
...I'M SURE PIOTR'S FINE.
YIKES.
SO WHERE WE GOING? HUH? HUH? WE'RE NOT FIGHTING MORE WENDIGO, ARE WE?
BECAUSE THAT SUCKED.
REALLY? THE REST OF US THOUGHT IT WAS A DELIGHT.
COLOSSUS THINKS THE RUBY THAT GIVES THE JUGGERNAUT HIS POWER IS BACK ON EARTH. WE HAVE TO GET TO IT BEFORE ANYONE ELSE DOES.
SO WHAT-- WHOEVER GETS THE ROCK BECOMES THE JUGGERNAUT? LIKE, IF I PICK IT UP, I'M THE JUGGERNAUT?
OKAY, FOR REAL. DO NOT PICK UP THE RUBY.
TO HELL WITH THAT! I'M GONNA BE THE JUGGERNAUT!
WHY DID WE BRING HIM AGAIN?
IN CASE SOMEONE HAS TO GET SACRIFICED.

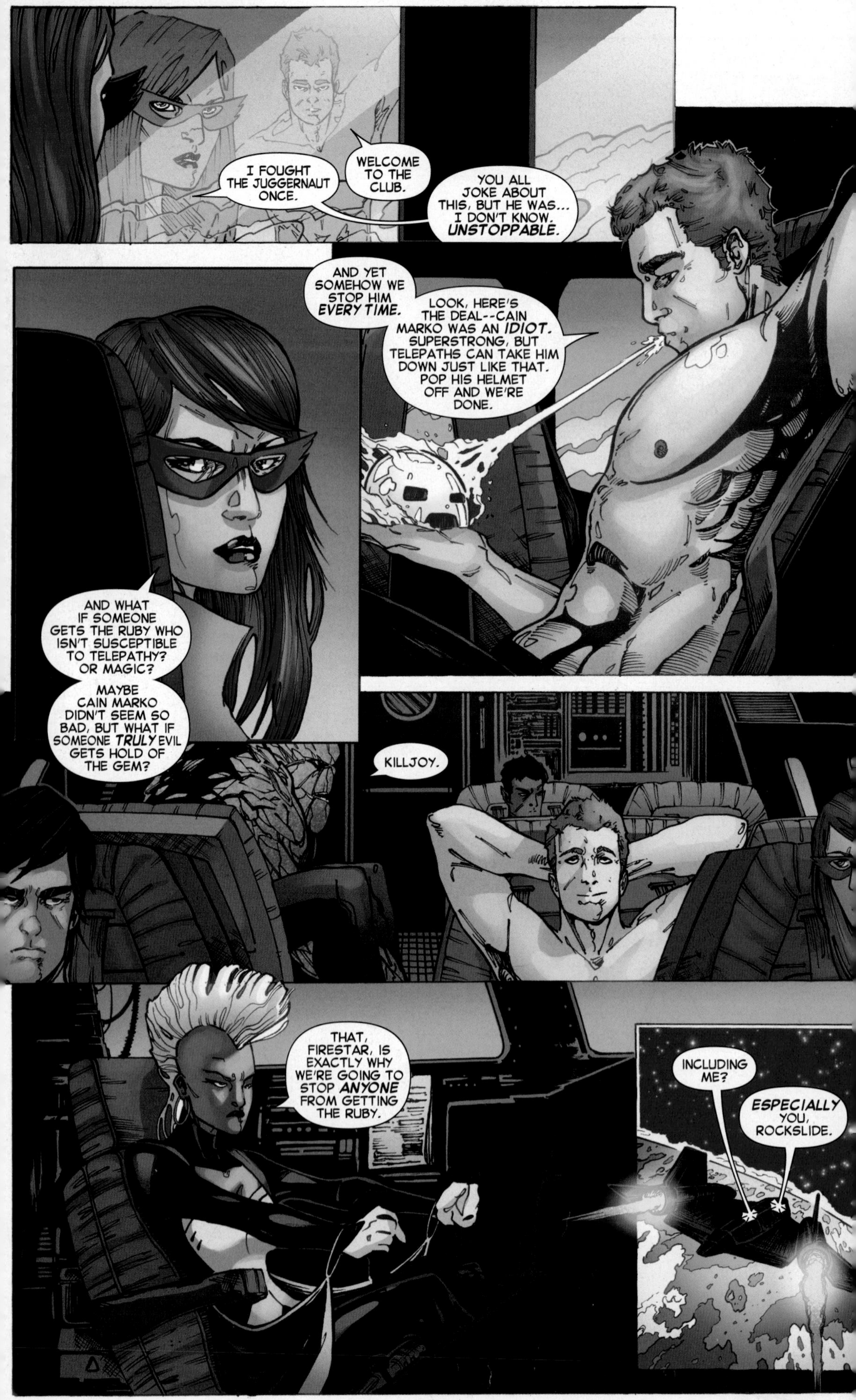
I FOUGHT THE JUGGERNAUT ONCE.
WELCOME TO THE CLUB.
YOU ALL JOKE ABOUT THIS, BUT HE WAS... I DON'T KNOW. UNSTOPPABLE.
AND YET SOMEHOW WE STOP HIM EVERY TIME.
LOOK, HERE'S THE DEAL--CAIN MARKO WAS AN IDIOT. SUPERSTRONG, BUT TELEPATHS CAN TAKE HIM DOWN JUST LIKE THAT. POP HIS HELMET OFF AND WE'RE DONE.
AND WHAT IF SOMEONE GETS THE RUBY WHO ISN'T SUSCEPTIBLE TO TELEPATHY? OR MAGIC?
MAYBE CAIN MARKO DIDN'T SEEM SO BAD, BUT WHAT IF SOMEONE TRULY EVIL GETS HOLD OF THE GEM?
KILLJOY.
THAT, FIRESTAR, IS EXACTLY WHY WE'RE GOING TO STOP ANYONE FROM GETTING THE RUBY.
INCLUDING ME?
ESPECIALLY YOU, ROCKSLIDE.

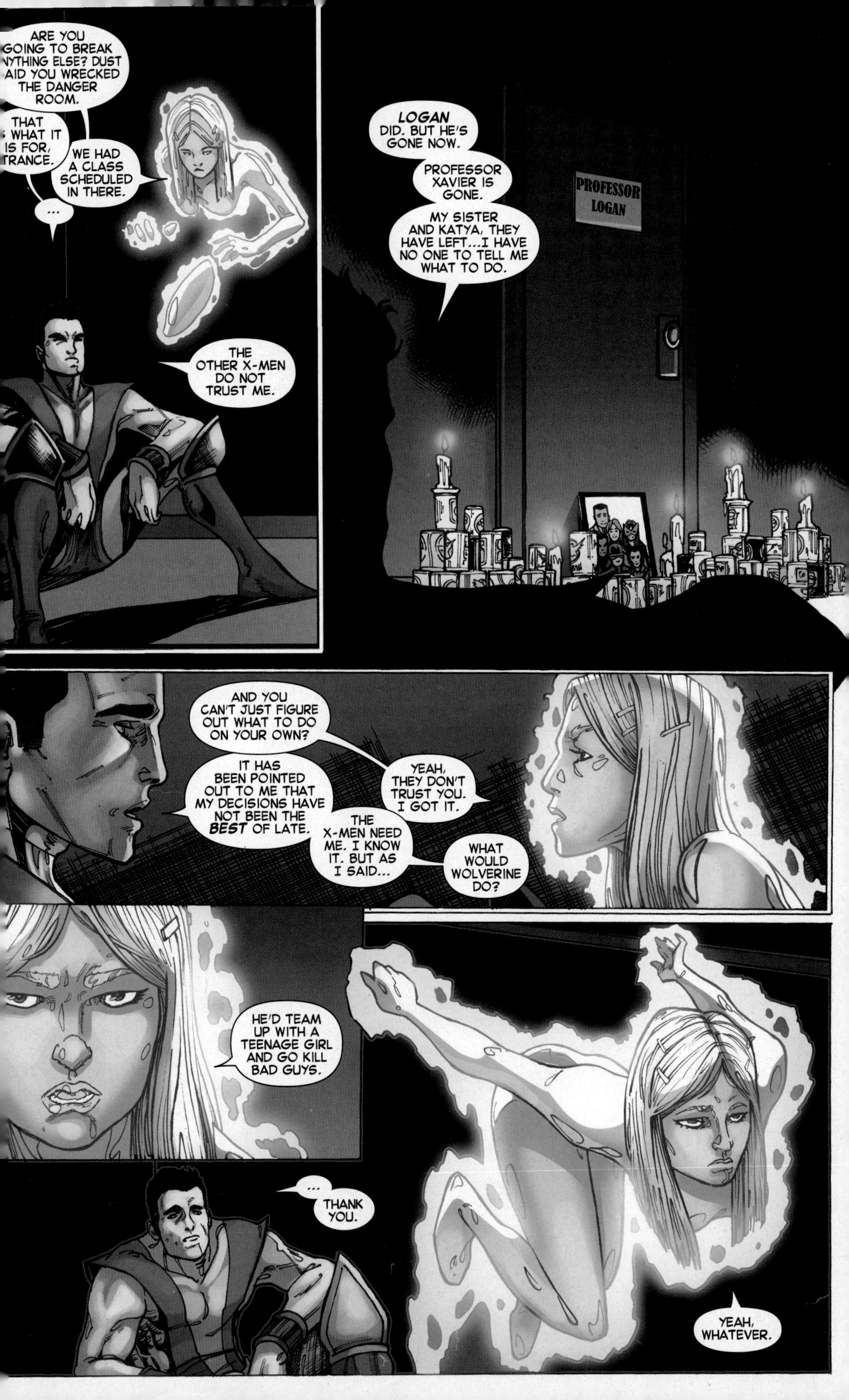
ARE YOU GOING TO BREAK NYTHING ELSE? DUST AID YOU WRECKED THE DANGER ROOM.
THAT S WHAT IT IS FOR, TRANCE.
WE HAD A CLASS SCHEDULED IN THERE.
...
THE OTHER X-MEN DO NOT TRUST ME.
LOGAN DID. BUT HE'S GONE NOW.
PROFESSOR XAVIER IS GONE.
MY SISTER AND KATYA, THEY HAVE LEFT...I HAVE NO ONE TO TELL ME WHAT TO DO.
PROFESSOR LOGAN
AND YOU CAN'T JUST FIGURE OUT WHAT TO DO ON YOUR OWN?
IT HAS BEEN POINTED OUT TO ME THAT MY DECISIONS HAVE NOT BEEN THE BEST OF LATE.
YEAH, THEY DON'T TRUST YOU. I GOT IT.
THE X-MEN NEED ME. I KNOW IT. BUT AS I SAID...
WHAT WOULD WOLVERINE DO?
HE'D TEAM UP WITH A TEENAGE GIRL AND GO KILL BAD GUYS.
... THANK YOU.
YEAH, WHATEVER.

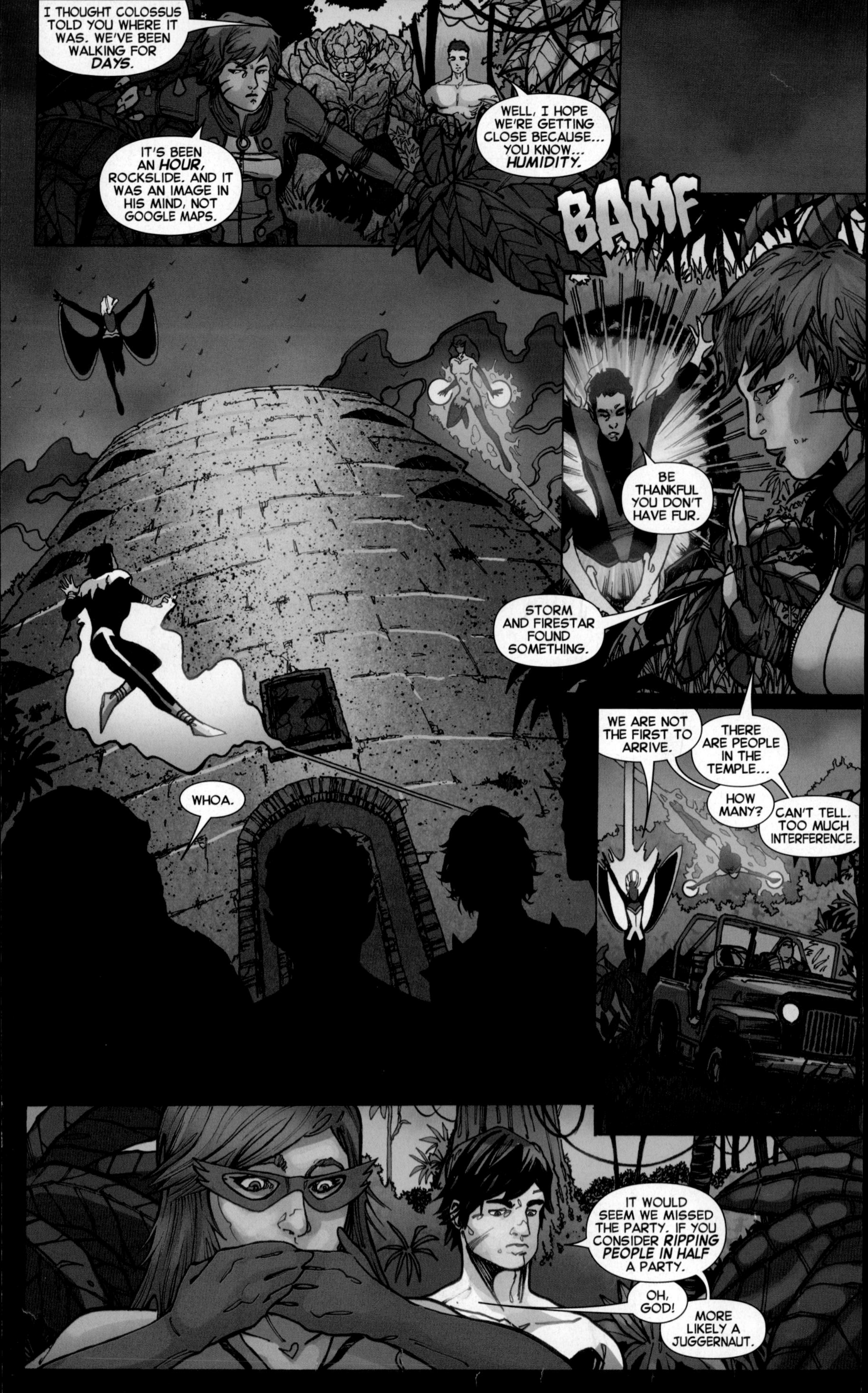
I THOUGHT COLOSSUS TOLD YOU WHERE IT WAS. WE'VE BEEN WALKING FOR DAYS.
IT'S BEEN AN HOUR, ROCKSLIDE. AND IT WAS AN IMAGE IN HIS MIND, NOT GOOGLE MAPS.
WELL, I HOPE WE'RE GETTING CLOSE BECAUSE... YOU KNOW... HUMIDITY.
BAMF
BE THANKFUL YOU DON'T HAVE FUR.
STORM AND FIRESTAR FOUND SOMETHING.
WHOA.
WE ARE NOT THE FIRST TO ARRIVE.
THERE ARE PEOPLE IN THE TEMPLE...
HOW MANY?
CAN'T TELL. TOO MUCH INTERFERENCE.
IT WOULD SEEM WE MISSED THE PARTY. IF YOU CONSIDER RIPPING PEOPLE IN HALF A PARTY.
OH, GOD!
MORE LIKELY A JUGGERNAUT.

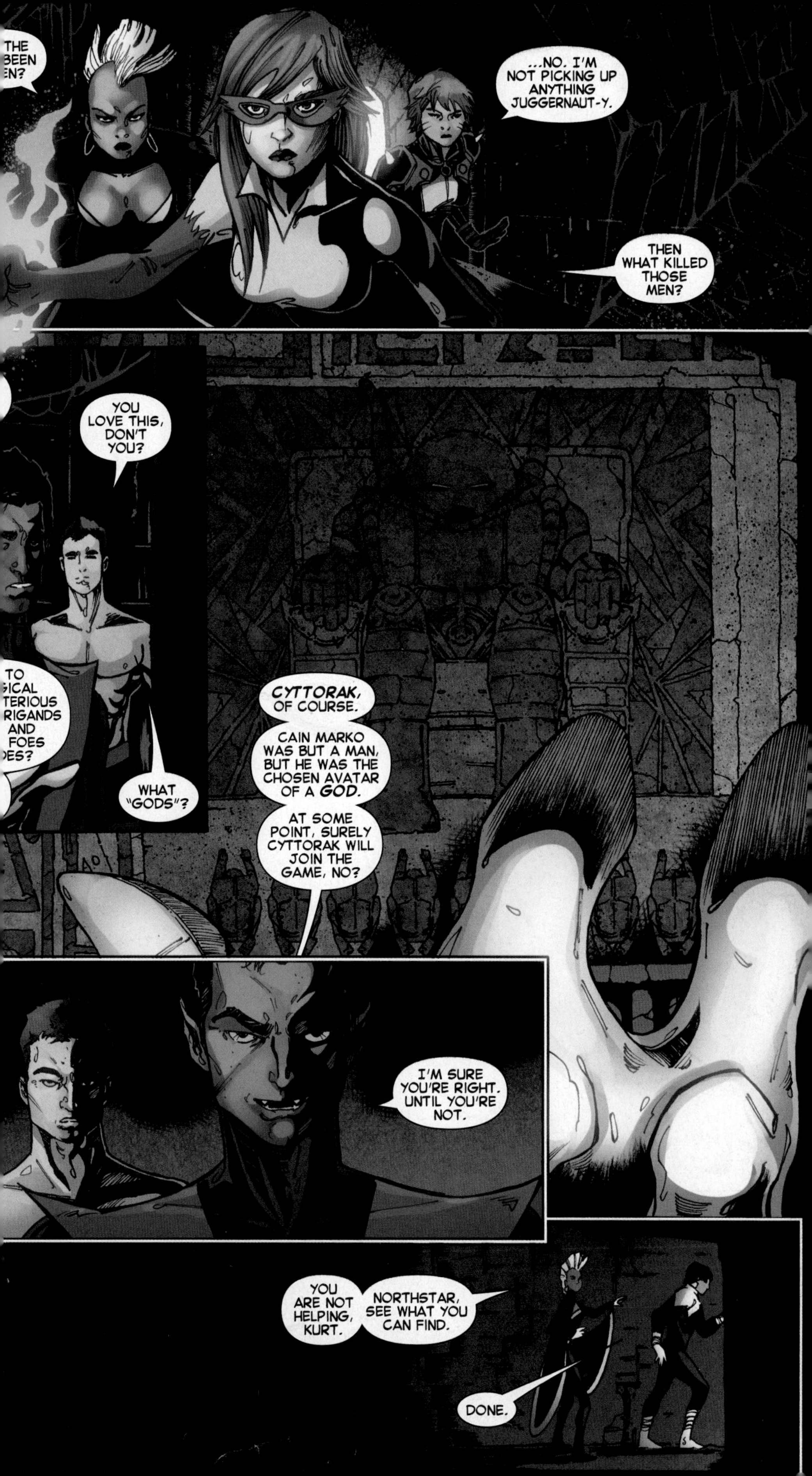
...NO. I'M NOT PICKING UP ANYTHING JUGGERNAUT-Y.
THEN WHAT KILLED THOSE MEN?
YOU LOVE THIS, DON'T YOU?
WHAT "GODS"?
CYTTORAK, OF COURSE.
CAIN MARKO WAS BUT A MAN, BUT HE WAS THE CHOSEN AVATAR OF A GOD.
AT SOME POINT, SURELY CYTTORAK WILL JOIN THE GAME, NO?
I'M SURE YOU'RE RIGHT. UNTIL YOU'RE NOT.
YOU ARE NOT HELPING, KURT.
NORTHSTAR, SEE WHAT YOU CAN FIND.
DONE.

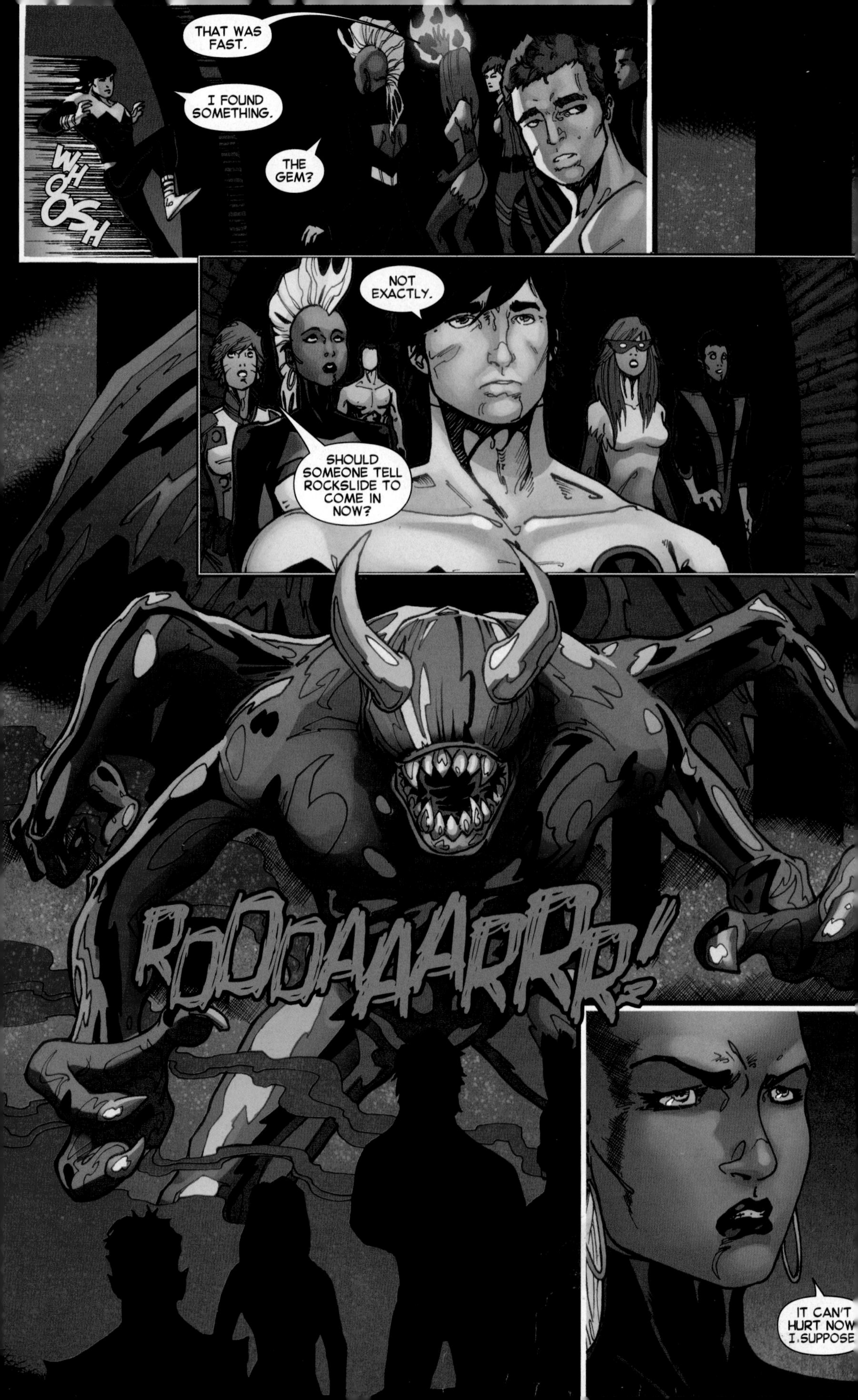
THAT WAS FAST.
I FOUND SOMETHING.
WHOOSH
THE GEM?
NOT EXACTLY.
SHOULD SOMEONE TELL ROCKSLIDE TO COME IN NOW?
ROOOAAARRR!
IT CAN'T HURT NOW I SUPPOSE

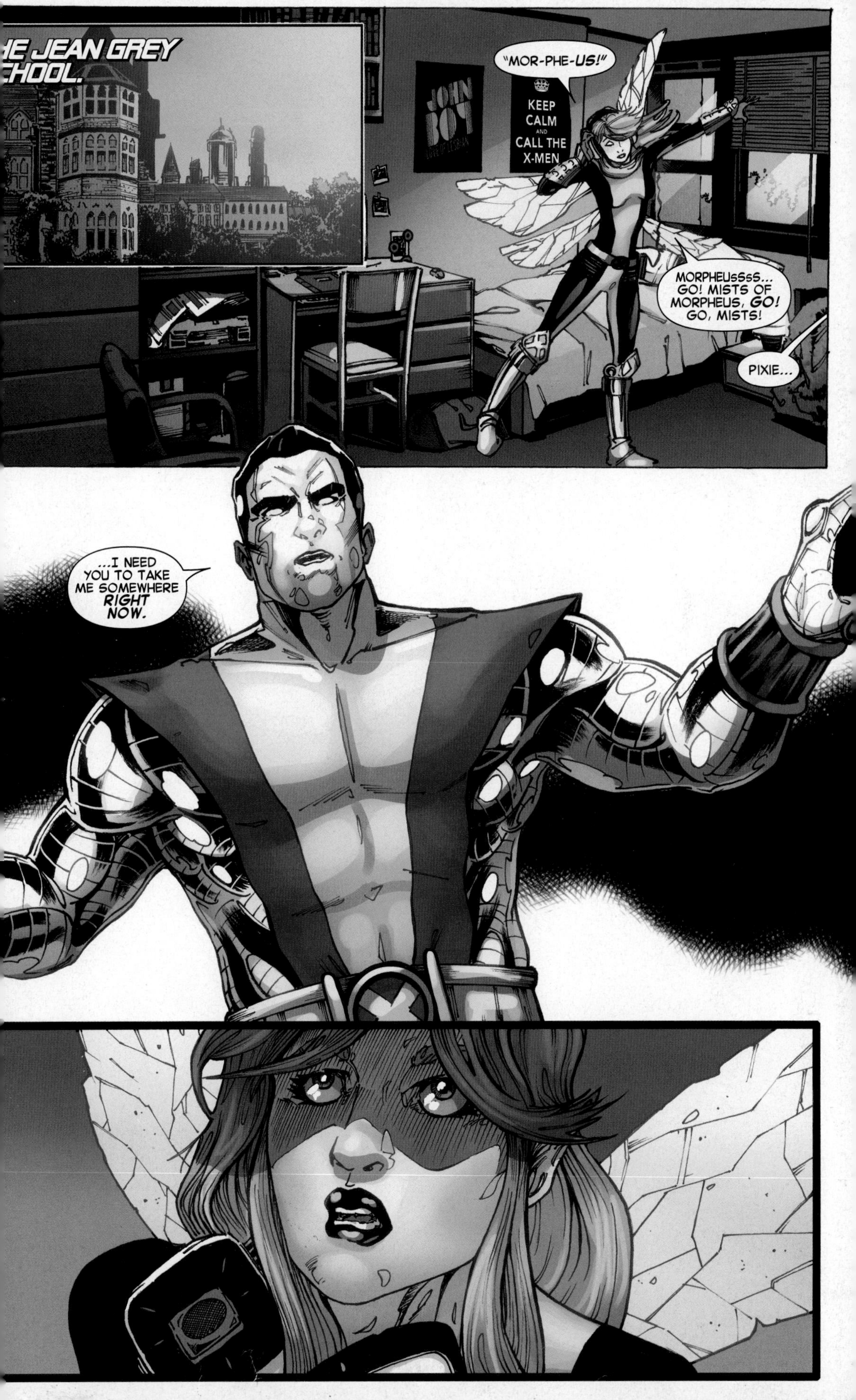
THE JEAN GREY SCHOOL.
"MOR-PHE-US!"
JOHN BOY
KEEP CALM AND CALL THE X-MEN
MORPHEUSSSS... GO! MISTS OF MORPHEUS, GO! GO, MISTS!
PIXIE...
...I NEED YOU TO TAKE ME SOMEWHERE RIGHT NOW.

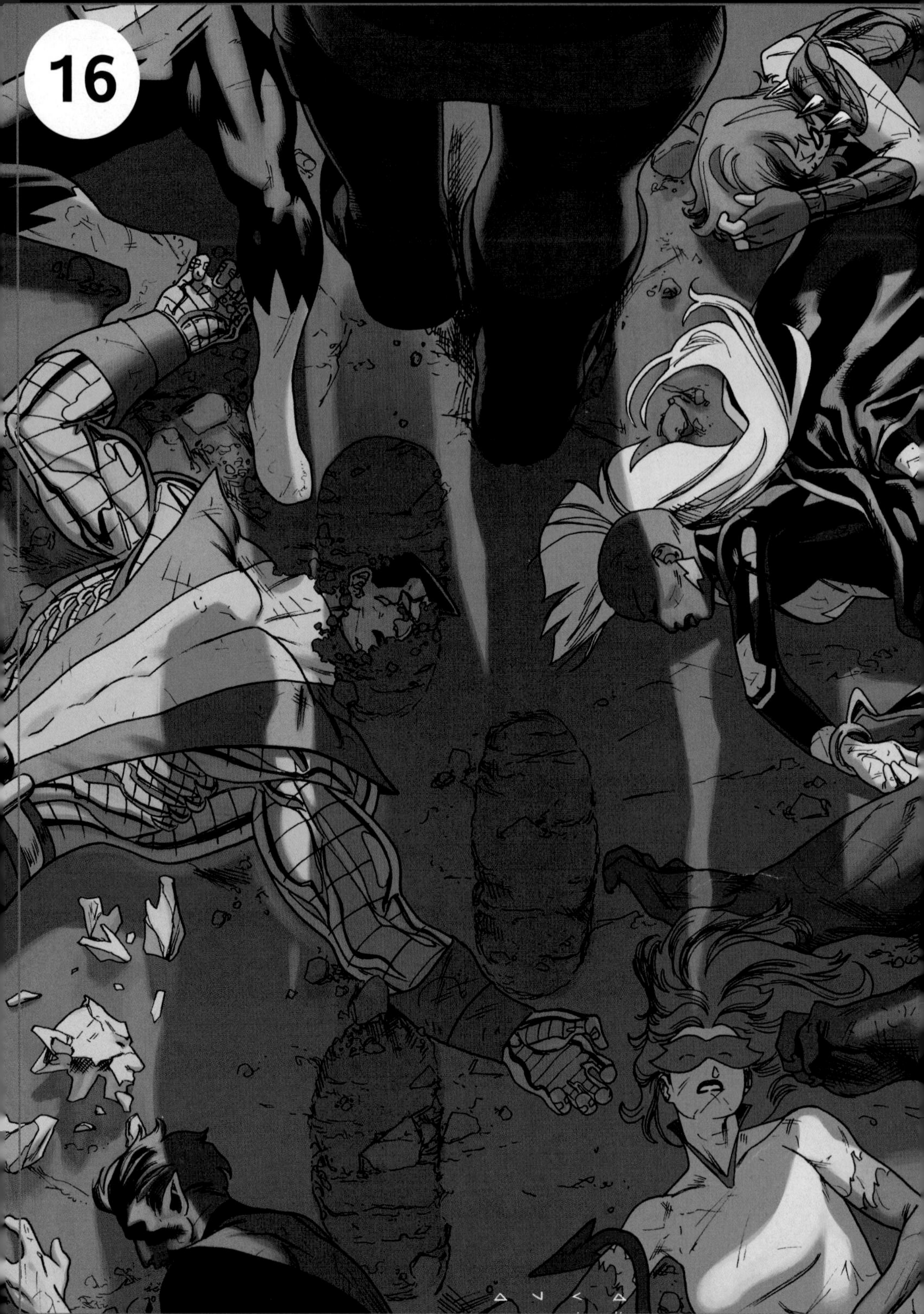
16

THE ONCE AND FUTURE JUGGERNAUT PART

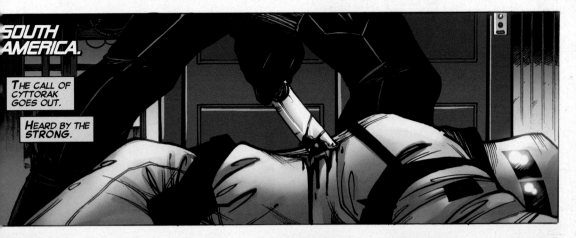

SOUTH AMERICA.

THE CALL OF CYTTORAK GOES OUT.

HEARD BY THE STRONG.

COLORADO.

HEARD BY THOSE FILLED WITH RAGE.

WITH THE DESIRE FOR POWER.

SAUDI ARABIA.

THOSE WHO CYTTORAK FELT COULD BE CONTROLLED.

THE SAHARA DESERT.

THOSE WHO WOULD SHOW THIS WORLD HIS POWER.

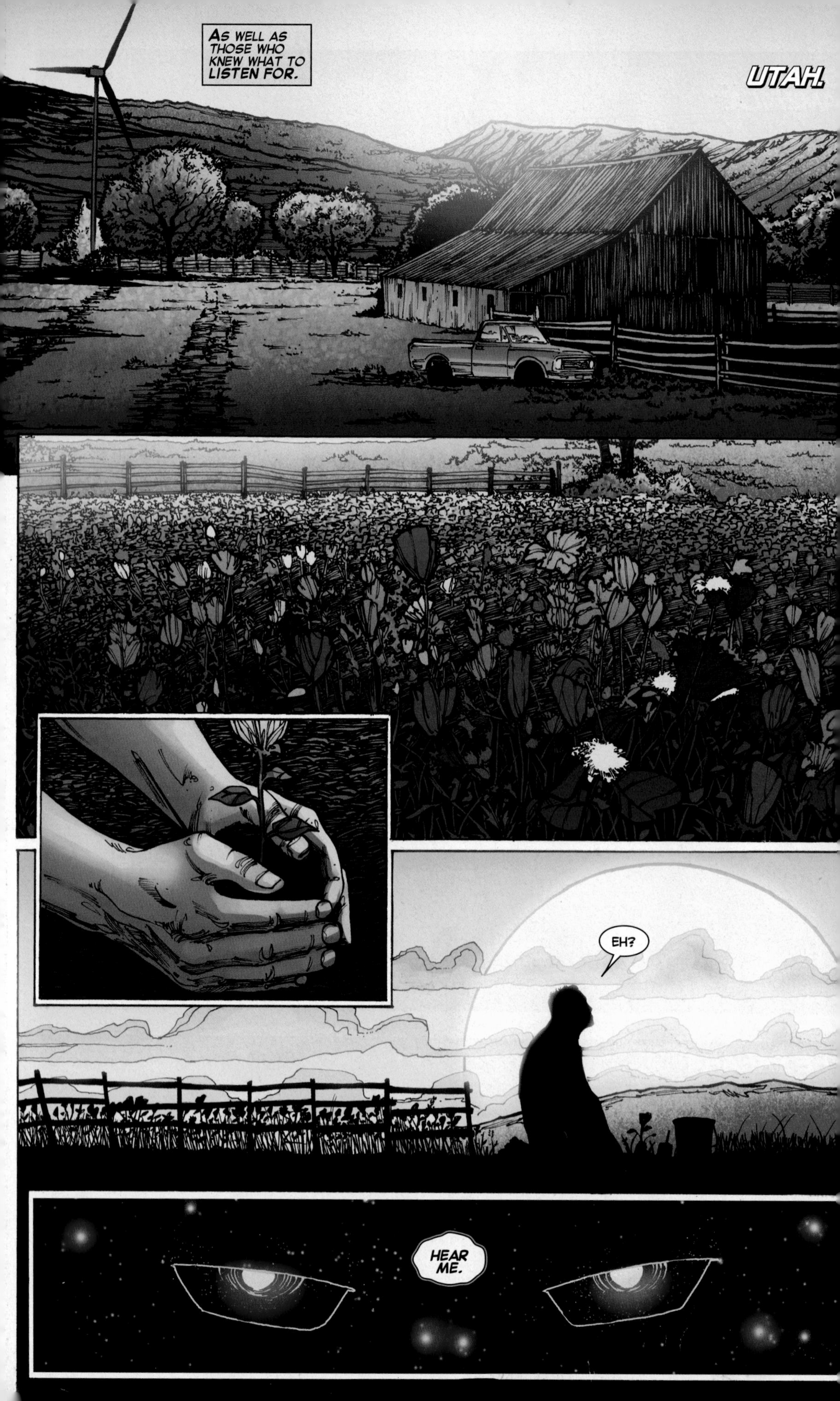
As well as those who knew what to listen for.
UTAH.
EH?
HEAR ME.

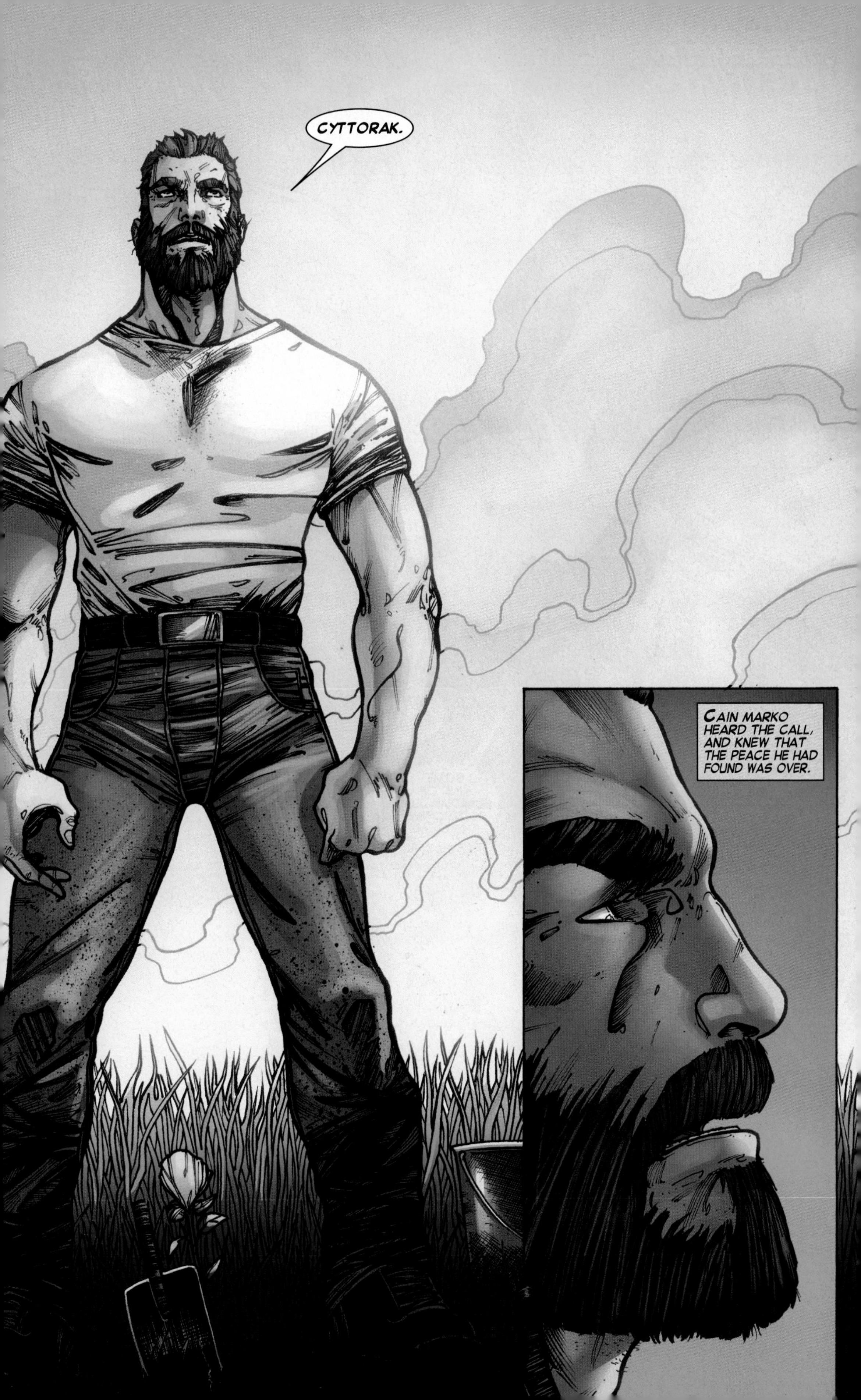
CYTTORAK.
CAIN MARKO HEARD THE CALL, AND KNEW THAT THE PEACE HE HAD FOUND WAS OVER.

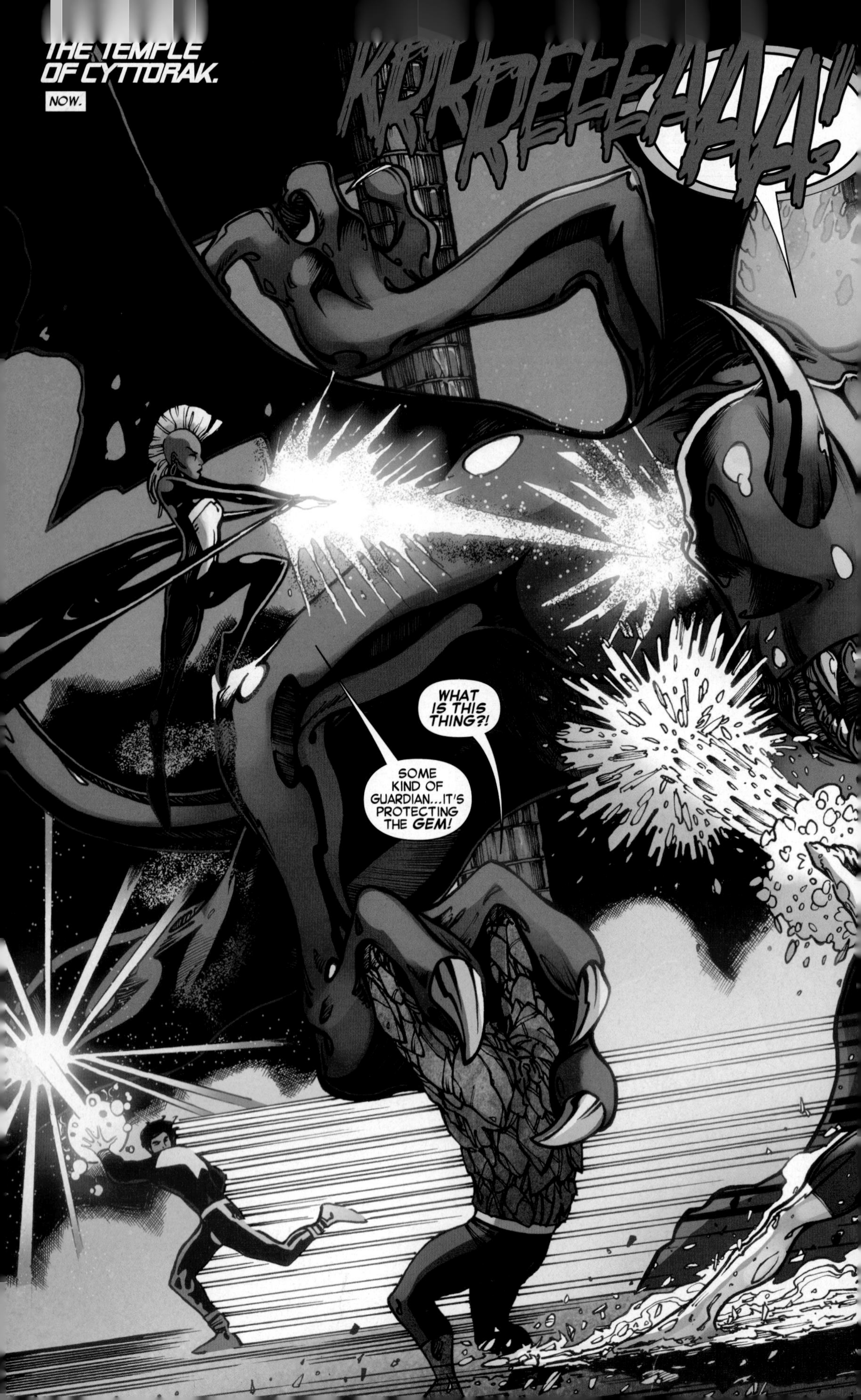
THE TEMPLE OF CYTTORAK.
NOW.
KRRKREEEAAAA!
WHAT IS THIS THING?!
SOME KIND OF GUARDIAN...IT'S PROTECTING THE GEM!

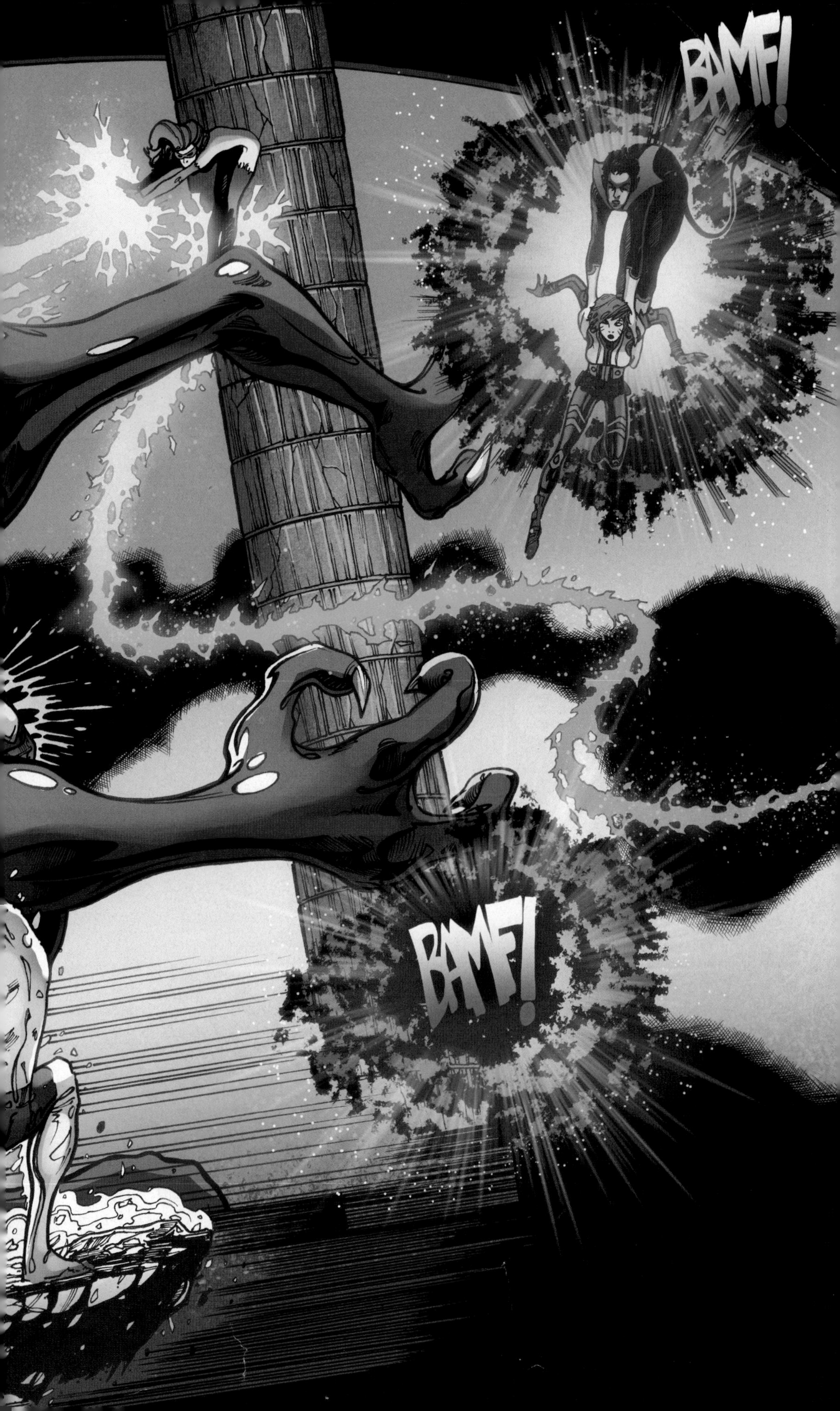
BAMF!
BAMF!

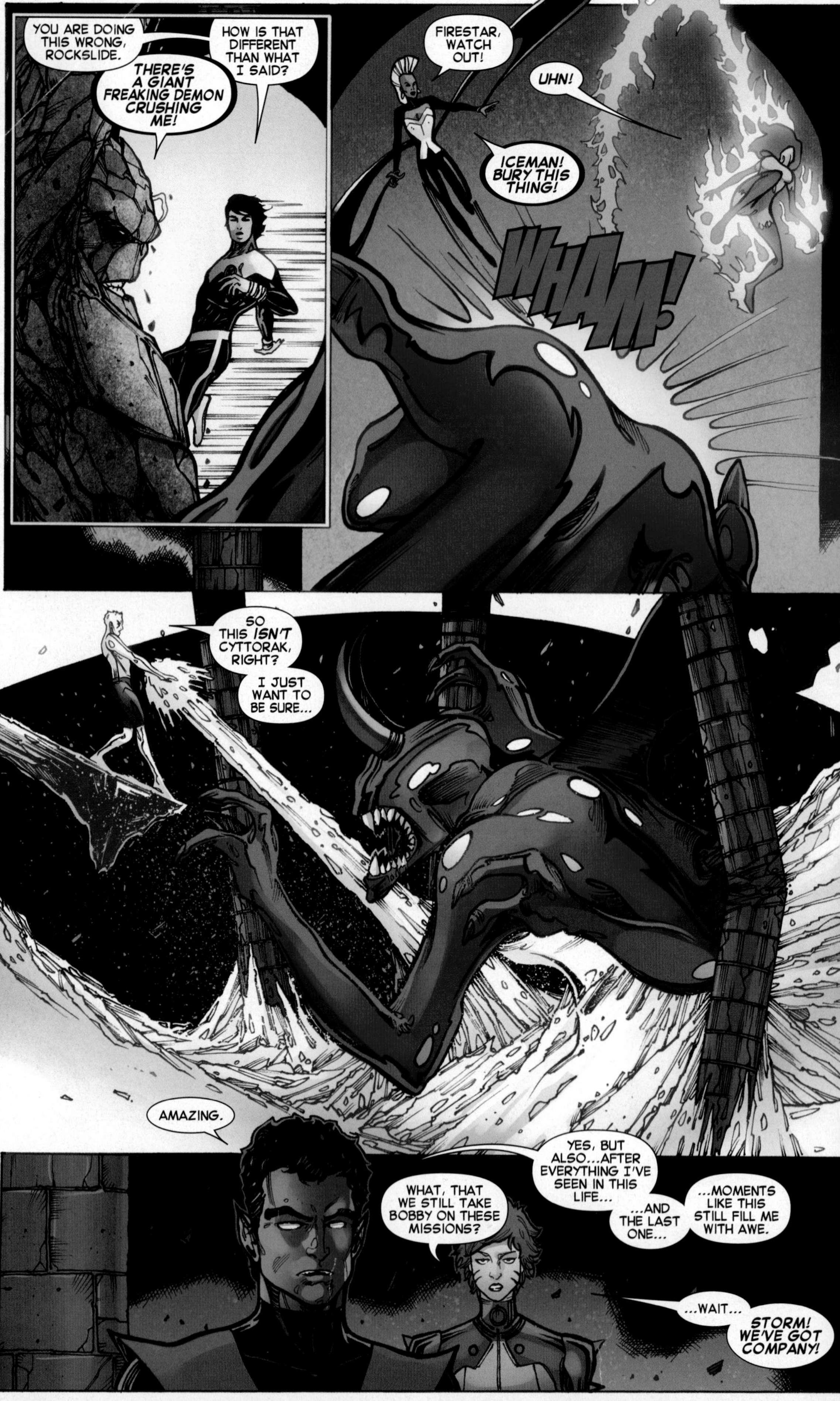
YOU ARE DOING THIS WRONG, ROCKSLIDE.
HOW IS THAT DIFFERENT THAN WHAT I SAID?
THERE'S A GIANT FREAKING DEMON CRUSHING ME!
FIRESTAR, WATCH OUT!
UHN!
ICEMAN! BURY THIS THING!
WHAM!
SO THIS ISN'T CYTTORAK, RIGHT?
I JUST WANT TO BE SURE...
AMAZING.
WHAT, THAT WE STILL TAKE BOBBY ON THESE MISSIONS?
YES, BUT ALSO...AFTER EVERYTHING I'VE SEEN IN THIS LIFE...
...AND THE LAST ONE...
...MOMENTS LIKE THIS STILL FILL ME WITH AWE.
...WAIT...
STORM! WE'VE GOT COMPANY!

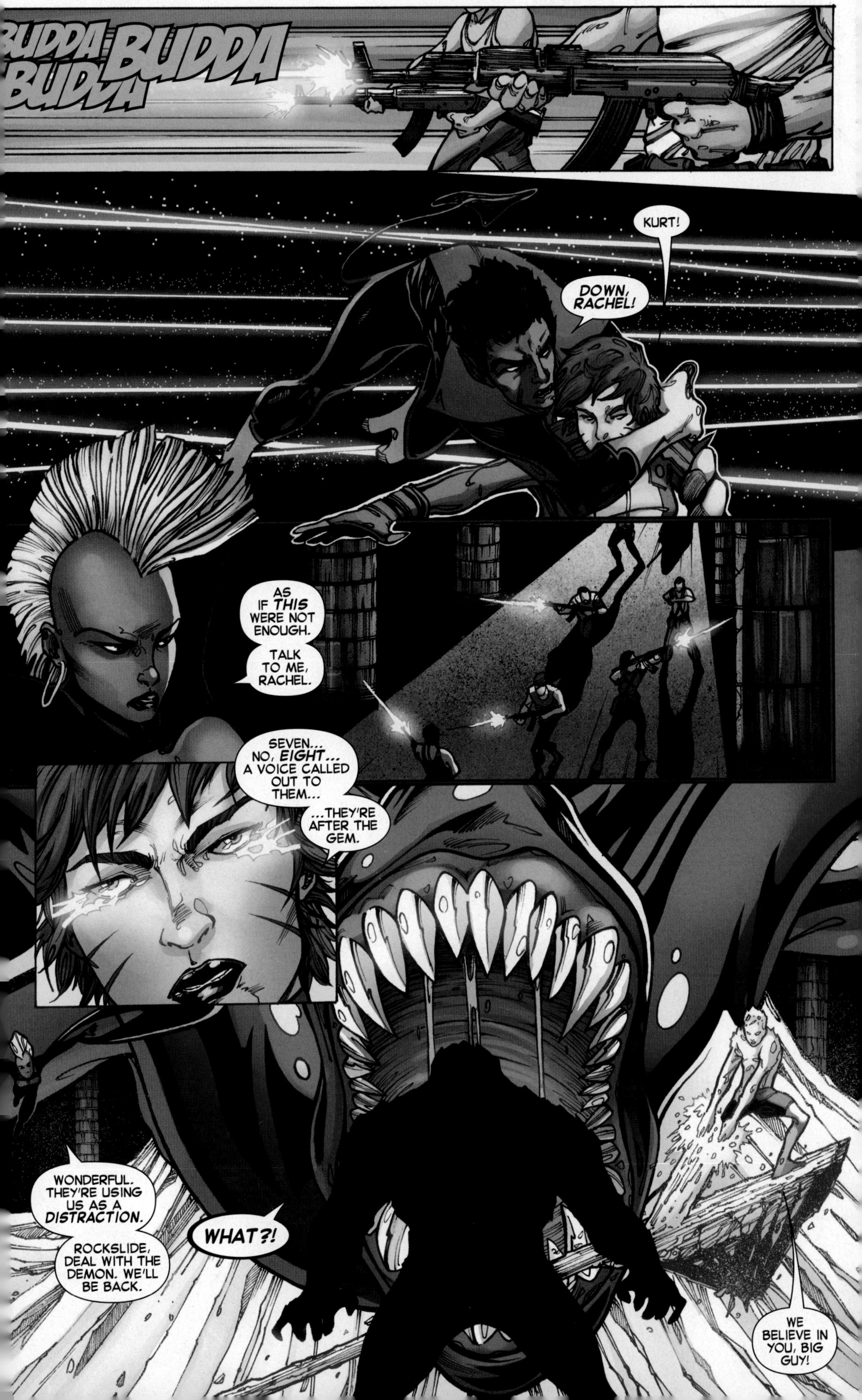
BUDDA BUDDA BUDDA BUDDA
KURT!
DOWN, RACHEL!
AS IF THIS WERE NOT ENOUGH.
TALK TO ME, RACHEL.
SEVEN... NO, EIGHT... A VOICE CALLED OUT TO THEM...
...THEY'RE AFTER THE GEM.
WONDERFUL. THEY'RE USING US AS A DISTRACTION.
ROCKSLIDE, DEAL WITH THE DEMON. WE'LL BE BACK.
WHAT?!
WE BELIEVE IN YOU, BIG GUY!

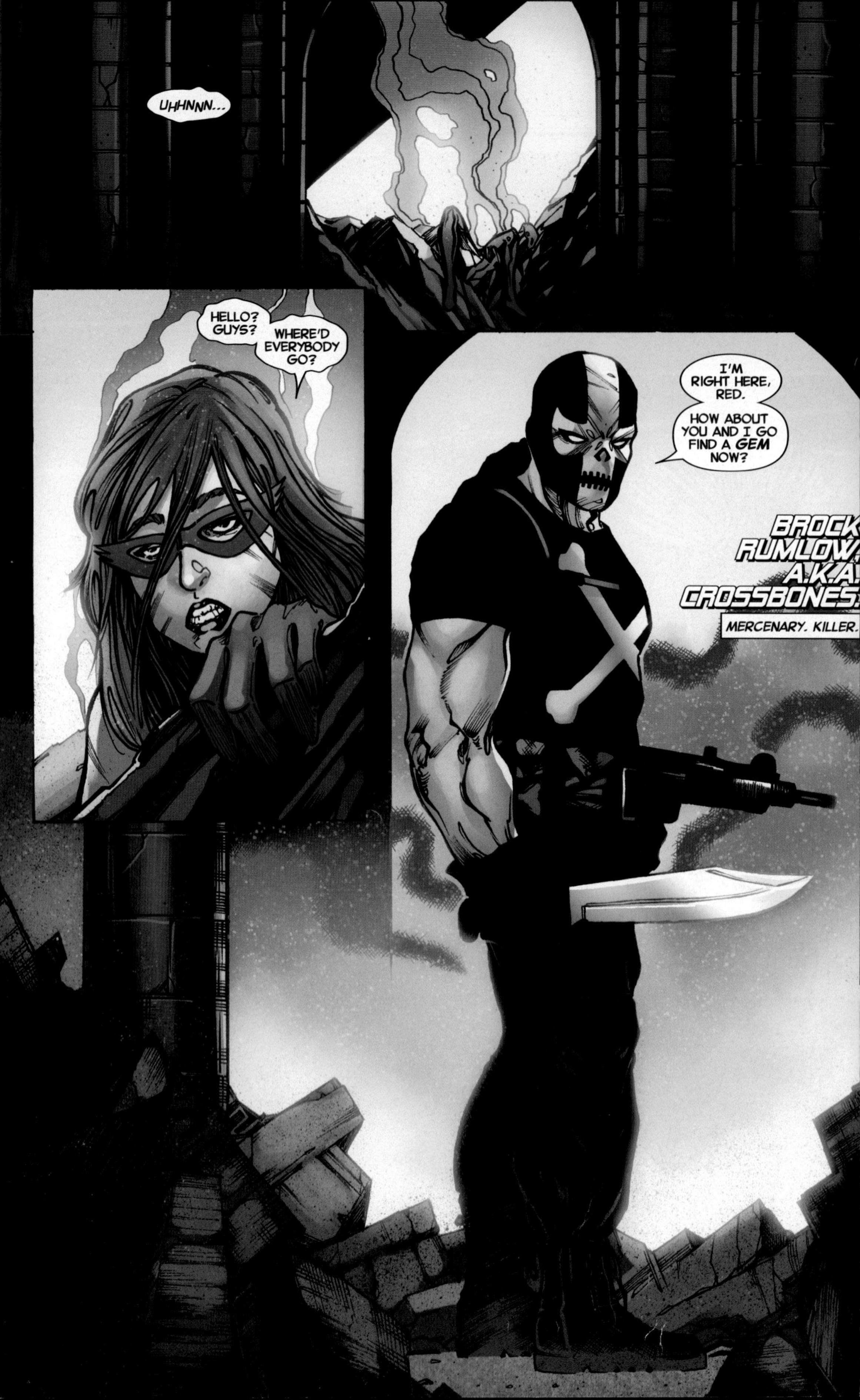
UHHNNN...
HELLO? GUYS?
WHERE'D EVERYBODY GO?
I'M RIGHT HERE, RED.
HOW ABOUT YOU AND I GO FIND A GEM NOW?
BROCK RUMLOW, A.K.A. CROSSBONES.
MERCENARY. KILLER.

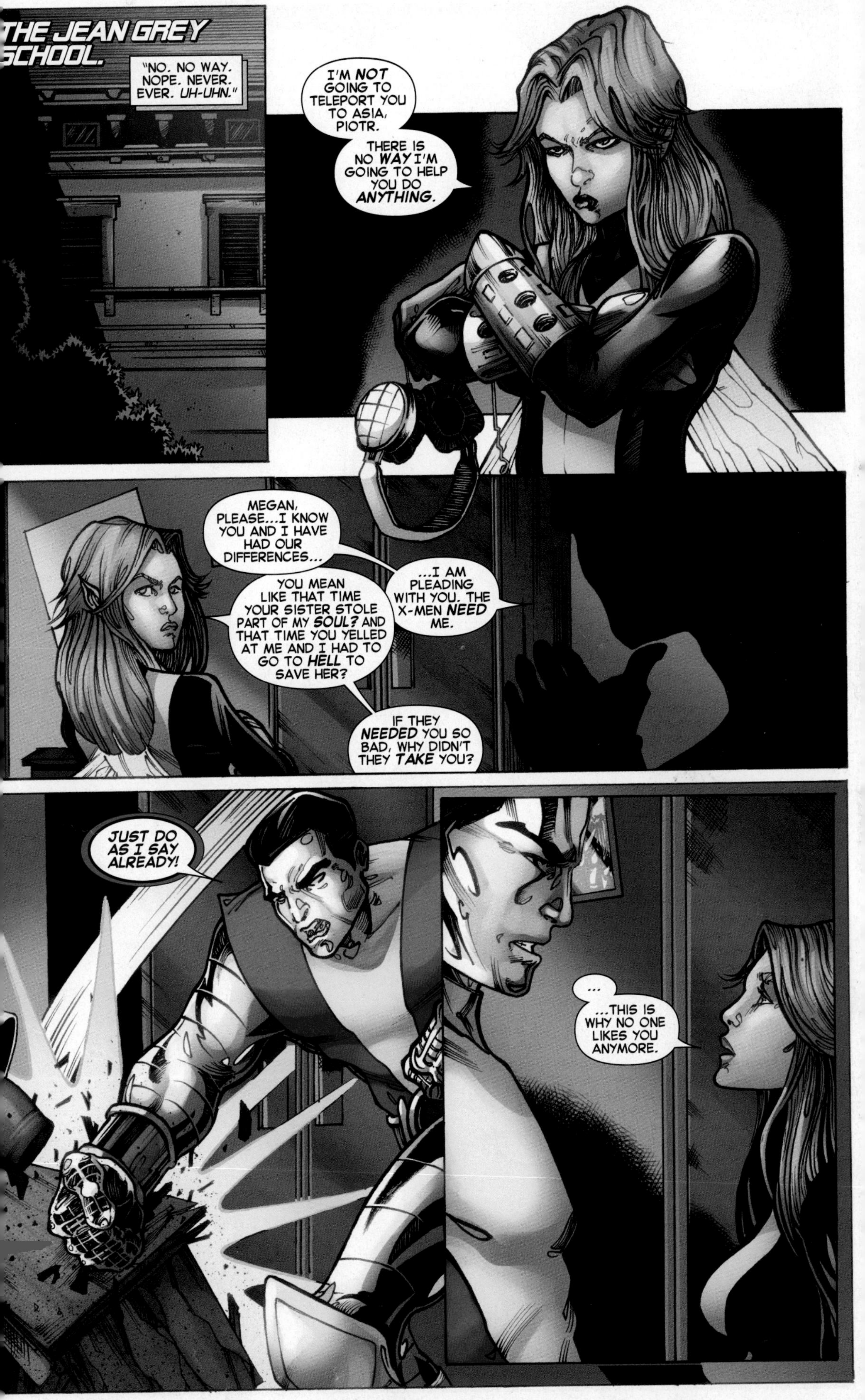
THE JEAN GREY SCHOOL.
"NO. NO WAY. NOPE. NEVER. EVER. UH-UHN."
I'M NOT GOING TO TELEPORT YOU TO ASIA, PIOTR.
THERE IS NO WAY I'M GOING TO HELP YOU DO ANYTHING.
MEGAN, PLEASE...I KNOW YOU AND I HAVE HAD OUR DIFFERENCES...
...I AM PLEADING WITH YOU. THE X-MEN NEED ME.
YOU MEAN LIKE THAT TIME YOUR SISTER STOLE PART OF MY SOUL? AND THAT TIME YOU YELLED AT ME AND I HAD TO GO TO HELL TO SAVE HER?
IF THEY NEEDED YOU SO BAD, WHY DIDN'T THEY TAKE YOU?
JUST DO AS I SAY ALREADY!
...
...THIS IS WHY NO ONE LIKES YOU ANYMORE.

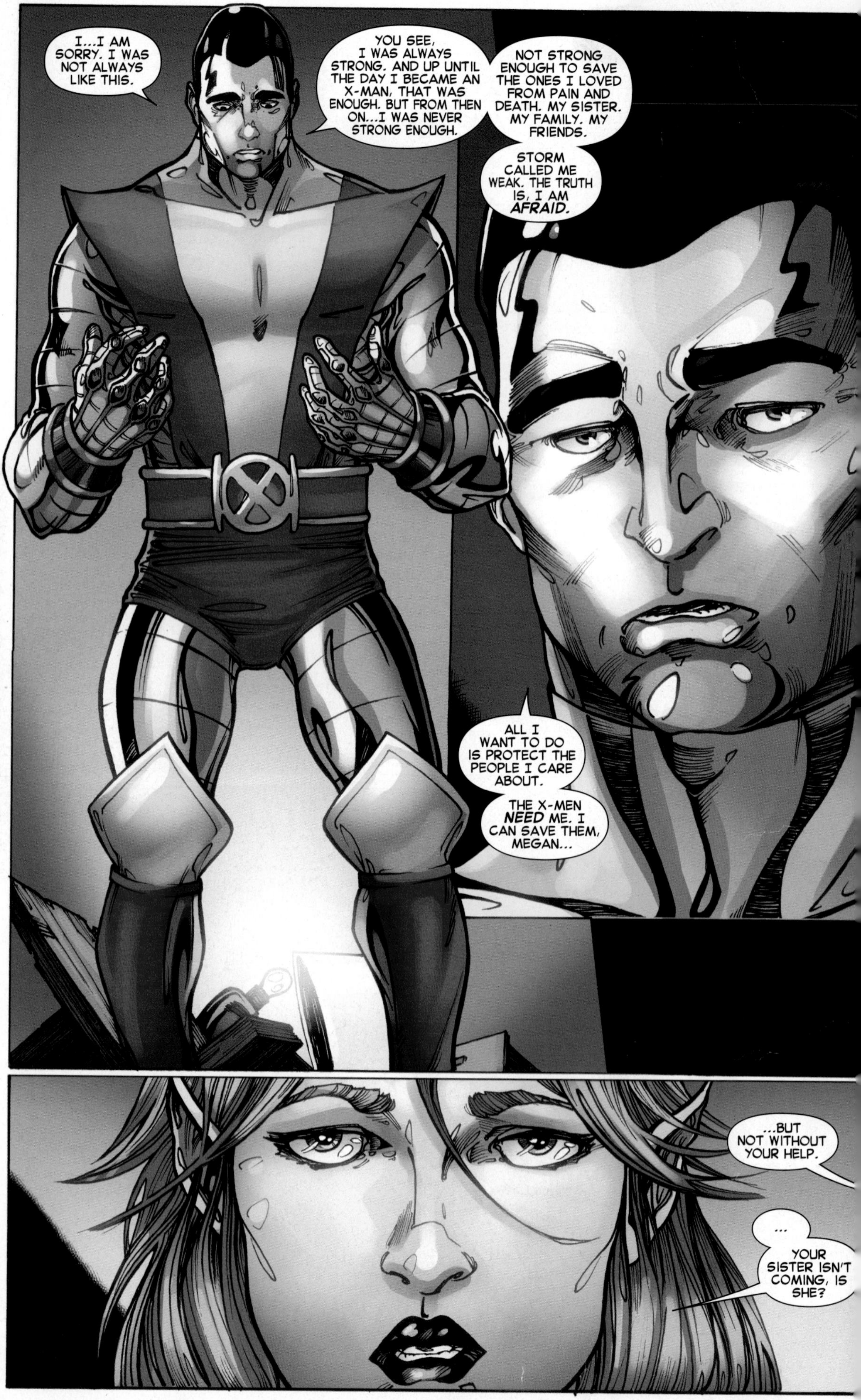

I...I AM SORRY. I WAS NOT ALWAYS LIKE THIS.
YOU SEE, I WAS ALWAYS STRONG. AND UP UNTIL THE DAY I BECAME AN X-MAN, THAT WAS ENOUGH. BUT FROM THEN ON...I WAS NEVER STRONG ENOUGH.
NOT STRONG ENOUGH TO SAVE THE ONES I LOVED FROM PAIN AND DEATH. MY SISTER. MY FAMILY. MY FRIENDS.
STORM CALLED ME WEAK. THE TRUTH IS, I AM *AFRAID.*
ALL I WANT TO DO IS PROTECT THE PEOPLE I CARE ABOUT.
THE X-MEN *NEED* ME. I CAN SAVE THEM, MEGAN...
...BUT NOT WITHOUT YOUR HELP.
...
YOUR SISTER ISN'T COMING, IS SHE?

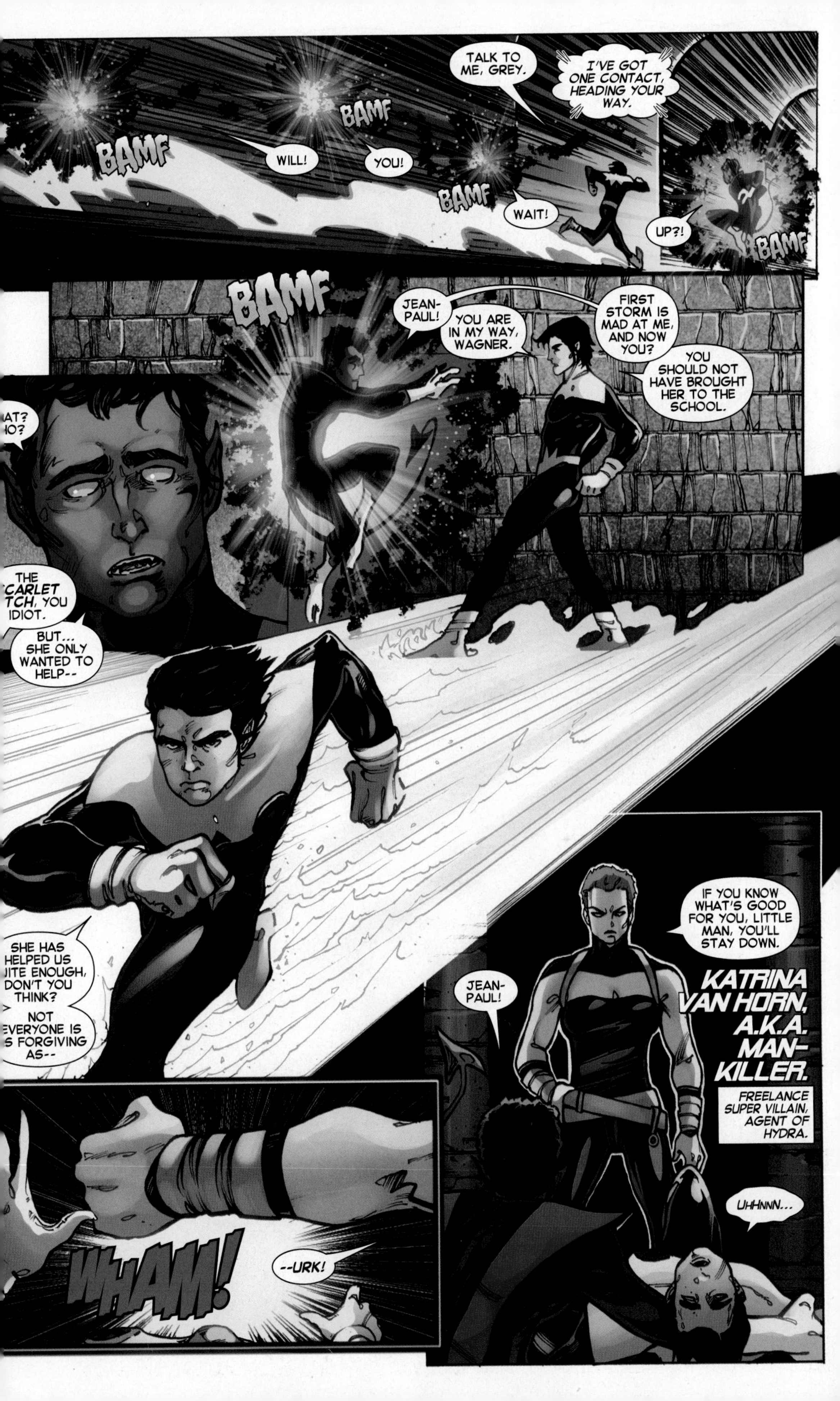

BAMF
WILL!
BAMF
YOU!
TALK TO ME, GREY.
I'VE GOT ONE CONTACT, HEADING YOUR WAY.
BAMF
WAIT!
UP?!
BAMF
BAMF
JEAN-PAUL!
YOU ARE IN MY WAY, WAGNER.
FIRST STORM IS MAD AT ME, AND NOW YOU?
YOU SHOULD NOT HAVE BROUGHT HER TO THE SCHOOL.
THE CARLET TCH, YOU IDIOT.
BUT... SHE ONLY WANTED TO HELP--
SHE HAS HELPED US JITE ENOUGH, DON'T YOU THINK?
NOT EVERYONE IS S FORGIVING AS--
WHAM!
--URK!
IF YOU KNOW WHAT'S GOOD FOR YOU, LITTLE MAN, YOU'LL STAY DOWN.
JEAN-PAUL!
KATRINA VAN HORN, A.K.A. MAN-KILLER.
FREELANCE SUPER VILLAIN, AGENT OF HYDRA.
UHHNNN...

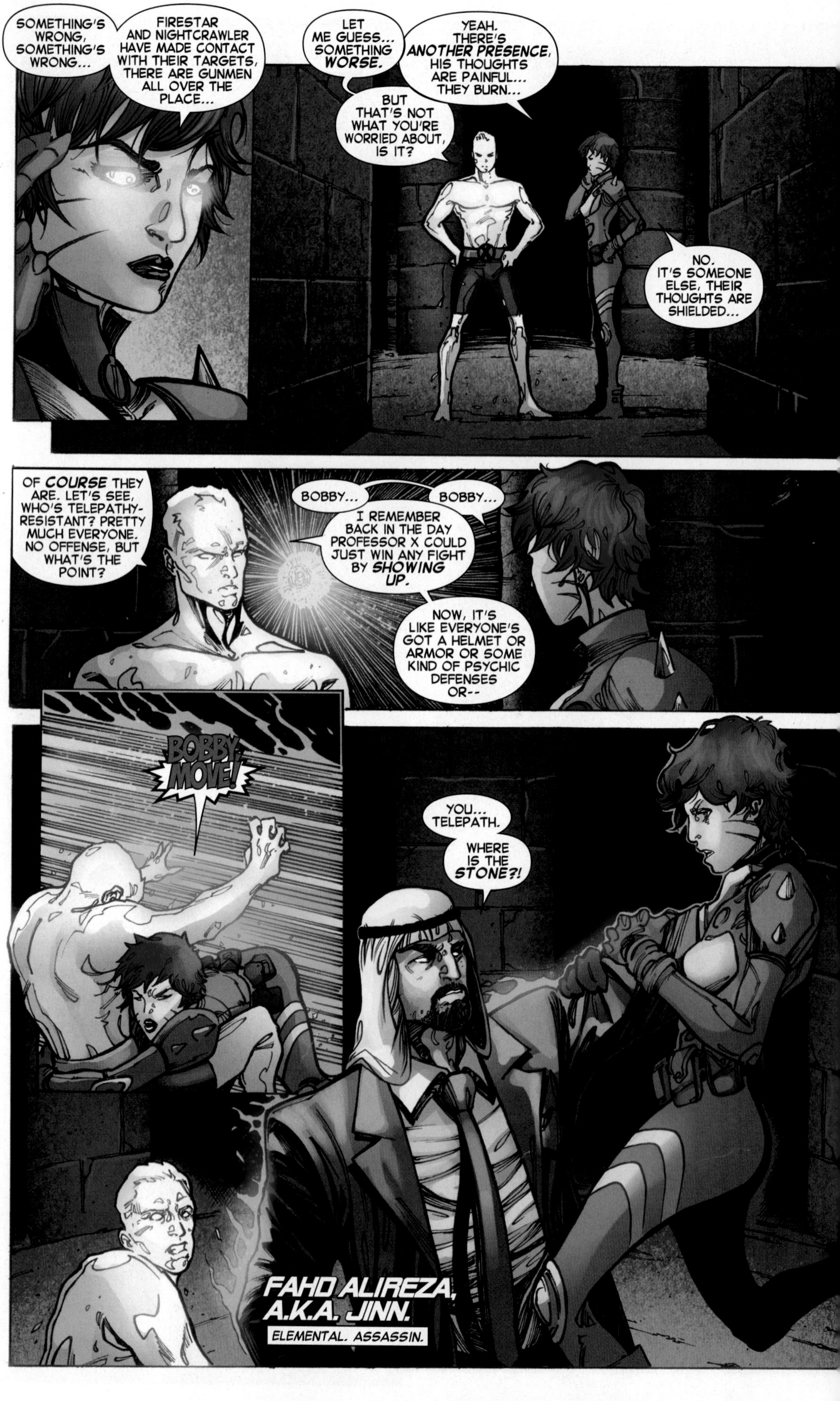

SOMETHING'S WRONG, SOMETHING'S WRONG...
FIRESTAR AND NIGHTCRAWLER HAVE MADE CONTACT WITH THEIR TARGETS, THERE ARE GUNMEN ALL OVER THE PLACE...
LET ME GUESS... SOMETHING WORSE.
BUT THAT'S NOT WHAT YOU'RE WORRIED ABOUT, IS IT?
YEAH. THERE'S ANOTHER PRESENCE, HIS THOUGHTS ARE PAINFUL... THEY BURN...
NO. IT'S SOMEONE ELSE, THEIR THOUGHTS ARE SHIELDED...
OF COURSE THEY ARE. LET'S SEE, WHO'S TELEPATHY-RESISTANT? PRETTY MUCH EVERYONE. NO OFFENSE, BUT WHAT'S THE POINT?
BOBBY...
BOBBY...
I REMEMBER BACK IN THE DAY PROFESSOR X COULD JUST WIN ANY FIGHT BY SHOWING UP.
NOW, IT'S LIKE EVERYONE'S GOT A HELMET OR ARMOR OR SOME KIND OF PSYCHIC DEFENSES OR--
BOBBY MOVE!
YOU... TELEPATH.
WHERE IS THE STONE?!
FAHD ALIREZA, A.K.A. JINN.
ELEMENTAL. ASSASSIN.

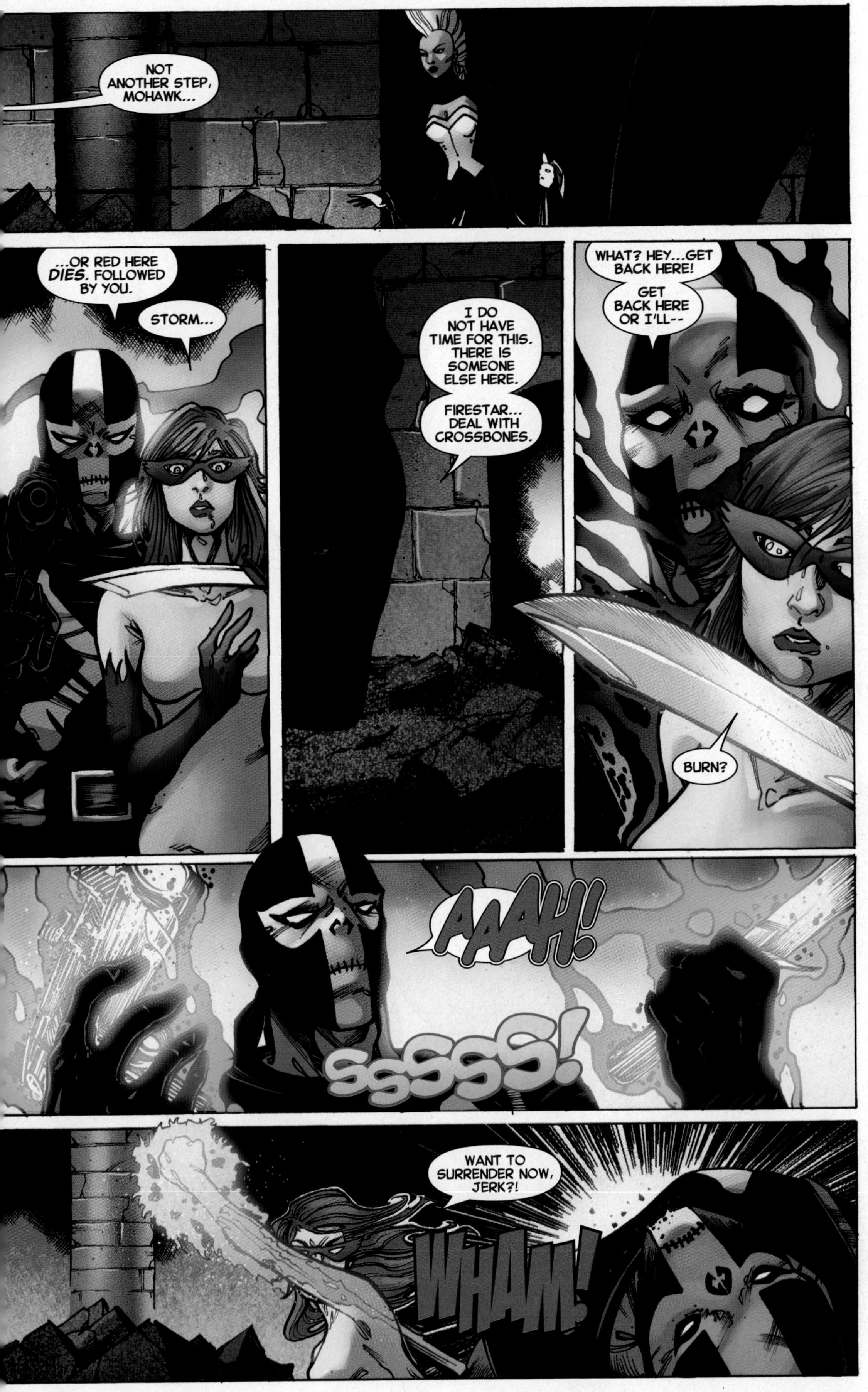
NOT ANOTHER STEP, MOHAWK...
...OR RED HERE *DIES.* FOLLOWED BY YOU.
STORM...
I DO NOT HAVE TIME FOR THIS. THERE IS SOMEONE ELSE HERE.
FIRESTAR... DEAL WITH CROSSBONES.
WHAT? HEY...GET BACK HERE!
GET BACK HERE OR I'LL--
BURN?
AAAH!
SSSSS!
WANT TO SURRENDER NOW, JERK?!
WHAM!

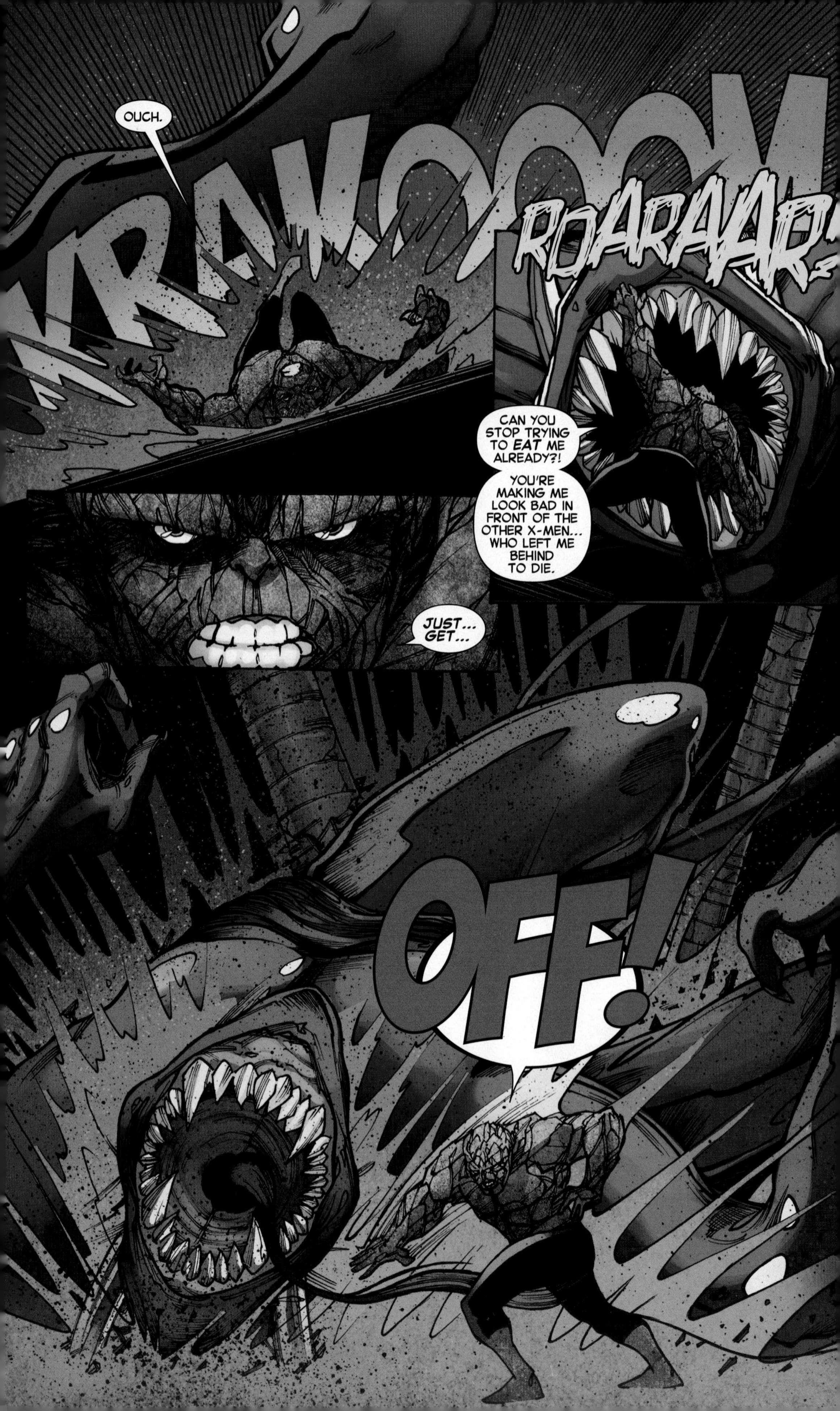
OUCH.
KRAKOOOM
ROARAAAR!
CAN YOU STOP TRYING TO EAT ME ALREADY?!
YOU'RE MAKING ME LOOK BAD IN FRONT OF THE OTHER X-MEN... WHO LEFT ME BEHIND TO DIE.
JUST... GET...
OFF!

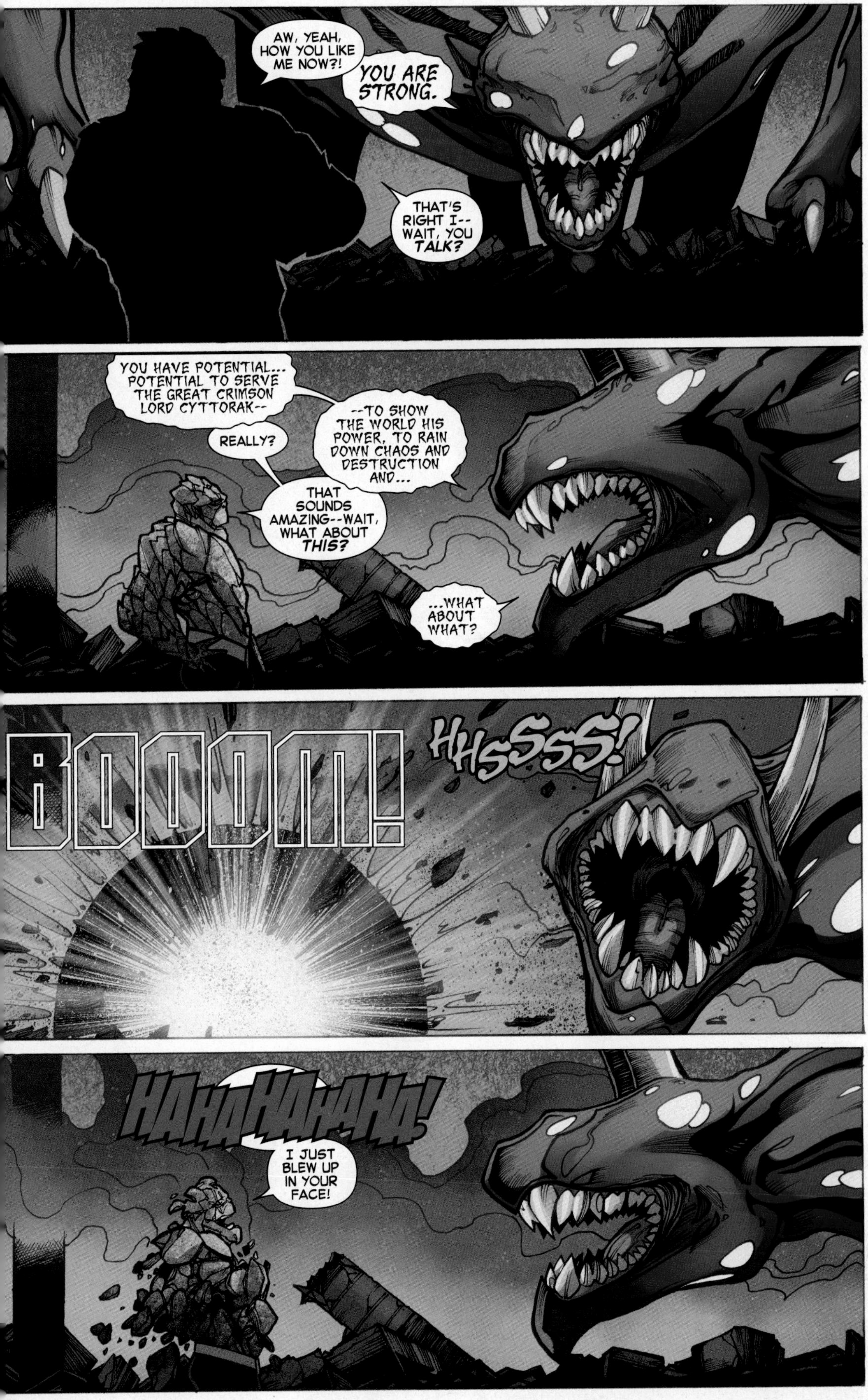

AW, YEAH, HOW YOU LIKE ME NOW?!
YOU ARE STRONG.
THAT'S RIGHT I-- WAIT, YOU TALK?
YOU HAVE POTENTIAL... POTENTIAL TO SERVE THE GREAT CRIMSON LORD CYTTORAK--
REALLY?
--TO SHOW THE WORLD HIS POWER, TO RAIN DOWN CHAOS AND DESTRUCTION AND...
THAT SOUNDS AMAZING--WAIT, WHAT ABOUT THIS?
...WHAT ABOUT WHAT?
BOOOM!
HHSSSS!
HAHAHAHAHA!
I JUST BLEW UP IN YOUR FACE!

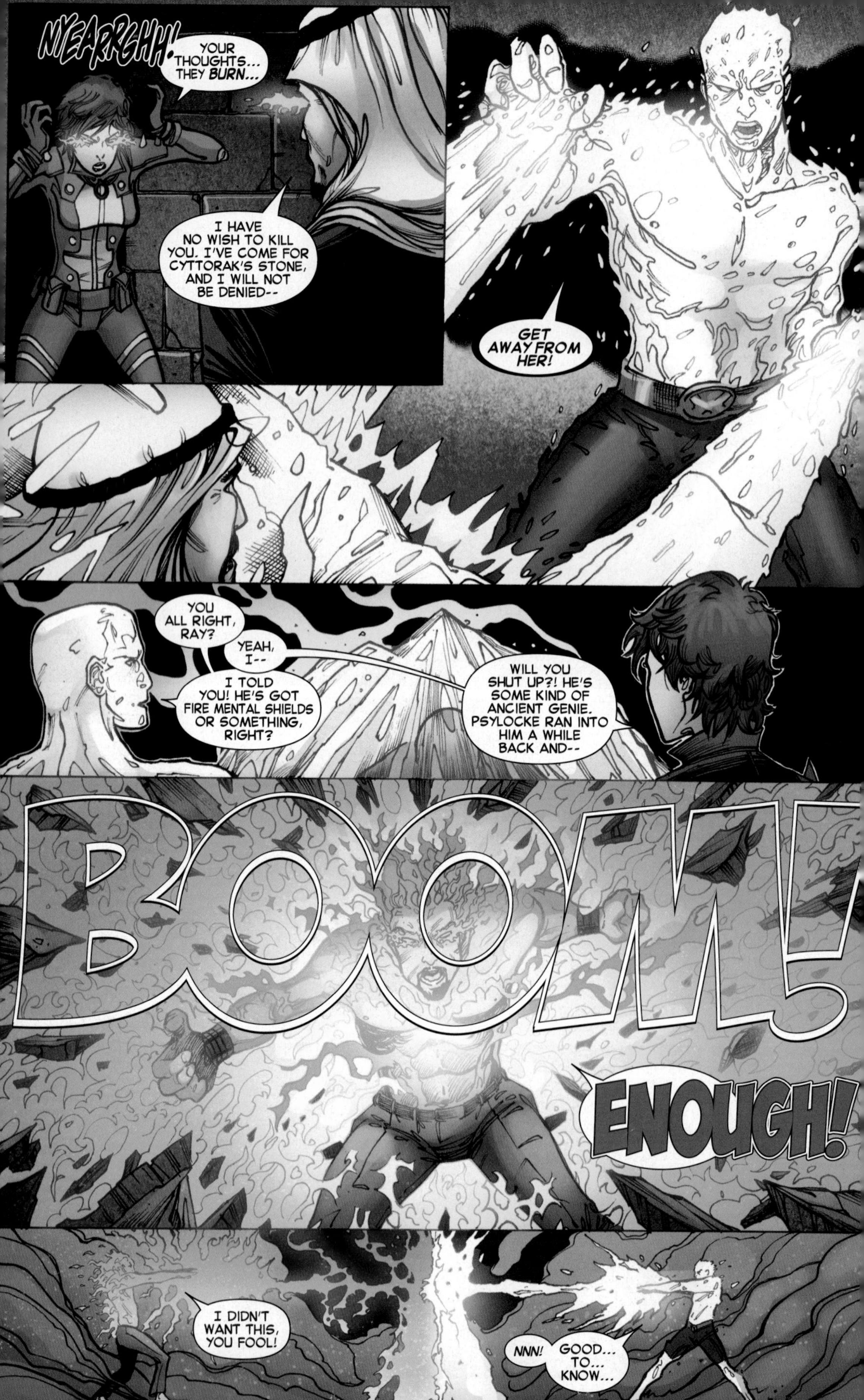
NYEARRGHH!
YOUR THOUGHTS... THEY BURN...
I HAVE NO WISH TO KILL YOU. I'VE COME FOR CYTTORAK'S STONE, AND I WILL NOT BE DENIED--
GET AWAY FROM HER!
YOU ALL RIGHT, RAY?
YEAH, I--
I TOLD YOU! HE'S GOT FIRE MENTAL SHIELDS OR SOMETHING, RIGHT?
WILL YOU SHUT UP?! HE'S SOME KIND OF ANCIENT GENIE. PSYLOCKE RAN INTO HIM A WHILE BACK AND--
BOOM!
ENOUGH!
I DIDN'T WANT THIS, YOU FOOL!
NNN!
GOOD... TO... KNOW...

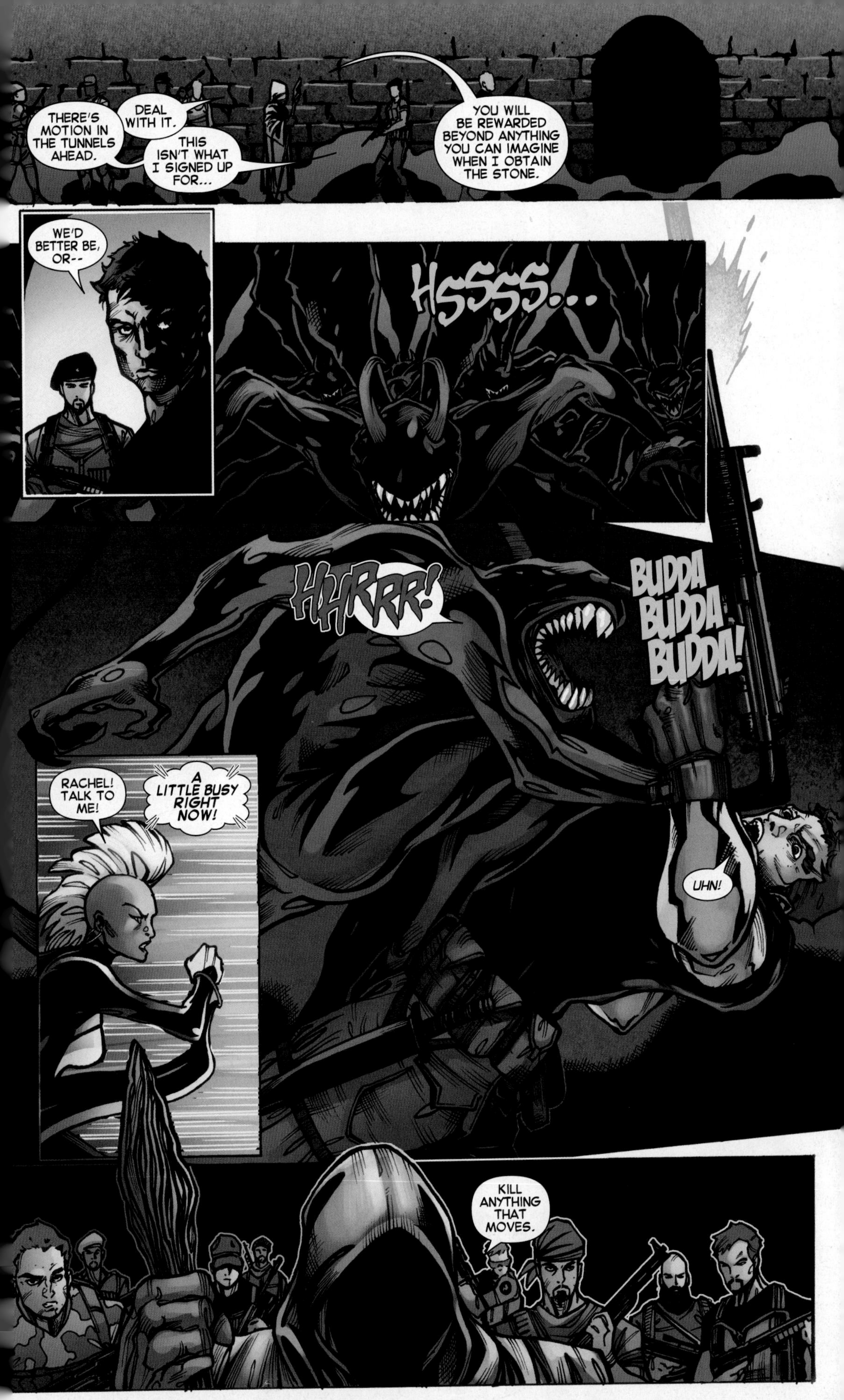
THERE'S MOTION IN THE TUNNELS AHEAD.
DEAL WITH IT.
THIS ISN'T WHAT I SIGNED UP FOR...
YOU WILL BE REWARDED BEYOND ANYTHING YOU CAN IMAGINE WHEN I OBTAIN THE STONE.
WE'D BETTER BE, OR--
HSSSS...
HHRRR!
BUDDA BUDDA BUDDA!
UHN!
RACHEL! TALK TO ME!
A LITTLE BUSY RIGHT NOW!
KILL ANYTHING THAT MOVES.

RACHEL--!
SPAK SPAK SPAK!
HT!
IT'S SOME CHICK! ARE WE--
NYEARGHH
LOGAN... HOW I WISH YOU WERE HERE TO KILL A LOT OF THINGS FOR ME.
BUT YOU'RE NOT.

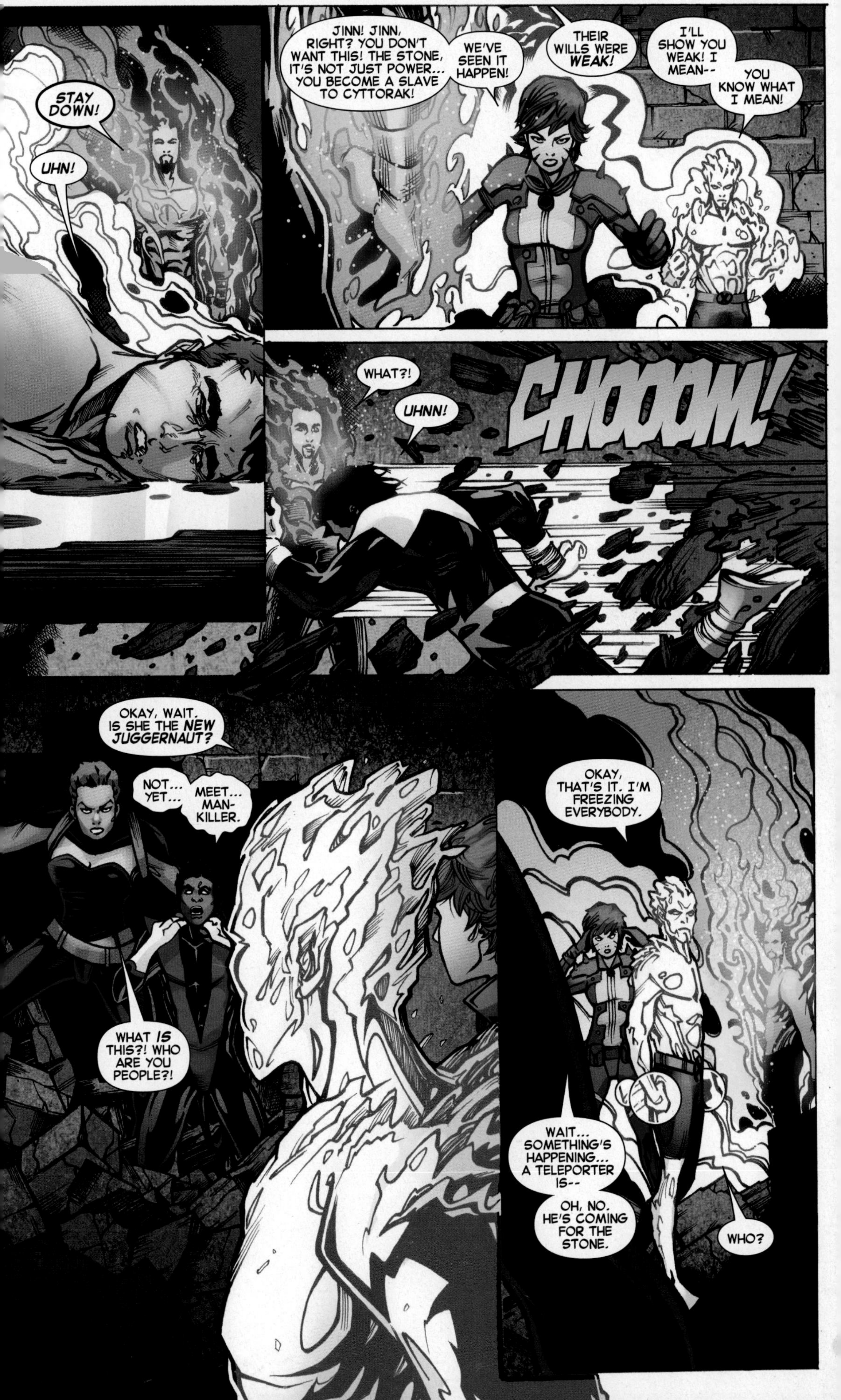
STAY DOWN!
UHN!
JINN! JINN, RIGHT? YOU DON'T WANT THIS! THE STONE, IT'S NOT JUST POWER... YOU BECOME A SLAVE TO CYTTORAK!
WE'VE SEEN IT HAPPEN!
THEIR WILLS WERE WEAK!
I'LL SHOW YOU WEAK! I MEAN--
YOU KNOW WHAT I MEAN!
WHAT?!
UHNN!
CHOOOM!
OKAY, WAIT. IS SHE THE NEW JUGGERNAUT?
NOT... YET...
MEET... MAN-KILLER.
WHAT IS THIS?! WHO ARE YOU PEOPLE?!
OKAY, THAT'S IT. I'M FREEZING EVERYBODY.
WAIT... SOMETHING'S HAPPENING... A TELEPORTER IS--
OH, NO. HE'S COMING FOR THE STONE.
WHO?

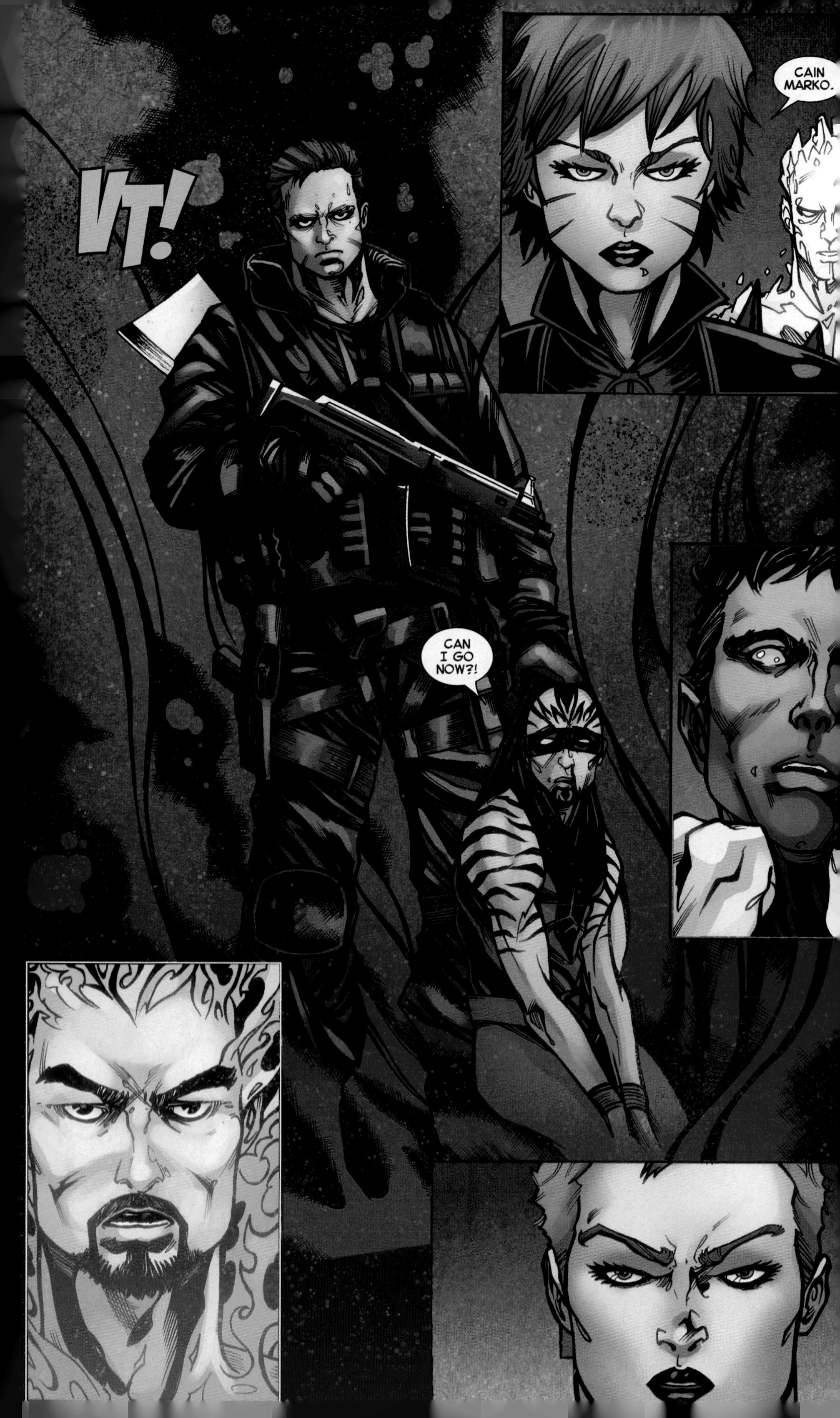
VT!
CAIN MARKO.
CAN I GO NOW?!

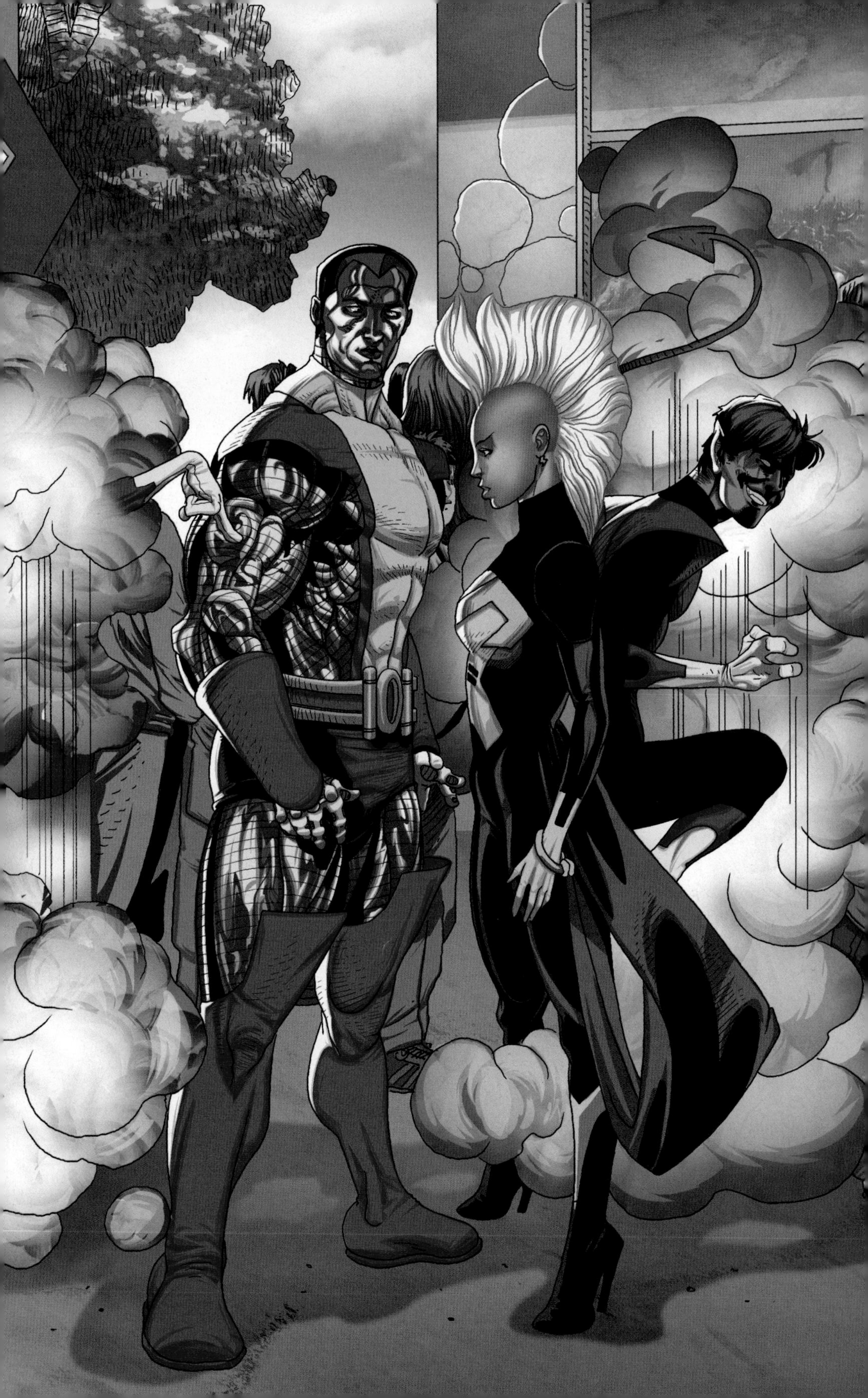

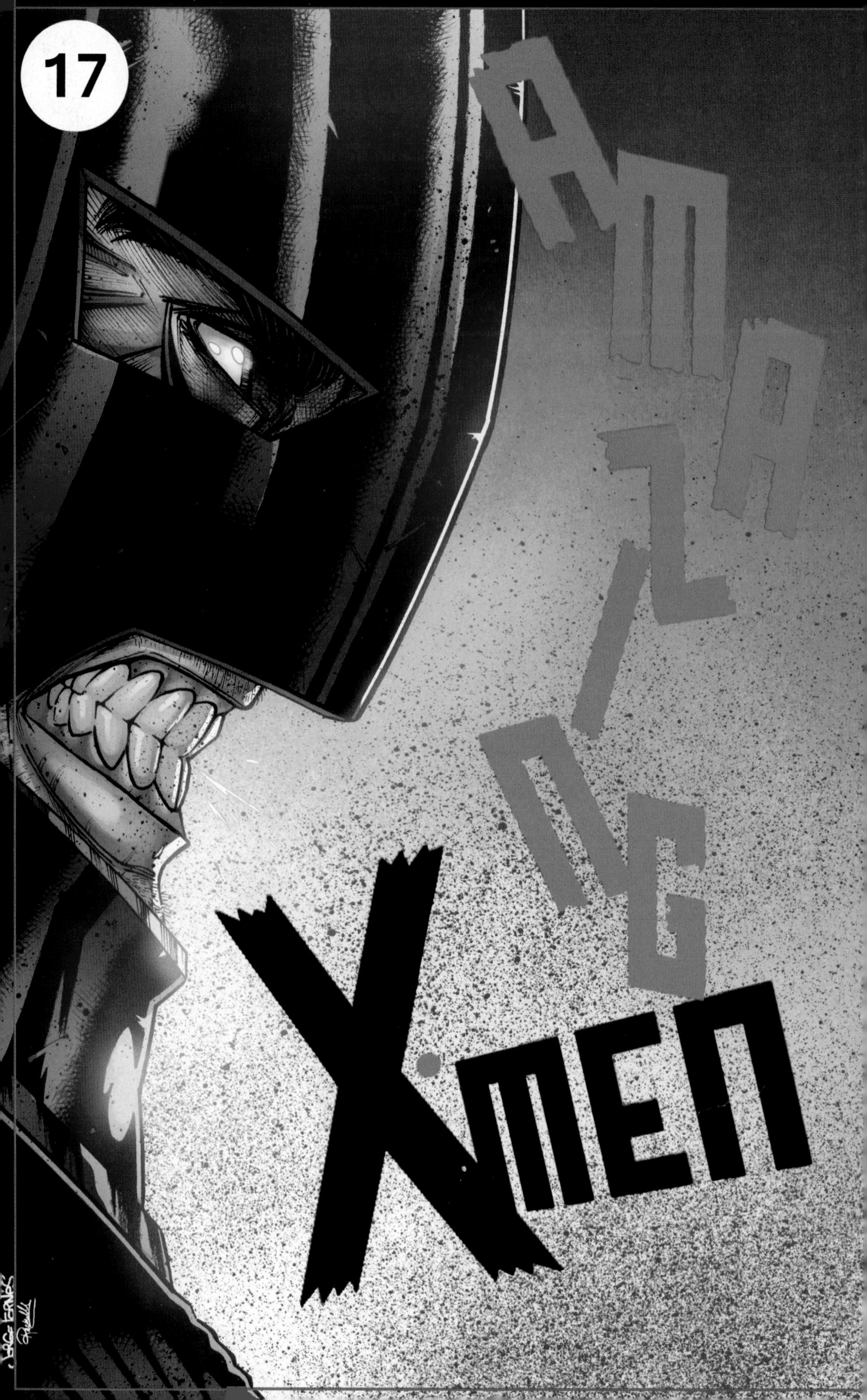
17
AMAZING
X-MEN

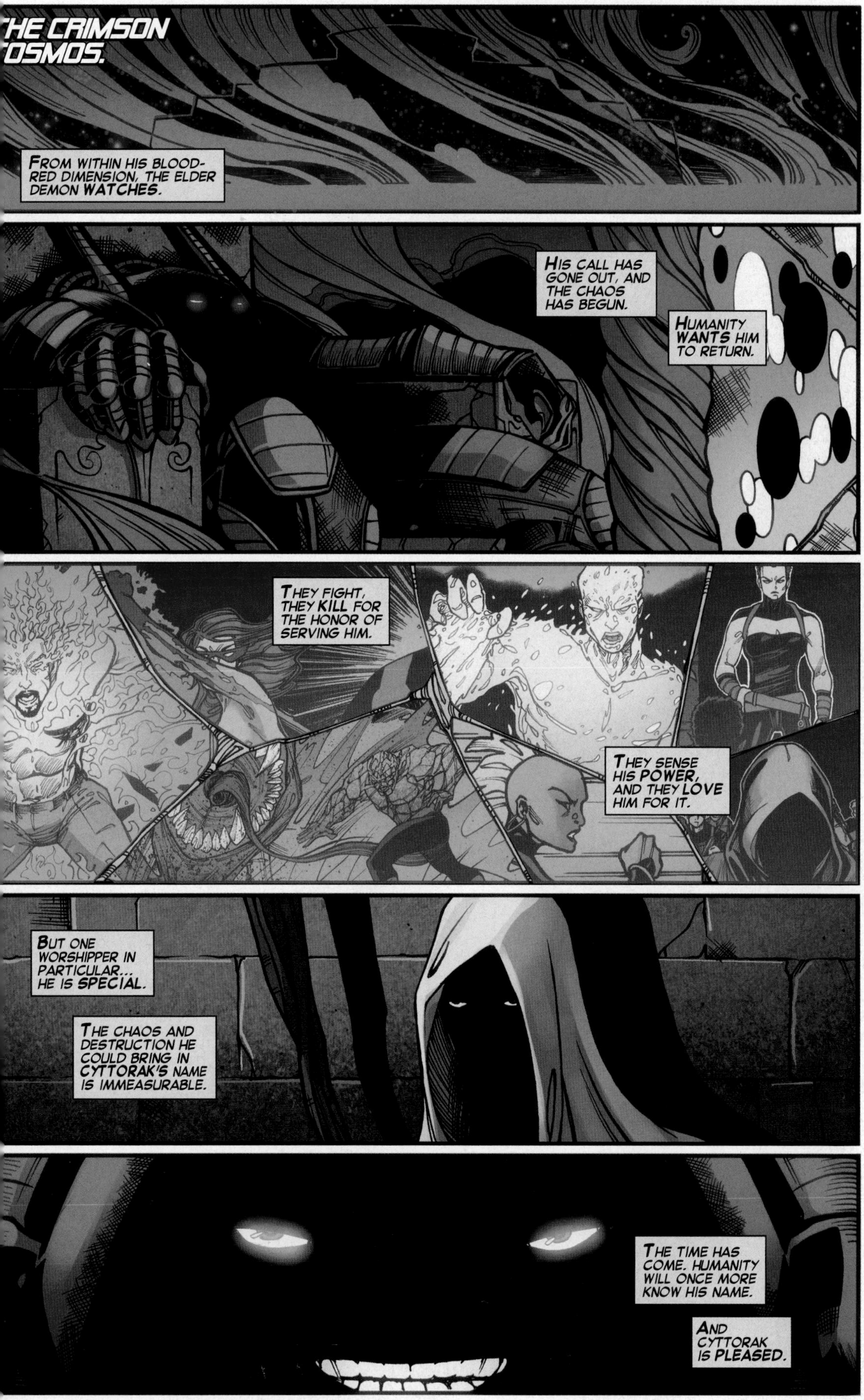
THE CRIMSON COSMOS.
FROM WITHIN HIS BLOOD-RED DIMENSION, THE ELDER DEMON WATCHES.
HIS CALL HAS GONE OUT, AND THE CHAOS HAS BEGUN.
HUMANITY WANTS HIM TO RETURN.
THEY FIGHT, THEY KILL FOR THE HONOR OF SERVING HIM.
THEY SENSE HIS POWER, AND THEY LOVE HIM FOR IT.
BUT ONE WORSHIPPER IN PARTICULAR... HE IS SPECIAL.
THE CHAOS AND DESTRUCTION HE COULD BRING IN CYTTORAK'S NAME IS IMMEASURABLE.
THE TIME HAS COME. HUMANITY WILL ONCE MORE KNOW HIS NAME.
AND CYTTORAK IS PLEASED.

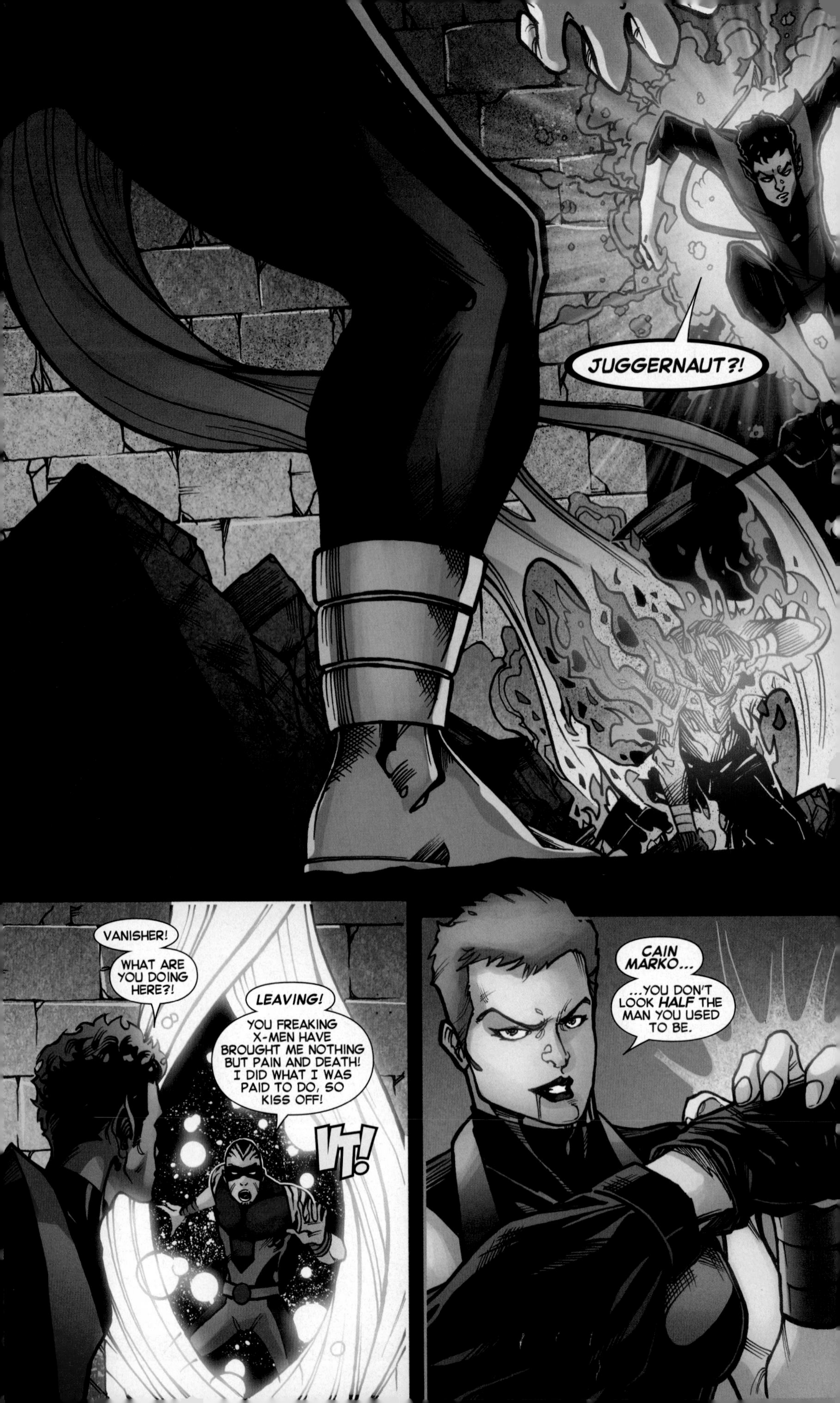
JUGGERNAUT?!
VANISHER!
WHAT ARE YOU DOING HERE?!
LEAVING!
YOU FREAKING X-MEN HAVE BROUGHT ME NOTHING BUT PAIN AND DEATH! I DID WHAT I WAS PAID TO DO, SO KISS OFF!
VT!
CAIN MARKO...
...YOU DON'T LOOK HALF THE MAN YOU USED TO BE.

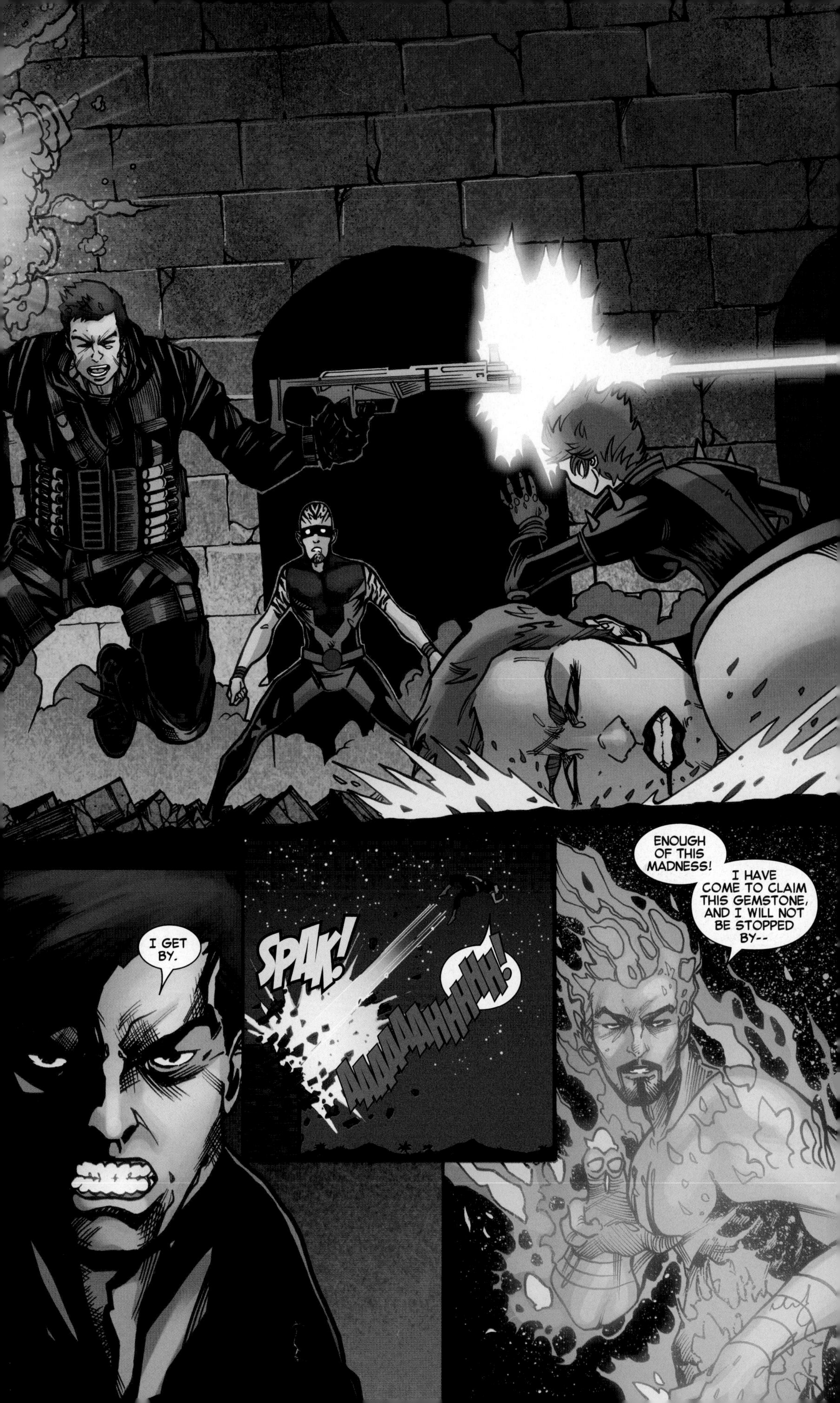
I GET BY.
SPAK!
AAAAAAHHHHH!
ENOUGH OF THIS MADNESS!
I HAVE COME TO CLAIM THIS GEMSTONE, AND I WILL NOT BE STOPPED BY--

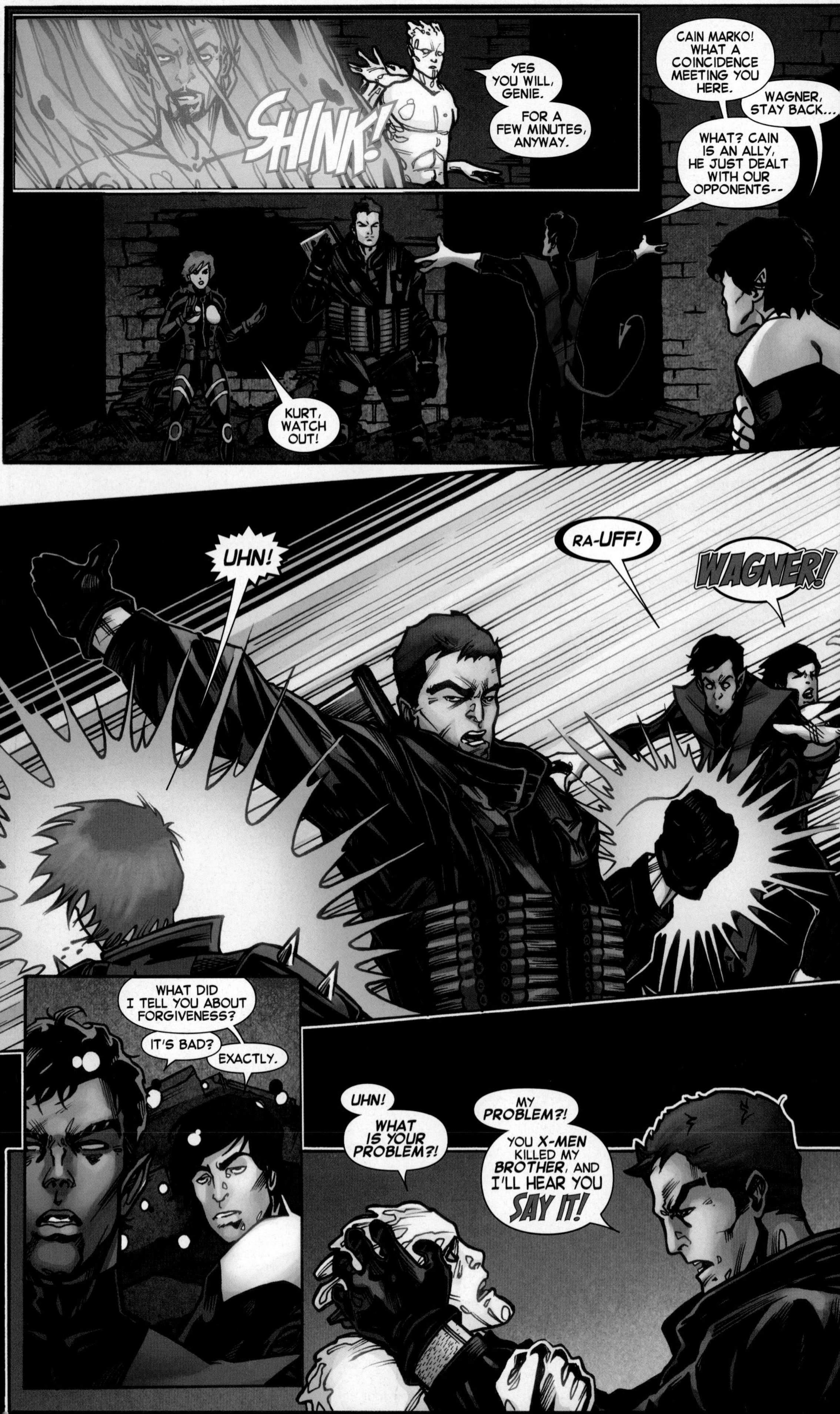

YES YOU WILL, GENIE.
FOR A FEW MINUTES, ANYWAY.
SHINK!
CAIN MARKO! WHAT A COINCIDENCE MEETING YOU HERE.
WAGNER, STAY BACK...
WHAT? CAIN IS AN ALLY, HE JUST DEALT WITH OUR OPPONENTS--
KURT, WATCH OUT!
UHN!
RA-UFF!
WAGNER!
WHAT DID I TELL YOU ABOUT FORGIVENESS?
IT'S BAD?
EXACTLY.
UHN!
WHAT IS YOUR PROBLEM?!
MY PROBLEM?!
YOU X-MEN KILLED MY BROTHER, AND I'LL HEAR YOU SAY IT!

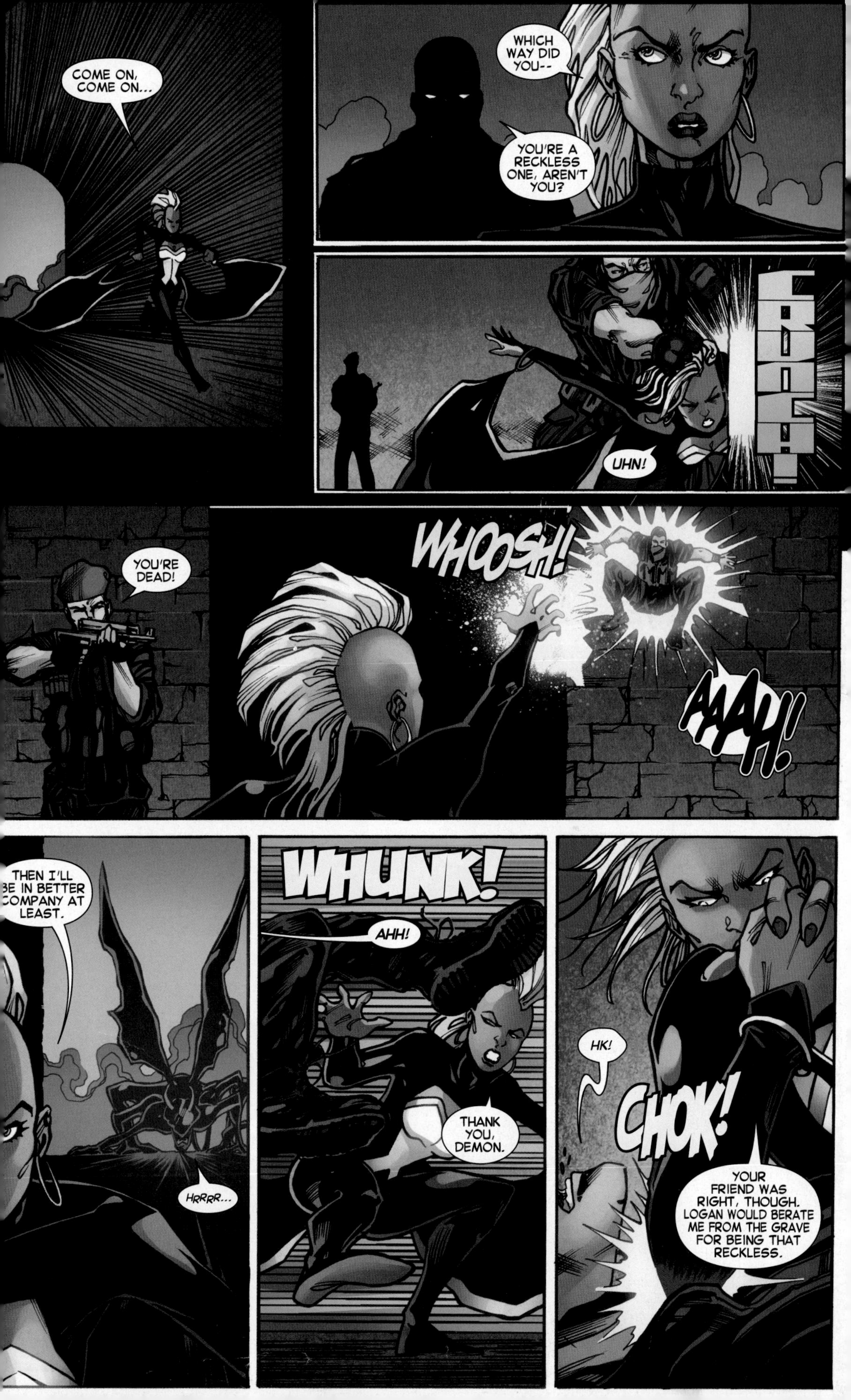

COME ON, COME ON...
WHICH WAY DID YOU--
YOU'RE A RECKLESS ONE, AREN'T YOU?
CRUNCH!
UHN!
YOU'RE DEAD!
WHOOSH!
AAAH!
THEN I'LL BE IN BETTER COMPANY AT LEAST.
HRRRR...
WHUNK!
AHH!
THANK YOU, DEMON.
HK!
CHOK!
YOUR FRIEND WAS RIGHT, THOUGH. LOGAN WOULD BERATE ME FROM THE GRAVE FOR BEING THAT RECKLESS.

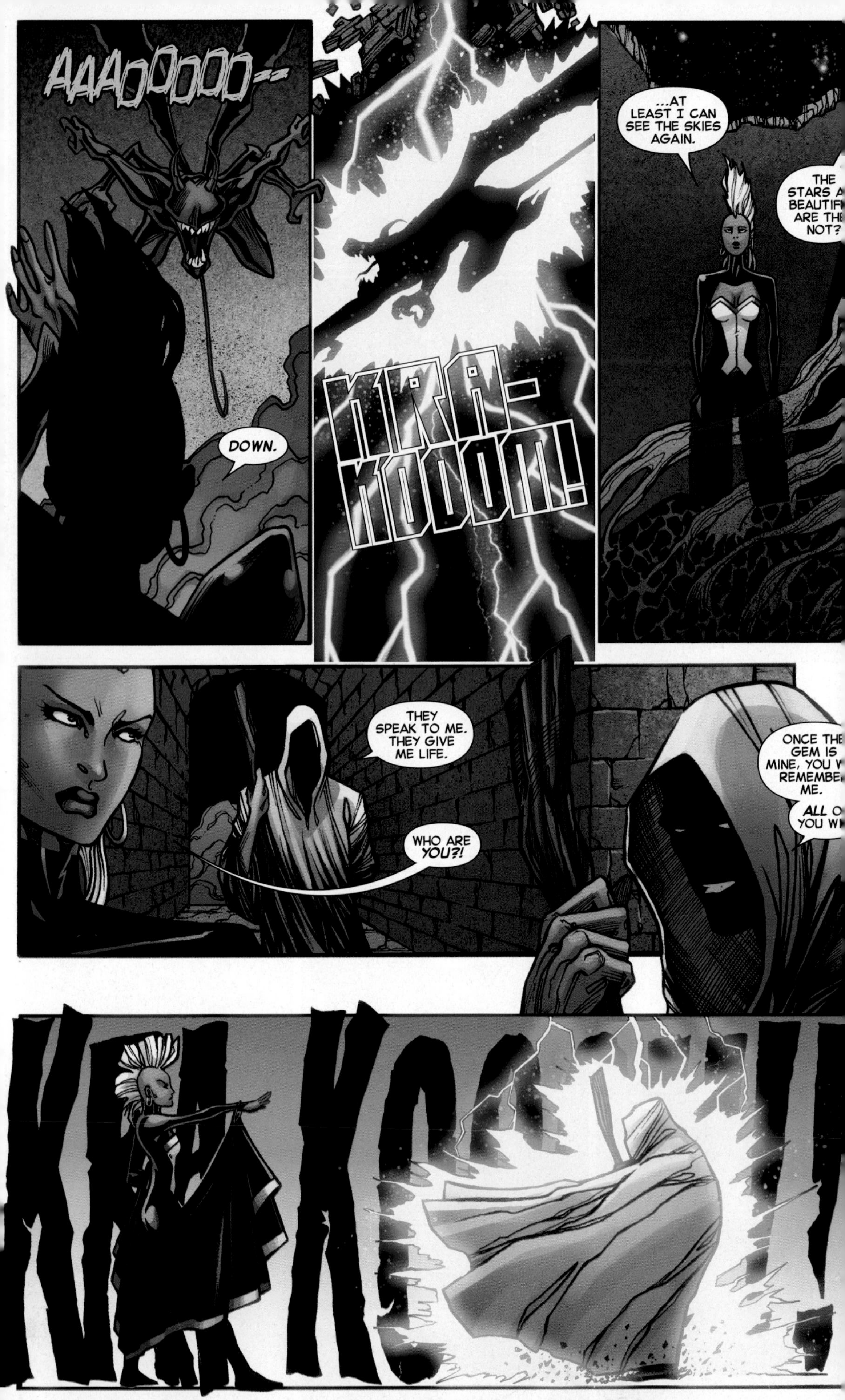
AAAOOOOO--
DOWN.
KRA-KOOOM!
...AT LEAST I CAN SEE THE SKIES AGAIN.
THEY SPEAK TO ME. THEY GIVE ME LIFE.
WHO ARE YOU?!

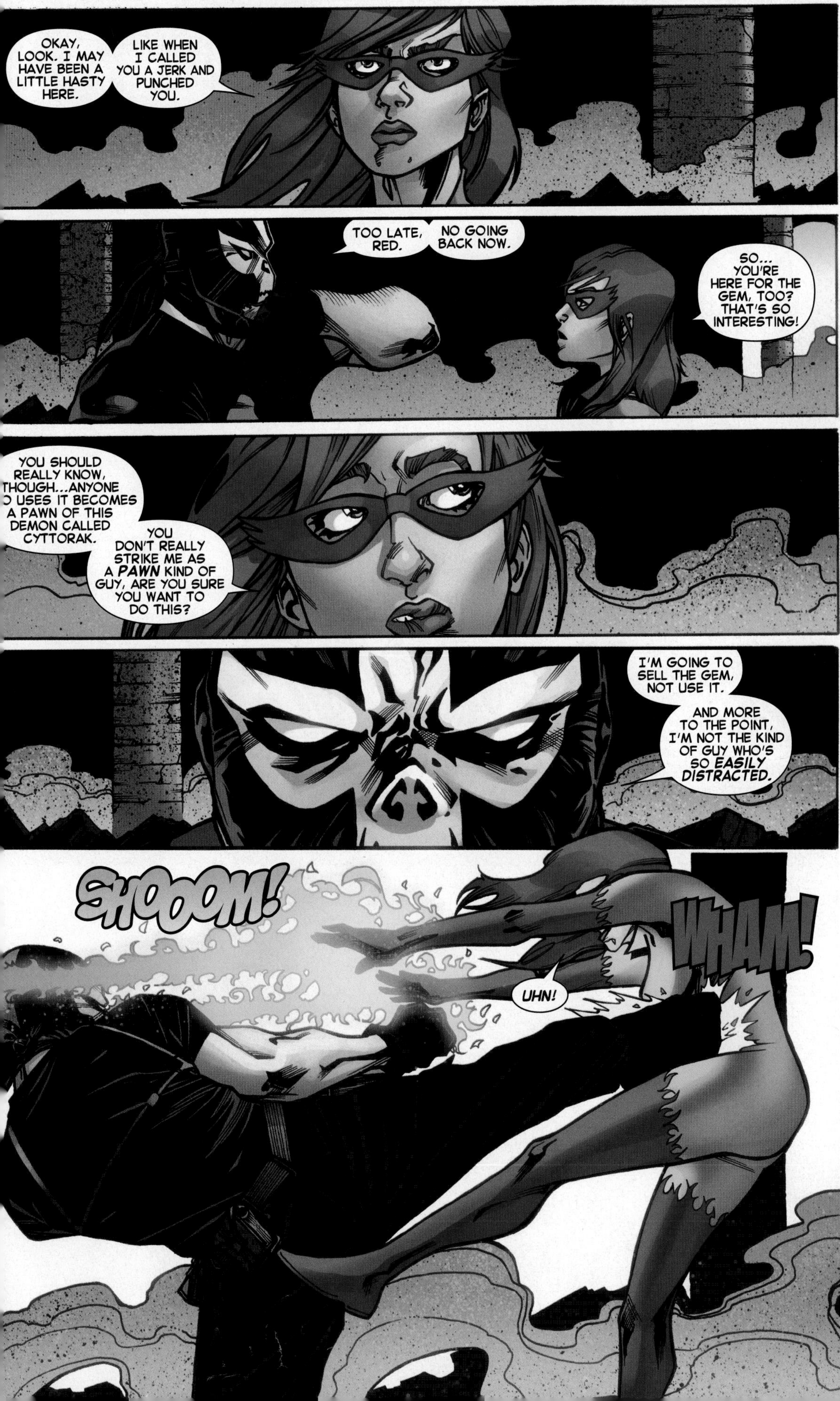
OKAY, LOOK. I MAY HAVE BEEN A LITTLE HASTY HERE.
LIKE WHEN I CALLED YOU A JERK AND PUNCHED YOU.
TOO LATE, RED.
NO GOING BACK NOW.
SO... YOU'RE HERE FOR THE GEM, TOO? THAT'S SO INTERESTING!
YOU SHOULD REALLY KNOW, THOUGH...ANYONE O USES IT BECOMES A PAWN OF THIS DEMON CALLED CYTTORAK.
YOU DON'T REALLY STRIKE ME AS A PAWN KIND OF GUY, ARE YOU SURE YOU WANT TO DO THIS?
I'M GOING TO SELL THE GEM, NOT USE IT.
AND MORE TO THE POINT, I'M NOT THE KIND OF GUY WHO'S SO EASILY DISTRACTED.
SHOOOM!
WHAM!
UHN!

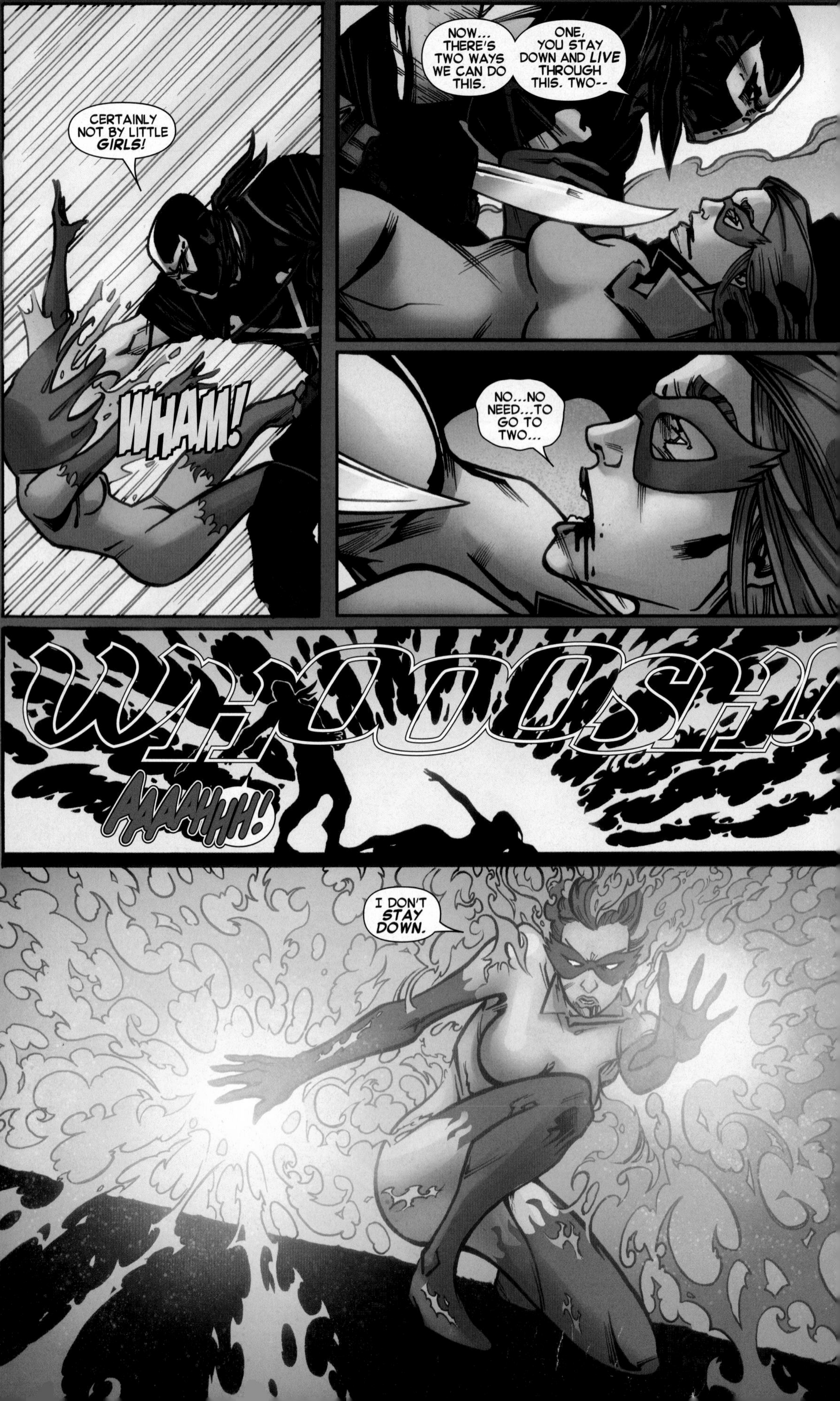
CERTAINLY NOT BY LITTLE GIRLS!
WHAM!
NOW... THERE'S TWO WAYS WE CAN DO THIS.
ONE, YOU STAY DOWN AND LIVE THROUGH THIS. TWO--
NO...NO NEED...TO GO TO TWO...
WHOOOSH!
AAAAHHH!
I DON'T STAY DOWN.

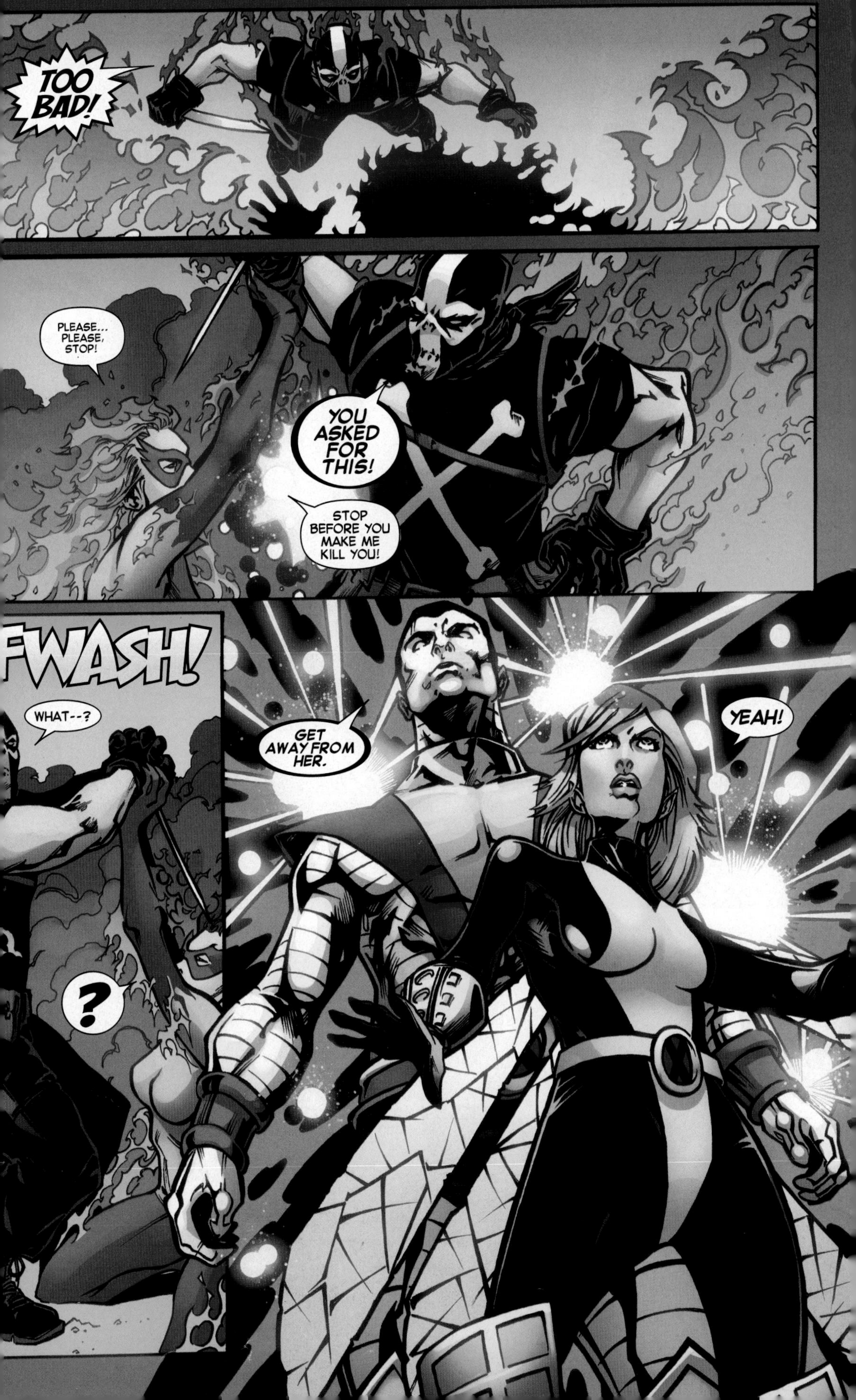
TOO BAD!
PLEASE... PLEASE, STOP!
YOU ASKED FOR THIS!
STOP BEFORE YOU MAKE ME KILL YOU!
FWASH!
WHAT--?
?
GET AWAY FROM HER.
YEAH!

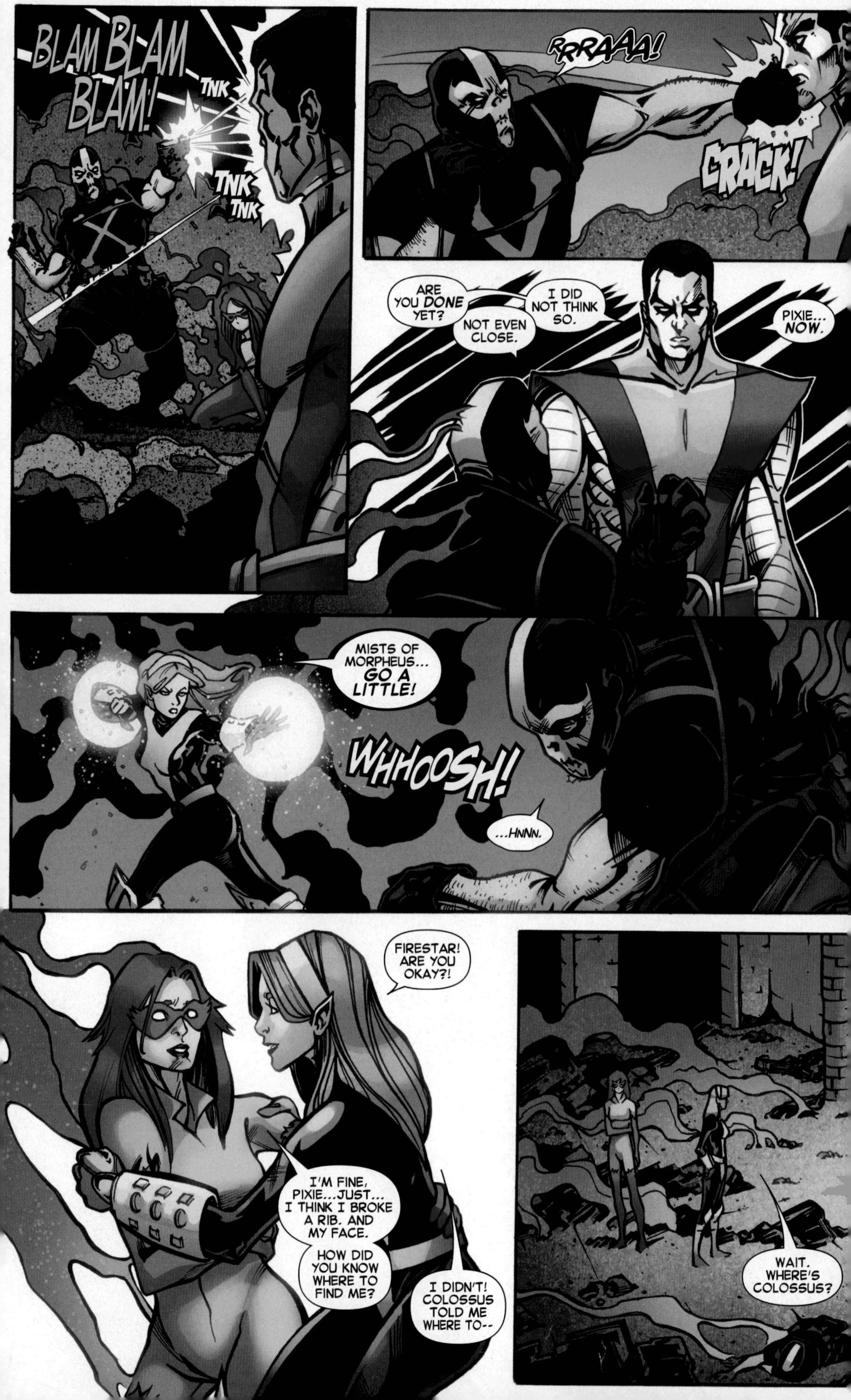
BLAM BLAM BLAM BLAM!
TNK
TNK TNK
RRRAAAA!
CRACK!
ARE YOU DONE YET?
NOT EVEN CLOSE.
I DID NOT THINK SO.
PIXIE... NOW.
MISTS OF MORPHEUS... GO A LITTLE!
WHHOOSH!
...HNNN.
FIRESTAR! ARE YOU OKAY?!
I'M FINE, PIXIE...JUST... I THINK I BROKE A RIB. AND MY FACE.
HOW DID YOU KNOW WHERE TO FIND ME?
I DIDN'T! COLOSSUS TOLD ME WHERE TO--
WAIT. WHERE'S COLOSSUS?

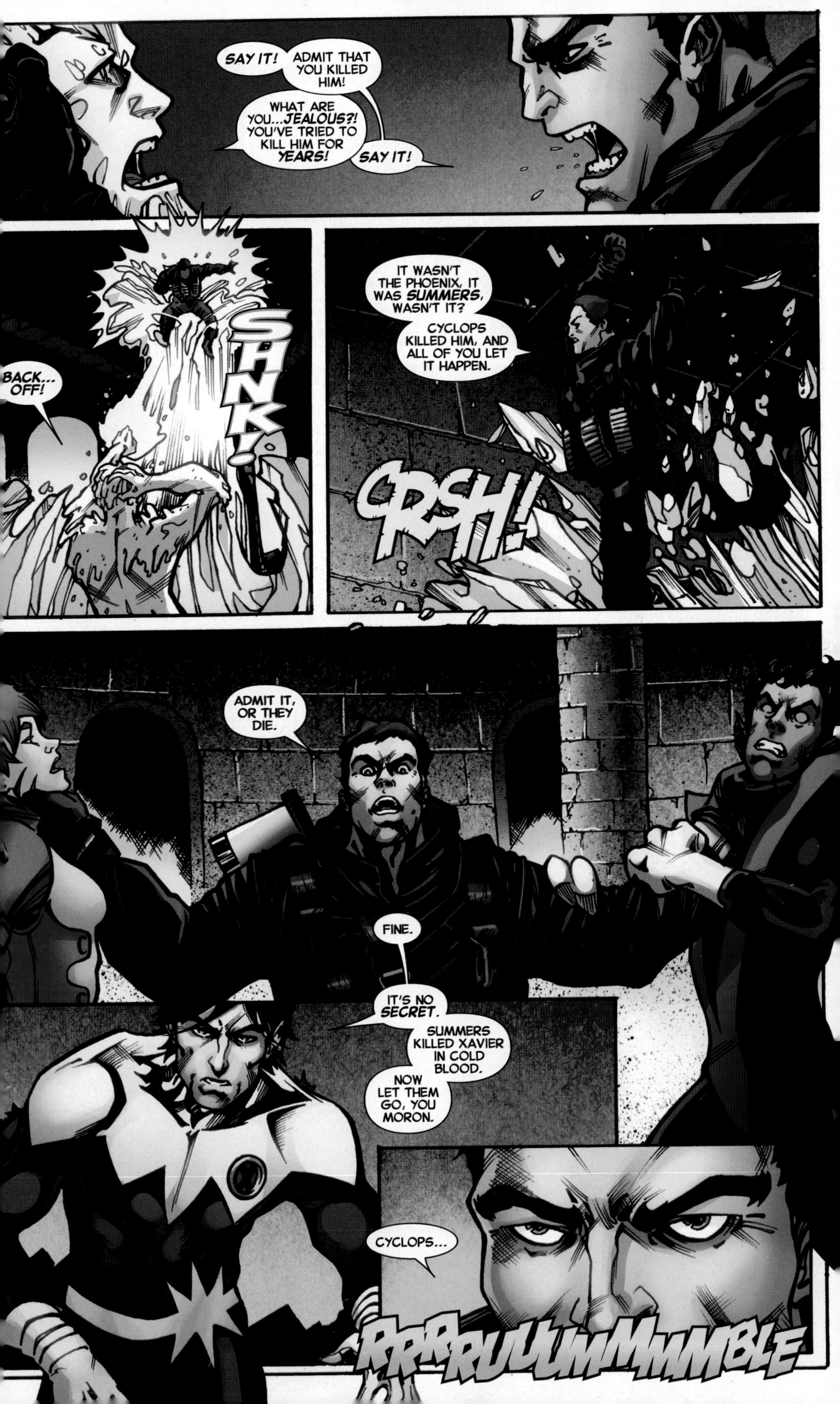
SAY IT!
ADMIT THAT YOU KILLED HIM!
WHAT ARE YOU...JEALOUS?! YOU'VE TRIED TO KILL HIM FOR YEARS!
SAY IT!
BACK... OFF!
SHNK!
IT WASN'T THE PHOENIX, IT WAS SUMMERS, WASN'T IT?
CYCLOPS KILLED HIM, AND ALL OF YOU LET IT HAPPEN.
CRSH!
ADMIT IT, OR THEY DIE.
FINE.
IT'S NO SECRET.
SUMMERS KILLED XAVIER IN COLD BLOOD.
NOW LET THEM GO, YOU MORON.
CYCLOPS...
RRRRUUUMMMMBLE

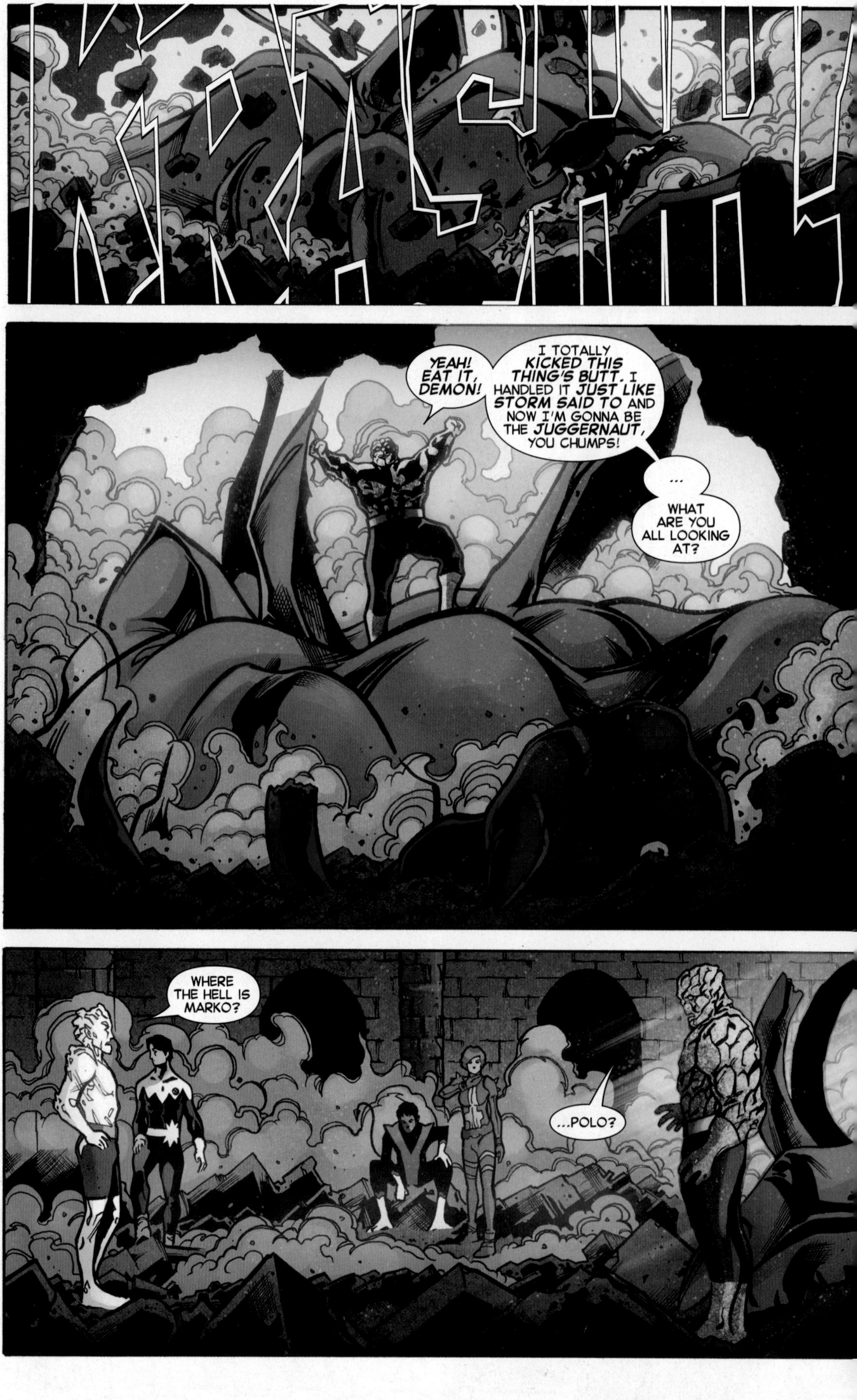
YEAH! EAT IT, DEMON!
I TOTALLY KICKED THIS THING'S BUTT. I HANDLED IT JUST LIKE STORM SAID TO AND NOW I'M GONNA BE THE JUGGERNAUT, YOU CHUMPS!
...
WHAT ARE YOU ALL LOOKING AT?
WHERE THE HELL IS MARKO?
...POLO?

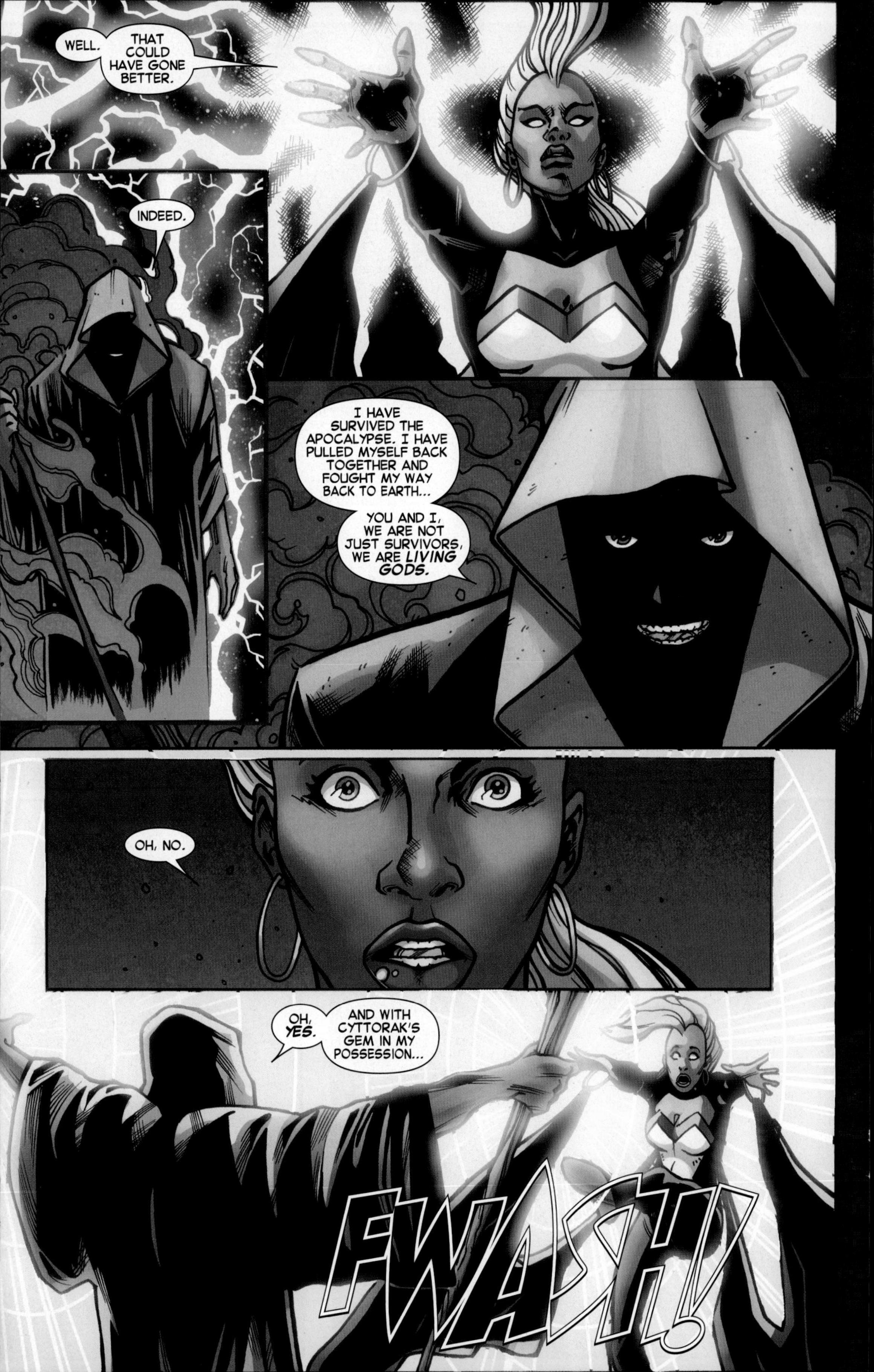
WELL.
THAT COULD HAVE GONE BETTER.
INDEED.
I HAVE SURVIVED THE APOCALYPSE. I HAVE PULLED MYSELF BACK TOGETHER AND FOUGHT MY WAY BACK TO EARTH...
YOU AND I, WE ARE NOT JUST SURVIVORS, WE ARE *LIVING GODS.*
OH, NO.
OH, *YES.*
AND WITH CYTTORAK'S GEM IN MY POSSESSION...
FWASH!!

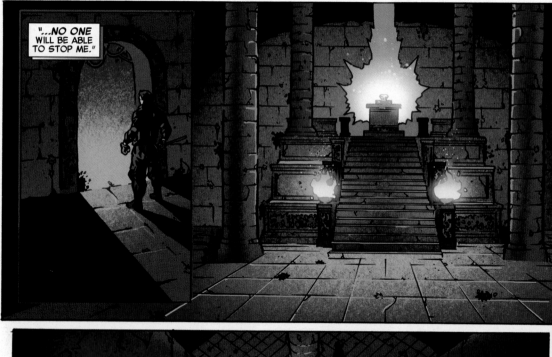

"...NO ONE WILL BE ABLE TO STOP ME."

YOU CALLED ME BACK.

WELL, HERE I--

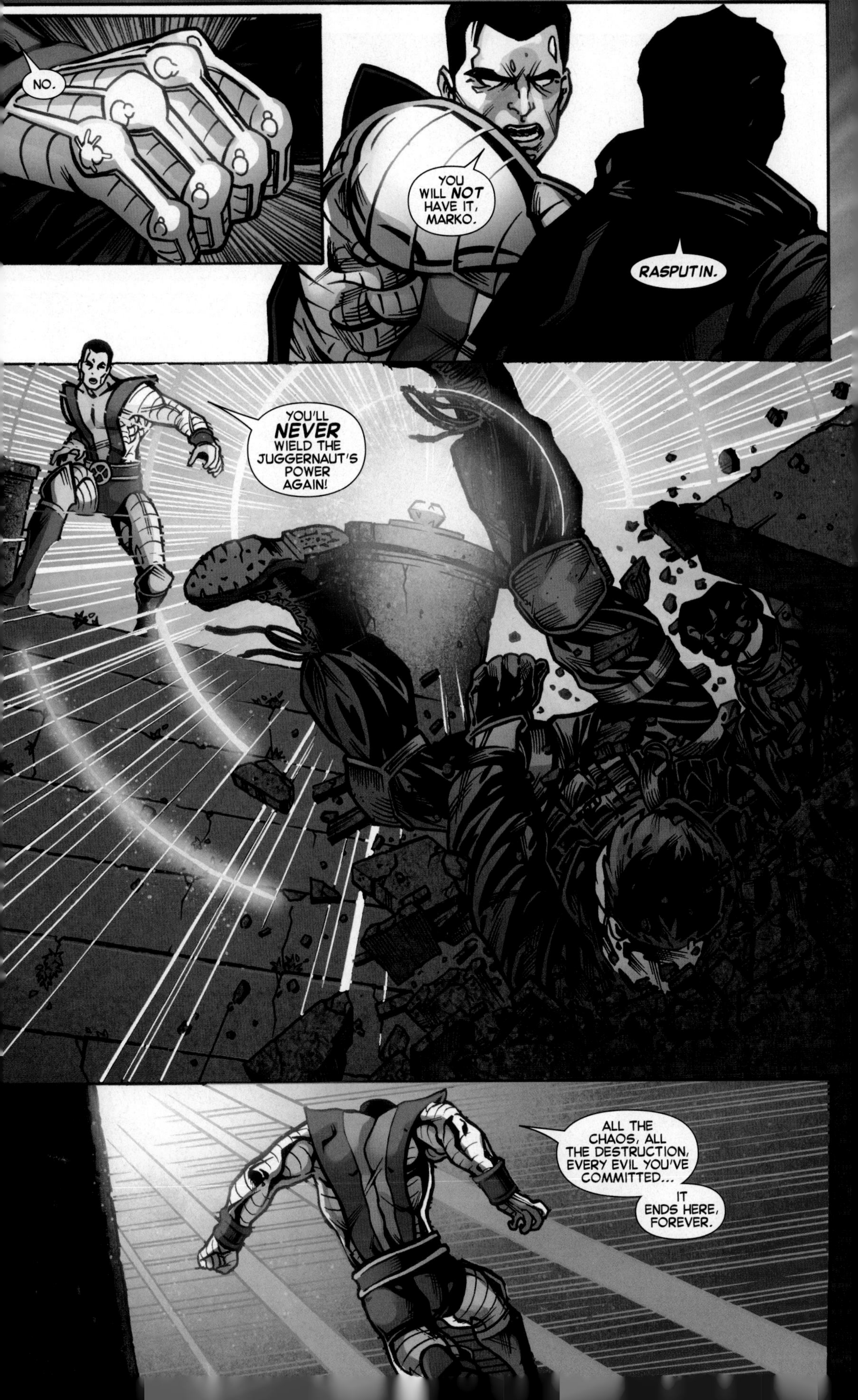
NO.
YOU WILL NOT HAVE IT, MARKO.
RASPUTIN.
YOU'LL NEVER WIELD THE JUGGERNAUT'S POWER AGAIN!
ALL THE CHAOS, ALL THE DESTRUCTION, EVERY EVIL YOU'VE COMMITTED...
IT ENDS HERE, FOREVER.

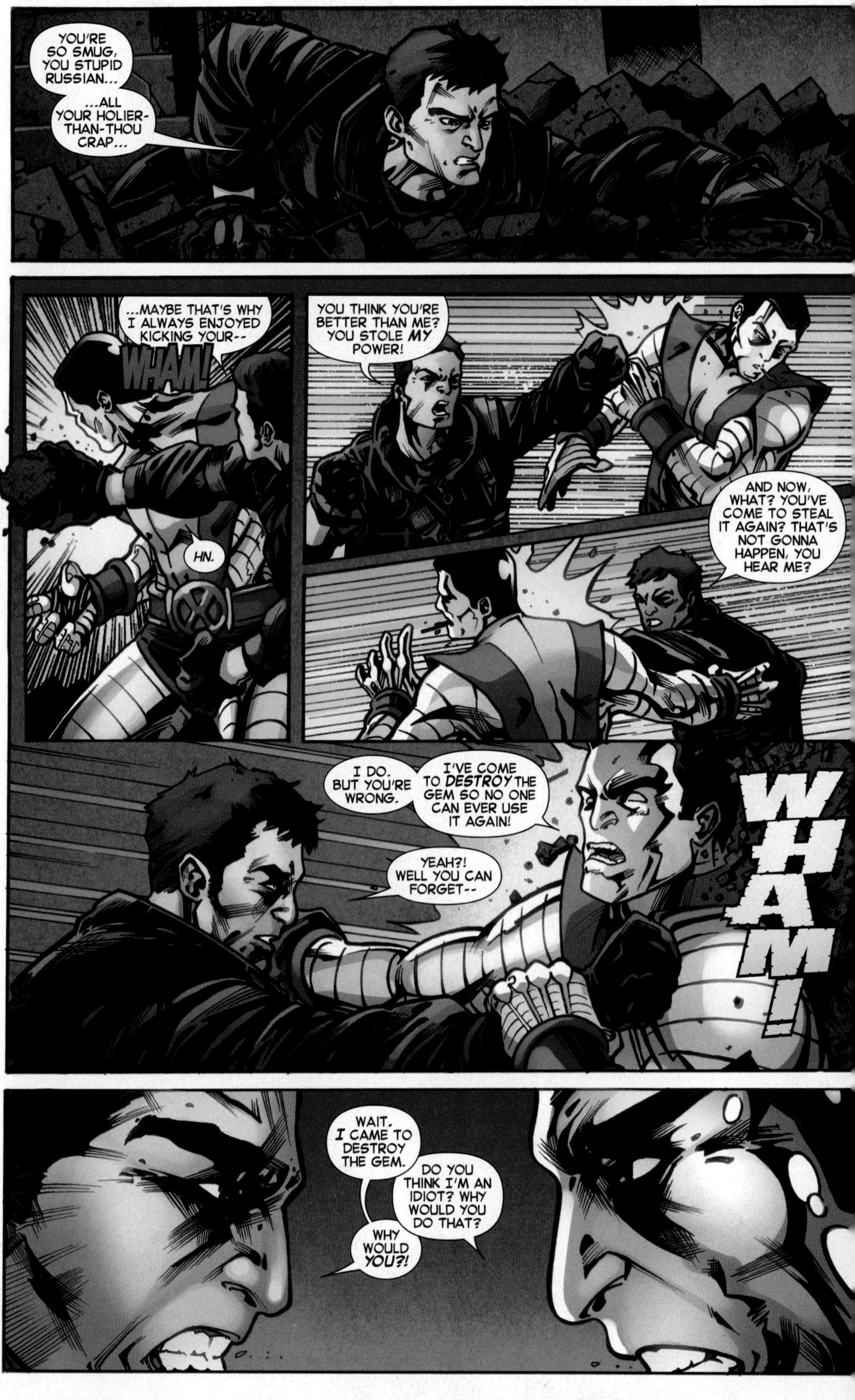
YOU'RE SO SMUG, YOU STUPID RUSSIAN...
...ALL YOUR HOLIER-THAN-THOU CRAP...
...MAYBE THAT'S WHY I ALWAYS ENJOYED KICKING YOUR--
WHAM!
HN.
YOU THINK YOU'RE BETTER THAN ME? YOU STOLE *MY* POWER!
AND NOW, WHAT? YOU'VE COME TO STEAL IT AGAIN? THAT'S NOT GONNA HAPPEN, YOU HEAR ME?
I DO. BUT YOU'RE WRONG.
I'VE COME TO *DESTROY* THE GEM SO NO ONE CAN EVER USE IT AGAIN!
YEAH?! WELL YOU CAN FORGET--
WHAM!
WAIT. *I* CAME TO DESTROY THE GEM.
DO YOU THINK I'M AN IDIOT? WHY WOULD YOU DO THAT?
WHY WOULD *YOU*?!

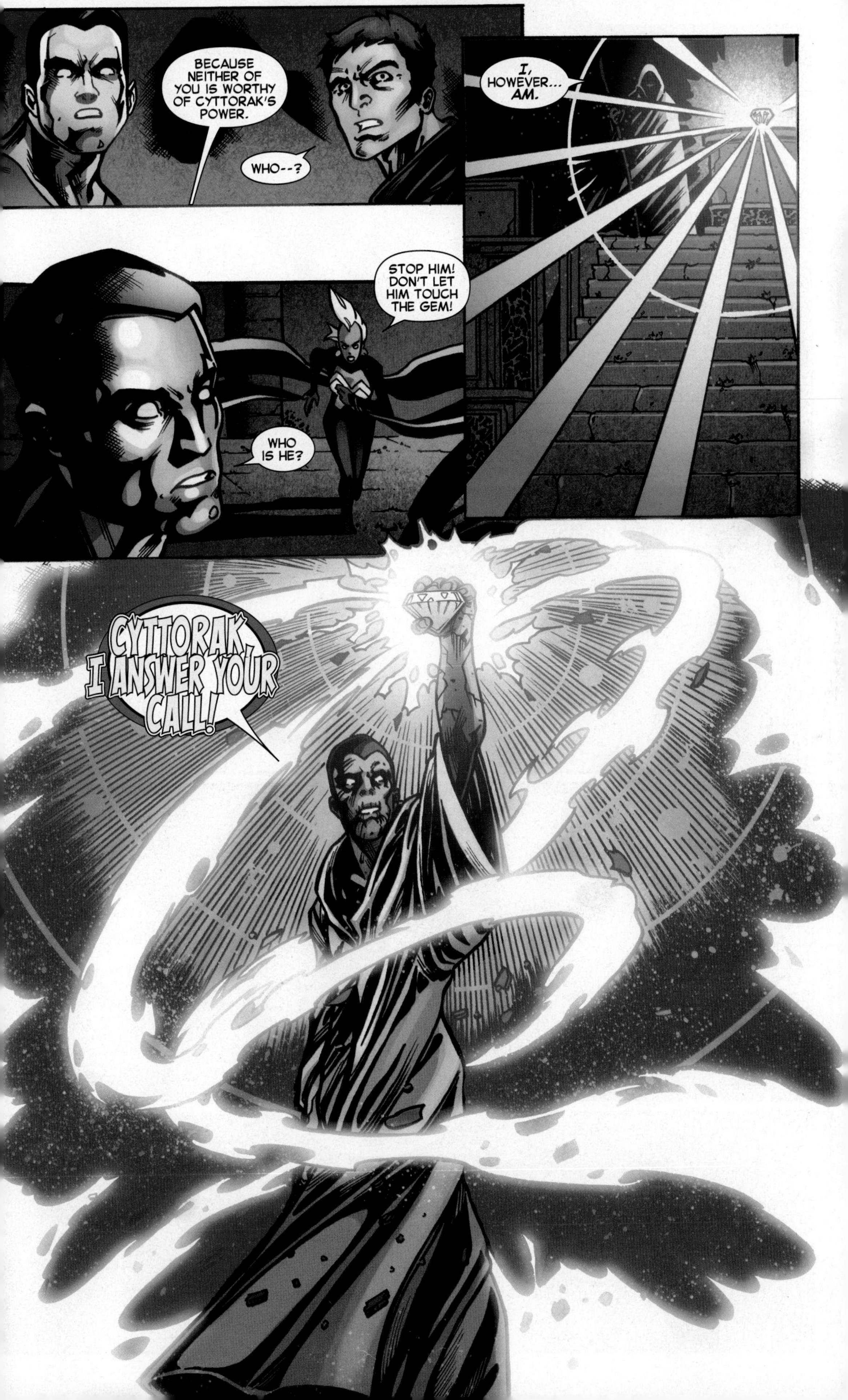

BECAUSE NEITHER OF YOU IS WORTHY OF CYTTORAK'S POWER.
WHO--?
I, HOWEVER... AM.
STOP HIM! DON'T LET HIM TOUCH THE GEM!
WHO IS HE?
CYTTORAK, I ANSWER YOUR CALL!

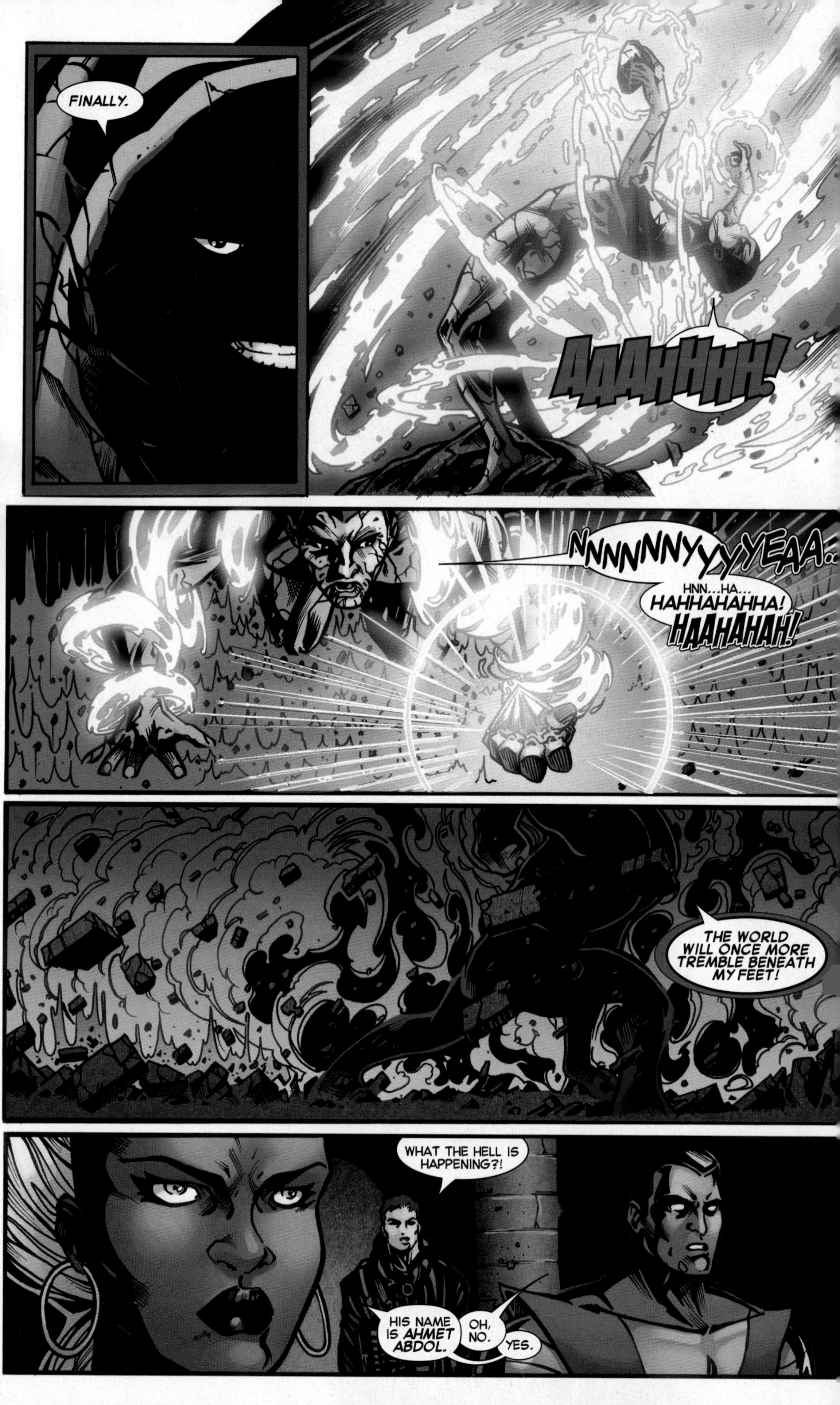
FINALLY.
AAAHHHH!
NNNNNNYYYYEAA..
HNN...HA...
HAHHAHAHHA!
HAAHAHAH!
THE WORLD WILL ONCE MORE TREMBLE BENEATH MY FEET!
WHAT THE HELL IS HAPPENING?!
HIS NAME IS AHMET ABDOL.
OH, NO.
YES.

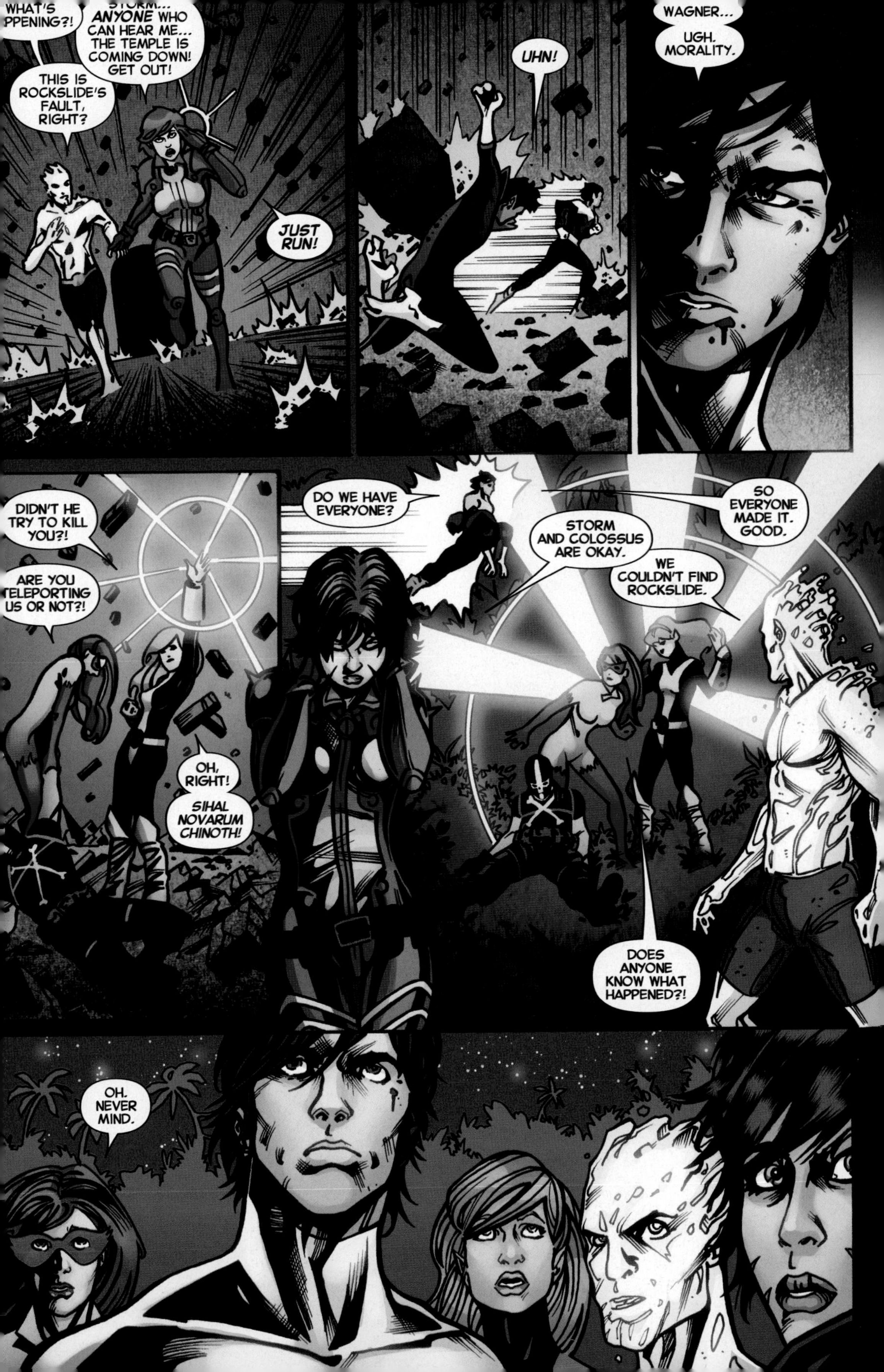
WHAT'S PPENING?!
THIS IS ROCKSLIDE'S FAULT, RIGHT?
STORM... ANYONE WHO CAN HEAR ME... THE TEMPLE IS COMING DOWN! GET OUT!
JUST RUN!
UHN!
WAGNER...
UGH. MORALITY.
DIDN'T HE TRY TO KILL YOU?!
ARE YOU TELEPORTING US OR NOT?!
OH, RIGHT!
SIHAL NOVARUM CHINOTH!
DO WE HAVE EVERYONE?
STORM AND COLOSSUS ARE OKAY.
SO EVERYONE MADE IT. GOOD.
WE COULDN'T FIND ROCKSLIDE.
DOES ANYONE KNOW WHAT HAPPENED?!
OH. NEVER MIND.

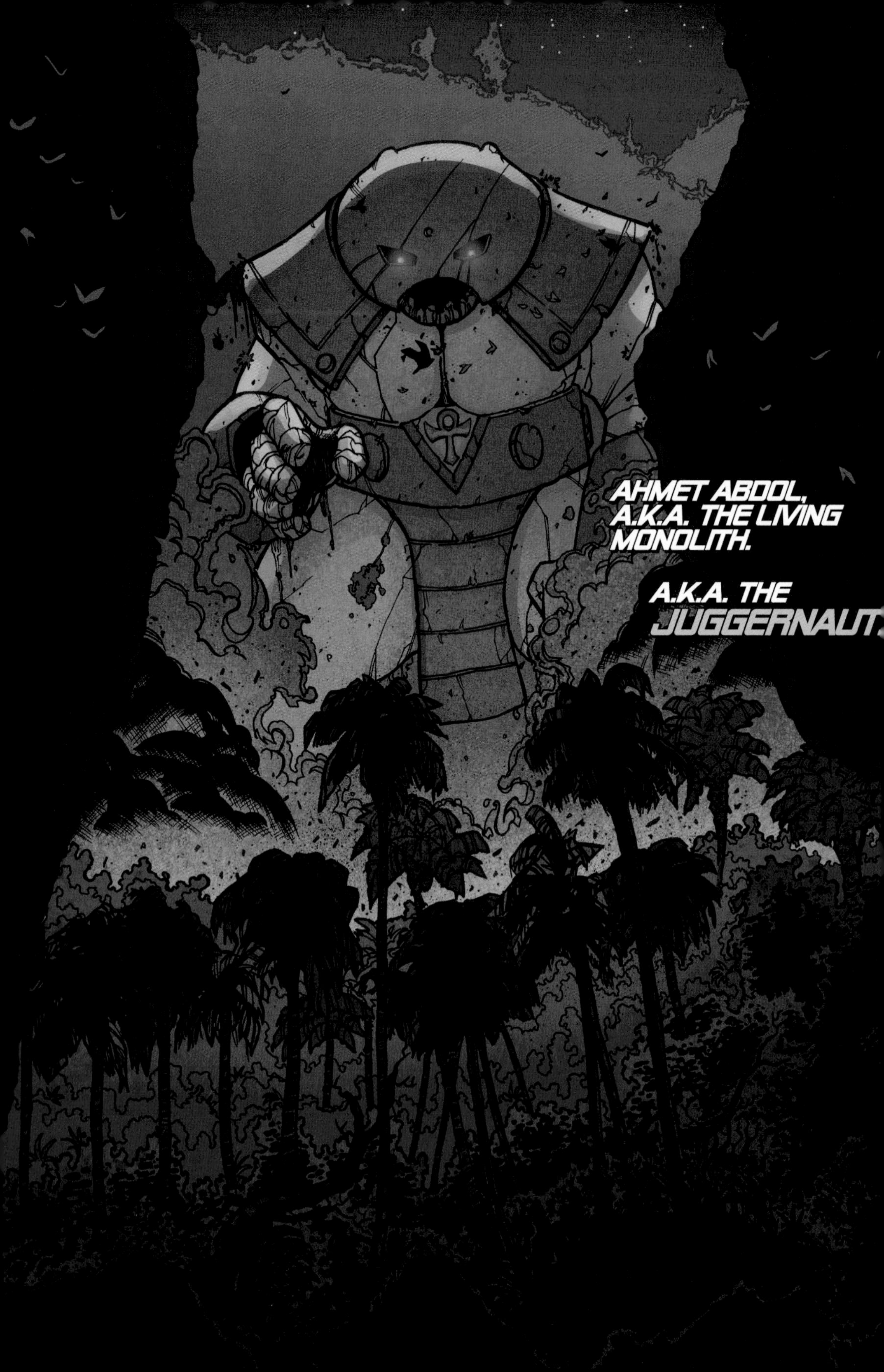
AHMET ABDOL, A.K.A. THE LIVING MONOLITH.
A.K.A. THE JUGGERNAUT.

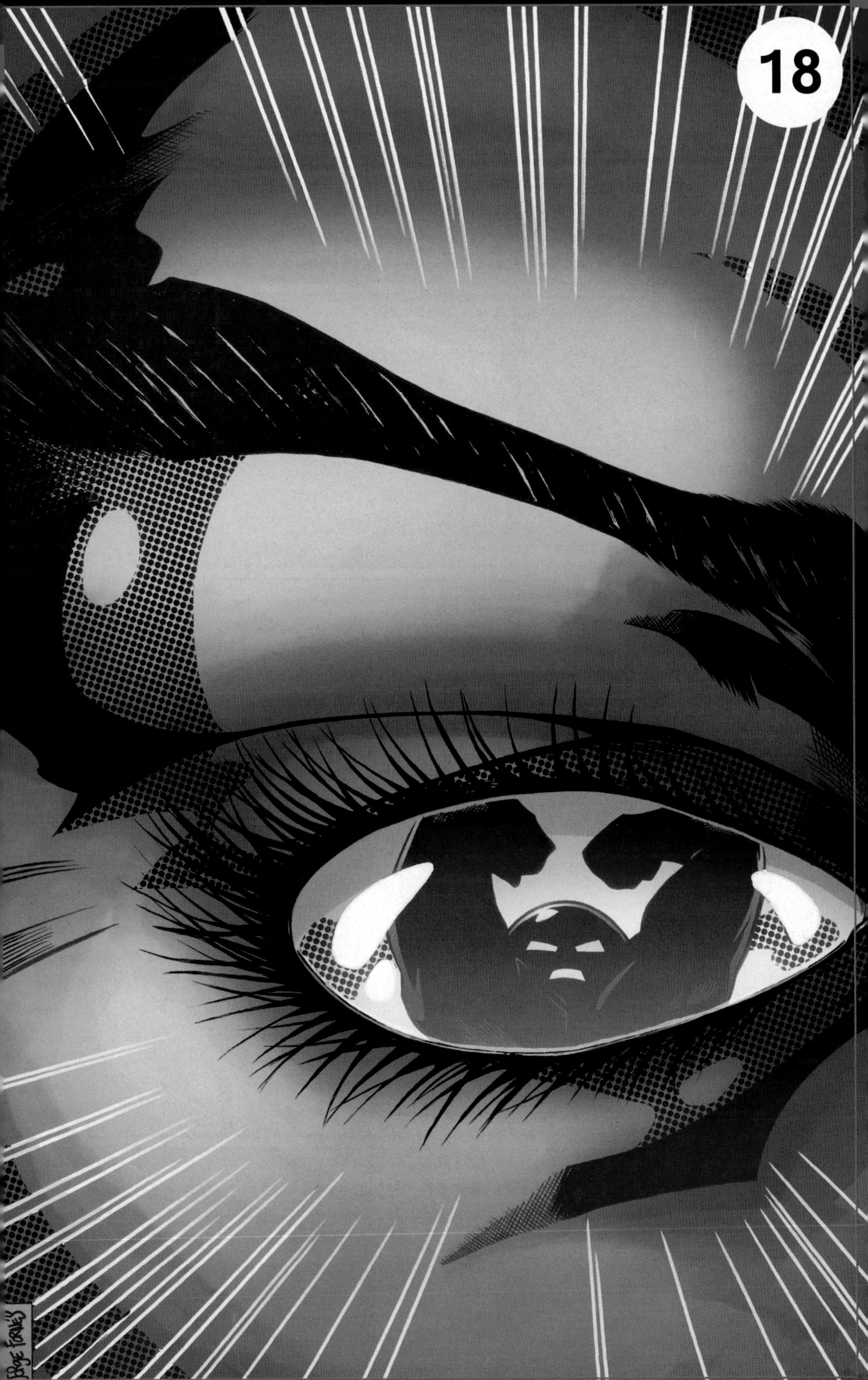
18

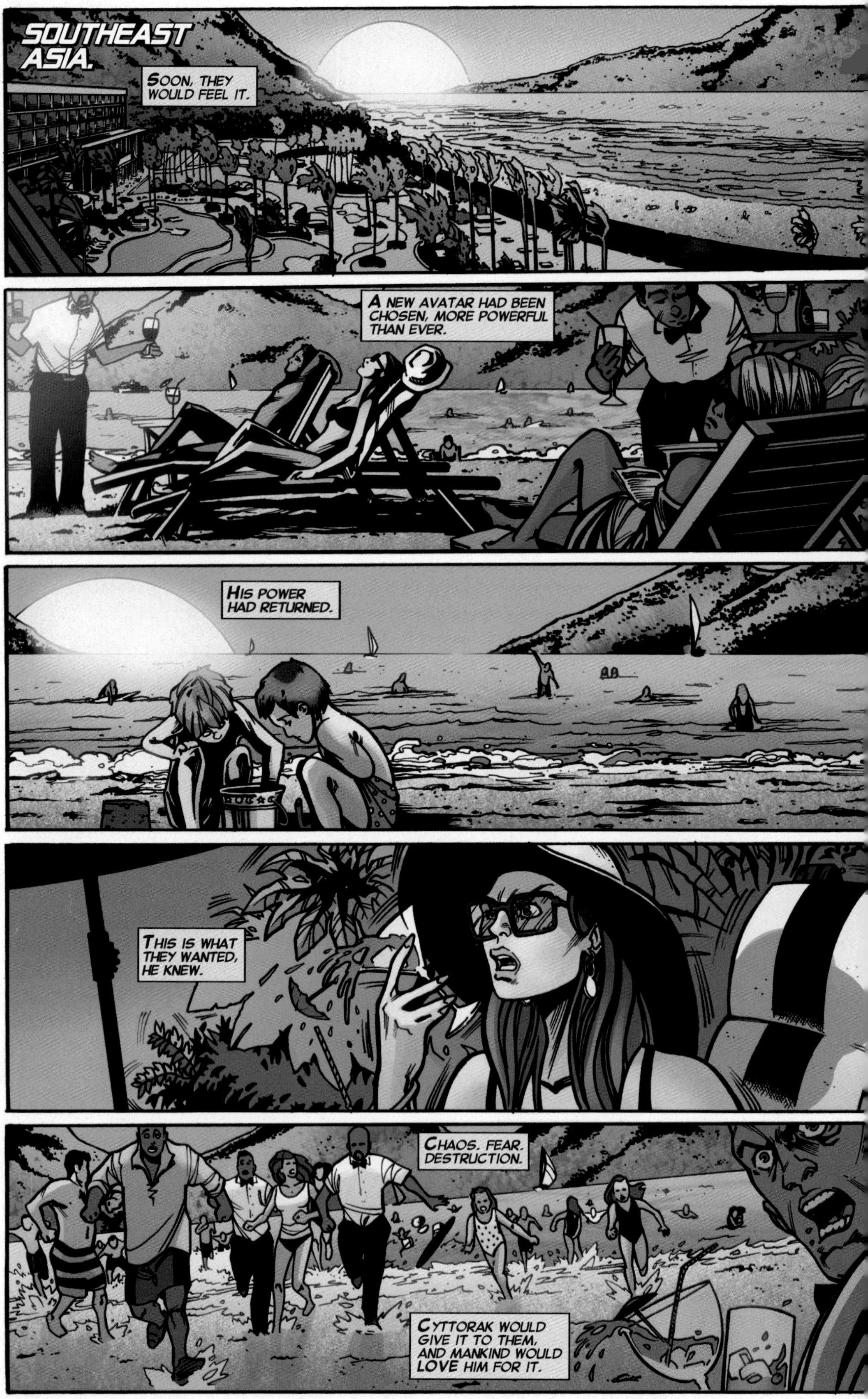
SOUTHEAST ASIA.
SOON, THEY WOULD FEEL IT.
A NEW AVATAR HAD BEEN CHOSEN, MORE POWERFUL THAN EVER.
HIS POWER HAD RETURNED.
THIS IS WHAT THEY WANTED, HE KNEW.
CHAOS. FEAR. DESTRUCTION.
CYTTORAK WOULD GIVE IT TO THEM, AND MANKIND WOULD LOVE HIM FOR IT.

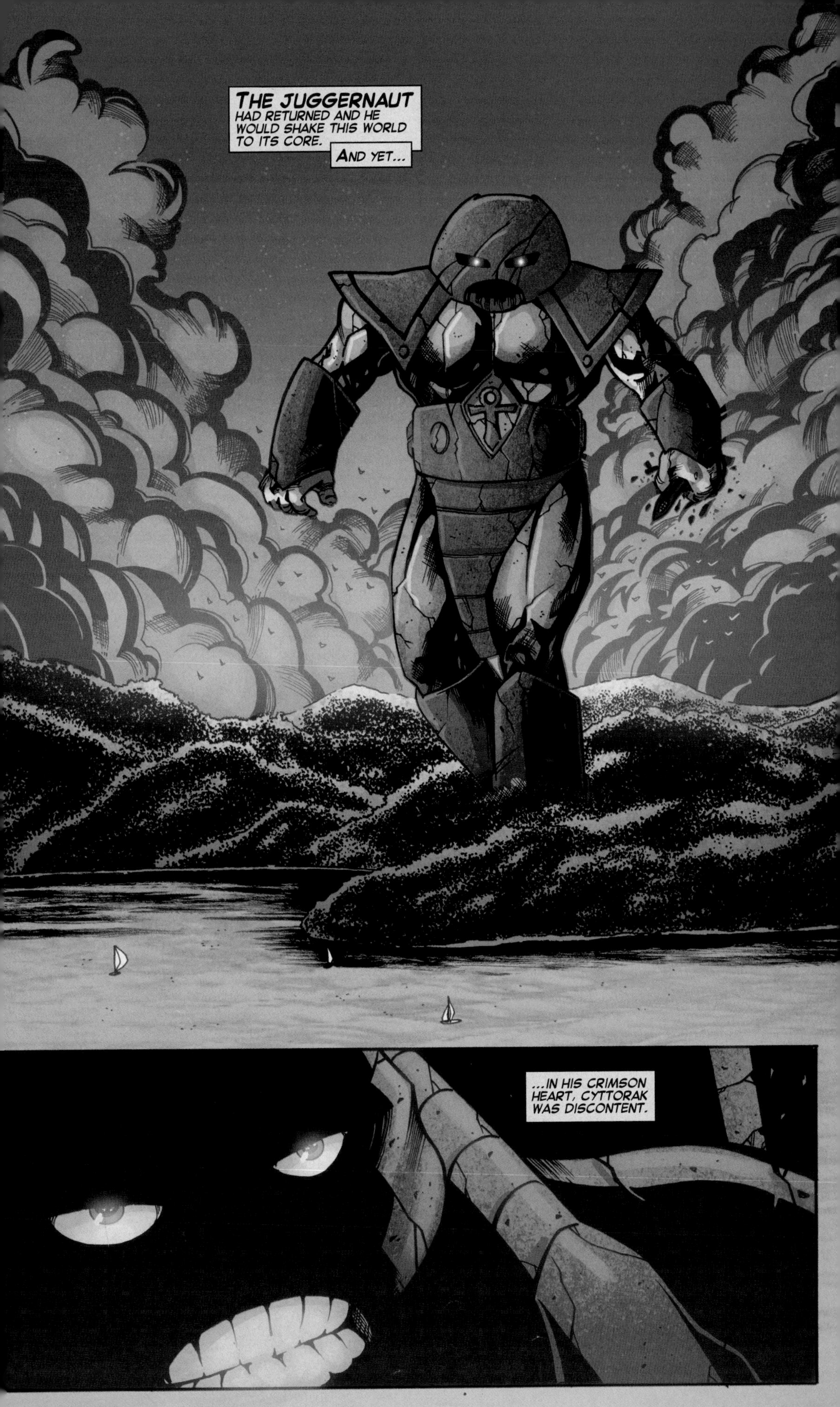
THE JUGGERNAUT HAD RETURNED AND HE WOULD SHAKE THIS WORLD TO ITS CORE.
AND YET...
...IN HIS CRIMSON HEART, CYTTORAK WAS DISCONTENT.

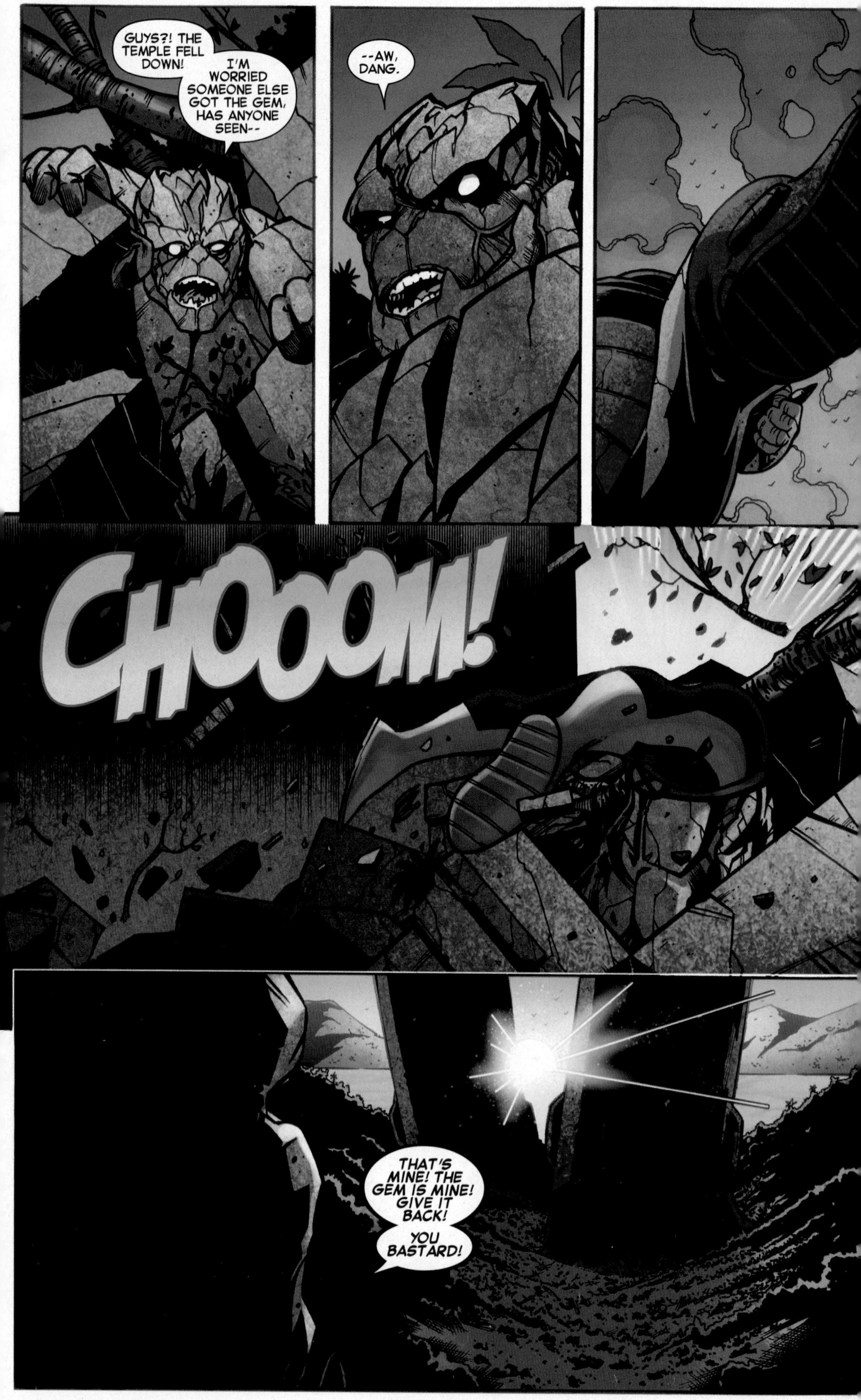
GUYS?! THE TEMPLE FELL DOWN!
I'M WORRIED SOMEONE ELSE GOT THE GEM, HAS ANYONE SEEN--
--AW, DANG.
CHOOOM!
THAT'S MINE! THE GEM IS MINE! GIVE IT BACK!
YOU BASTARD!

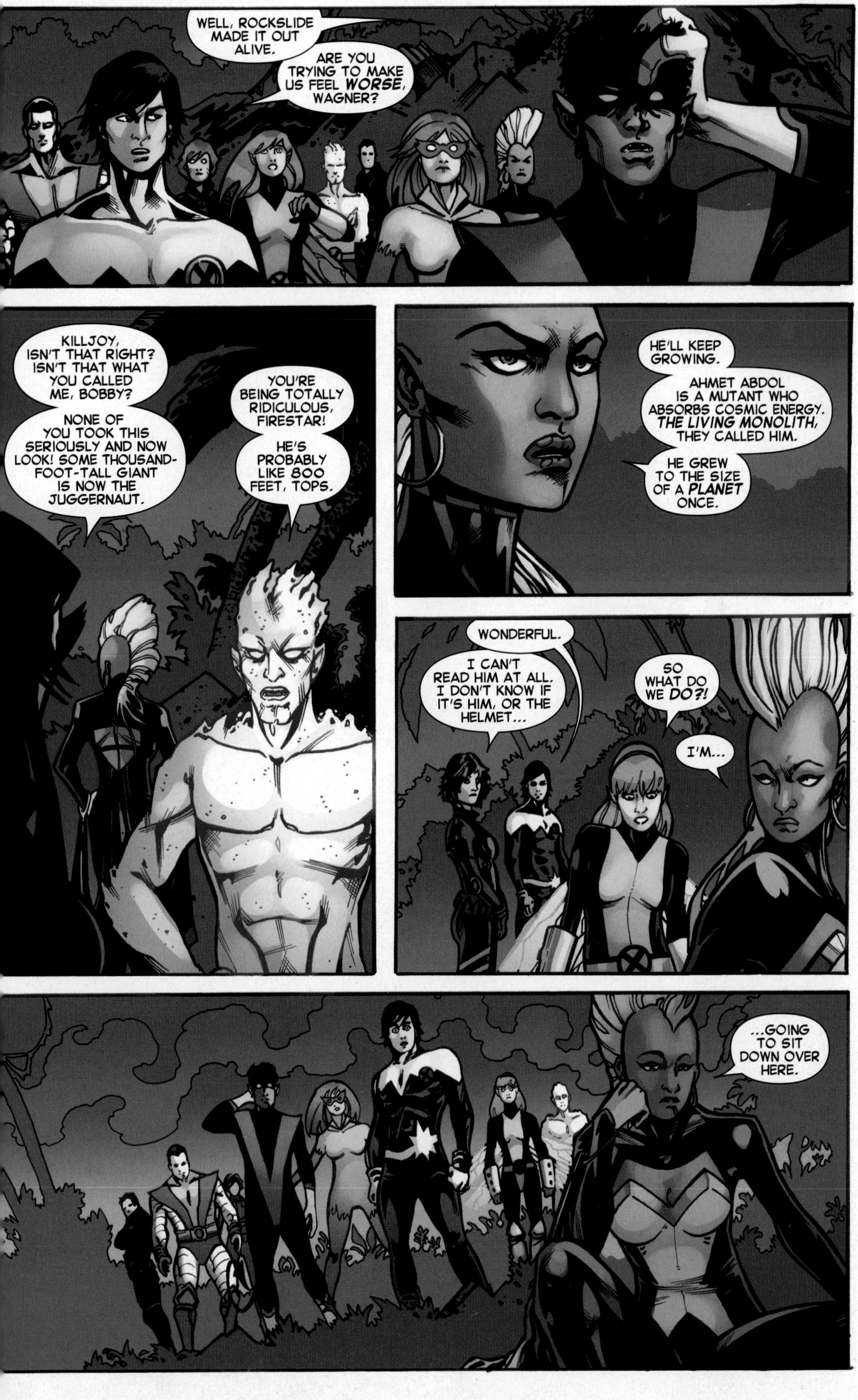
WELL, ROCKSLIDE MADE IT OUT ALIVE.
ARE YOU TRYING TO MAKE US FEEL *WORSE*, WAGNER?
KILLJOY, ISN'T THAT RIGHT? ISN'T THAT WHAT YOU CALLED ME, BOBBY?
NONE OF YOU TOOK THIS SERIOUSLY AND NOW LOOK! SOME THOUSAND-FOOT-TALL GIANT IS NOW THE JUGGERNAUT.
YOU'RE BEING TOTALLY RIDICULOUS, FIRESTAR!
HE'S PROBABLY LIKE 800 FEET, TOPS.
HE'LL KEEP GROWING.
AHMET ABDOL IS A MUTANT WHO ABSORBS COSMIC ENERGY. *THE LIVING MONOLITH,* THEY CALLED HIM.
HE GREW TO THE SIZE OF A *PLANET* ONCE.
WONDERFUL.
I CAN'T READ HIM AT ALL. I DON'T KNOW IF IT'S HIM, OR THE HELMET...
SO WHAT DO WE *DO?!*
I'M...
...GOING TO SIT DOWN OVER HERE.

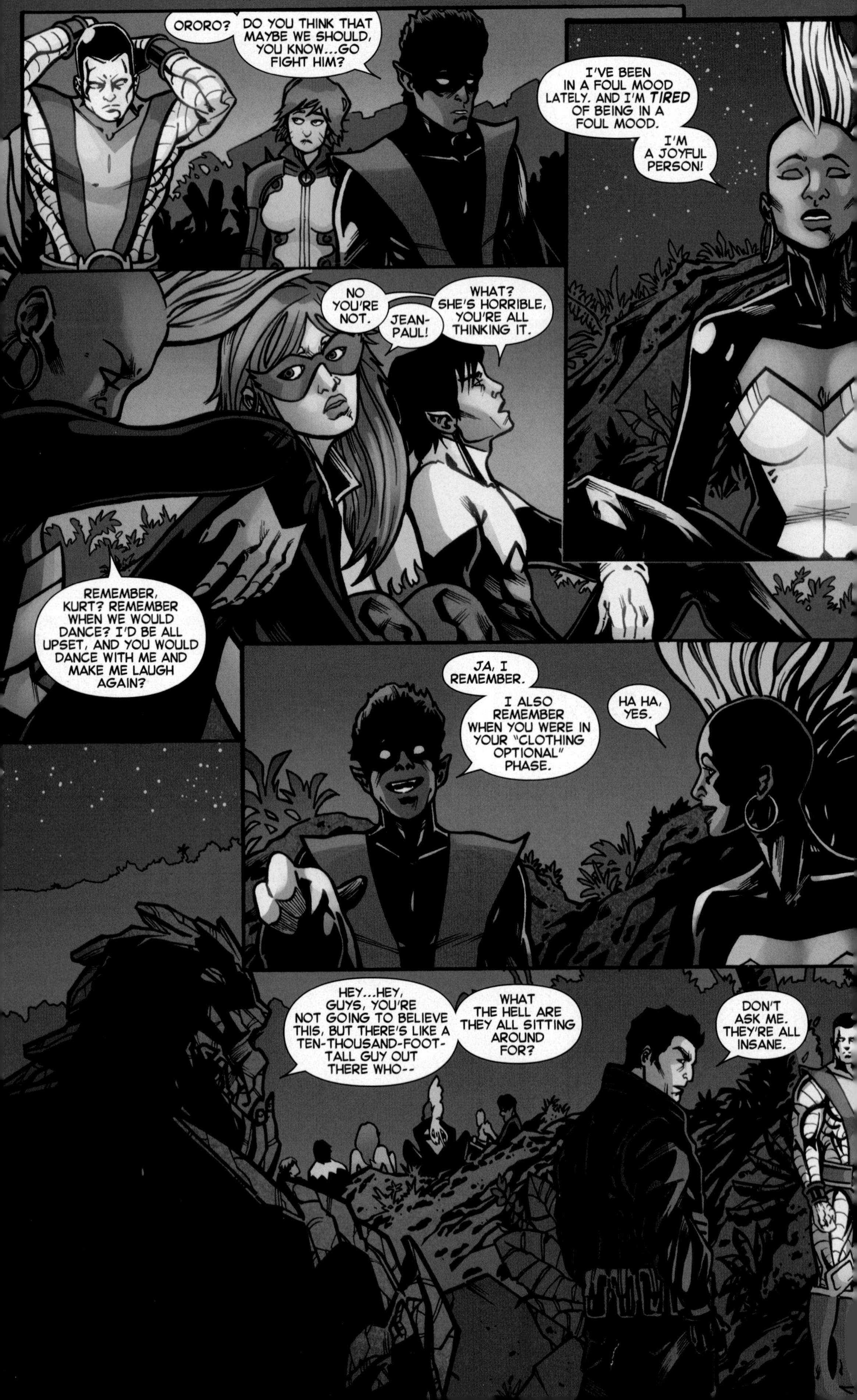

ORORO?
DO YOU THINK THAT MAYBE WE SHOULD, YOU KNOW...GO FIGHT HIM?
I'VE BEEN IN A FOUL MOOD LATELY. AND I'M *TIRED* OF BEING IN A FOUL MOOD.
I'M A JOYFUL PERSON!
NO YOU'RE NOT.
WHAT? SHE'S HORRIBLE, YOU'RE ALL THINKING IT.
JEAN-PAUL!
REMEMBER, KURT? REMEMBER WHEN WE WOULD DANCE? I'D BE ALL UPSET, AND YOU WOULD DANCE WITH ME AND MAKE ME LAUGH AGAIN?
JA, I REMEMBER.
I ALSO REMEMBER WHEN YOU WERE IN YOUR "CLOTHING OPTIONAL" PHASE.
HA HA, YES.
HEY...HEY, GUYS, YOU'RE NOT GOING TO BELIEVE THIS, BUT THERE'S LIKE A TEN-THOUSAND-FOOT-TALL GUY OUT THERE WHO--
WHAT THE HELL ARE THEY ALL SITTING AROUND FOR?
DON'T ASK ME. THEY'RE ALL INSANE.

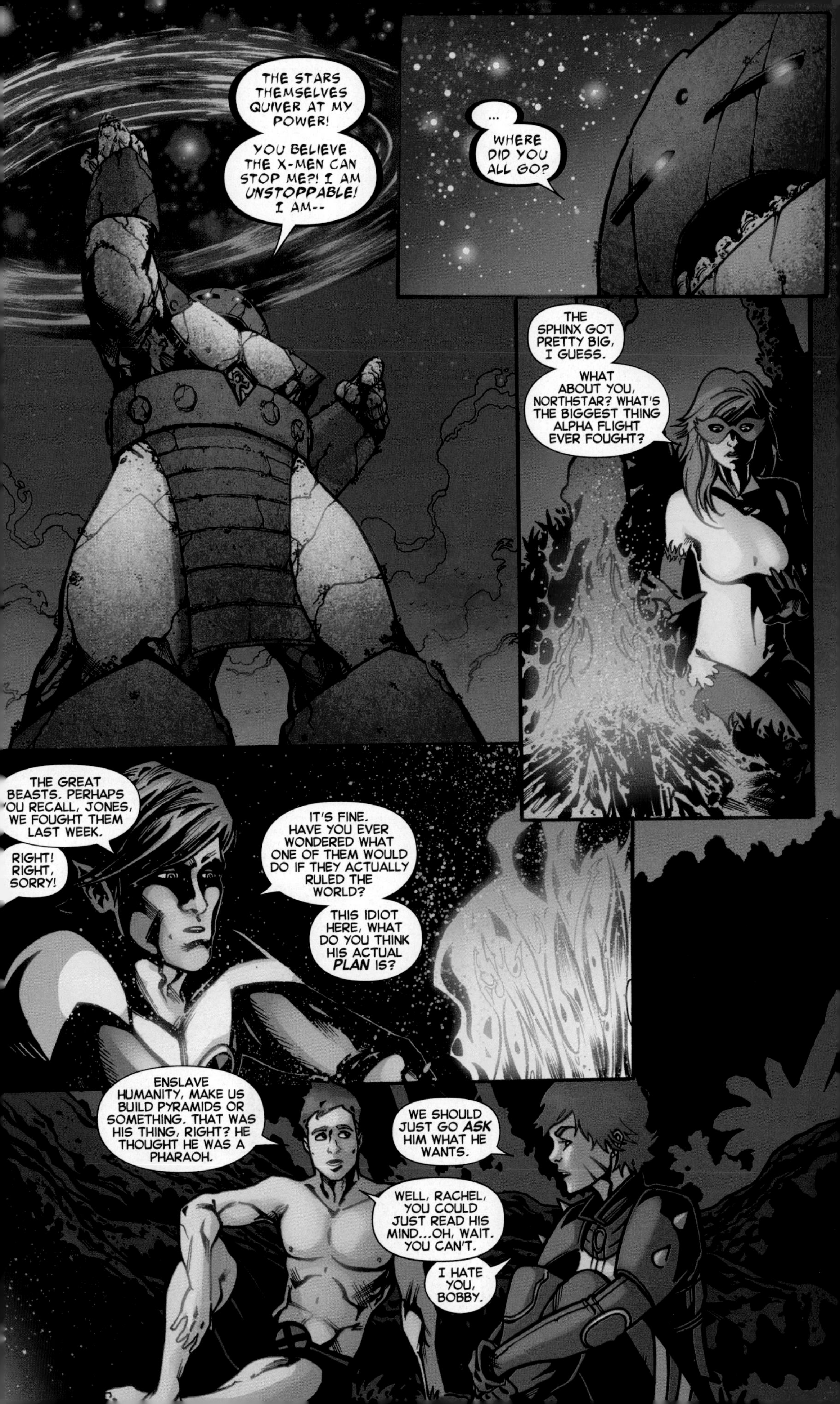
THE STARS THEMSELVES QUIVER AT MY POWER!
YOU BELIEVE THE X-MEN CAN STOP ME?! I AM UNSTOPPABLE! I AM--
... WHERE DID YOU ALL GO?
THE SPHINX GOT PRETTY BIG, I GUESS.
WHAT ABOUT YOU, NORTHSTAR? WHAT'S THE BIGGEST THING ALPHA FLIGHT EVER FOUGHT?
THE GREAT BEASTS. PERHAPS YOU RECALL, JONES, WE FOUGHT THEM LAST WEEK.
RIGHT! RIGHT, SORRY!
IT'S FINE. HAVE YOU EVER WONDERED WHAT ONE OF THEM WOULD DO IF THEY ACTUALLY RULED THE WORLD?
THIS IDIOT HERE, WHAT DO YOU THINK HIS ACTUAL PLAN IS?
ENSLAVE HUMANITY, MAKE US BUILD PYRAMIDS OR SOMETHING. THAT WAS HIS THING, RIGHT? HE THOUGHT HE WAS A PHARAOH.
WE SHOULD JUST GO ASK HIM WHAT HE WANTS.
WELL, RACHEL, YOU COULD JUST READ HIS MIND...OH, WAIT. YOU CAN'T.
I HATE YOU, BOBBY.

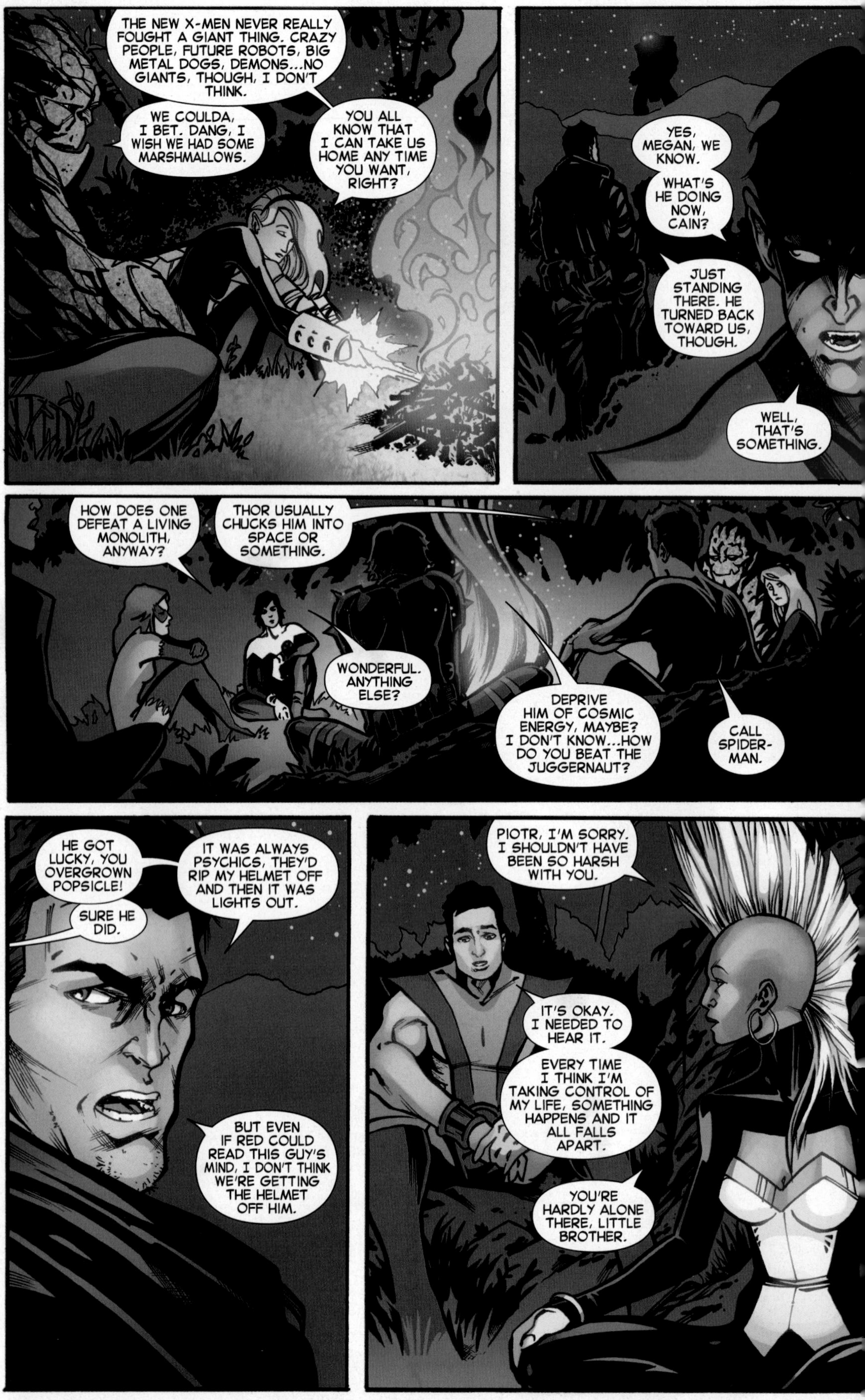
THE NEW X-MEN NEVER REALLY FOUGHT A GIANT THING. CRAZY PEOPLE, FUTURE ROBOTS, BIG METAL DOGS, DEMONS...NO GIANTS, THOUGH, I DON'T THINK.
WE COULDA, I BET. DANG, I WISH WE HAD SOME MARSHMALLOWS.
YOU ALL KNOW THAT I CAN TAKE US HOME ANY TIME YOU WANT, RIGHT?
YES, MEGAN, WE KNOW.
WHAT'S HE DOING NOW, CAIN?
JUST STANDING THERE. HE TURNED BACK TOWARD US, THOUGH.
WELL, THAT'S SOMETHING.
HOW DOES ONE DEFEAT A LIVING MONOLITH, ANYWAY?
THOR USUALLY CHUCKS HIM INTO SPACE OR SOMETHING.
WONDERFUL. ANYTHING ELSE?
DEPRIVE HIM OF COSMIC ENERGY, MAYBE? I DON'T KNOW...HOW DO YOU BEAT THE JUGGERNAUT?
CALL SPIDER-MAN.
HE GOT LUCKY, YOU OVERGROWN POPSICLE!
SURE HE DID.
IT WAS ALWAYS PSYCHICS, THEY'D RIP MY HELMET OFF AND THEN IT WAS LIGHTS OUT.
BUT EVEN IF RED COULD READ THIS GUY'S MIND, I DON'T THINK WE'RE GETTING THE HELMET OFF HIM.
PIOTR, I'M SORRY. I SHOULDN'T HAVE BEEN SO HARSH WITH YOU.
IT'S OKAY. I NEEDED TO HEAR IT.
EVERY TIME I THINK I'M TAKING CONTROL OF MY LIFE, SOMETHING HAPPENS AND IT ALL FALLS APART.
YOU'RE HARDLY ALONE THERE, LITTLE BROTHER.

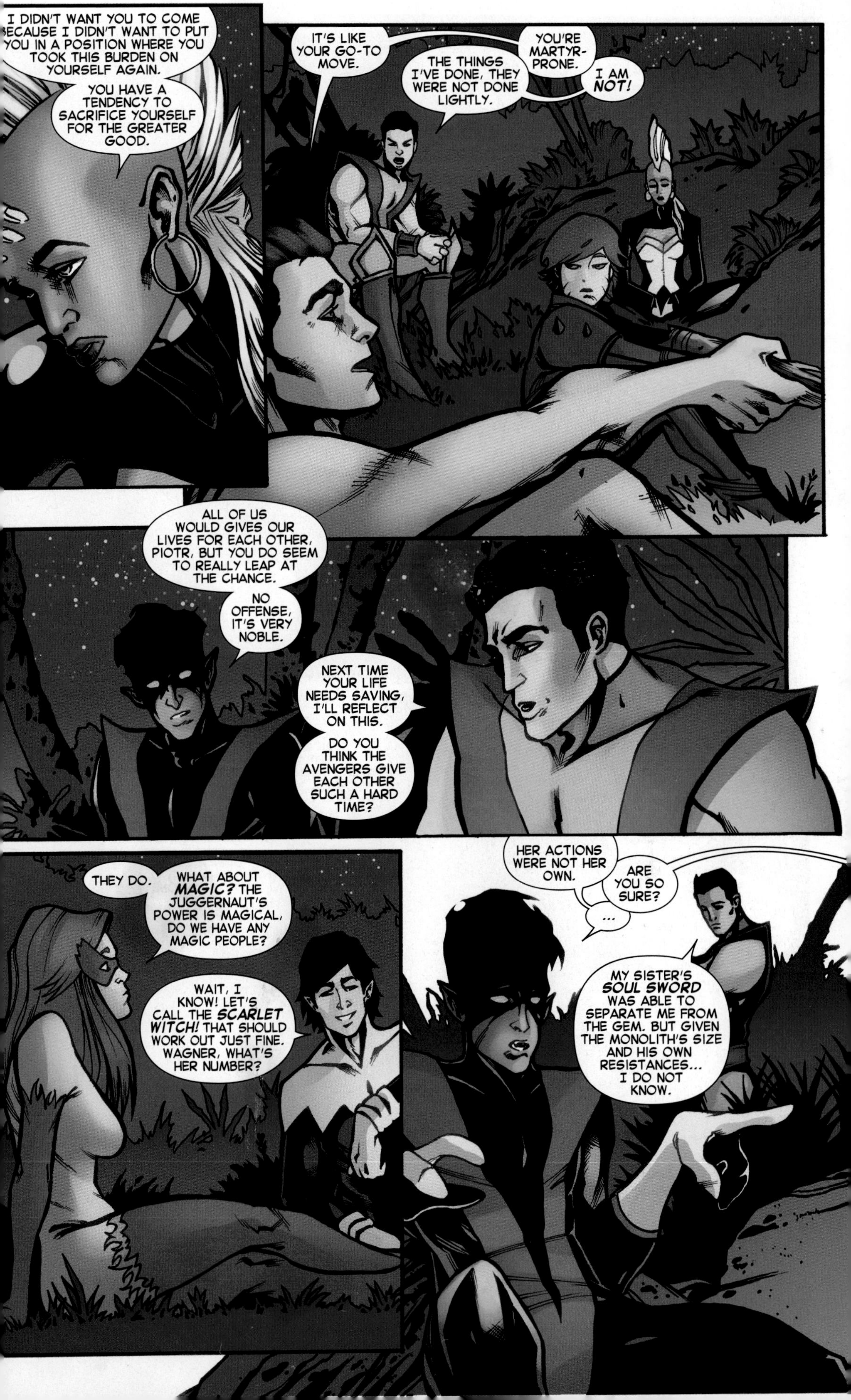
I DIDN'T WANT YOU TO COME BECAUSE I DIDN'T WANT TO PUT YOU IN A POSITION WHERE YOU TOOK THIS BURDEN ON YOURSELF AGAIN.
YOU HAVE A TENDENCY TO SACRIFICE YOURSELF FOR THE GREATER GOOD.
IT'S LIKE YOUR GO-TO MOVE.
YOU'RE MARTYR-PRONE.
THE THINGS I'VE DONE, THEY WERE NOT DONE LIGHTLY.
I AM NOT!
ALL OF US WOULD GIVES OUR LIVES FOR EACH OTHER, PIOTR, BUT YOU DO SEEM TO REALLY LEAP AT THE CHANCE.
NO OFFENSE, IT'S VERY NOBLE.
NEXT TIME YOUR LIFE NEEDS SAVING, I'LL REFLECT ON THIS.
DO YOU THINK THE AVENGERS GIVE EACH OTHER SUCH A HARD TIME?
THEY DO.
WHAT ABOUT MAGIC? THE JUGGERNAUT'S POWER IS MAGICAL, DO WE HAVE ANY MAGIC PEOPLE?
WAIT, I KNOW! LET'S CALL THE SCARLET WITCH! THAT SHOULD WORK OUT JUST FINE. WAGNER, WHAT'S HER NUMBER?
HER ACTIONS WERE NOT HER OWN.
ARE YOU SO SURE?
...
MY SISTER'S SOUL SWORD WAS ABLE TO SEPARATE ME FROM THE GEM. BUT GIVEN THE MONOLITH'S SIZE AND HIS OWN RESISTANCES... I DO NOT KNOW.

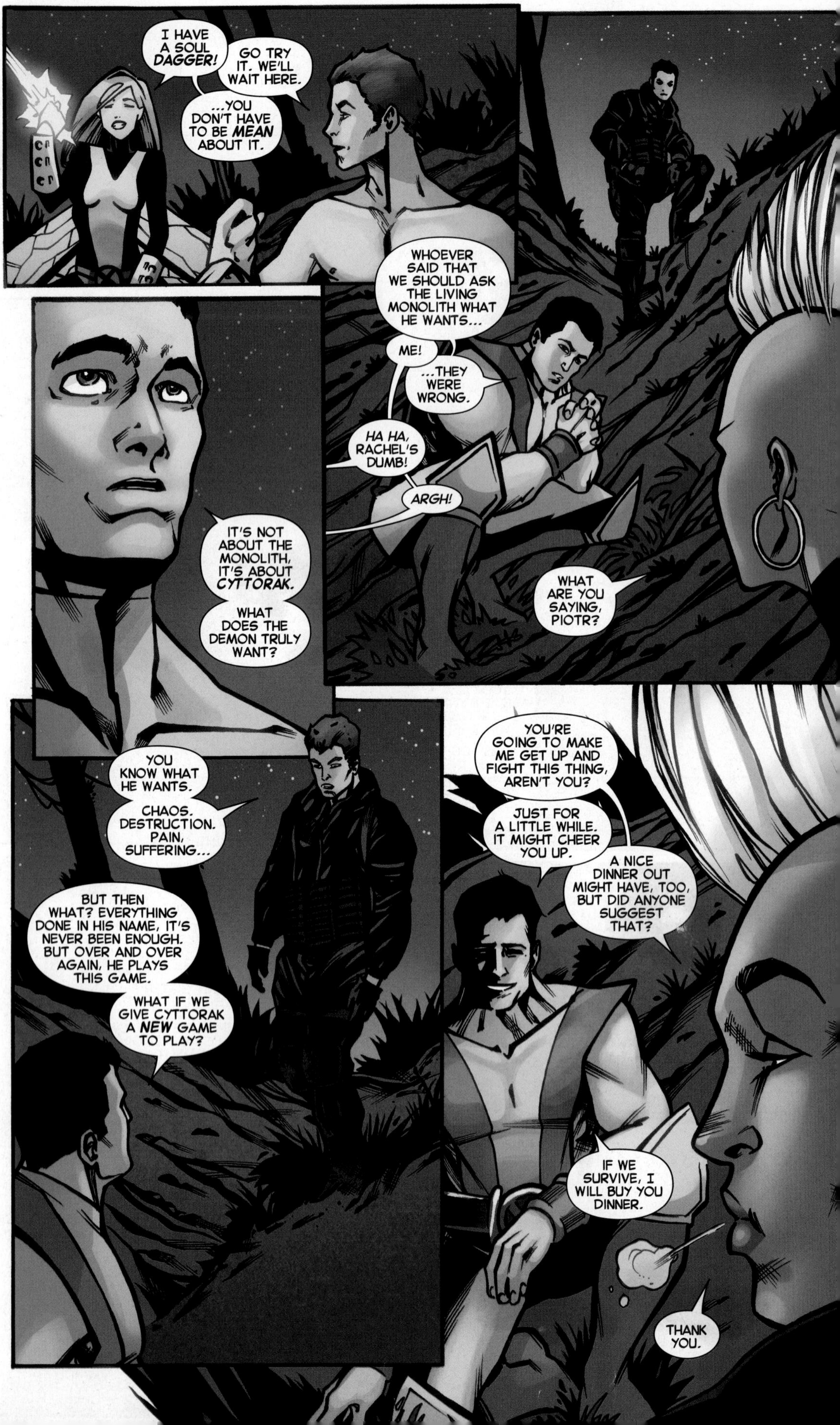
I HAVE A SOUL DAGGER!
GO TRY IT. WE'LL WAIT HERE.
...YOU DON'T HAVE TO BE MEAN ABOUT IT.
WHOEVER SAID THAT WE SHOULD ASK THE LIVING MONOLITH WHAT HE WANTS...
ME!
...THEY WERE WRONG.
HA HA, RACHEL'S DUMB!
ARGH!
IT'S NOT ABOUT THE MONOLITH, IT'S ABOUT CYTTORAK.
WHAT DOES THE DEMON TRULY WANT?
WHAT ARE YOU SAYING, PIOTR?
YOU KNOW WHAT HE WANTS.
CHAOS. DESTRUCTION. PAIN, SUFFERING...
BUT THEN WHAT? EVERYTHING DONE IN HIS NAME, IT'S NEVER BEEN ENOUGH. BUT OVER AND OVER AGAIN, HE PLAYS THIS GAME.
WHAT IF WE GIVE CYTTORAK A NEW GAME TO PLAY?
YOU'RE GOING TO MAKE ME GET UP AND FIGHT THIS THING, AREN'T YOU?
JUST FOR A LITTLE WHILE. IT MIGHT CHEER YOU UP.
A NICE DINNER OUT MIGHT HAVE, TOO, BUT DID ANYONE SUGGEST THAT?
IF WE SURVIVE, I WILL BUY YOU DINNER.
THANK YOU.

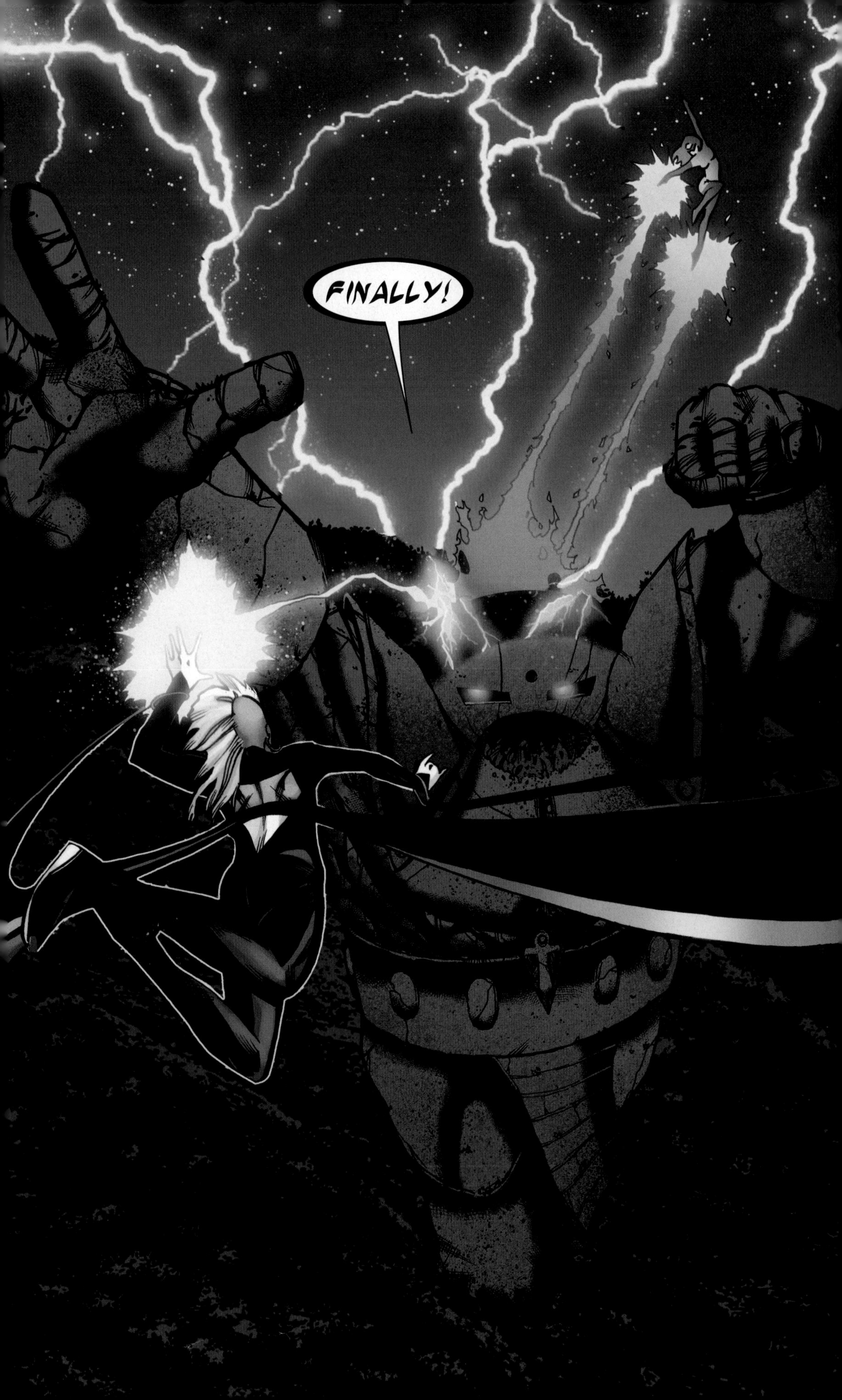
FINALLY!

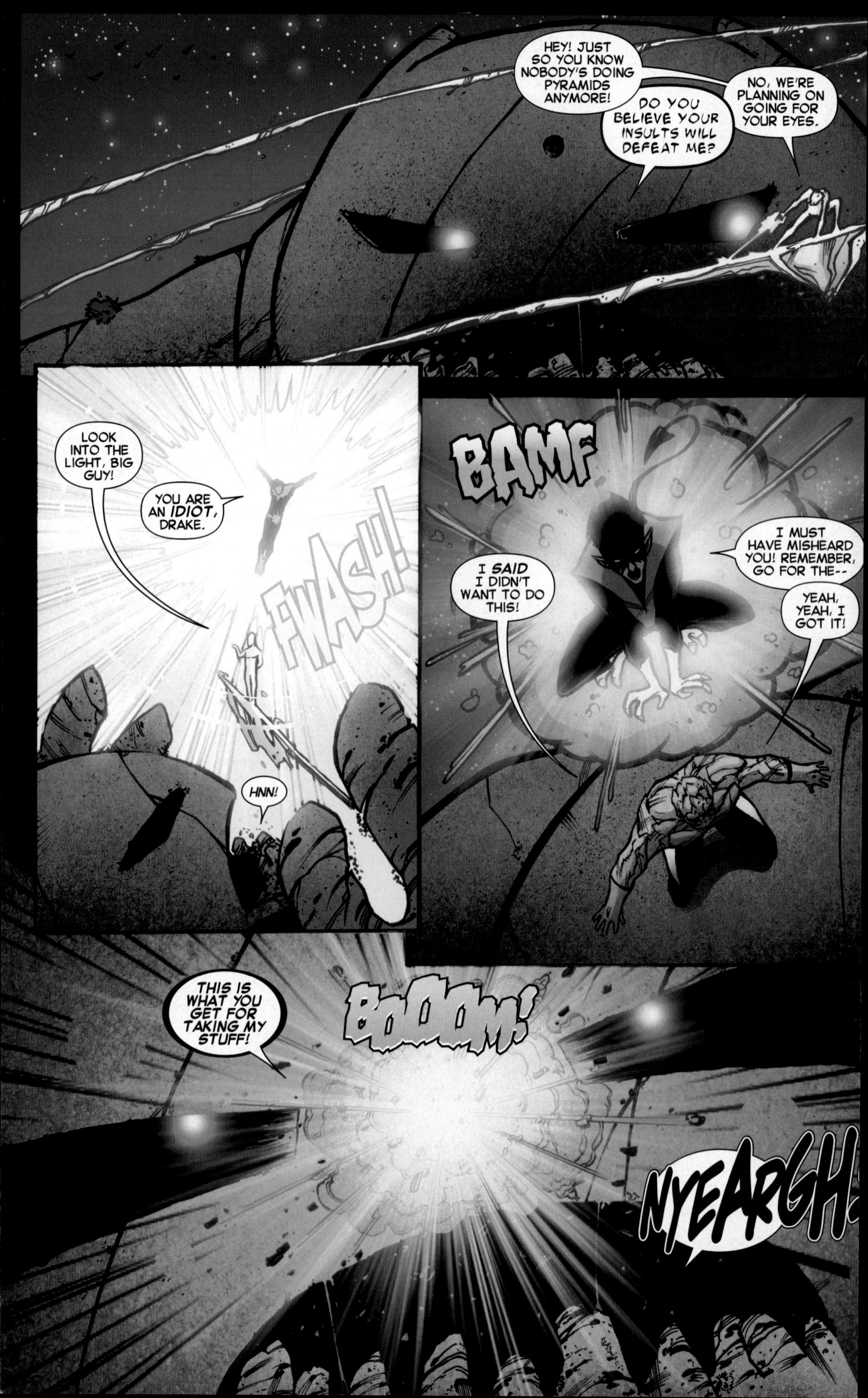
HEY! JUST SO YOU KNOW NOBODY'S DOING PYRAMIDS ANYMORE!
DO YOU BELIEVE YOUR INSULTS WILL DEFEAT ME?
NO, WE'RE PLANNING ON GOING FOR YOUR EYES.
LOOK INTO THE LIGHT, BIG GUY!
YOU ARE AN *IDIOT*, DRAKE.
FWASH!
HNN!
BAMF
I *SAID* I DIDN'T WANT TO DO THIS!
I MUST HAVE MISHEARD YOU! REMEMBER, GO FOR THE--
YEAH, YEAH, I GOT IT!
THIS IS WHAT YOU GET FOR TAKING MY STUFF!
BOOOM!
NYEARGH!

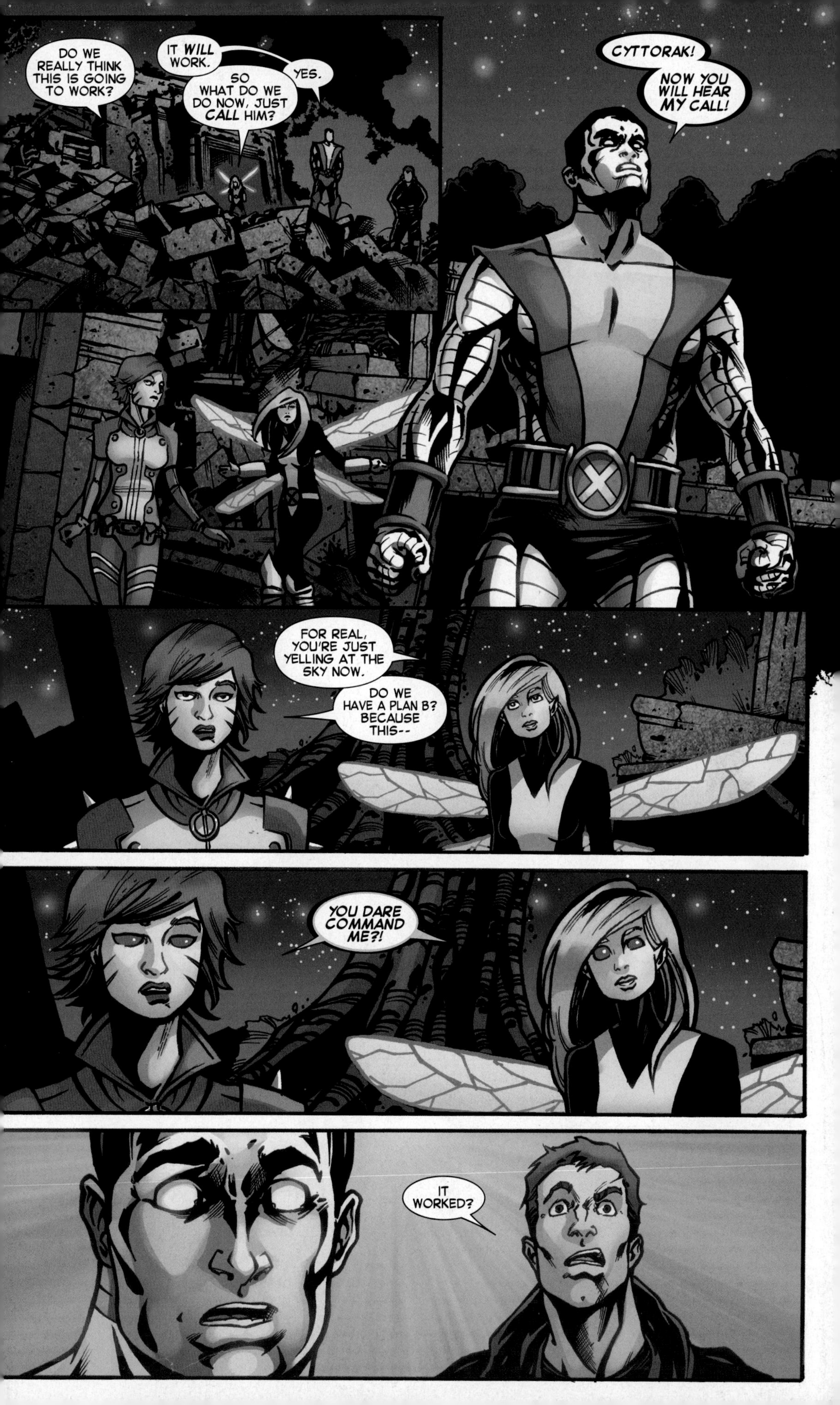
DO WE REALLY THINK THIS IS GOING TO WORK?
IT WILL WORK.
YES.
SO WHAT DO WE DO NOW, JUST CALL HIM?
CYTTORAK!
NOW YOU WILL HEAR MY CALL!
FOR REAL, YOU'RE JUST YELLING AT THE SKY NOW.
DO WE HAVE A PLAN B? BECAUSE THIS--
YOU DARE COMMAND ME?!
IT WORKED?

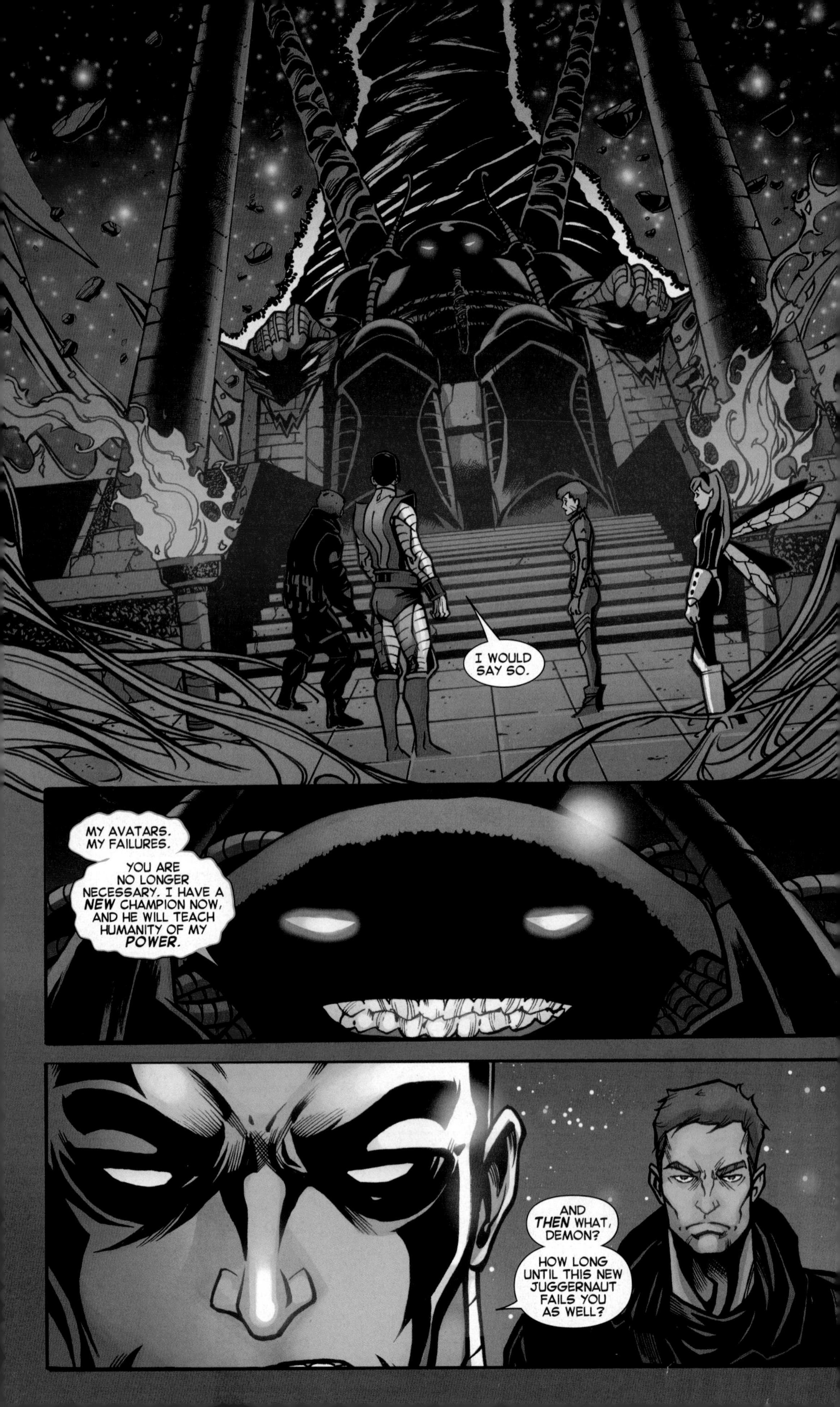

I WOULD SAY SO.
MY AVATARS. MY FAILURES.
YOU ARE NO LONGER NECESSARY. I HAVE A *NEW* CHAMPION NOW, AND HE WILL TEACH HUMANITY OF MY *POWER*.
AND *THEN* WHAT, DEMON?
HOW LONG UNTIL THIS NEW JUGGERNAUT FAILS YOU AS WELL?

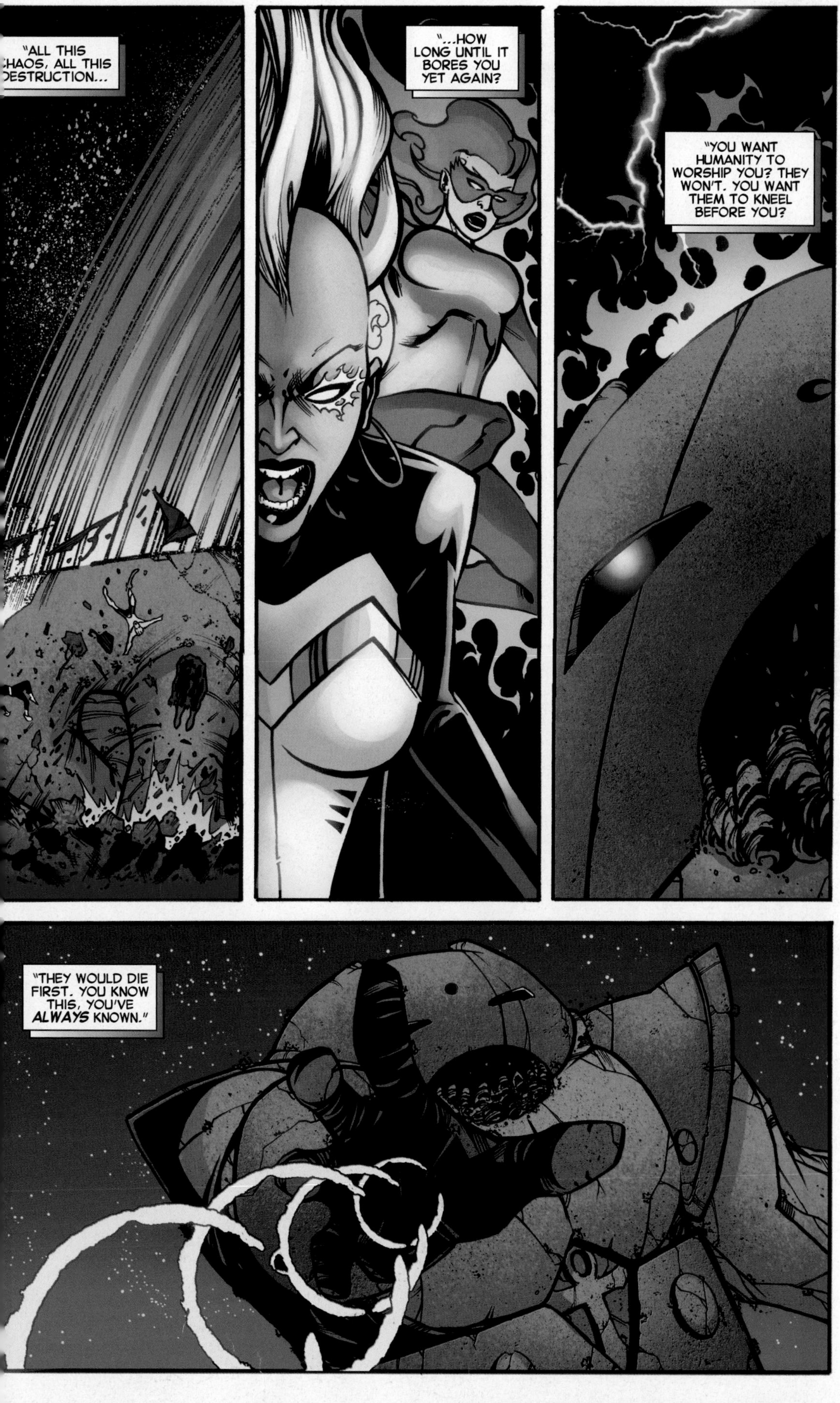
"ALL THIS CHAOS, ALL THIS DESTRUCTION...
"...HOW LONG UNTIL IT BORES YOU YET AGAIN?
"YOU WANT HUMANITY TO WORSHIP YOU? THEY WON'T. YOU WANT THEM TO KNEEL BEFORE YOU?
"THEY WOULD DIE FIRST. YOU KNOW THIS, YOU'VE *ALWAYS* KNOWN."

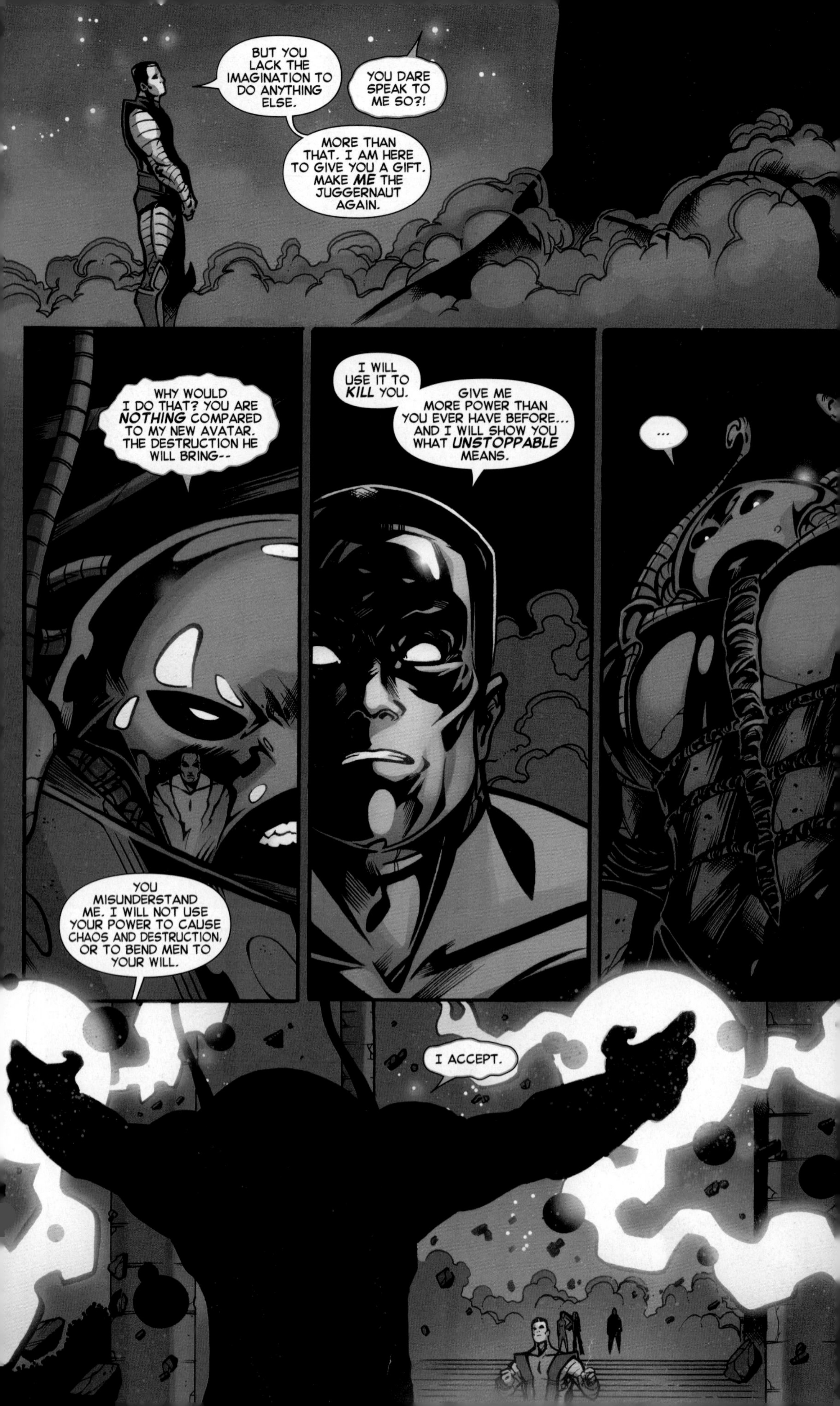
BUT YOU LACK THE IMAGINATION TO DO ANYTHING ELSE.
YOU DARE SPEAK TO ME SO?!
MORE THAN THAT. I AM HERE TO GIVE YOU A GIFT. MAKE ME THE JUGGERNAUT AGAIN.
WHY WOULD I DO THAT? YOU ARE NOTHING COMPARED TO MY NEW AVATAR. THE DESTRUCTION HE WILL BRING--
YOU MISUNDERSTAND ME. I WILL NOT USE YOUR POWER TO CAUSE CHAOS AND DESTRUCTION, OR TO BEND MEN TO YOUR WILL.
I WILL USE IT TO KILL YOU.
GIVE ME MORE POWER THAN YOU EVER HAVE BEFORE... AND I WILL SHOW YOU WHAT UNSTOPPABLE MEANS.
...
I ACCEPT.

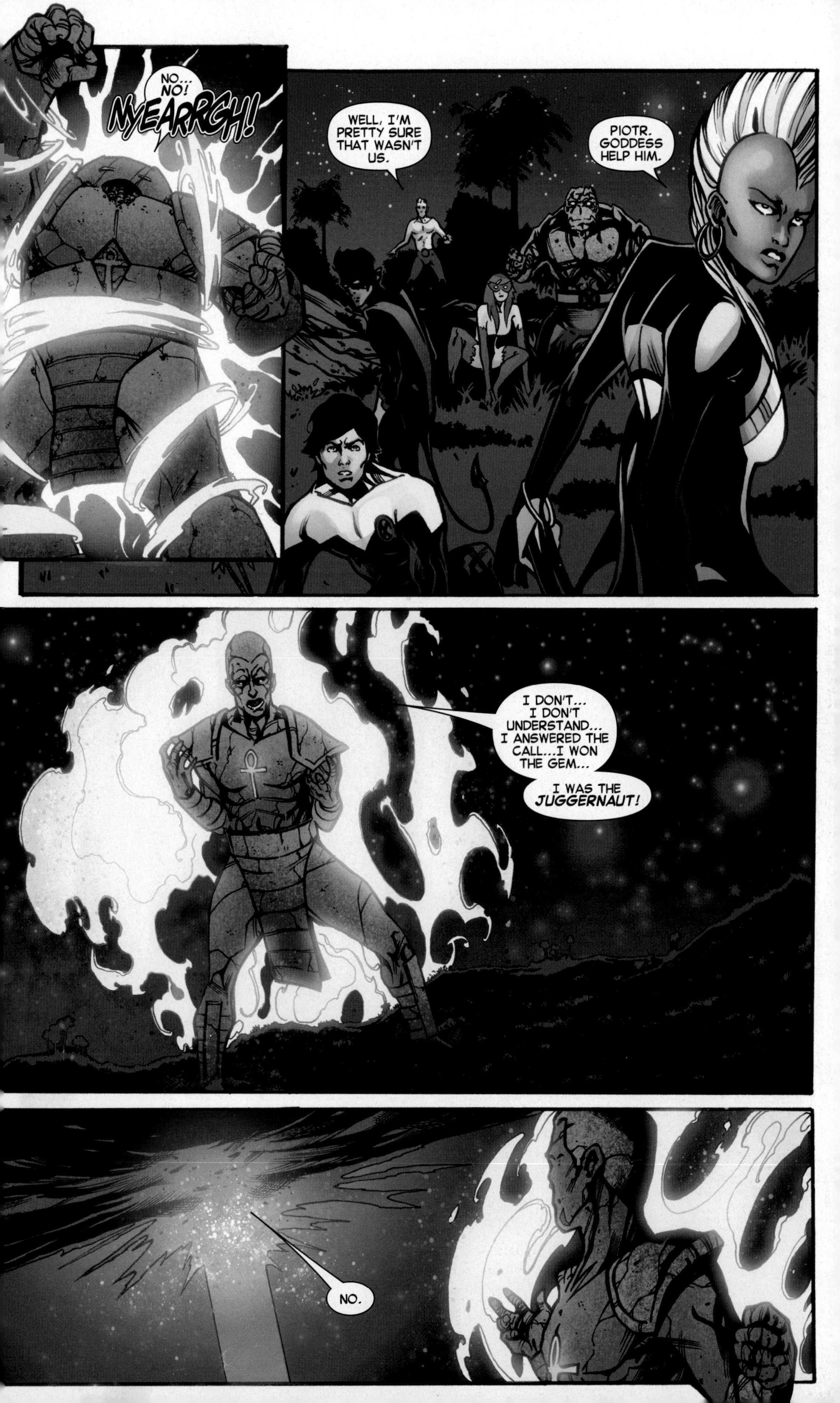

NO... NO!
NYEARRRGH!
WELL, I'M PRETTY SURE THAT WASN'T US.
PIOTR. GODDESS HELP HIM.
I DON'T... I DON'T UNDERSTAND... I ANSWERED THE CALL...I WON THE GEM...
I WAS THE JUGGERNAUT!
NO.

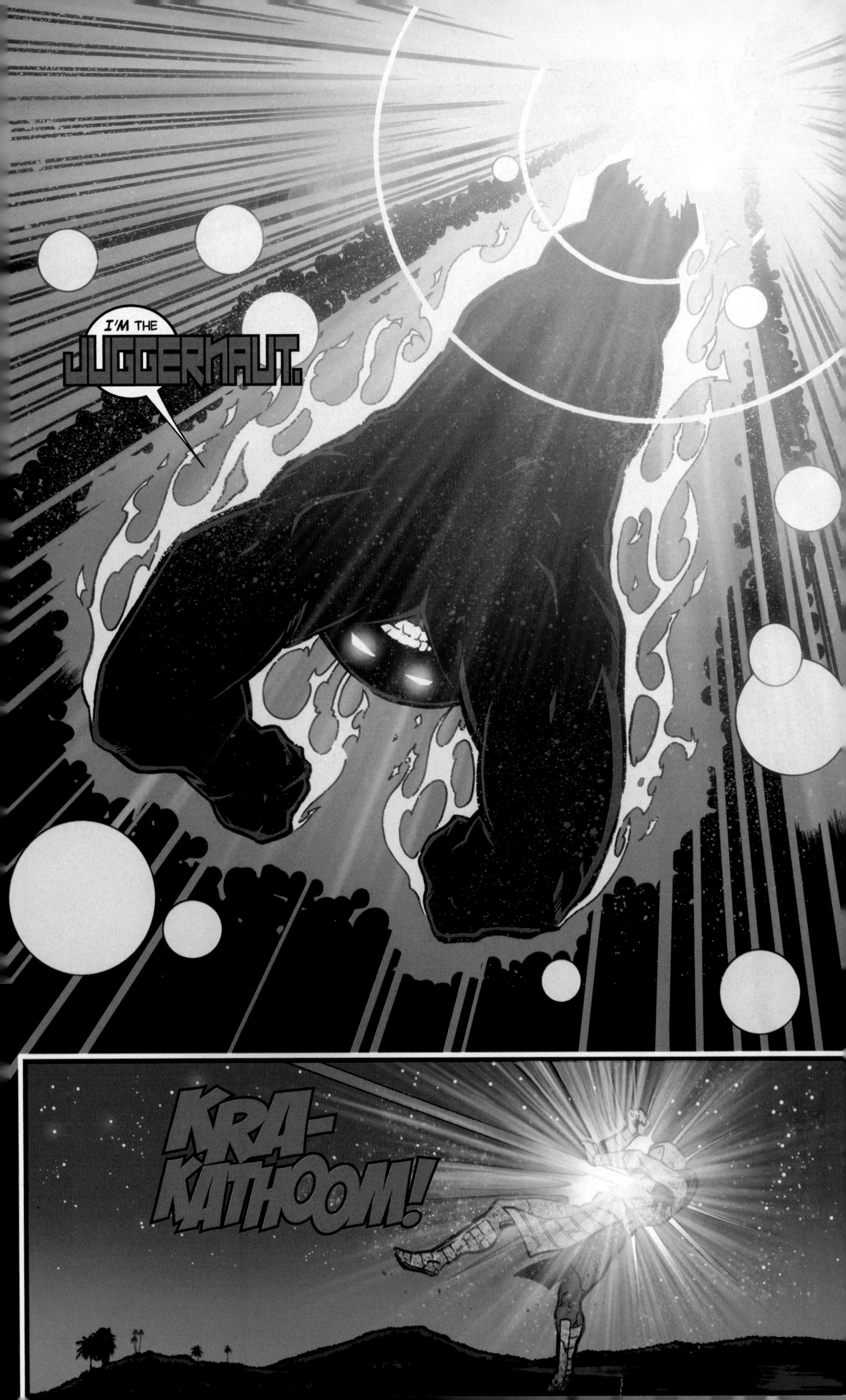
I'M THE JUGGERNAUT.
KRA-KATHOOM!

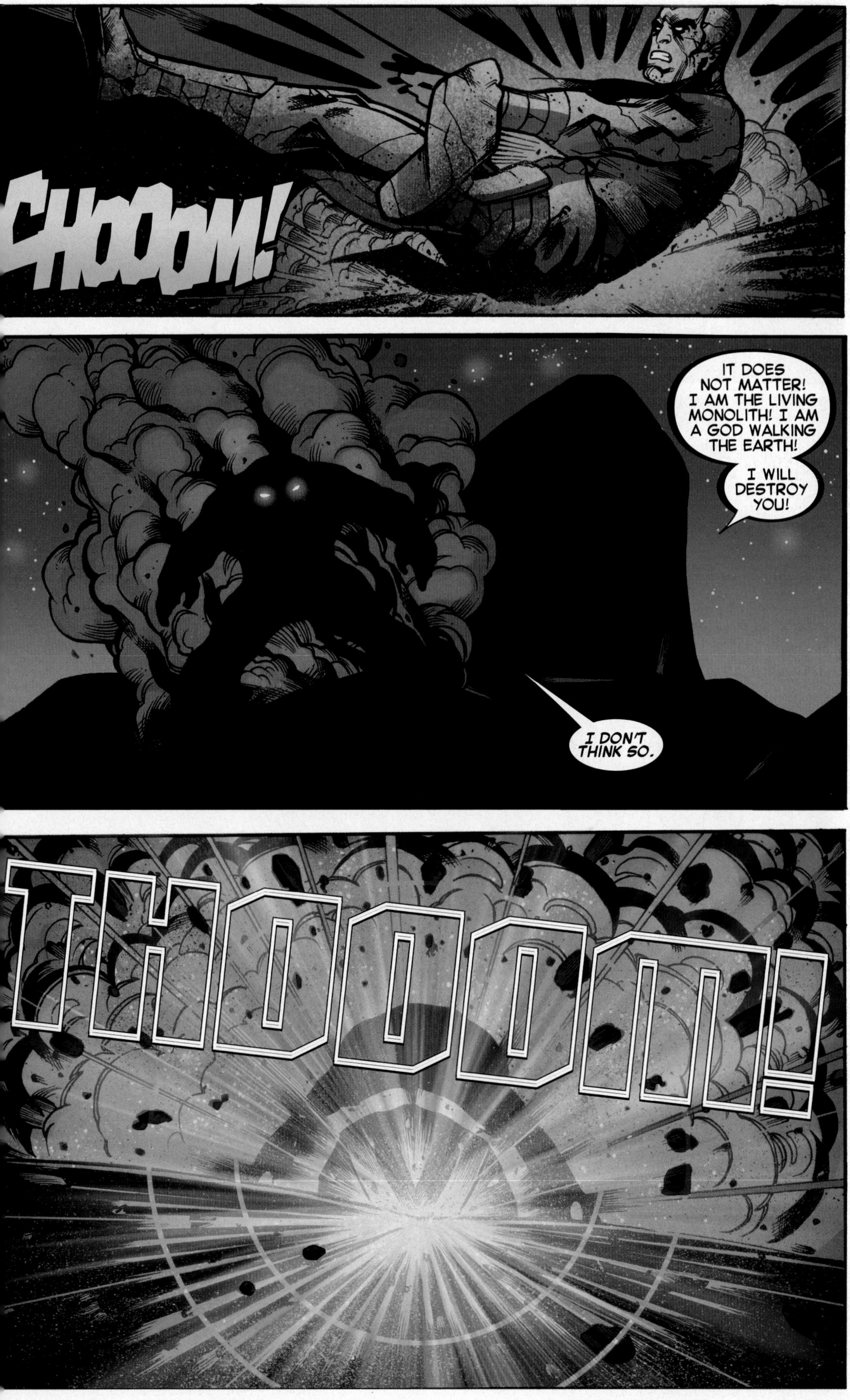
CHOOOM!
IT DOES NOT MATTER! I AM THE LIVING MONOLITH! I AM A GOD WALKING THE EARTH!
I WILL DESTROY YOU!
I DON'T THINK SO.
THOOOM!

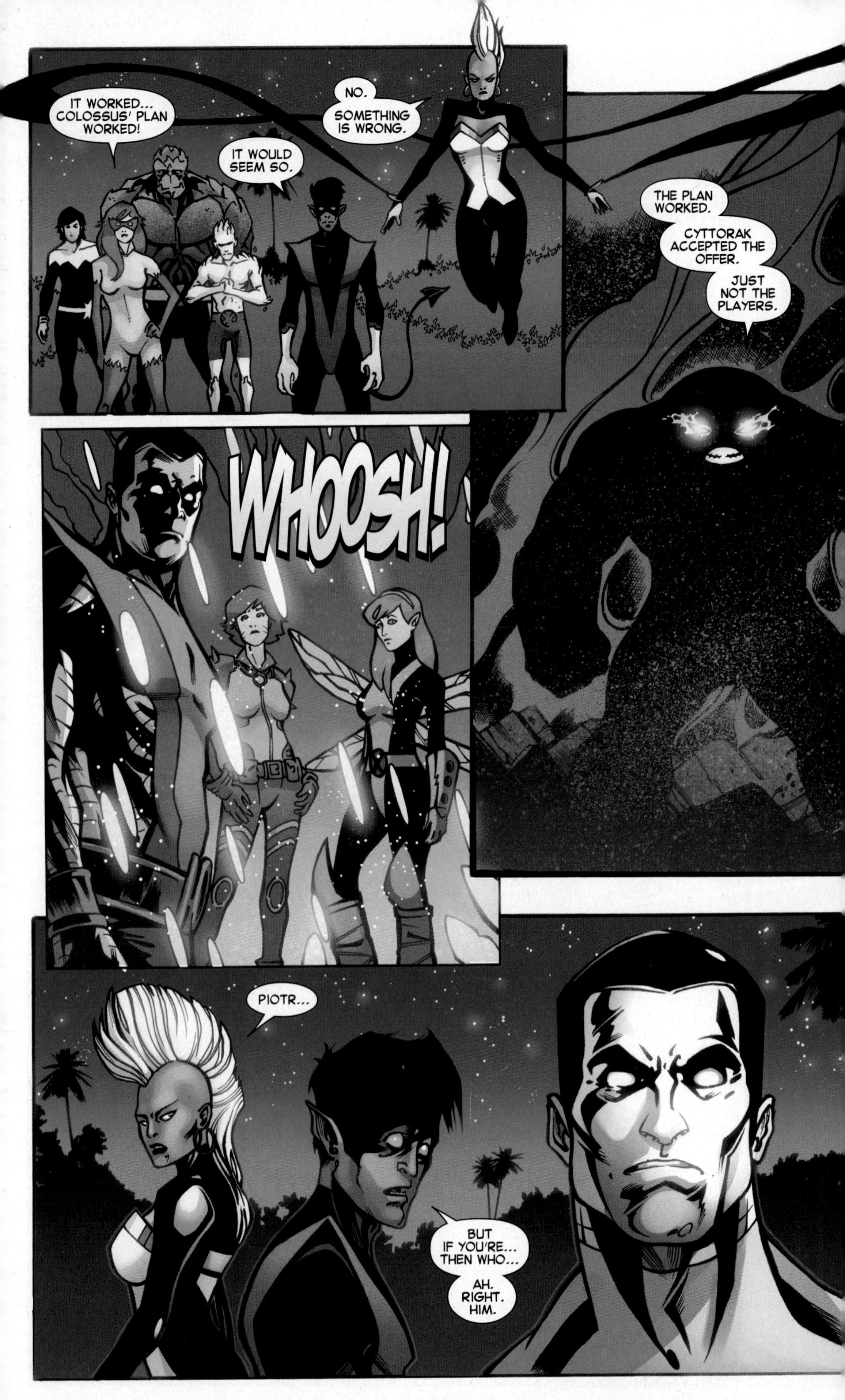
IT WORKED... COLOSSUS' PLAN WORKED!
IT WOULD SEEM SO.
NO.
SOMETHING IS WRONG.
THE PLAN WORKED.
CYTTORAK ACCEPTED THE OFFER.
JUST NOT THE PLAYERS.
WHOOSH!
PIOTR...
BUT IF YOU'RE... THEN WHO...
AH. RIGHT. HIM.

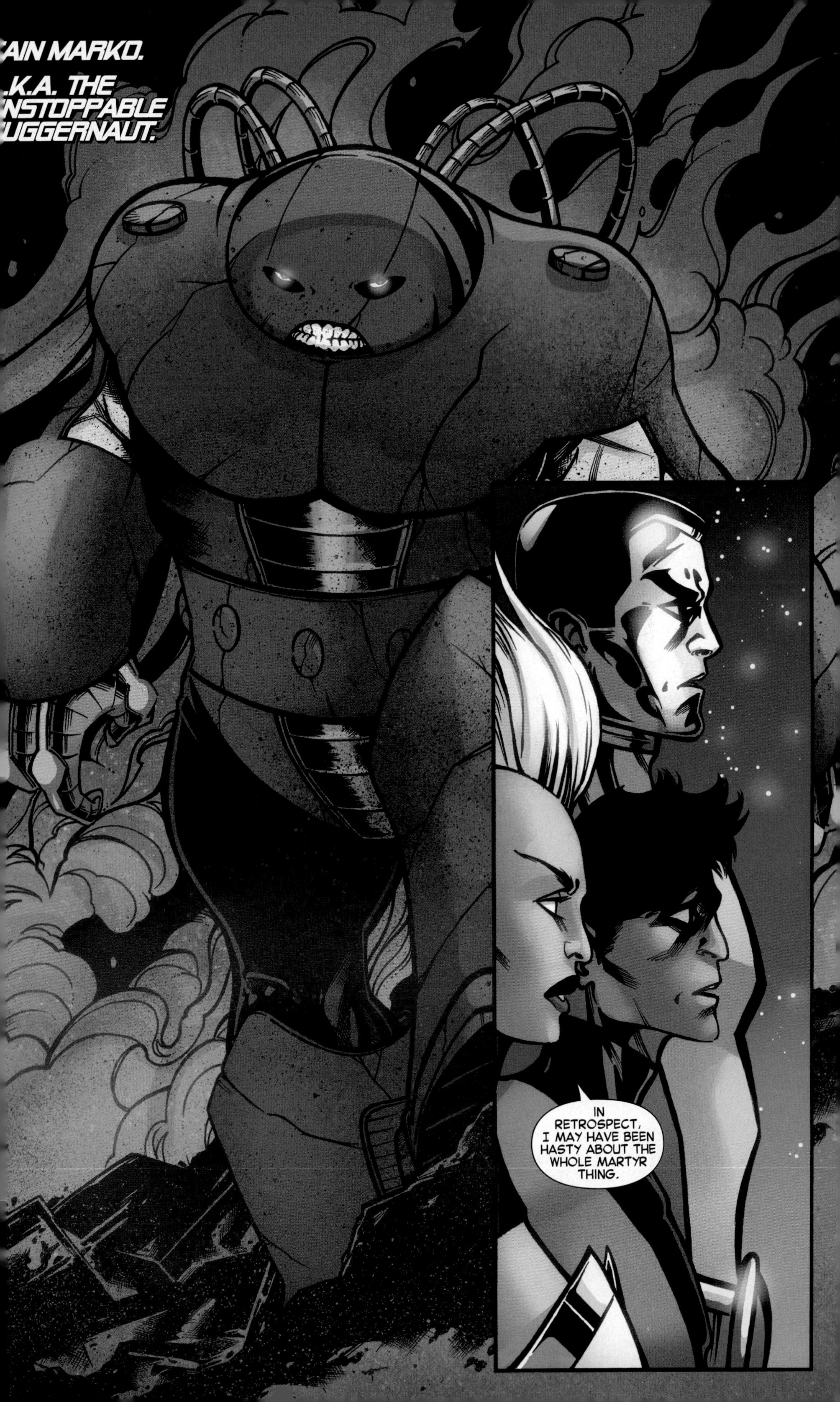
AIN MARKO.
.K.A. THE
NSTOPPABLE
UGGERNAUT.
IN RETROSPECT, I MAY HAVE BEEN HASTY ABOUT THE WHOLE MARTYR THING.

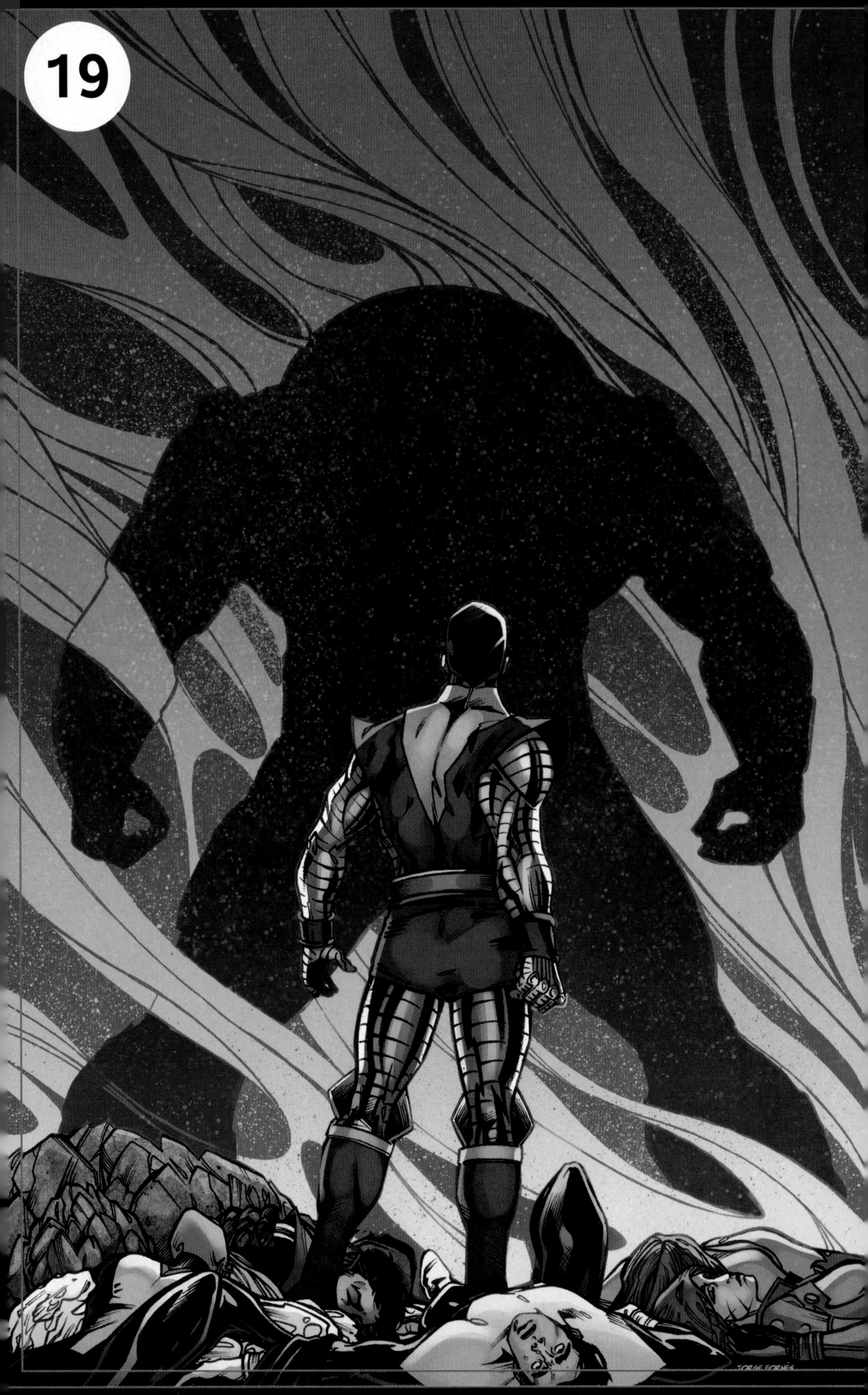
19
JORGE FORNÉS

THE ONCE AND FUTURE JUGGERNAUT EPILOGUE: ENOUG

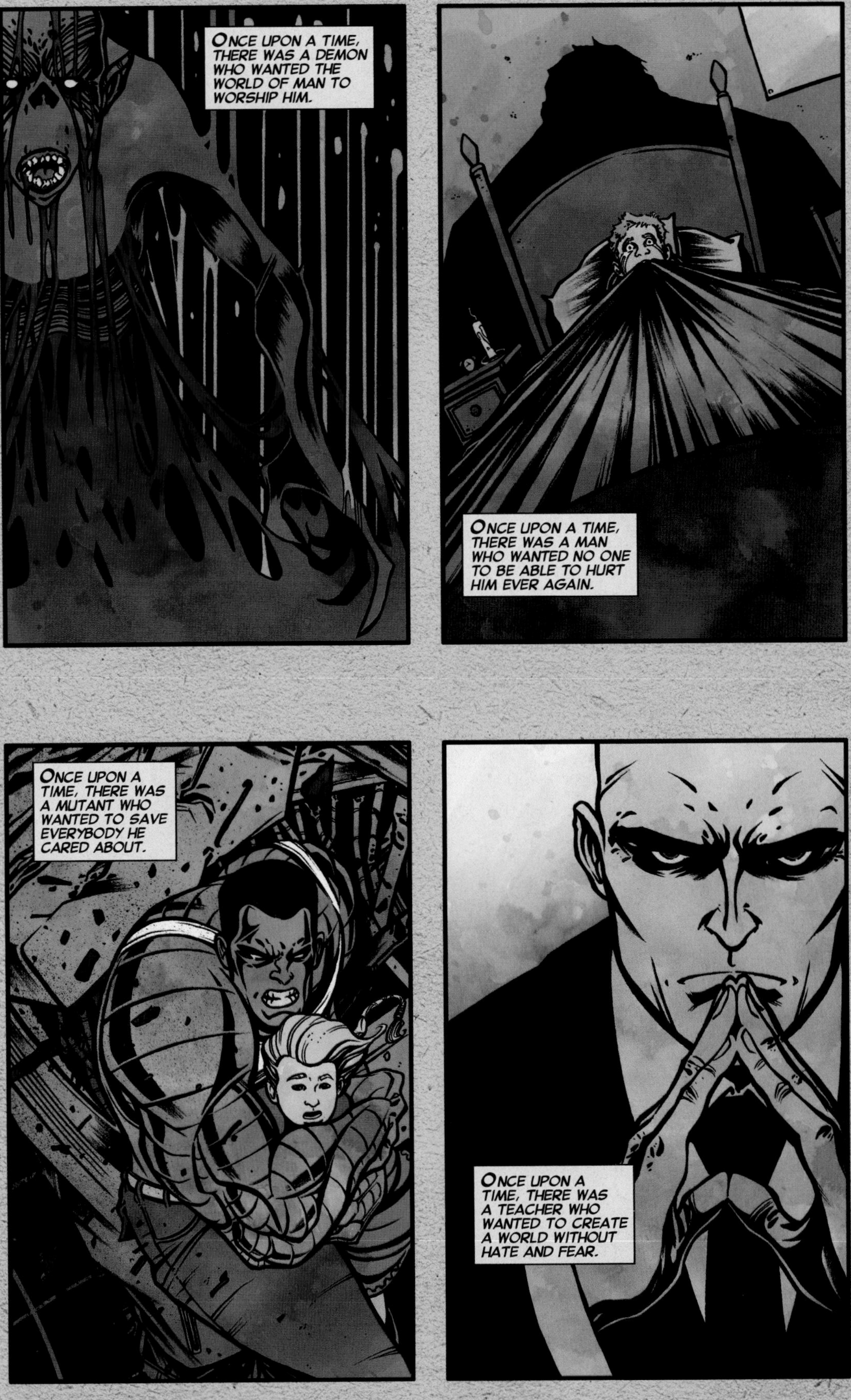
ONCE UPON A TIME, THERE WAS A DEMON WHO WANTED THE WORLD OF MAN TO WORSHIP HIM.
ONCE UPON A TIME, THERE WAS A MAN WHO WANTED NO ONE TO BE ABLE TO HURT HIM EVER AGAIN.
ONCE UPON A TIME, THERE WAS A MUTANT WHO WANTED TO SAVE EVERYBODY HE CARED ABOUT.
ONCE UPON A TIME, THERE WAS A TEACHER WHO WANTED TO CREATE A WORLD WITHOUT HATE AND FEAR.

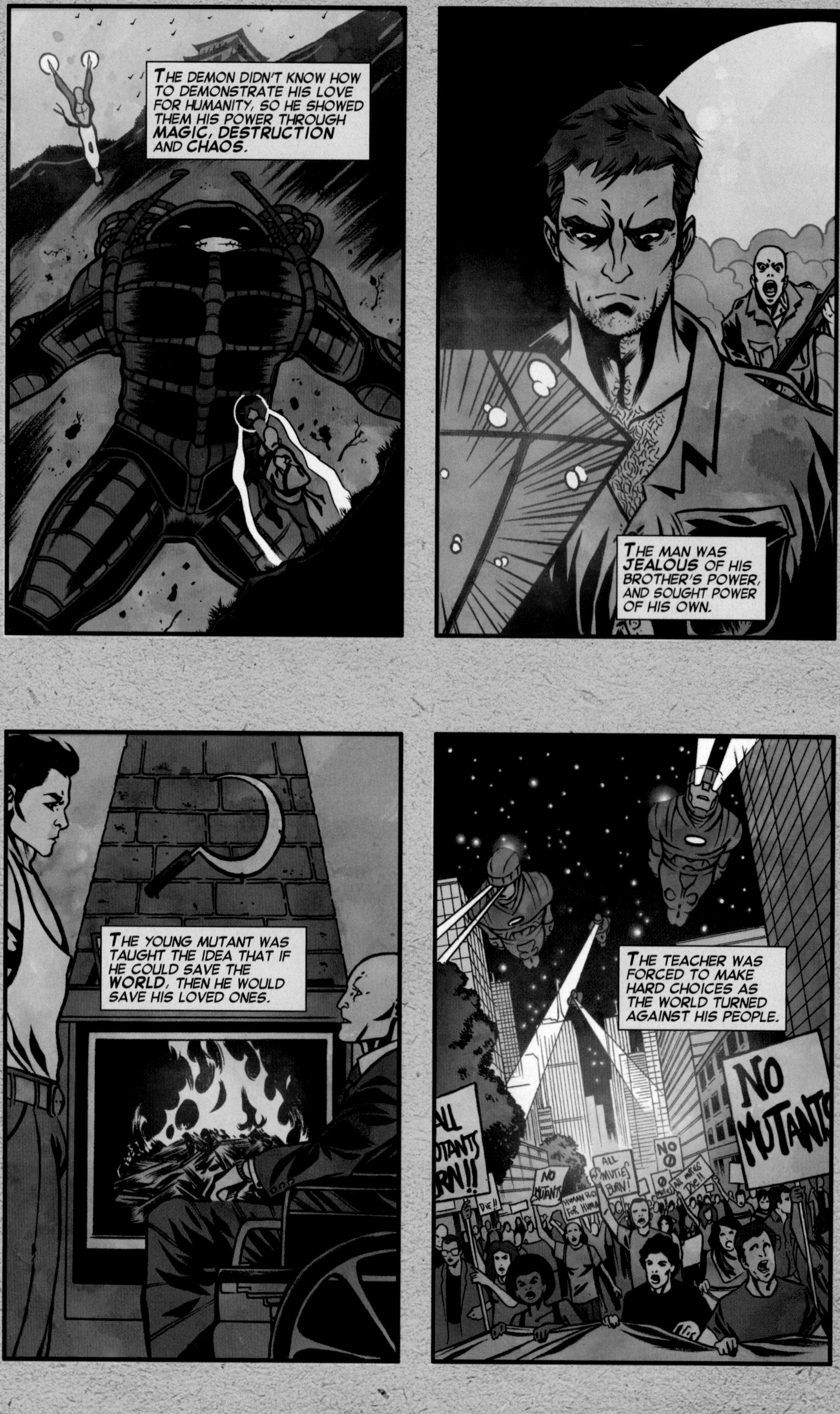
THE DEMON DIDN'T KNOW HOW TO DEMONSTRATE HIS LOVE FOR HUMANITY, SO HE SHOWED THEM HIS POWER THROUGH MAGIC, DESTRUCTION AND CHAOS.
THE MAN WAS JEALOUS OF HIS BROTHER'S POWER, AND SOUGHT POWER OF HIS OWN.
THE YOUNG MUTANT WAS TAUGHT THE IDEA THAT IF HE COULD SAVE THE WORLD, THEN HE WOULD SAVE HIS LOVED ONES.
THE TEACHER WAS FORCED TO MAKE HARD CHOICES AS THE WORLD TURNED AGAINST HIS PEOPLE.
NO MUTANTS

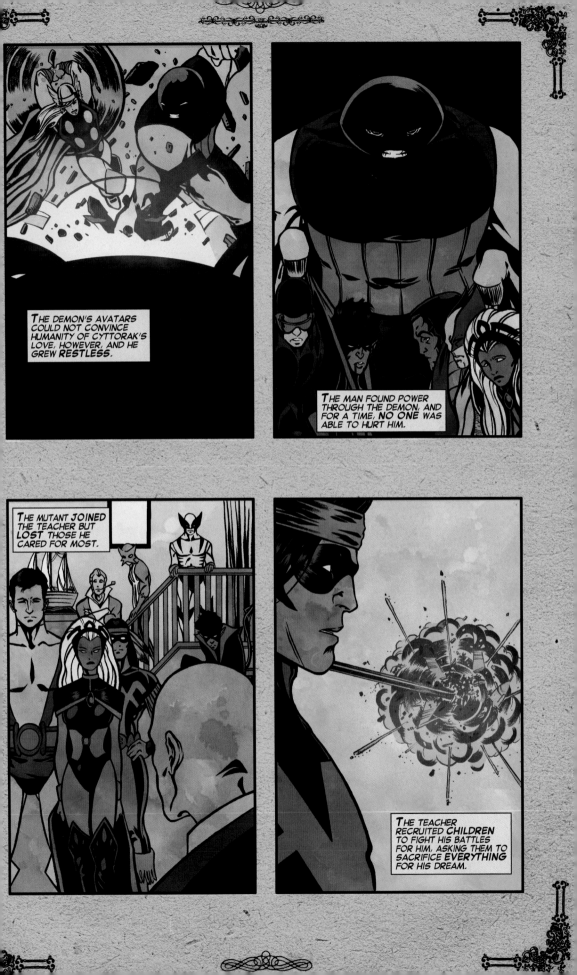

THE DEMON'S AVATARS COULD NOT CONVINCE HUMANITY OF CYTTORAK'S LOVE, HOWEVER, AND HE GREW RESTLESS.

THE MAN FOUND POWER THROUGH THE DEMON, AND FOR A TIME, NO ONE WAS ABLE TO HURT HIM.

THE MUTANT JOINED THE TEACHER BUT LOST THOSE HE CARED FOR MOST.

THE TEACHER RECRUITED CHILDREN TO FIGHT HIS BATTLES FOR HIM, ASKING THEM TO SACRIFICE EVERYTHING FOR HIS DREAM.

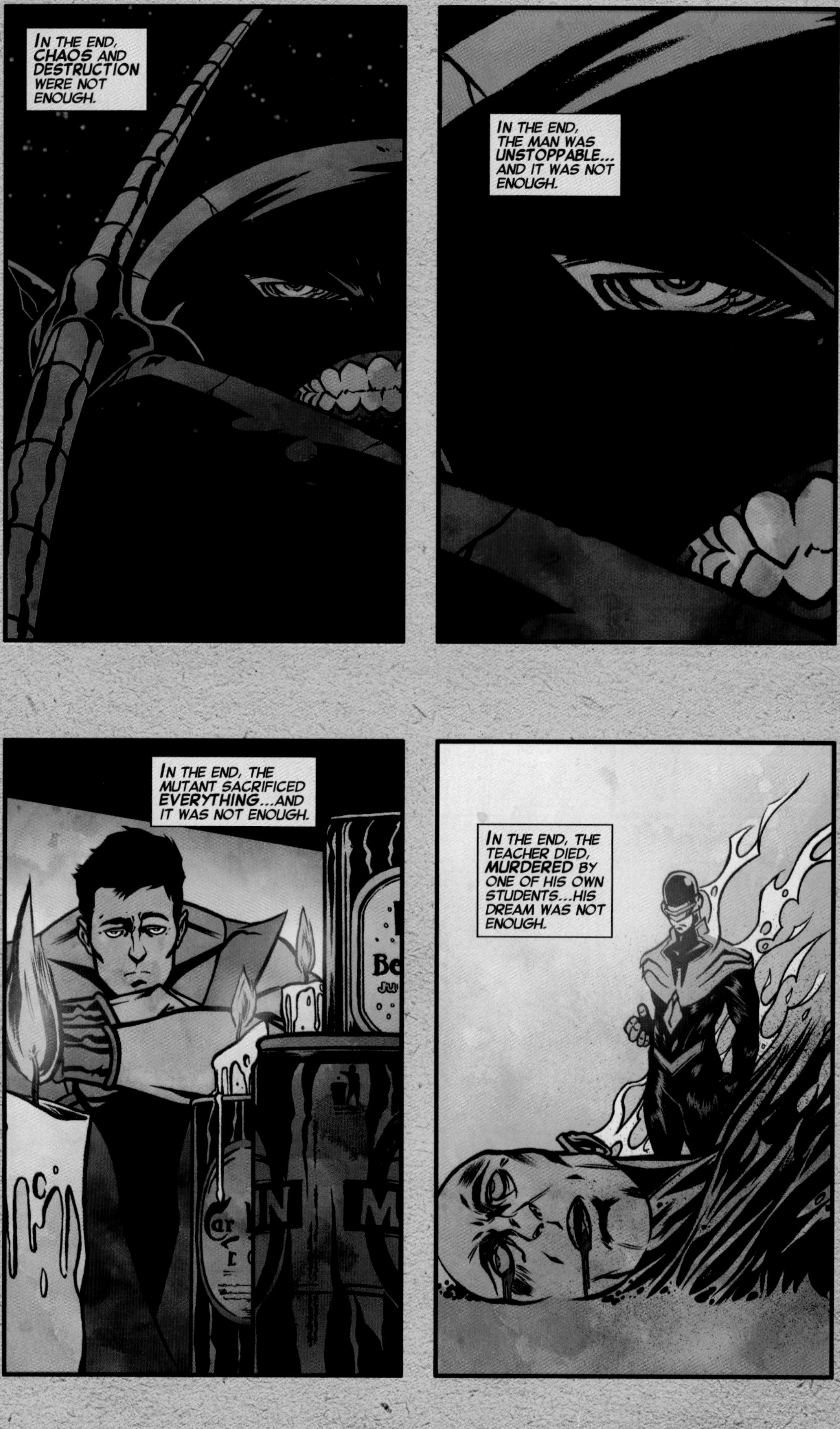
IN THE END, CHAOS AND DESTRUCTION WERE NOT ENOUGH.
IN THE END, THE MAN WAS UNSTOPPABLE... AND IT WAS NOT ENOUGH.
IN THE END, THE MUTANT SACRIFICED EVERYTHING...AND IT WAS NOT ENOUGH.
IN THE END, THE TEACHER DIED, MURDERED BY ONE OF HIS OWN STUDENTS...HIS DREAM WAS NOT ENOUGH.

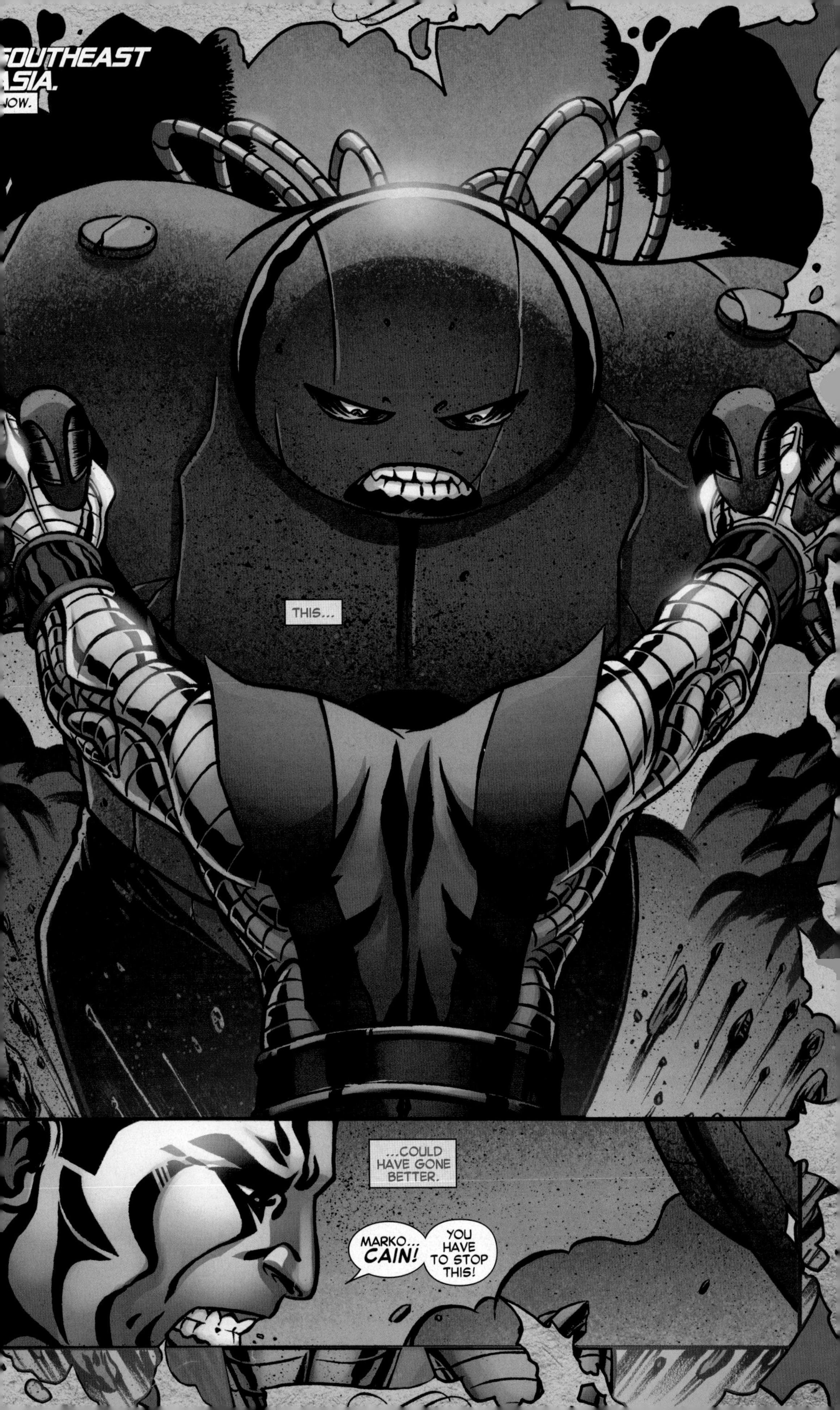
SOUTHEAST ASIA.
NOW.
THIS...
...COULD HAVE GONE BETTER.
MARKO... CAIN!
YOU HAVE TO STOP THIS!

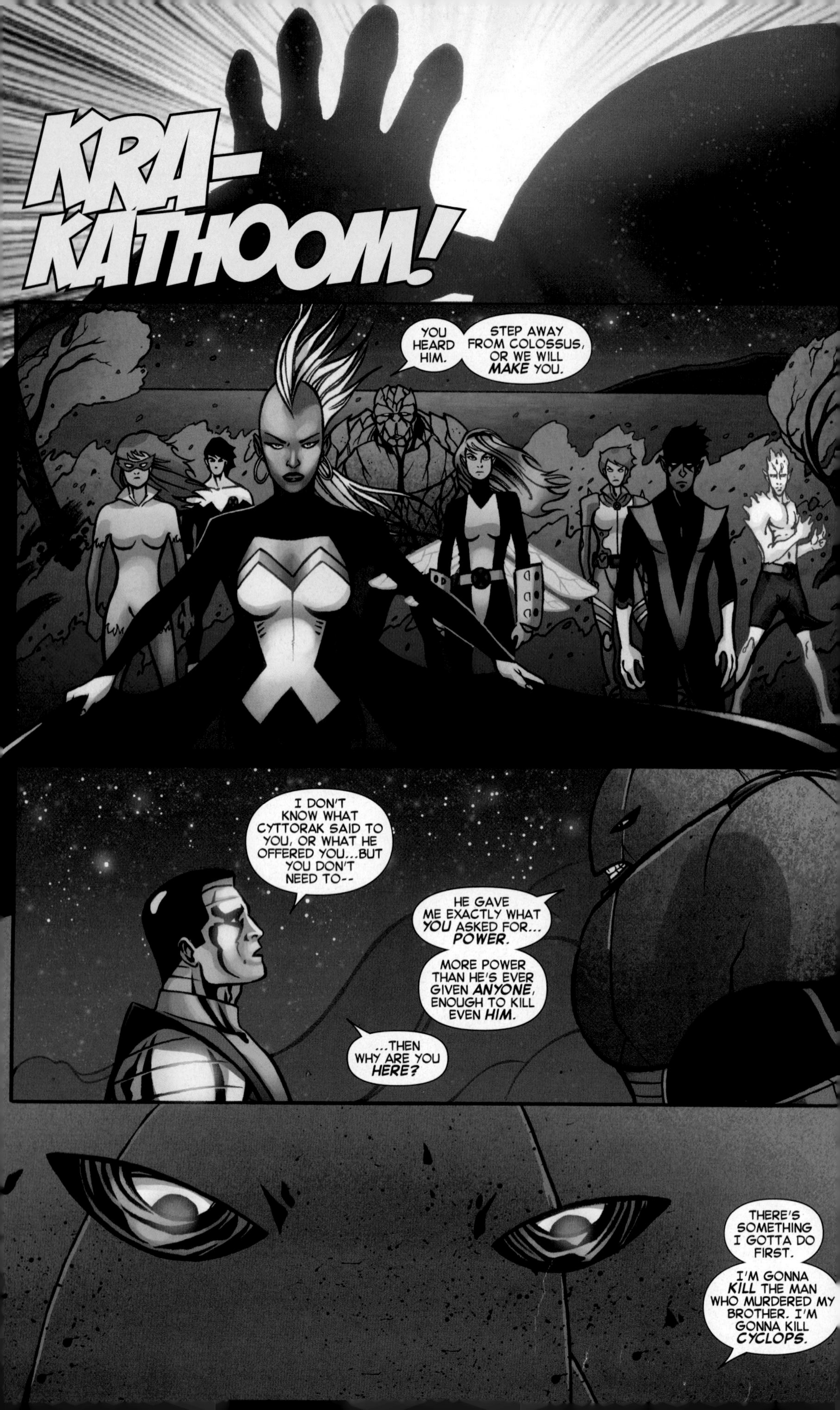
KRA-KATHOOM!
YOU HEARD HIM.
STEP AWAY FROM COLOSSUS, OR WE WILL MAKE YOU.
I DON'T KNOW WHAT CYTTORAK SAID TO YOU, OR WHAT HE OFFERED YOU...BUT YOU DON'T NEED TO--
HE GAVE ME EXACTLY WHAT YOU ASKED FOR... POWER.
MORE POWER THAN HE'S EVER GIVEN ANYONE, ENOUGH TO KILL EVEN HIM.
...THEN WHY ARE YOU HERE?
THERE'S SOMETHING I GOTTA DO FIRST.
I'M GONNA KILL THE MAN WHO MURDERED MY BROTHER. I'M GONNA KILL CYCLOPS.

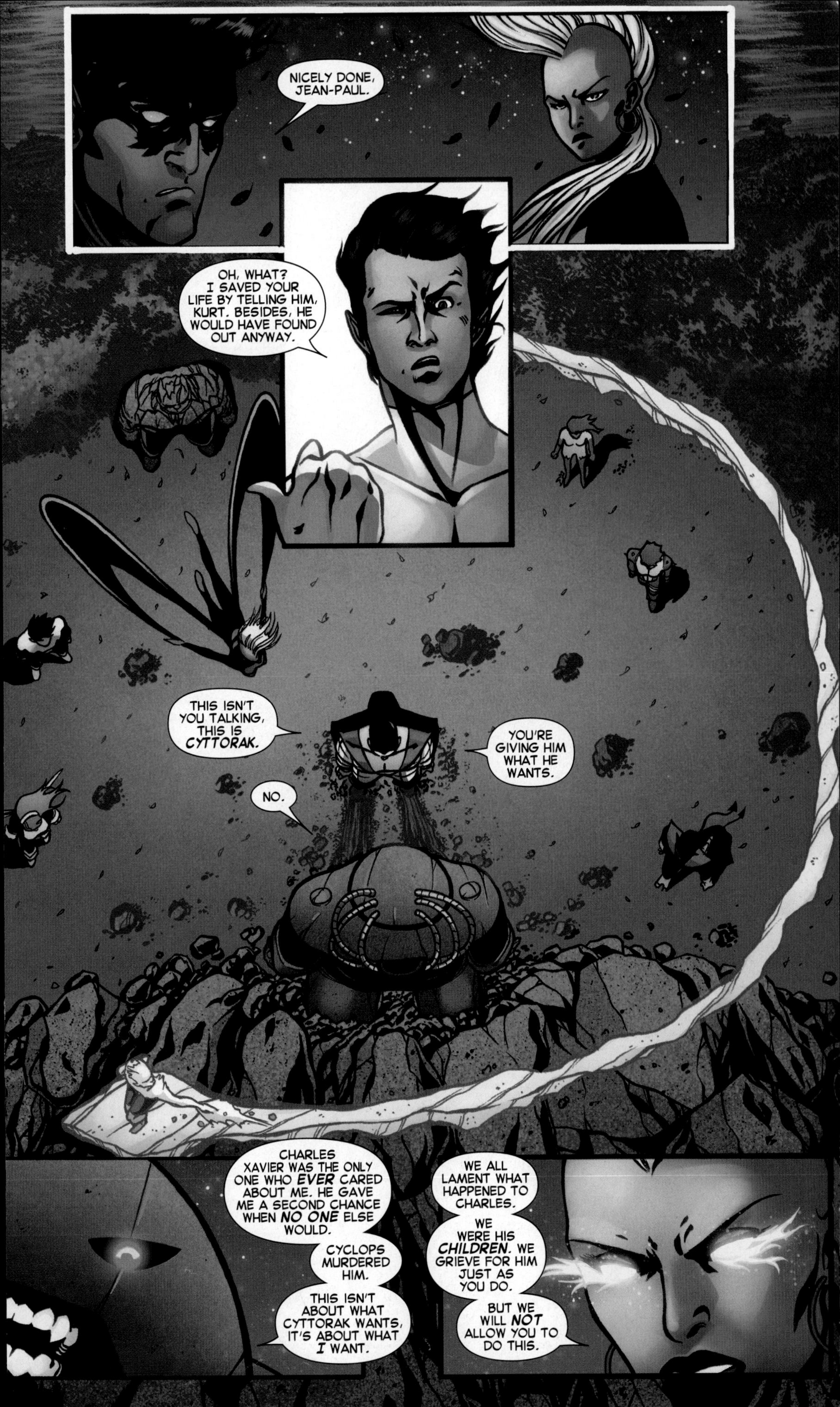
NICELY DONE, JEAN-PAUL.
OH, WHAT? I SAVED YOUR LIFE BY TELLING HIM, KURT. BESIDES, HE WOULD HAVE FOUND OUT ANYWAY.
THIS ISN'T YOU TALKING, THIS IS CYTTORAK.
YOU'RE GIVING HIM WHAT HE WANTS.
NO.
CHARLES XAVIER WAS THE ONLY ONE WHO EVER CARED ABOUT ME. HE GAVE ME A SECOND CHANCE WHEN NO ONE ELSE WOULD.
CYCLOPS MURDERED HIM.
THIS ISN'T ABOUT WHAT CYTTORAK WANTS, IT'S ABOUT WHAT I WANT.
WE ALL LAMENT WHAT HAPPENED TO CHARLES.
WE WERE HIS CHILDREN. WE GRIEVE FOR HIM JUST AS YOU DO.
BUT WE WILL NOT ALLOW YOU TO DO THIS.

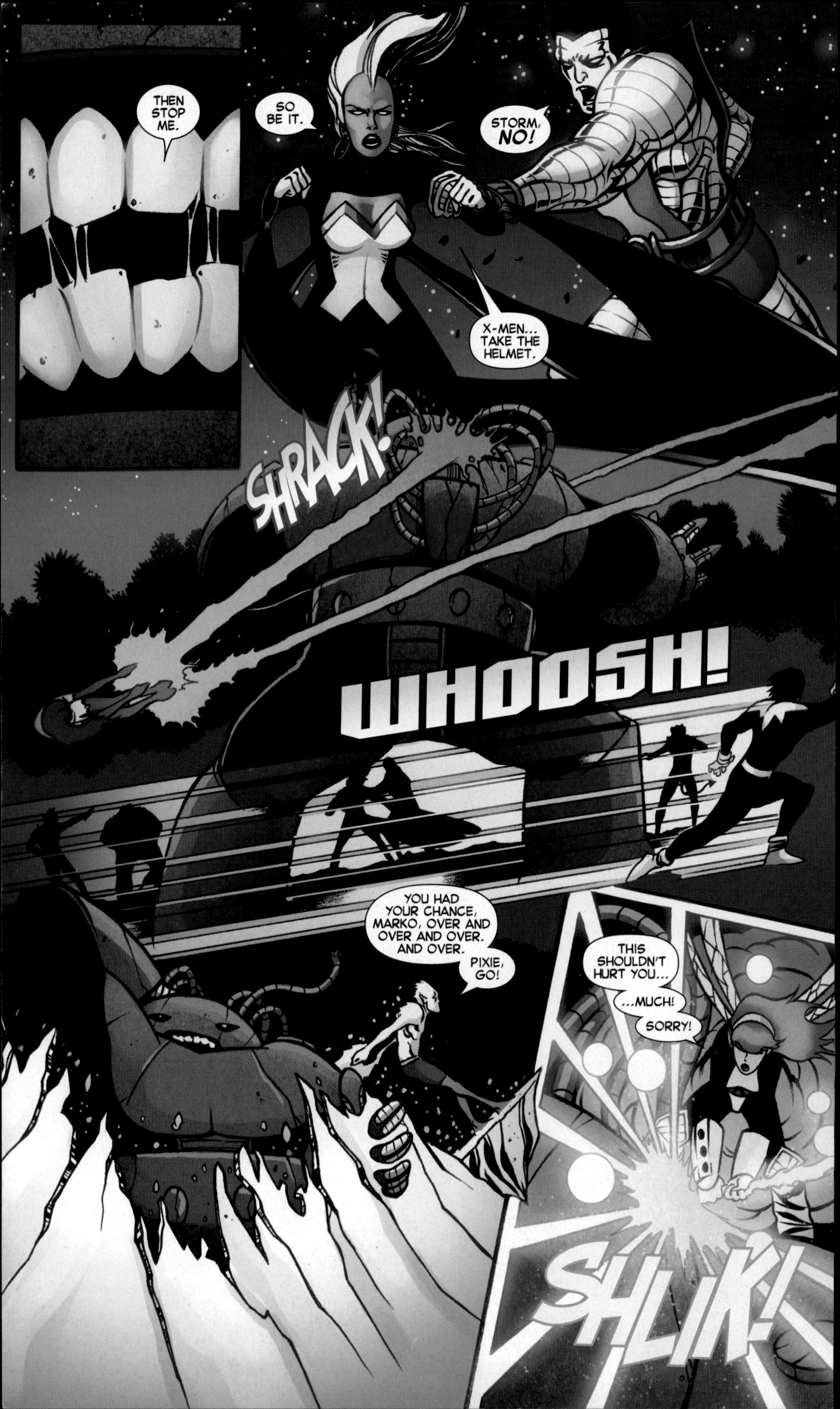
THEN STOP ME.
SO BE IT.
STORM, NO!
X-MEN... TAKE THE HELMET.
SHRACK!
WHOOSH!
YOU HAD YOUR CHANCE, MARKO, OVER AND OVER AND OVER. AND OVER.
PIXIE, GO!
THIS SHOULDN'T HURT YOU...
...MUCH!
SORRY!
SHLIK!

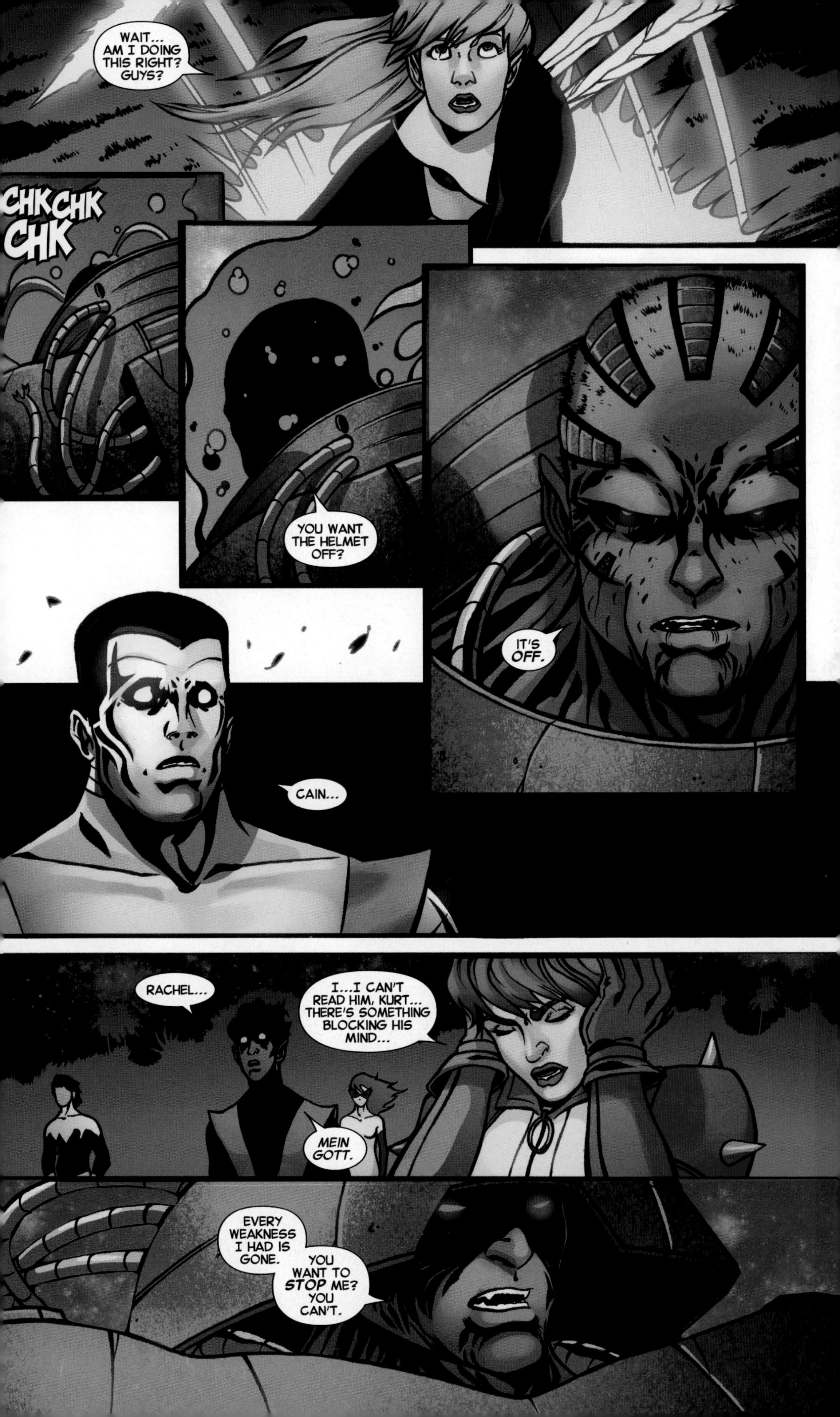
WAIT... AM I DOING THIS RIGHT? GUYS?
CHKCHK CHK
YOU WANT THE HELMET OFF?
IT'S OFF.
CAIN...
RACHEL...
I...I CAN'T READ HIM, KURT... THERE'S SOMETHING BLOCKING HIS MIND...
MEIN GOTT.
EVERY WEAKNESS I HAD IS GONE.
YOU WANT TO STOP ME? YOU CAN'T.

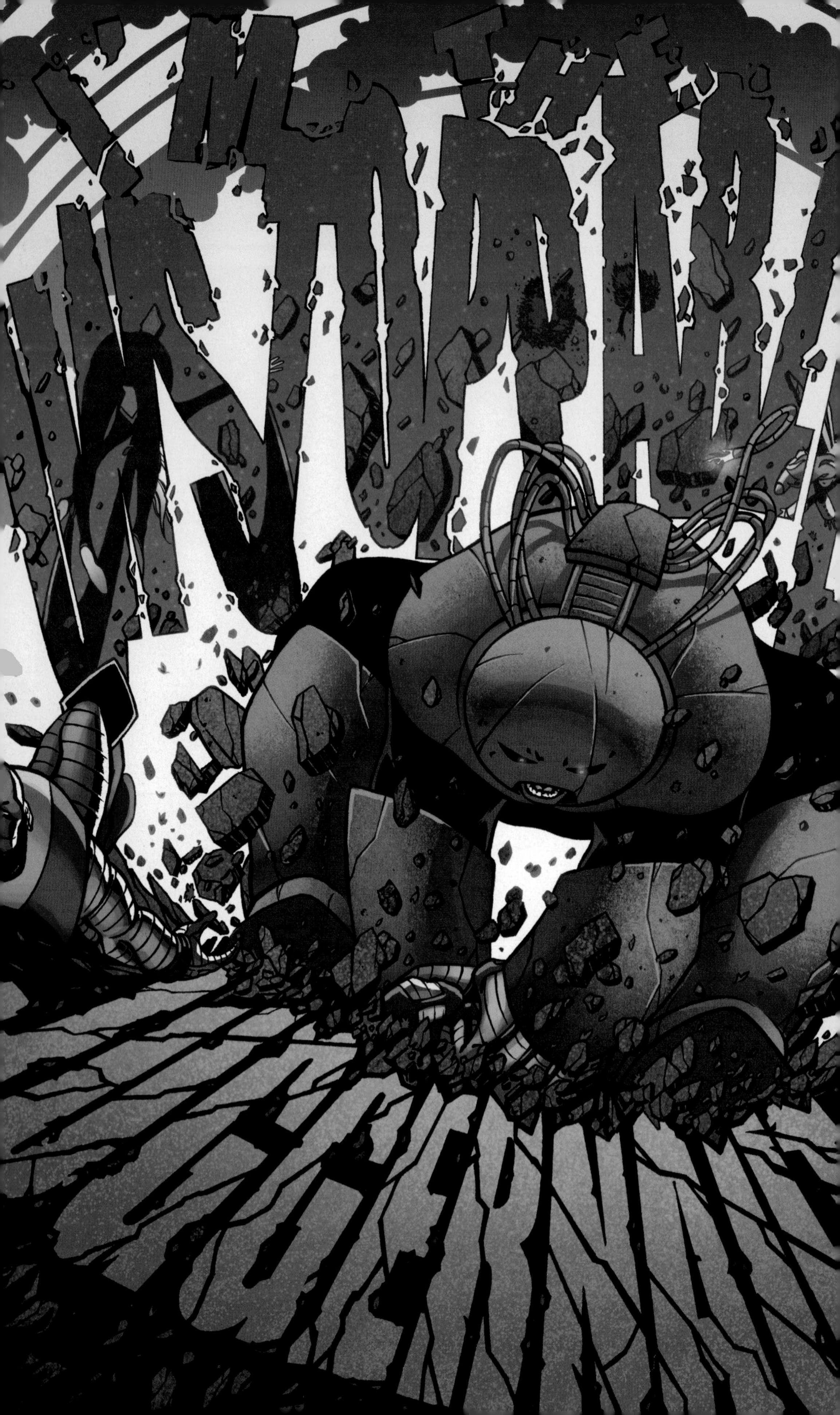

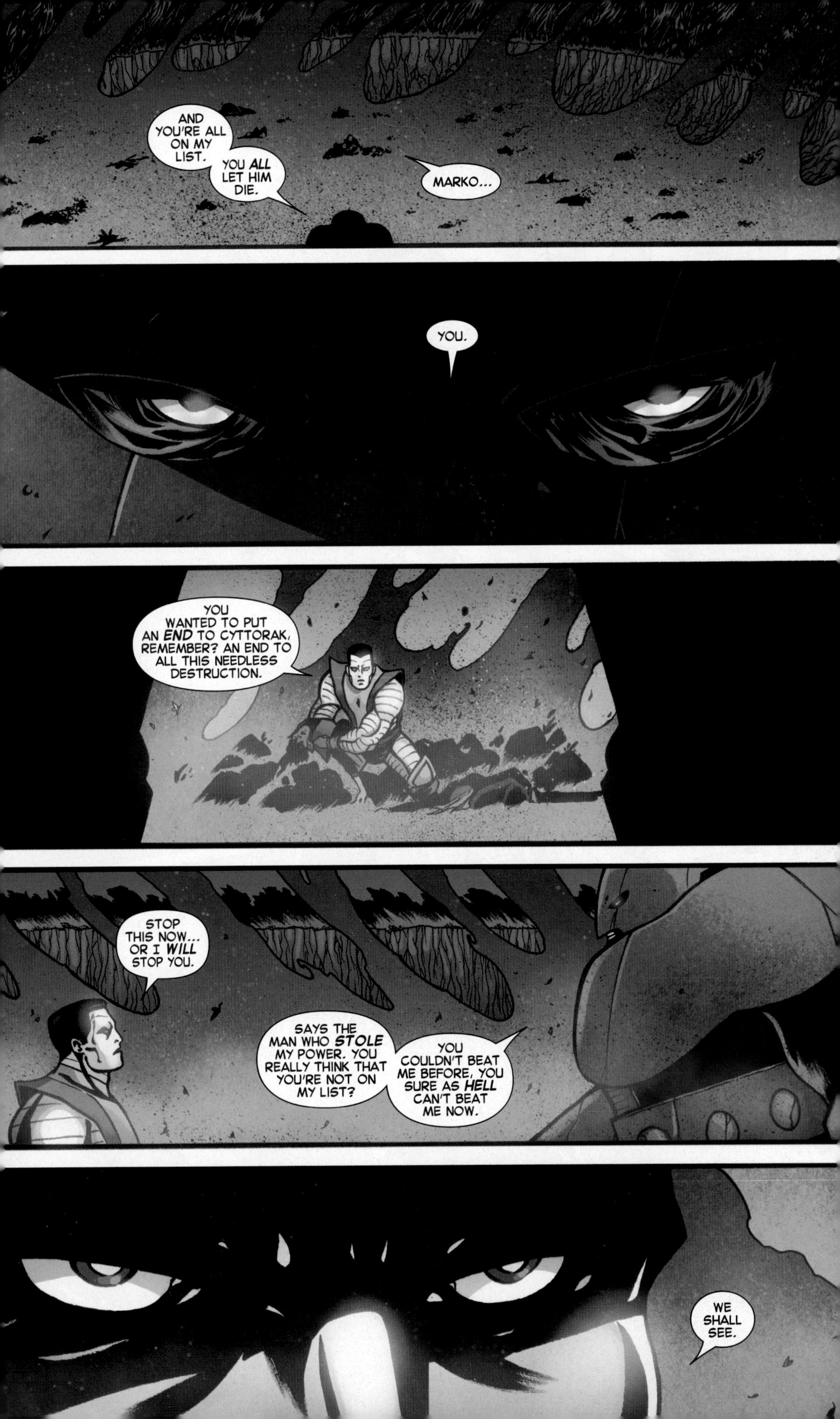
AND YOU'RE ALL ON MY LIST.
YOU ALL LET HIM DIE.
MARKO...
YOU.
YOU WANTED TO PUT AN END TO CYTTORAK, REMEMBER? AN END TO ALL THIS NEEDLESS DESTRUCTION.
STOP THIS NOW... OR I WILL STOP YOU.
SAYS THE MAN WHO STOLE MY POWER. YOU REALLY THINK THAT YOU'RE NOT ON MY LIST?
YOU COULDN'T BEAT ME BEFORE, YOU SURE AS HELL CAN'T BEAT ME NOW.
WE SHALL SEE.

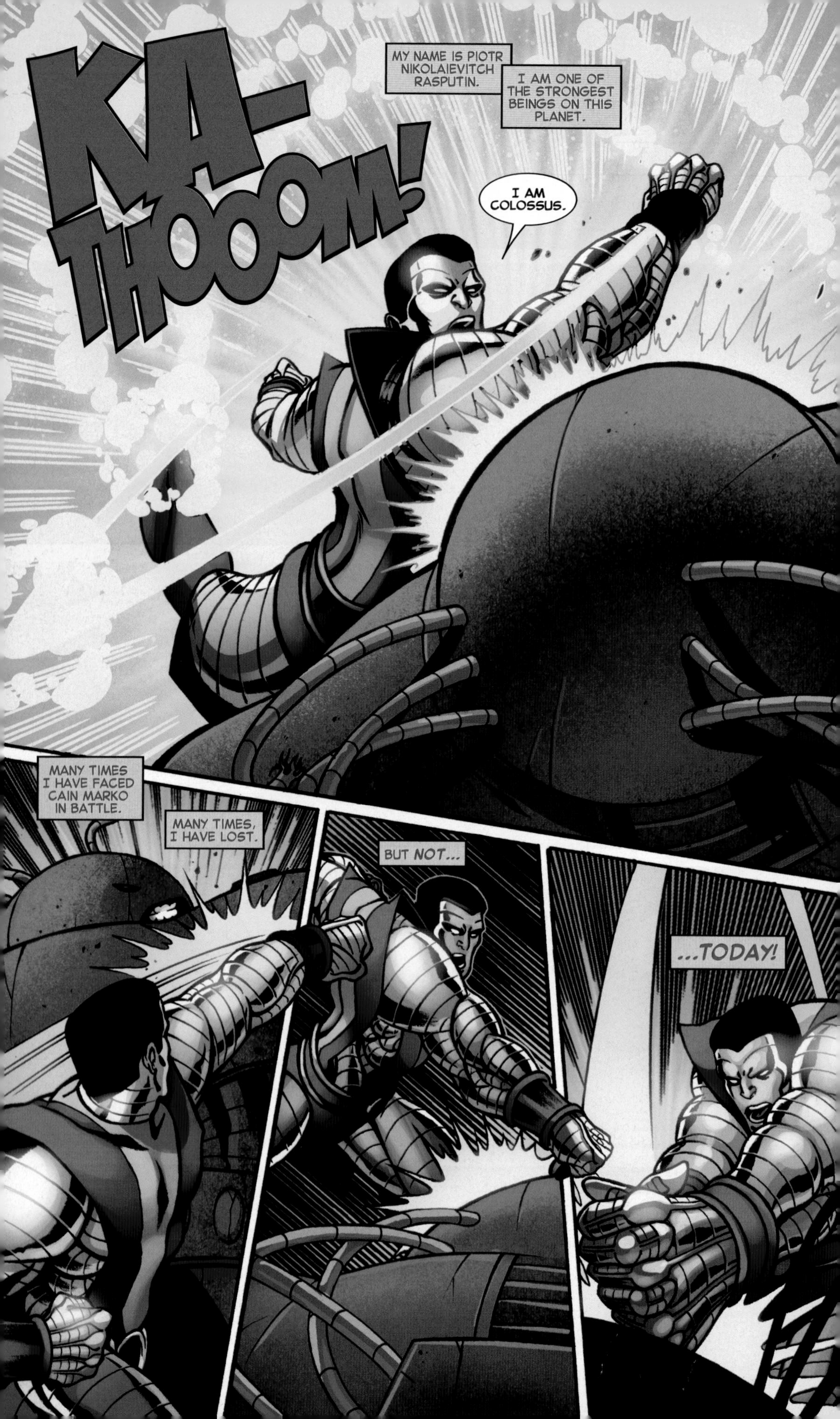
KA-THOOOM!
MY NAME IS PIOTR NIKOLAIEVITCH RASPUTIN.
I AM ONE OF THE STRONGEST BEINGS ON THIS PLANET.
I AM COLOSSUS.
MANY TIMES I HAVE FACED CAIN MARKO IN BATTLE.
MANY TIMES, I HAVE LOST.
BUT NOT...
...TODAY!

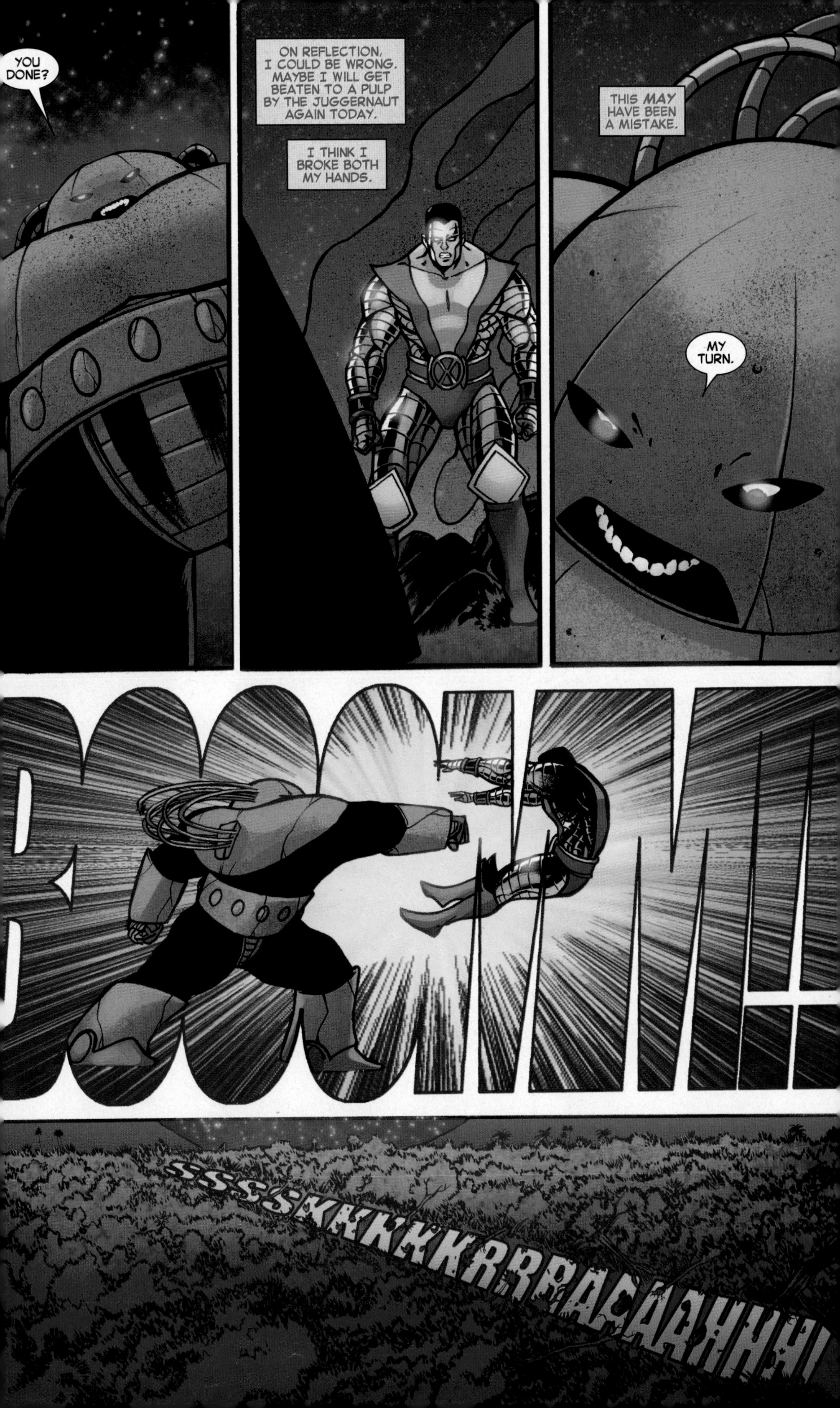
YOU DONE?
ON REFLECTION, I COULD BE WRONG. MAYBE I WILL GET BEATEN TO A PULP BY THE JUGGERNAUT AGAIN TODAY.
I THINK I BROKE BOTH MY HANDS.
THIS MAY HAVE BEEN A MISTAKE.
MY TURN.
BOOOOMM!!!
SSSSKKKKKKRRRRAAAAHHHH!

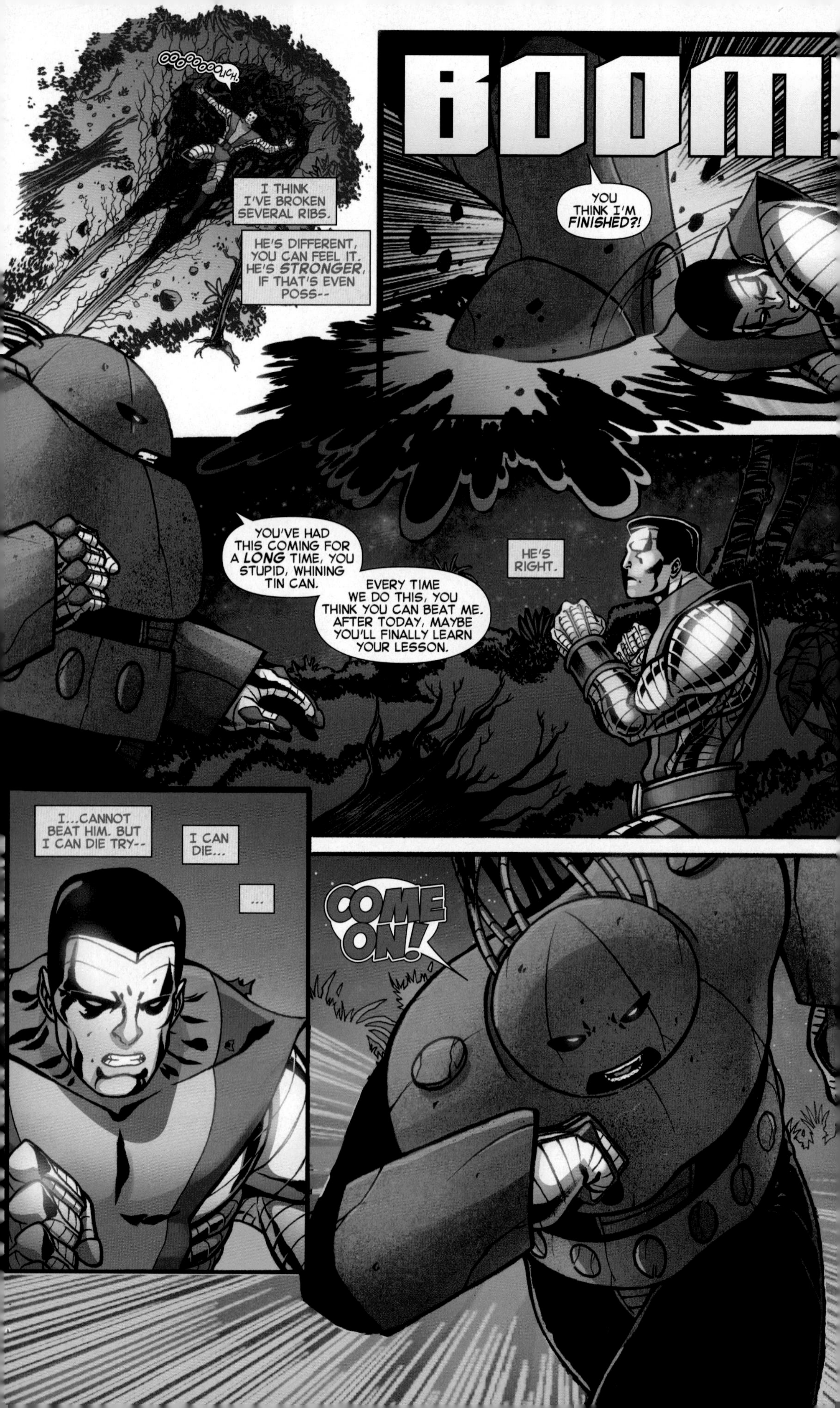
OOOOOOOOUCH.
I THINK I'VE BROKEN SEVERAL RIBS.
HE'S DIFFERENT, YOU CAN FEEL IT. HE'S STRONGER, IF THAT'S EVEN POSS--
BOOM!
YOU THINK I'M FINISHED?!
YOU'VE HAD THIS COMING FOR A LONG TIME, YOU STUPID, WHINING TIN CAN.
EVERY TIME WE DO THIS, YOU THINK YOU CAN BEAT ME. AFTER TODAY, MAYBE YOU'LL FINALLY LEARN YOUR LESSON.
HE'S RIGHT.
I...CANNOT BEAT HIM. BUT I CAN DIE TRY--
I CAN DIE...
...
COME ON!

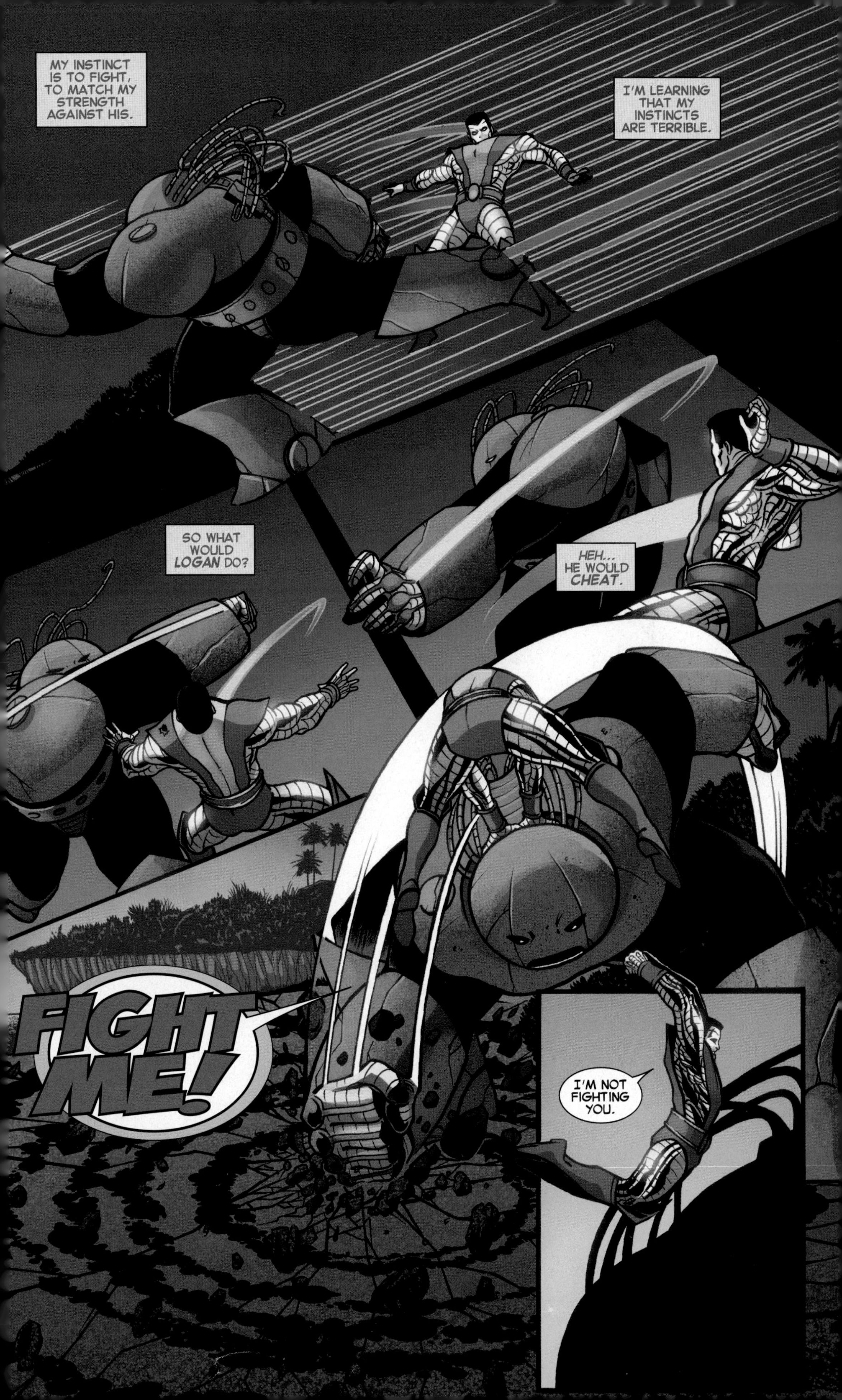
MY INSTINCT IS TO FIGHT, TO MATCH MY STRENGTH AGAINST HIS.
I'M LEARNING THAT MY INSTINCTS ARE TERRIBLE.
SO WHAT WOULD LOGAN DO?
HEH... HE WOULD CHEAT.
FIGHT ME!
I'M NOT FIGHTING YOU.

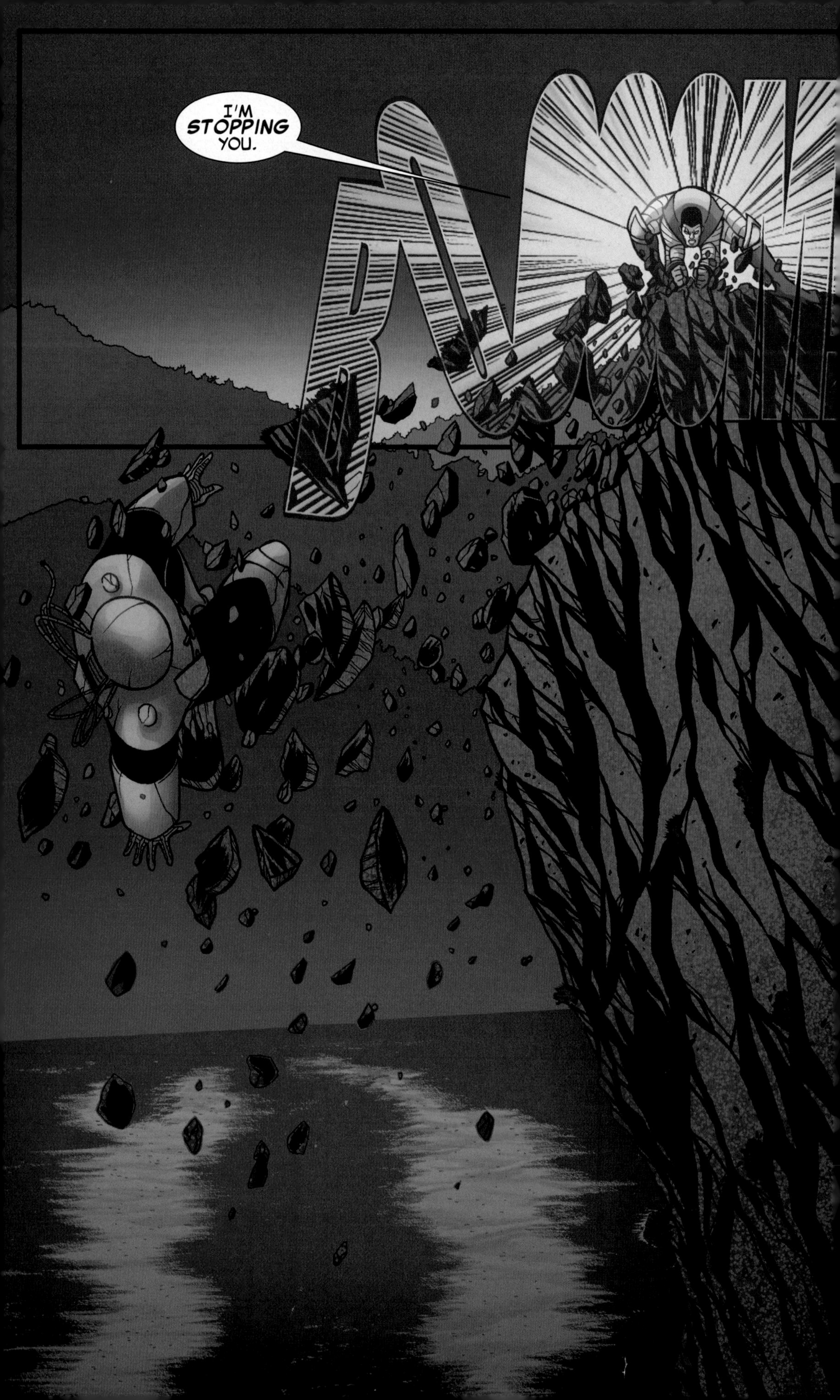
I'M STOPPING YOU.

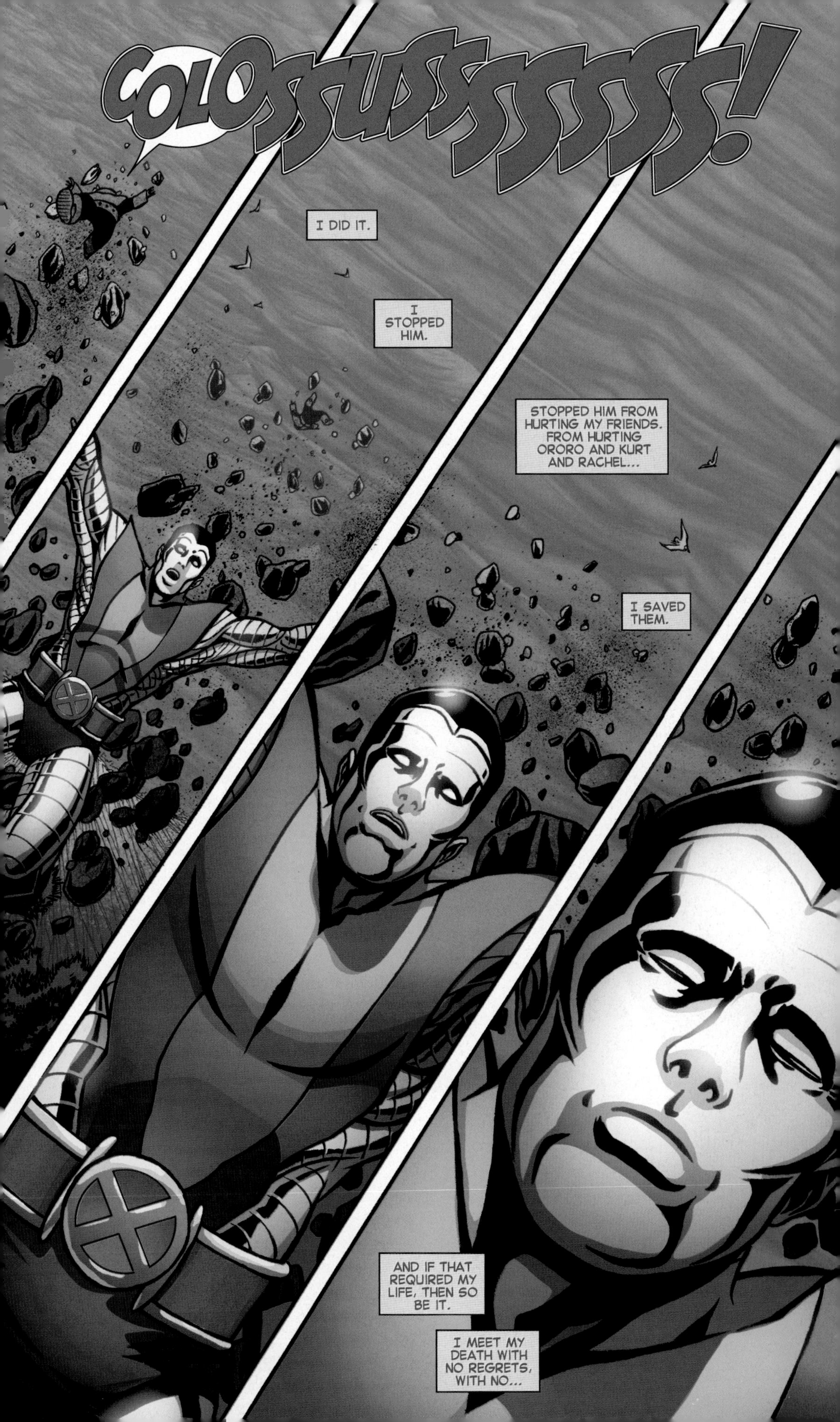
COLOSSUSSSSSSSS!
I DID IT.
I STOPPED HIM.
STOPPED HIM FROM HURTING MY FRIENDS. FROM HURTING ORORO AND KURT AND RACHEL...
I SAVED THEM.
AND IF THAT REQUIRED MY LIFE, THEN SO BE IT.
I MEET MY DEATH WITH NO REGRETS, WITH NO...

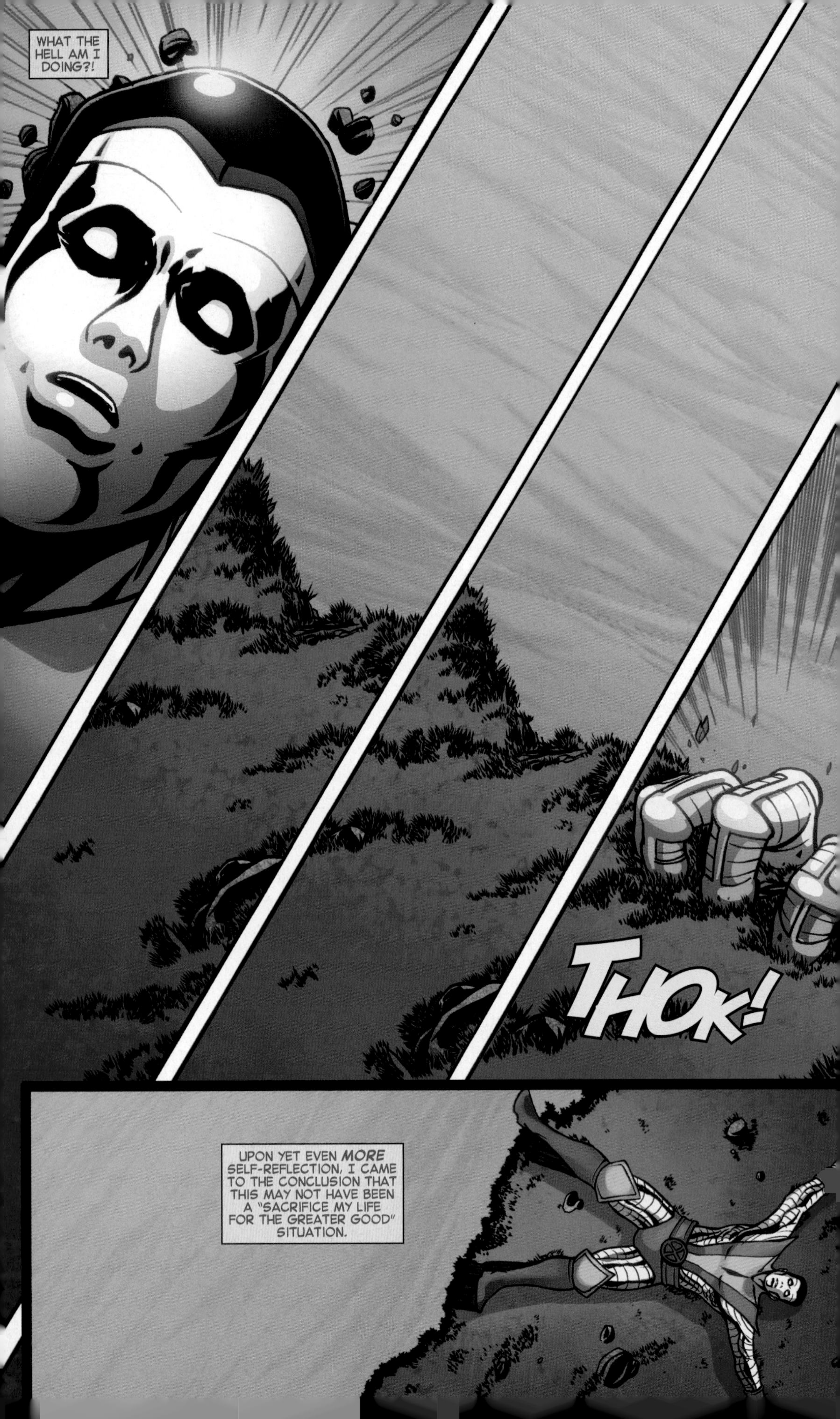
WHAT THE HELL AM I DOING?!
THOK!
UPON YET EVEN MORE SELF-REFLECTION, I CAME TO THE CONCLUSION THAT THIS MAY NOT HAVE BEEN A "SACRIFICE MY LIFE FOR THE GREATER GOOD" SITUATION.

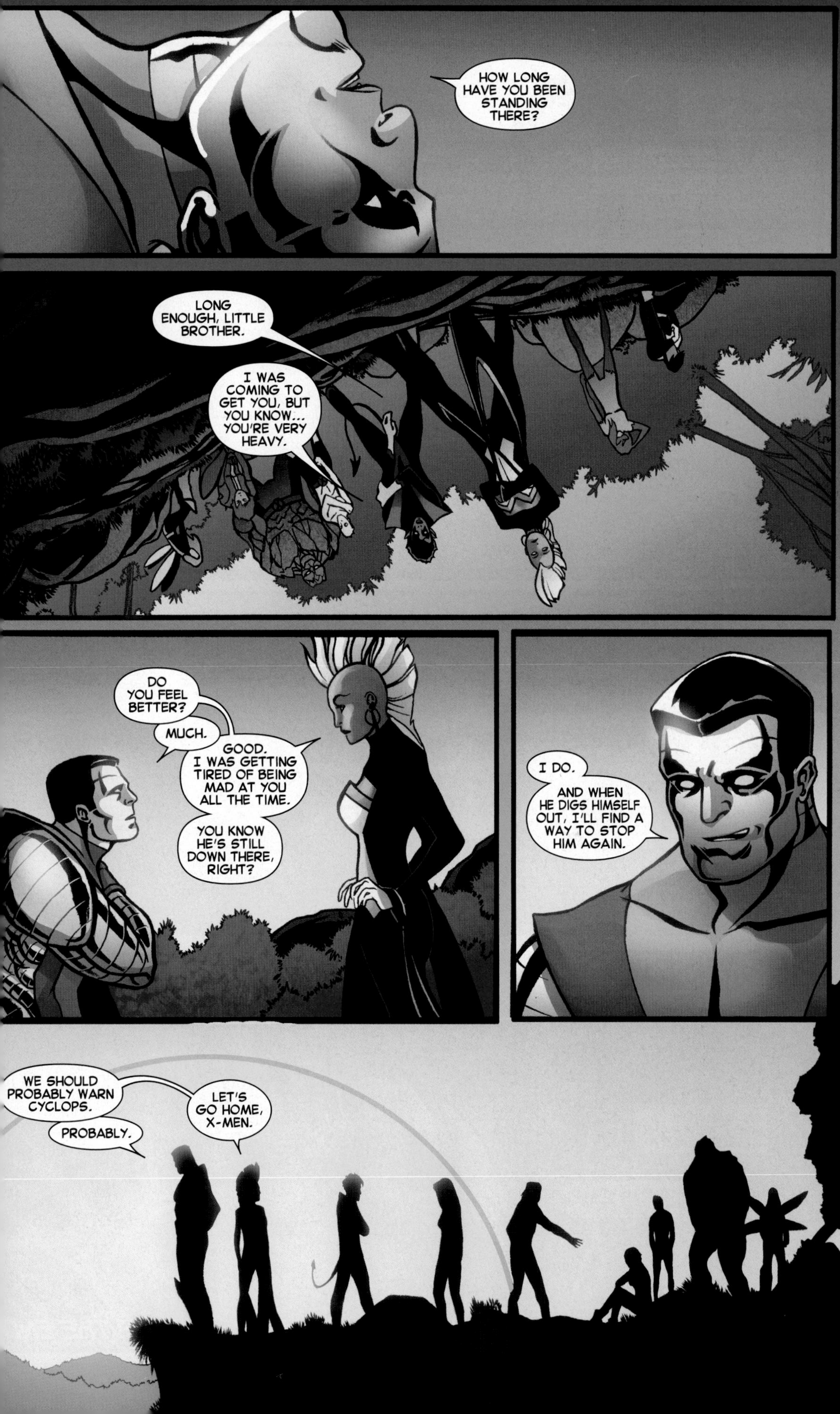

HOW LONG HAVE YOU BEEN STANDING THERE?
LONG ENOUGH, LITTLE BROTHER.
I WAS COMING TO GET YOU, BUT YOU KNOW... YOU'RE VERY HEAVY.
DO YOU FEEL BETTER?
MUCH.
GOOD. I WAS GETTING TIRED OF BEING MAD AT YOU ALL THE TIME.
YOU KNOW HE'S STILL DOWN THERE, RIGHT?
I DO.
AND WHEN HE DIGS HIMSELF OUT, I'LL FIND A WAY TO STOP HIM AGAIN.
WE SHOULD PROBABLY WARN CYCLOPS.
PROBABLY.
LET'S GO HOME, X-MEN.

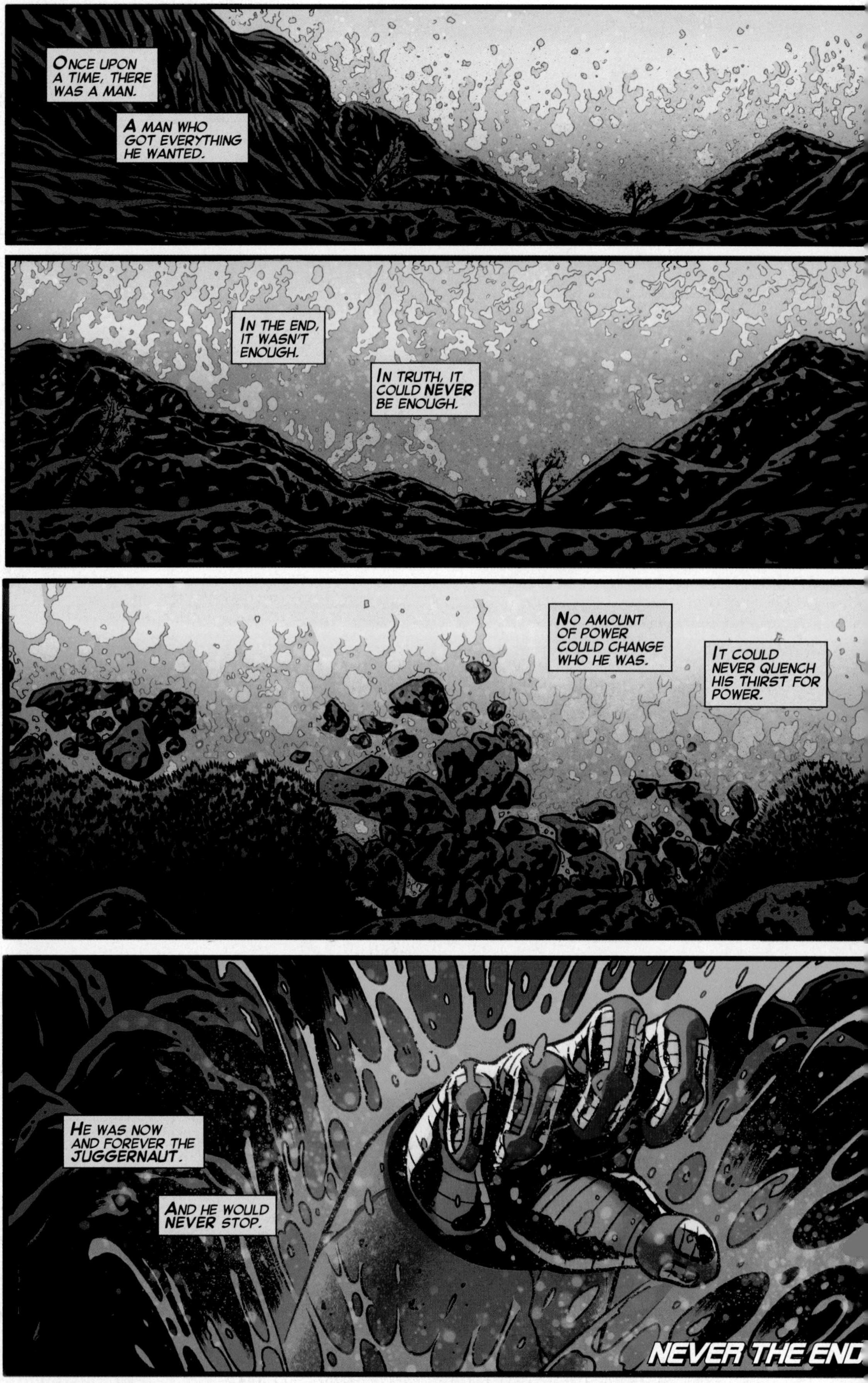
ONCE UPON A TIME, THERE WAS A MAN.
A MAN WHO GOT EVERYTHING HE WANTED.
IN THE END, IT WASN'T ENOUGH.
IN TRUTH, IT COULD NEVER BE ENOUGH.
NO AMOUNT OF POWER COULD CHANGE WHO HE WAS.
IT COULD NEVER QUENCH HIS THIRST FOR POWER.
HE WAS NOW AND FOREVER THE JUGGERNAUT.
AND HE WOULD NEVER STOP.
NEVER THE END

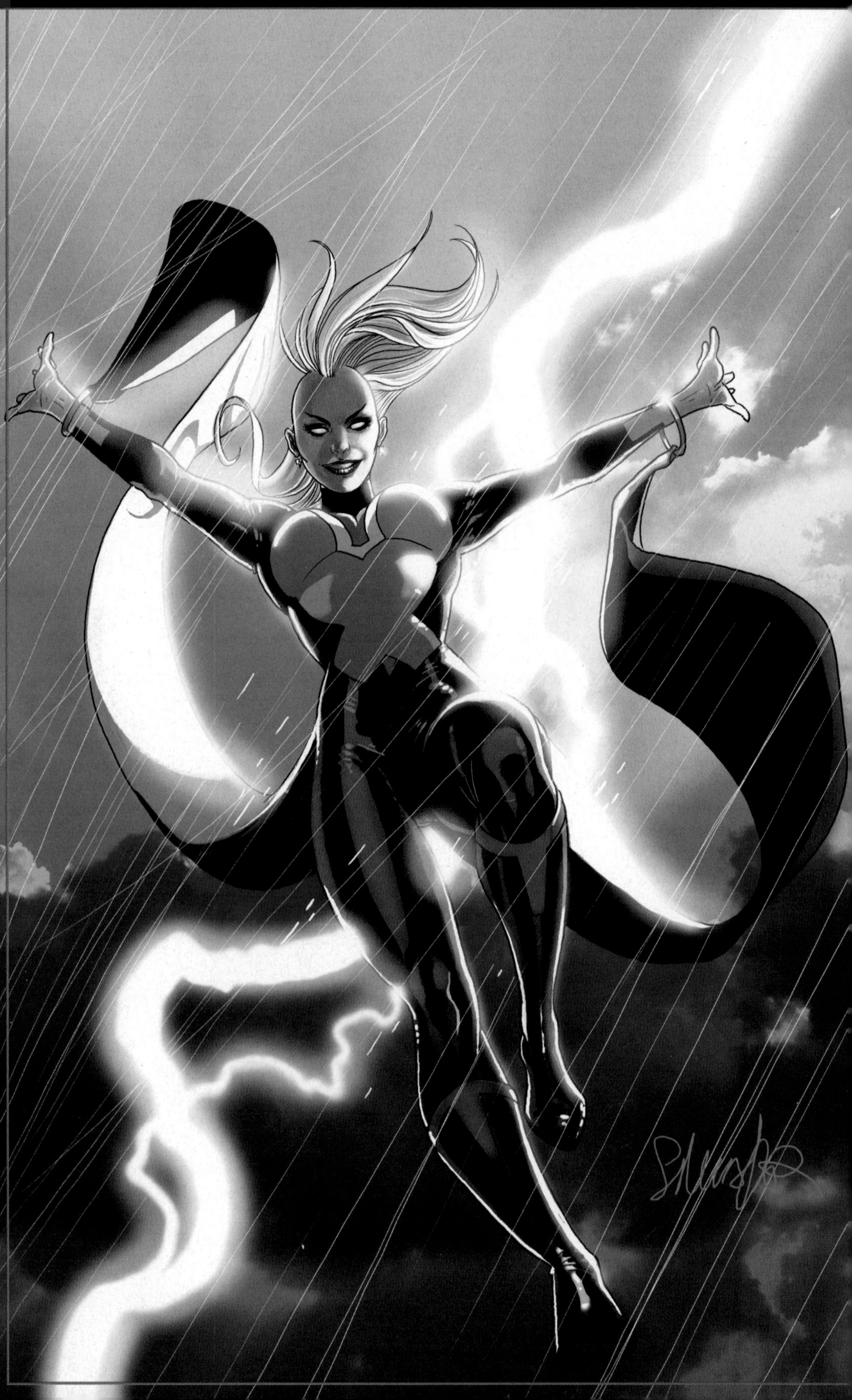

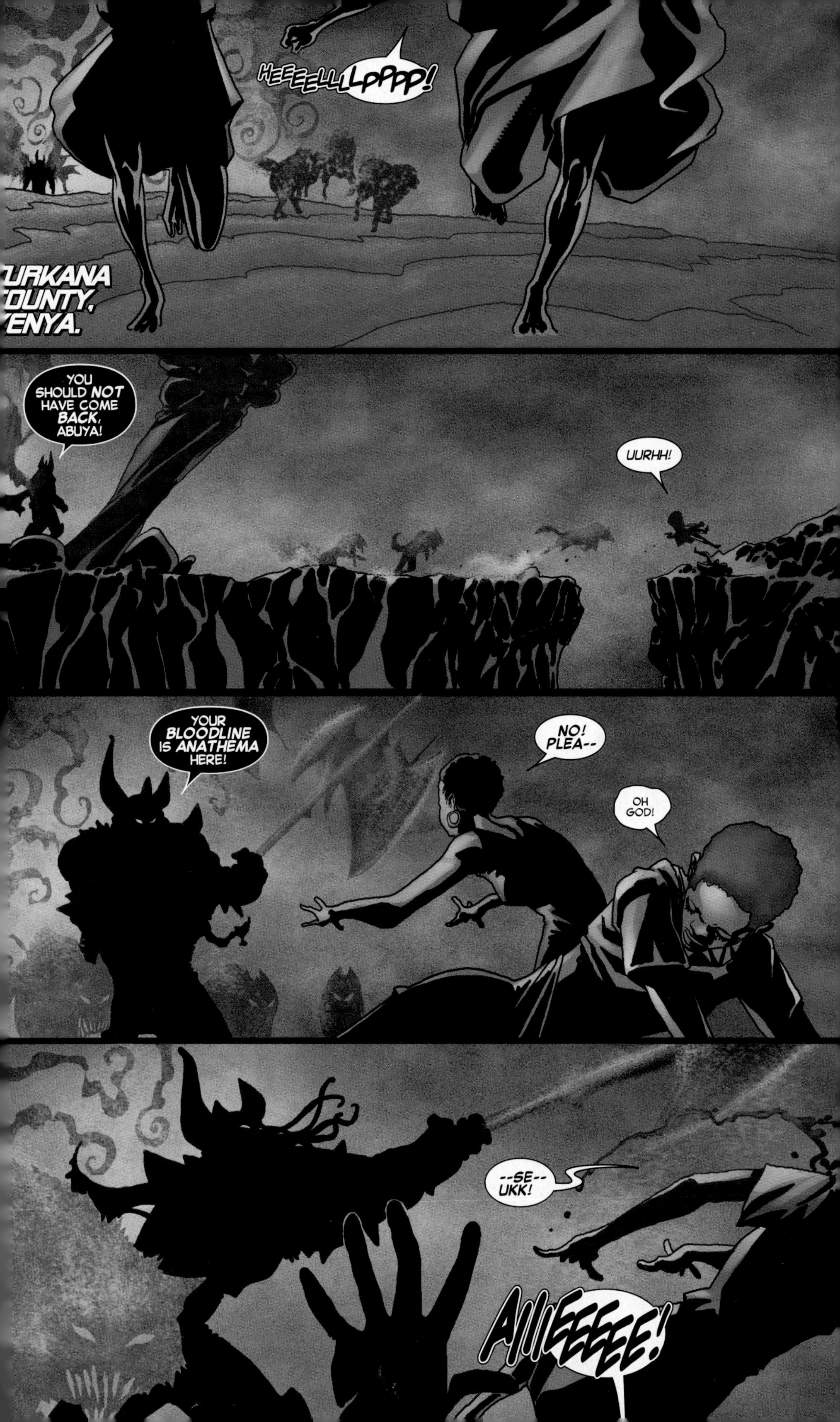
HEEEELLLLPPPP!
URKANA
OUNTY,
ENYA.
YOU SHOULD NOT HAVE COME BACK, ABUYA!
UURHH!
YOUR BLOODLINE IS ANATHEMA HERE!
NO! PLEA--
OH GOD!
--SE-- UKK!
AIIEEEEE!

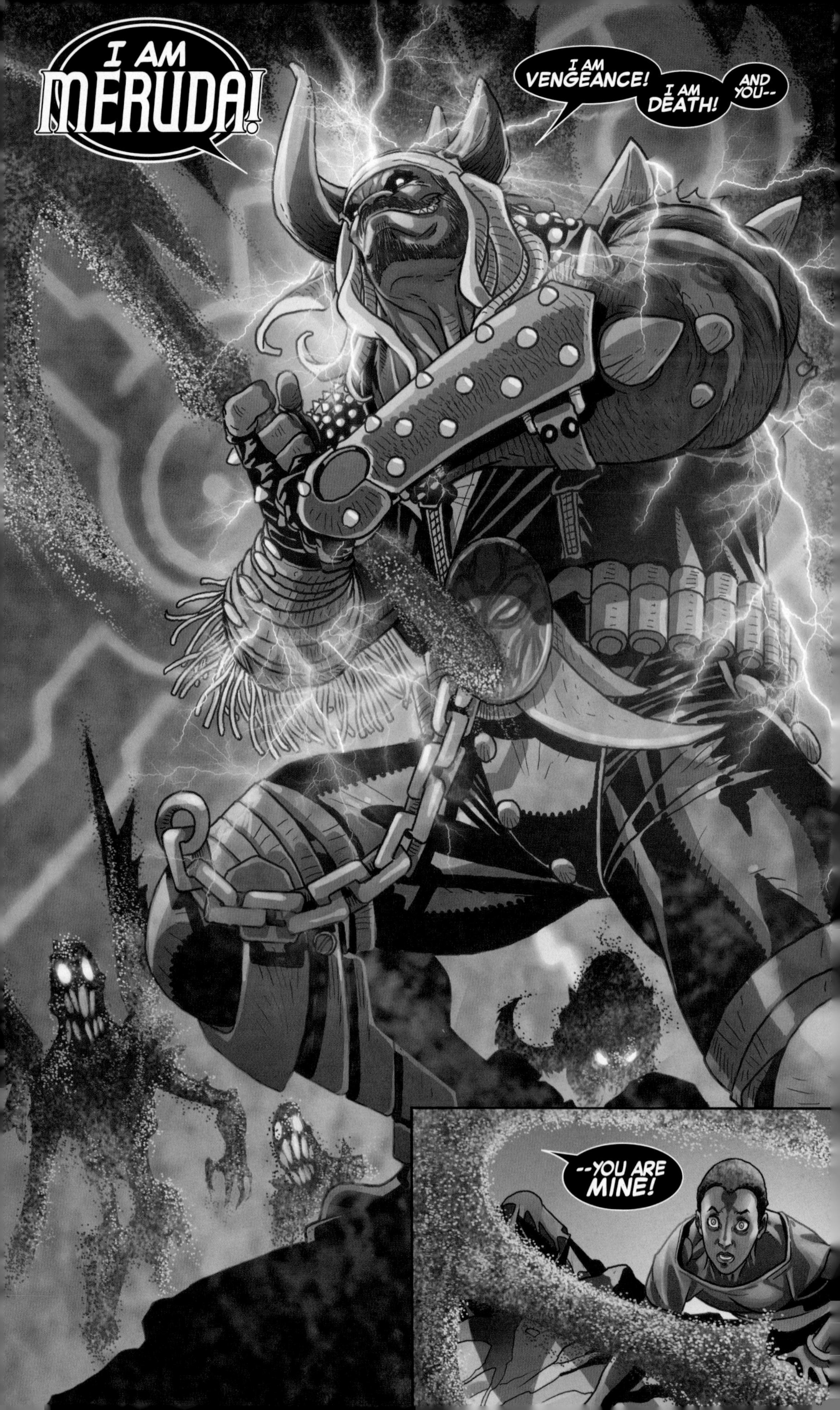
I AM MERUDA!
I AM VENGEANCE!
I AM DEATH!
AND YOU--
--YOU ARE MINE!

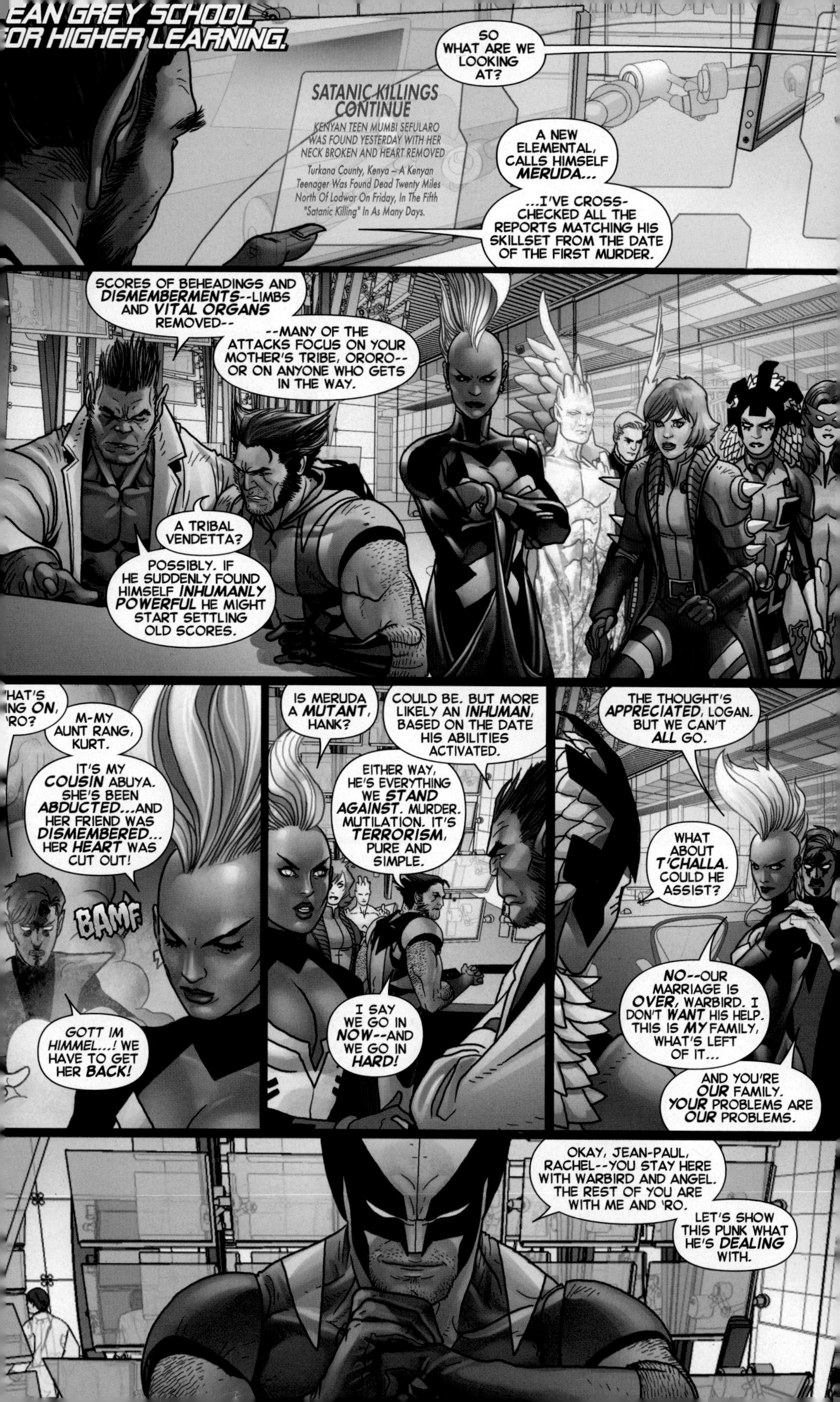
EAN GREY SCHOOL
OR HIGHER LEARNING.
SO WHAT ARE WE LOOKING AT?
SATANIC KILLINGS CONTINUE
KENYAN TEEN MUMBI SEFULARO WAS FOUND YESTERDAY WITH HER NECK BROKEN AND HEART REMOVED
Turkana County, Kenya – A Kenyan Teenager Was Found Dead Twenty Miles North Of Lodwar On Friday, In The Fifth "Satanic Killing" In As Many Days.
A NEW ELEMENTAL, CALLS HIMSELF MERUDA...
...I'VE CROSS-CHECKED ALL THE REPORTS MATCHING HIS SKILLSET FROM THE DATE OF THE FIRST MURDER.
SCORES OF BEHEADINGS AND DISMEMBERMENTS--LIMBS AND VITAL ORGANS REMOVED--
--MANY OF THE ATTACKS FOCUS ON YOUR MOTHER'S TRIBE, ORORO--OR ON ANYONE WHO GETS IN THE WAY.
A TRIBAL VENDETTA?
POSSIBLY. IF HE SUDDENLY FOUND HIMSELF INHUMANLY POWERFUL HE MIGHT START SETTLING OLD SCORES.
'HAT'S
ING ON,
'RO?
M-MY AUNT RANG, KURT.
IT'S MY COUSIN ABUYA. SHE'S BEEN ABDUCTED...AND HER FRIEND WAS DISMEMBERED... HER HEART WAS CUT OUT!
BAMF
GOTT IM HIMMEL...! WE HAVE TO GET HER BACK!
IS MERUDA A MUTANT, HANK?
COULD BE. BUT MORE LIKELY AN INHUMAN, BASED ON THE DATE HIS ABILITIES ACTIVATED.
EITHER WAY, HE'S EVERYTHING WE STAND AGAINST. MURDER. MUTILATION. IT'S TERRORISM, PURE AND SIMPLE.
I SAY WE GO IN NOW--AND WE GO IN HARD!
THE THOUGHT'S APPRECIATED, LOGAN. BUT WE CAN'T ALL GO.
WHAT ABOUT T'CHALLA. COULD HE ASSIST?
NO--OUR MARRIAGE IS OVER, WARBIRD. I DON'T WANT HIS HELP. THIS IS MY FAMILY, WHAT'S LEFT OF IT...
AND YOU'RE OUR FAMILY. YOUR PROBLEMS ARE OUR PROBLEMS.
OKAY, JEAN-PAUL, RACHEL--YOU STAY HERE WITH WARBIRD AND ANGEL. THE REST OF YOU ARE WITH ME AND 'RO.
LET'S SHOW THIS PUNK WHAT HE'S DEALING WITH.

TURKANA COUNTY, KENYA.

I DIDN'T EVEN KNOW 'RO *HAD* A COUSIN, TO BE HONEST. I THOUGHT HER FAMILY DIED IN CAIRO.

SHE DOESN'T *TALK* ABOUT THEM MUCH.

SHE TRIES TO *PROTECT* THEM...HIDE THEM FROM SCRUTINY. THIS IS HER *WORST* NIGHTMARE.

SHE DOES SEEM *QUIET*... COLDER, SOMEHOW.

YEAH, I KNOW THAT MOOD! I WOULDN'T LIKE TO BE THE GUY THAT *DID* THIS WHEN WE *FIND* HIM.

IF WE FIND HIM.

OH, WE'LL FIND HIM...

"...LOGAN'S THE BEST THERE IS."

WHAT WAS ABUYA *DOING* OUT HERE ANYWAY?

GETTING IN TOUCH WITH H[ER] ROOTS. I DI[D] SIMILAR THIN[G] WHEN I WAS YOUNG. I WAL[KED] FROM CAIRO T[O] THE HEART [OF] AFRICA, TRYIN[G] TO *FIND* MYSELF.

ANY LUCK?

AIN'T A *MATTER* OF LUCK. CAN'T MISS THE SCENT OF *BLOOD 'N' FEAR*--OR THE *TRACKS* THIS CREEP LEAVES.

HE CHASED HER THROUGH *HERE*... BROUGHT HER DOWN *THERE*... CUT THE *OTHER* GIRL'S HEART OUT WHERE SHE FELL... THEN CARRIED ABUYA OFF *THAT* WAY.

HANK, START SCANNING THOSE *CRATERS* 50 MILES WEST OF HERE.

WILL DO.

HEADS UP. HERE COMES YOUR FAN CLUB.

ORORO...GREAT *GODDESS* OF THE *STORM*...

OUR CROPS *WITHER*... OUR CAT[TLE] *HUNGER*. HUMBLY B[EFORE] YOU--

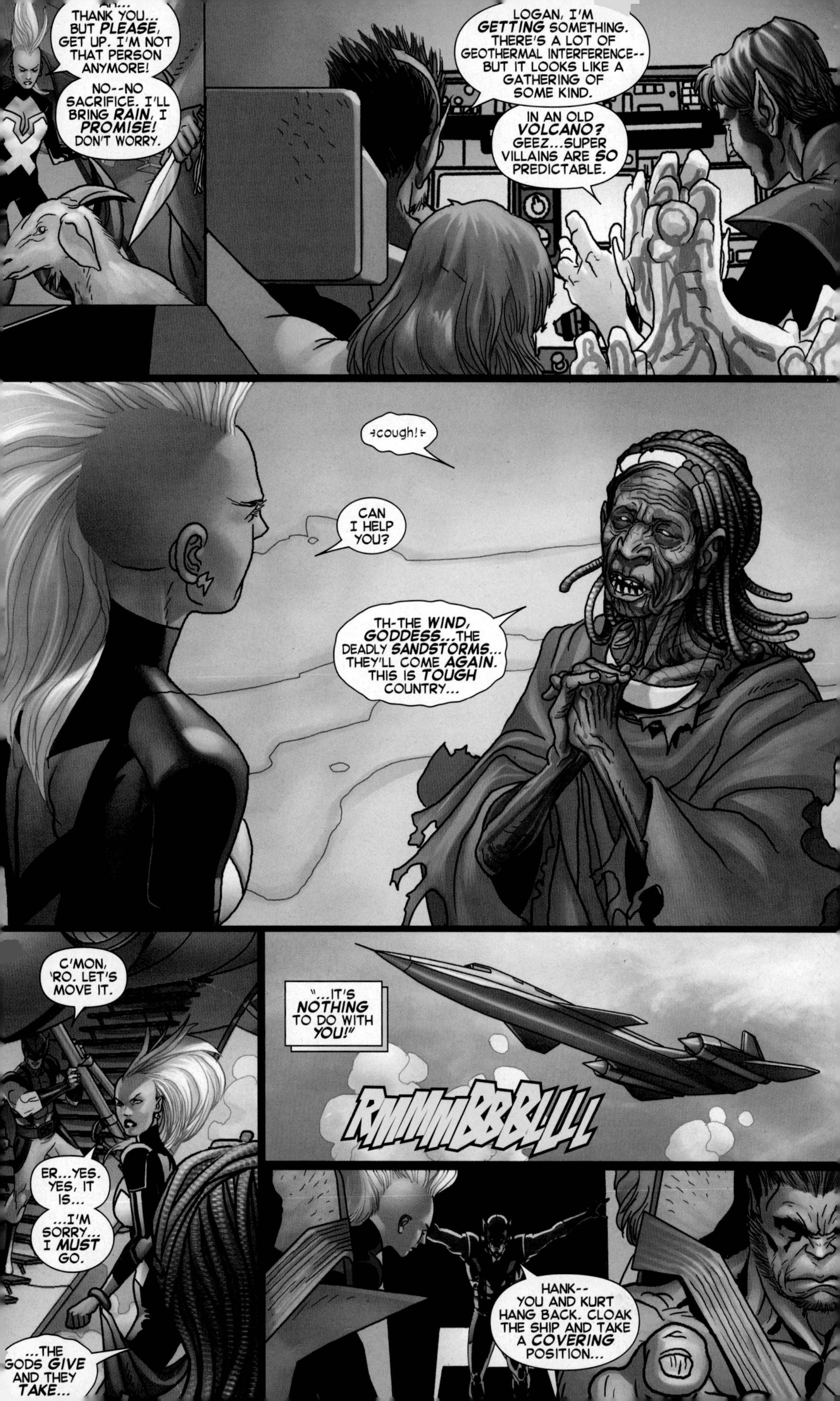
THANK YOU... BUT PLEASE, GET UP. I'M NOT THAT PERSON ANYMORE!
NO--NO SACRIFICE. I'LL BRING RAIN, I PROMISE! DON'T WORRY.
LOGAN, I'M GETTING SOMETHING. THERE'S A LOT OF GEOTHERMAL INTERFERENCE--BUT IT LOOKS LIKE A GATHERING OF SOME KIND.
IN AN OLD VOLCANO? GEEZ...SUPER VILLAINS ARE SO PREDICTABLE.
cough!
CAN I HELP YOU?
TH-THE WIND, GODDESS...THE DEADLY SANDSTORMS... THEY'LL COME AGAIN. THIS IS TOUGH COUNTRY...
C'MON, 'RO. LET'S MOVE IT.
ER...YES. YES, IT IS...
...I'M SORRY... I MUST GO.
...THE GODS GIVE AND THEY TAKE...
"...IT'S NOTHING TO DO WITH YOU!"
RMMMBBBLLLL
HANK--YOU AND KURT HANG BACK. CLOAK THE SHIP AND TAKE A COVERING POSITION...

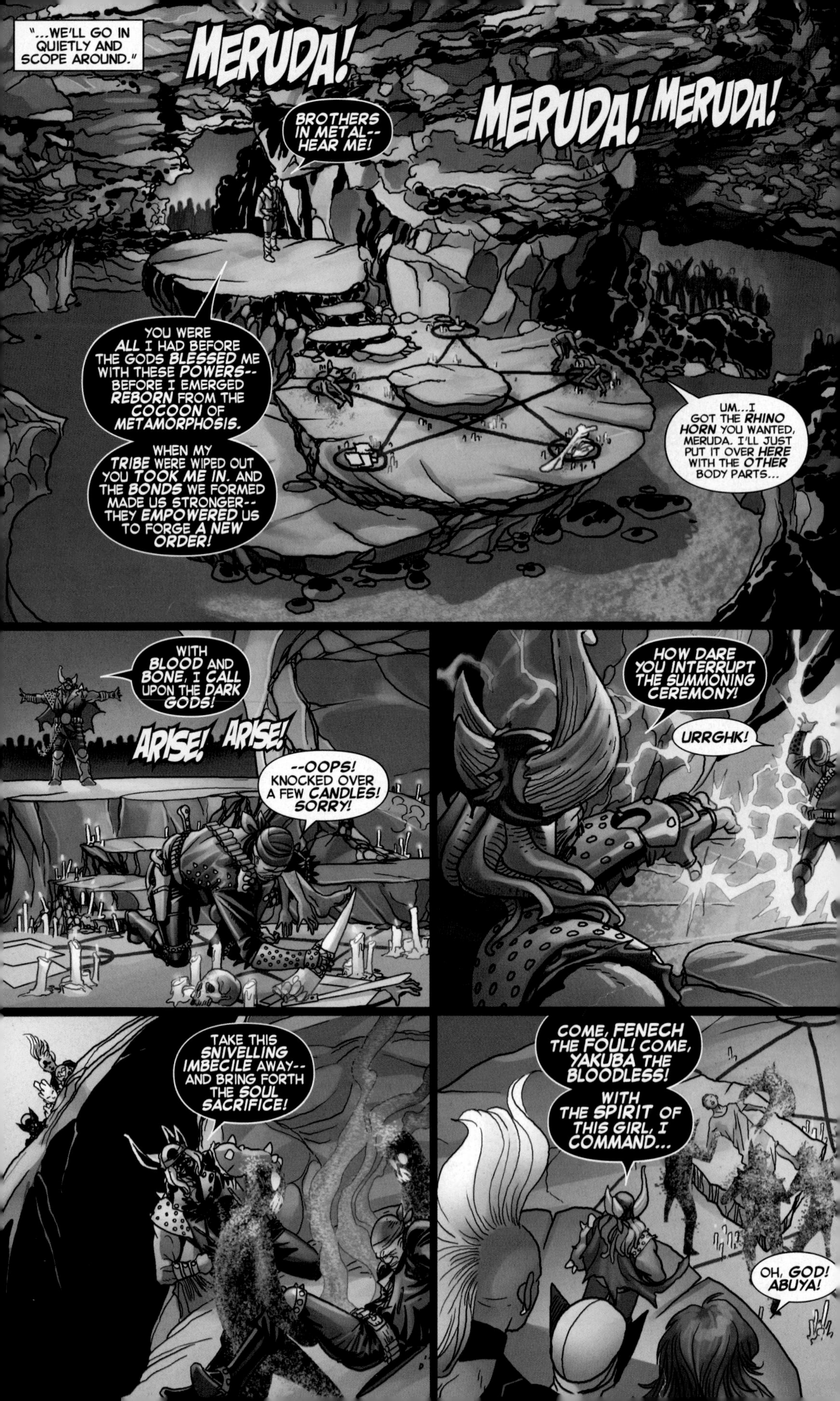
"...WE'LL GO IN QUIETLY AND SCOPE AROUND."
MERUDA!
MERUDA! MERUDA!
BROTHERS IN METAL-- HEAR ME!
YOU WERE ALL I HAD BEFORE THE GODS BLESSED ME WITH THESE POWERS-- BEFORE I EMERGED REBORN FROM THE COCOON OF METAMORPHOSIS.
WHEN MY TRIBE WERE WIPED OUT YOU TOOK ME IN. AND THE BONDS WE FORMED MADE US STRONGER-- THEY EMPOWERED US TO FORGE A NEW ORDER!
UM...I GOT THE RHINO HORN YOU WANTED, MERUDA. I'LL JUST PUT IT OVER HERE WITH THE OTHER BODY PARTS...
WITH BLOOD AND BONE, I CALL UPON THE DARK GODS!
ARISE! ARISE!
--OOPS! KNOCKED OVER A FEW CANDLES! SORRY!
HOW DARE YOU INTERRUPT THE SUMMONING CEREMONY!
URRGHK!
TAKE THIS SNIVELLING IMBECILE AWAY-- AND BRING FORTH THE SOUL SACRIFICE!
COME, FENECH THE FOUL! COME, YAKUBA THE BLOODLESS!
WITH THE SPIRIT OF THIS GIRL, I COMMAND...
OH, GOD! ABUYA!

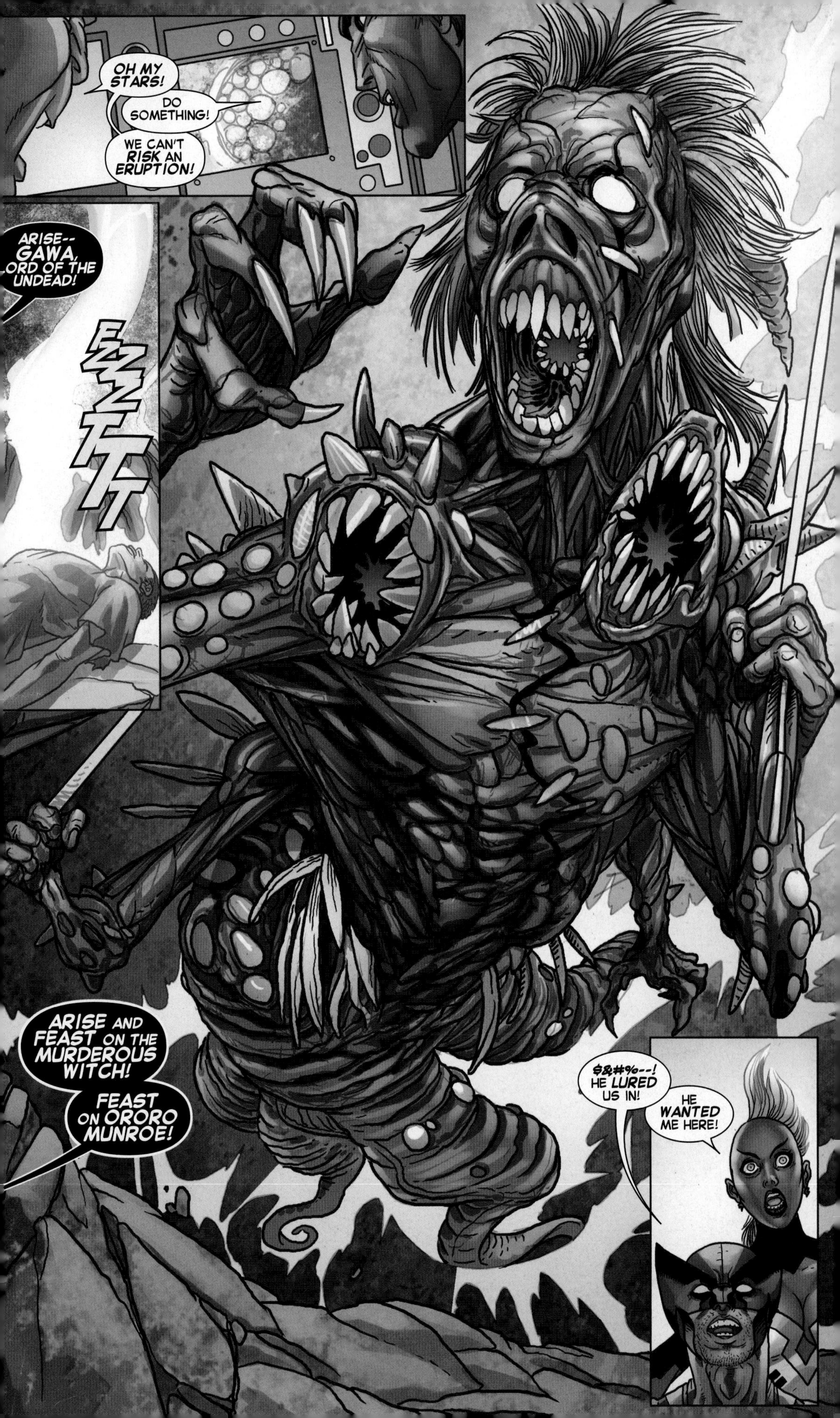
OH MY STARS!
DO SOMETHING!
WE CAN'T RISK AN ERUPTION!
ARISE-- GAWA, ORD OF THE UNDEAD!
FZZZTTT
ARISE AND FEAST ON THE MURDEROUS WITCH!
FEAST ON ORORO MUNROE!
$&#%--! HE LURED US IN!
HE WANTED ME HERE!

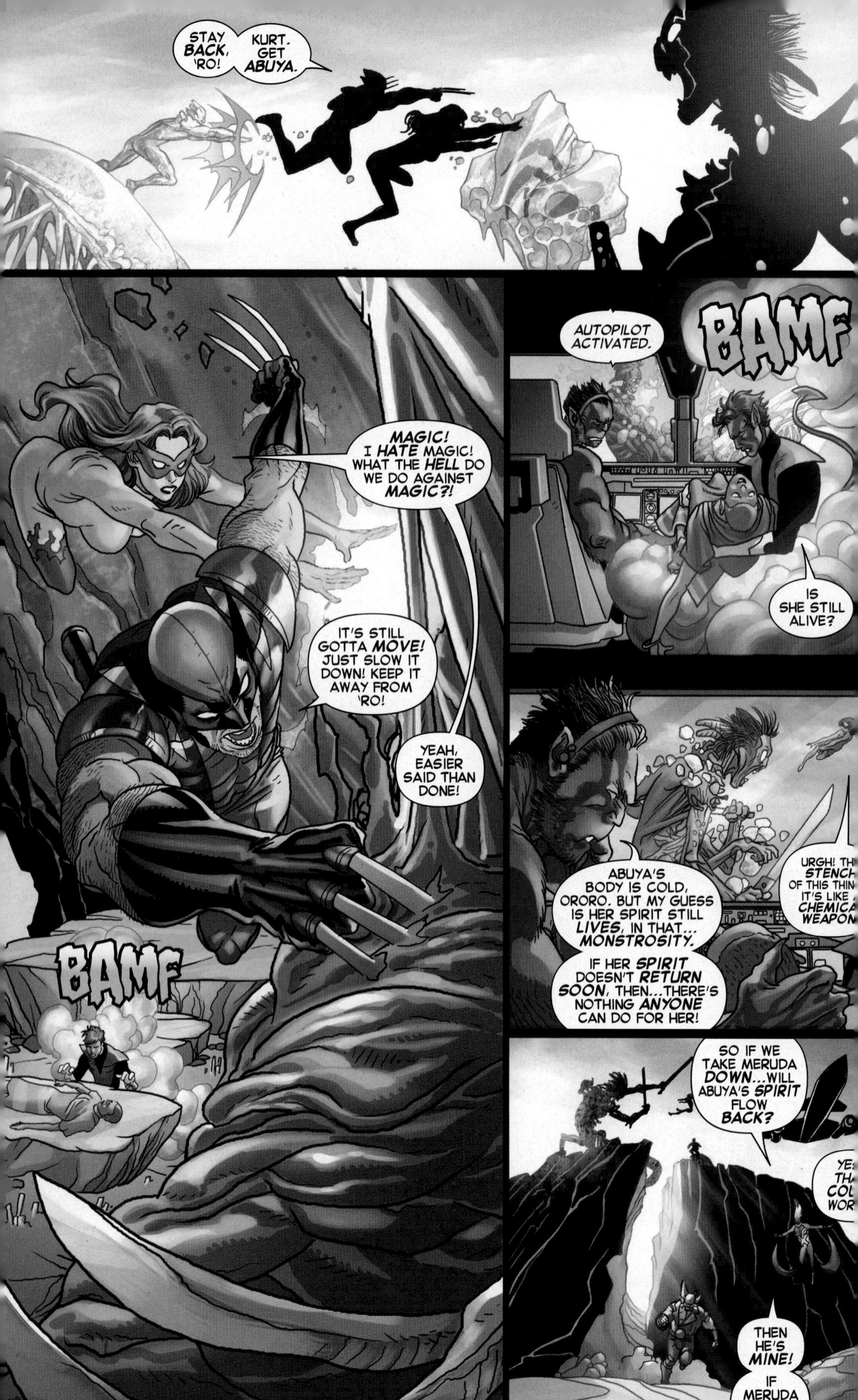

STAY BACK, 'RO!
KURT. GET ABUYA.
MAGIC! I HATE MAGIC! WHAT THE HELL DO WE DO AGAINST MAGIC?!
IT'S STILL GOTTA MOVE! JUST SLOW IT DOWN! KEEP IT AWAY FROM 'RO!
YEAH, EASIER SAID THAN DONE!
BAMF
AUTOPILOT ACTIVATED.
BAMF
IS SHE STILL ALIVE?
ABUYA'S BODY IS COLD, ORORO. BUT MY GUESS IS HER SPIRIT STILL LIVES, IN THAT... MONSTROSITY.
IF HER SPIRIT DOESN'T RETURN SOON, THEN...THERE'S NOTHING ANYONE CAN DO FOR HER!
SO IF WE TAKE MERUDA DOWN...WILL ABUYA'S SPIRIT FLOW BACK?
THEN HE'S MINE!
IF MERUDA WANTS WAR...

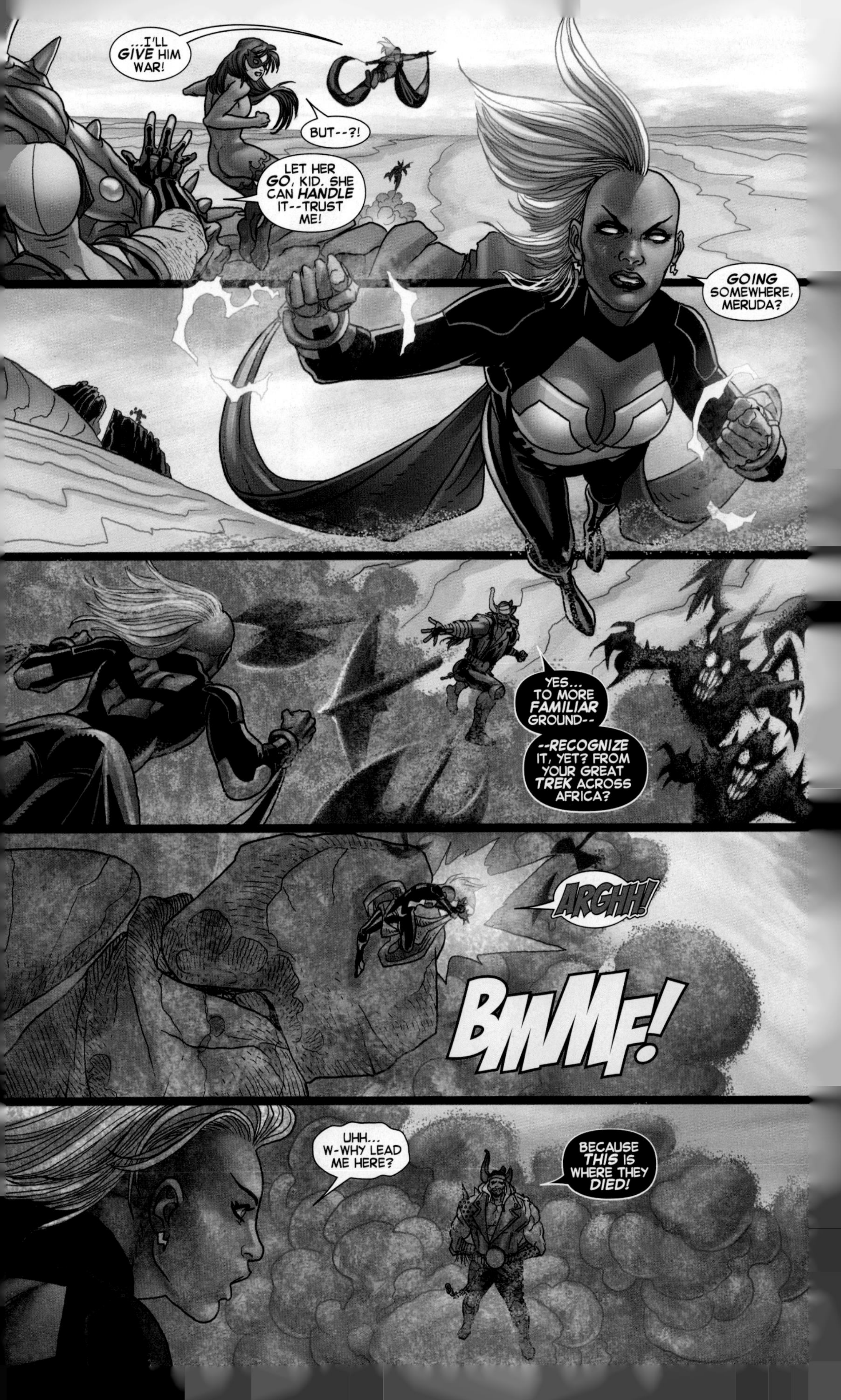

...I'LL GIVE HIM WAR!
BUT--?!
LET HER GO, KID. SHE CAN HANDLE IT--TRUST ME!
GOING SOMEWHERE, MERUDA?
YES... TO MORE FAMILIAR GROUND--
--RECOGNIZE IT, YET? FROM YOUR GREAT TREK ACROSS AFRICA?
ARGHH!
BMMF!
UHH... W-WHY LEAD ME HERE?
BECAUSE THIS IS WHERE THEY DIED!

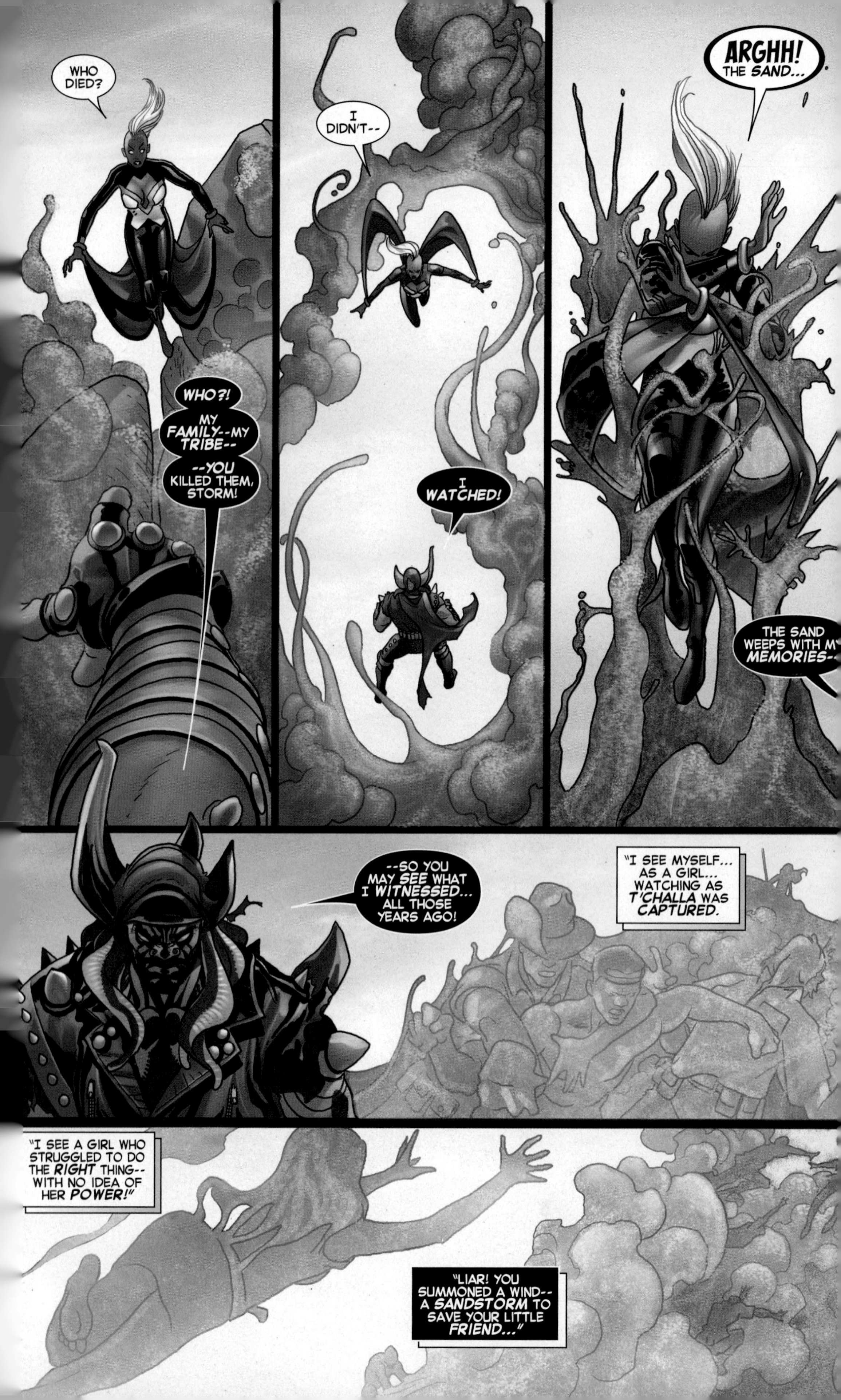

WHO DIED?
WHO?! MY FAMILY--MY TRIBE--
--YOU KILLED THEM, STORM!
I DIDN'T--
I WATCHED!
ARGHH! THE SAND...
THE SAND WEEPS WITH M MEMORIES-
--SO YOU MAY SEE WHAT I WITNESSED... ALL THOSE YEARS AGO!
"I SEE MYSELF... AS A GIRL... WATCHING AS T'CHALLA WAS CAPTURED.
"I SEE A GIRL WHO STRUGGLED TO DO THE RIGHT THING--WITH NO IDEA OF HER POWER!"
"LIAR! YOU SUMMONED A WIND--A SANDSTORM TO SAVE YOUR LITTLE FRIEND..."

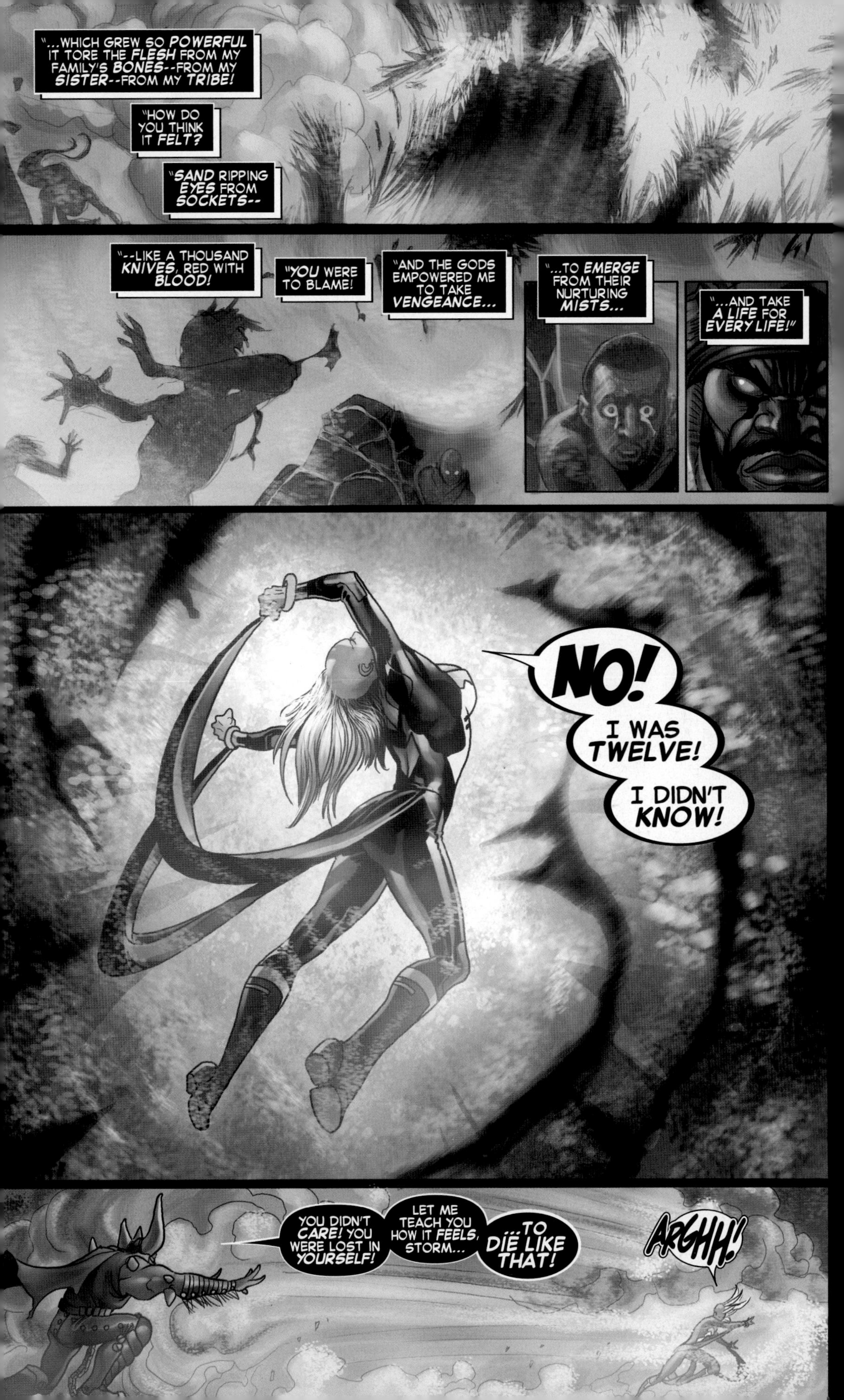
"...WHICH GREW SO POWERFUL IT TORE THE FLESH FROM MY FAMILY'S BONES--FROM MY SISTER--FROM MY TRIBE!
"HOW DO YOU THINK IT FELT?
"SAND RIPPING EYES FROM SOCKETS--
"--LIKE A THOUSAND KNIVES, RED WITH BLOOD!
"YOU WERE TO BLAME!
"AND THE GODS EMPOWERED ME TO TAKE VENGEANCE...
"...TO EMERGE FROM THEIR NURTURING MISTS...
"...AND TAKE A LIFE FOR EVERY LIFE!"
NO!
I WAS TWELVE!
I DIDN'T KNOW!
YOU DIDN'T CARE! YOU WERE LOST IN YOURSELF!
LET ME TEACH YOU HOW IT FEELS, STORM...
...TO DIE LIKE THAT!
ARGHH!

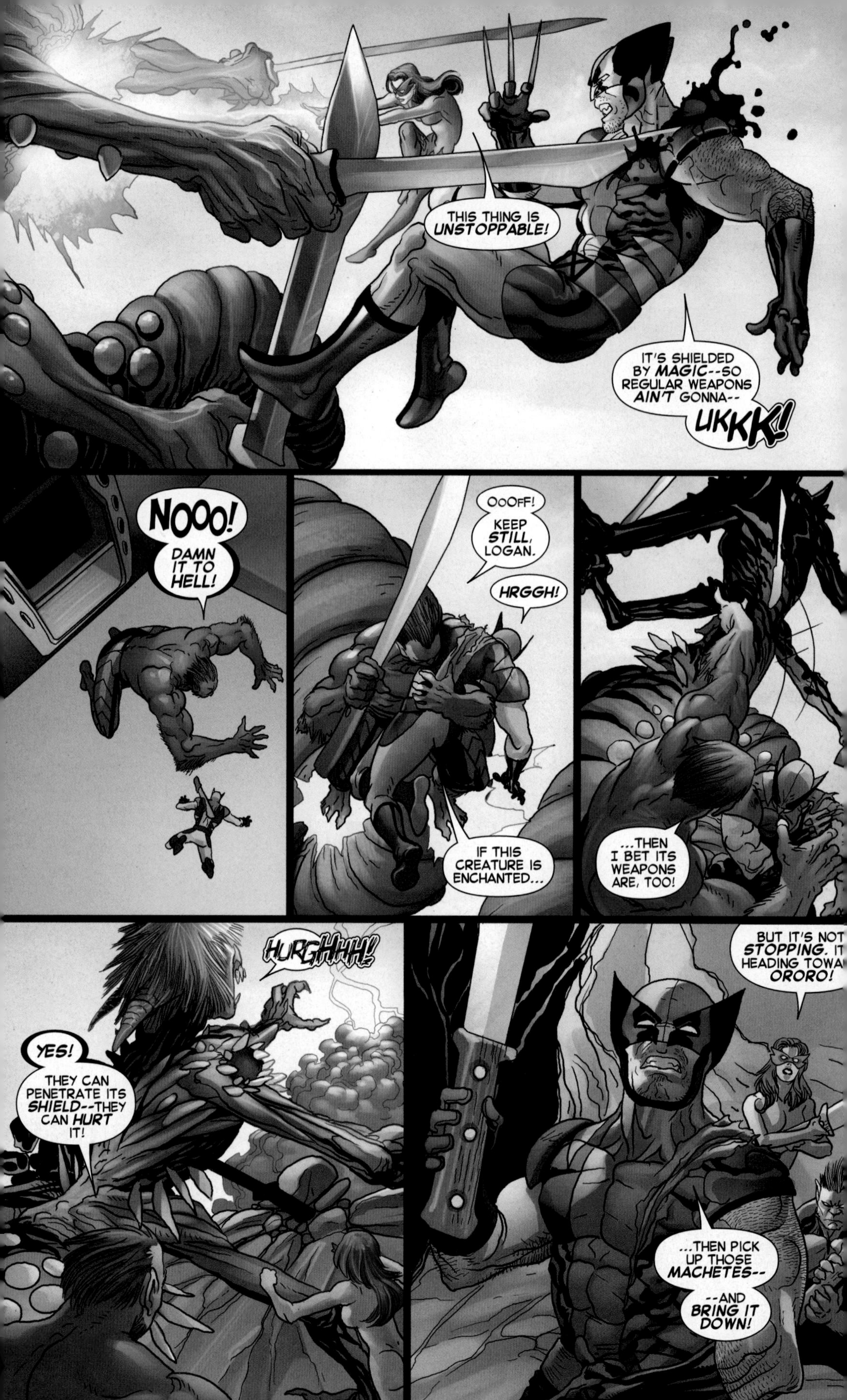
THIS THING IS UNSTOPPABLE!
IT'S SHIELDED BY MAGIC--SO REGULAR WEAPONS AIN'T GONNA--
UKKK!
NOOO!
DAMN IT TO HELL!
OOOFF! KEEP STILL, LOGAN.
HRGGH!
IF THIS CREATURE IS ENCHANTED...
...THEN I BET ITS WEAPONS ARE, TOO!
HURGHHH!
YES!
THEY CAN PENETRATE ITS SHIELD--THEY CAN HURT IT!
BUT IT'S NOT STOPPING. IT HEADING TOWA ORORO!
...THEN PICK UP THOSE MACHETES--
--AND BRING IT DOWN!

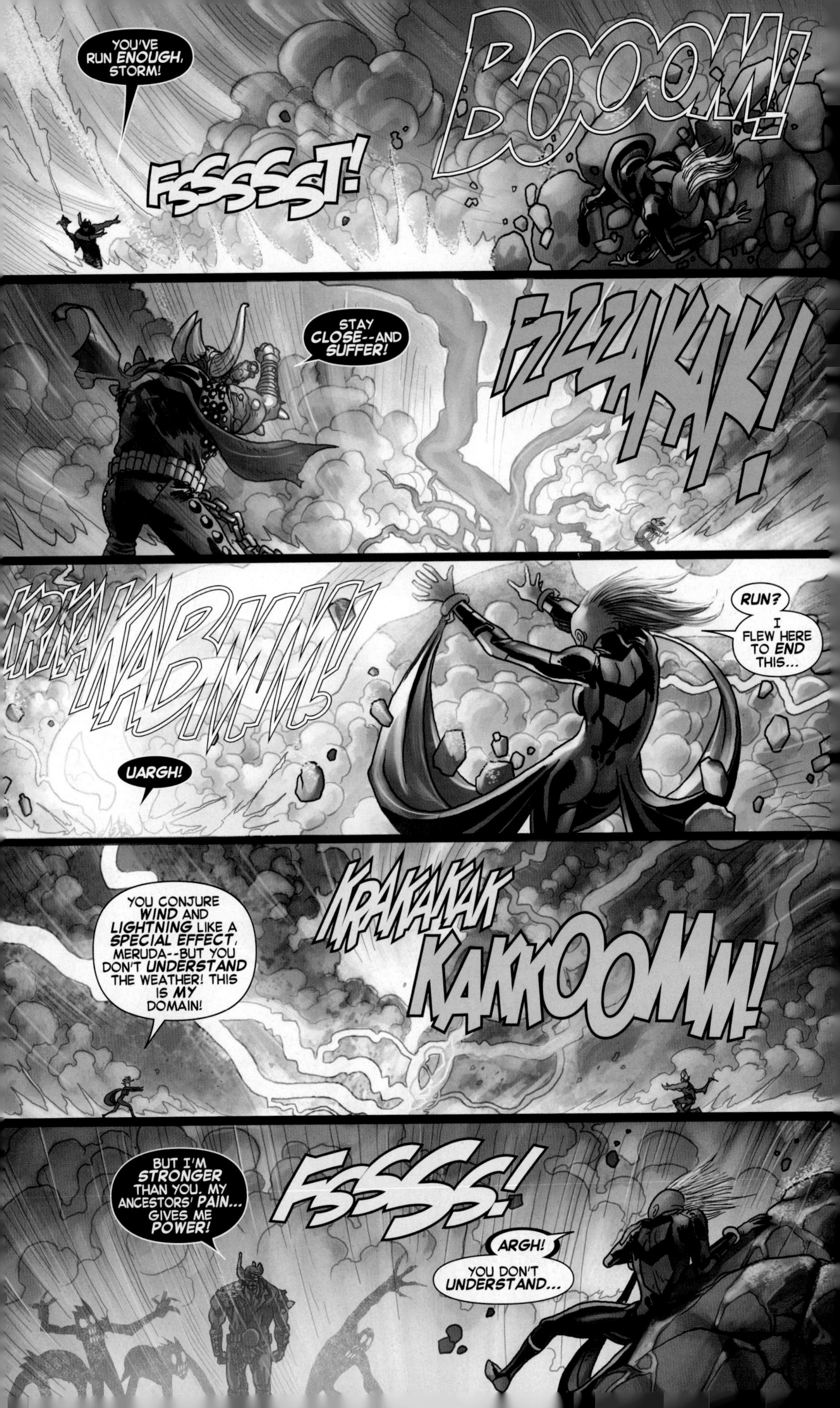
YOU'VE RUN ENOUGH, STORM!
BOOOM!
FSSSSST!
STAY CLOSE--AND SUFFER!
FZZZAKAK!
KRAKAKABOOOM!
RUN?
I FLEW HERE TO END THIS...
UARGH!
YOU CONJURE WIND AND LIGHTNING LIKE A SPECIAL EFFECT, MERUDA--BUT YOU DON'T UNDERSTAND THE WEATHER! THIS IS MY DOMAIN!
KRAKAKAK
KAKROOMM!
BUT I'M STRONGER THAN YOU. MY ANCESTORS' PAIN... GIVES ME POWER!
FSSSS!
ARGH!
YOU DON'T UNDERSTAND...

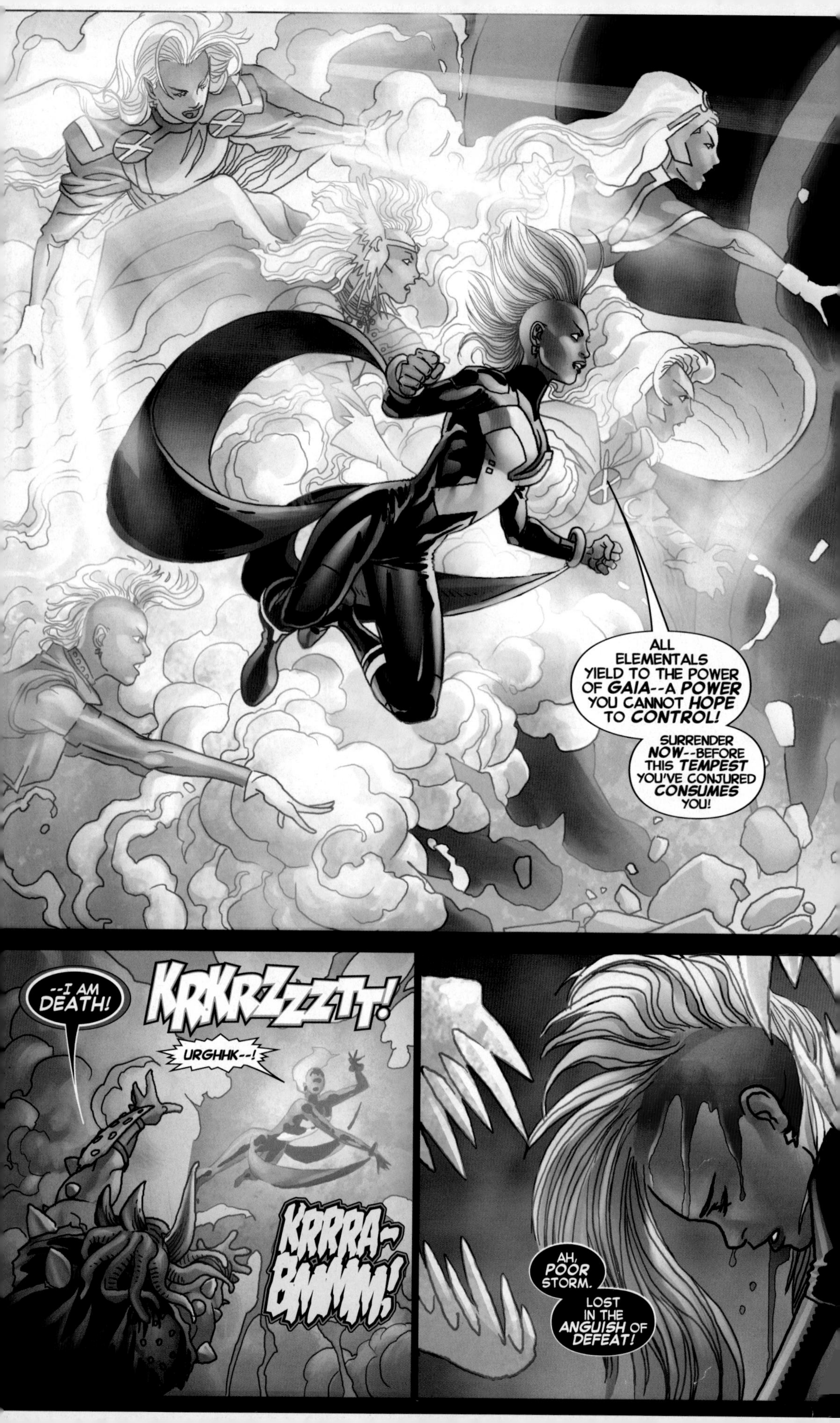
ALL ELEMENTALS YIELD TO THE POWER OF GAIA--A POWER YOU CANNOT HOPE TO CONTROL!
SURRENDER NOW--BEFORE THIS TEMPEST YOU'VE CONJURED CONSUMES YOU!
--I AM DEATH!
KRKRZZZTT!
URGHHK--!
KRRRA-BMMM!
AH, POOR STORM.
LOST IN THE ANGUISH OF DEFEAT!

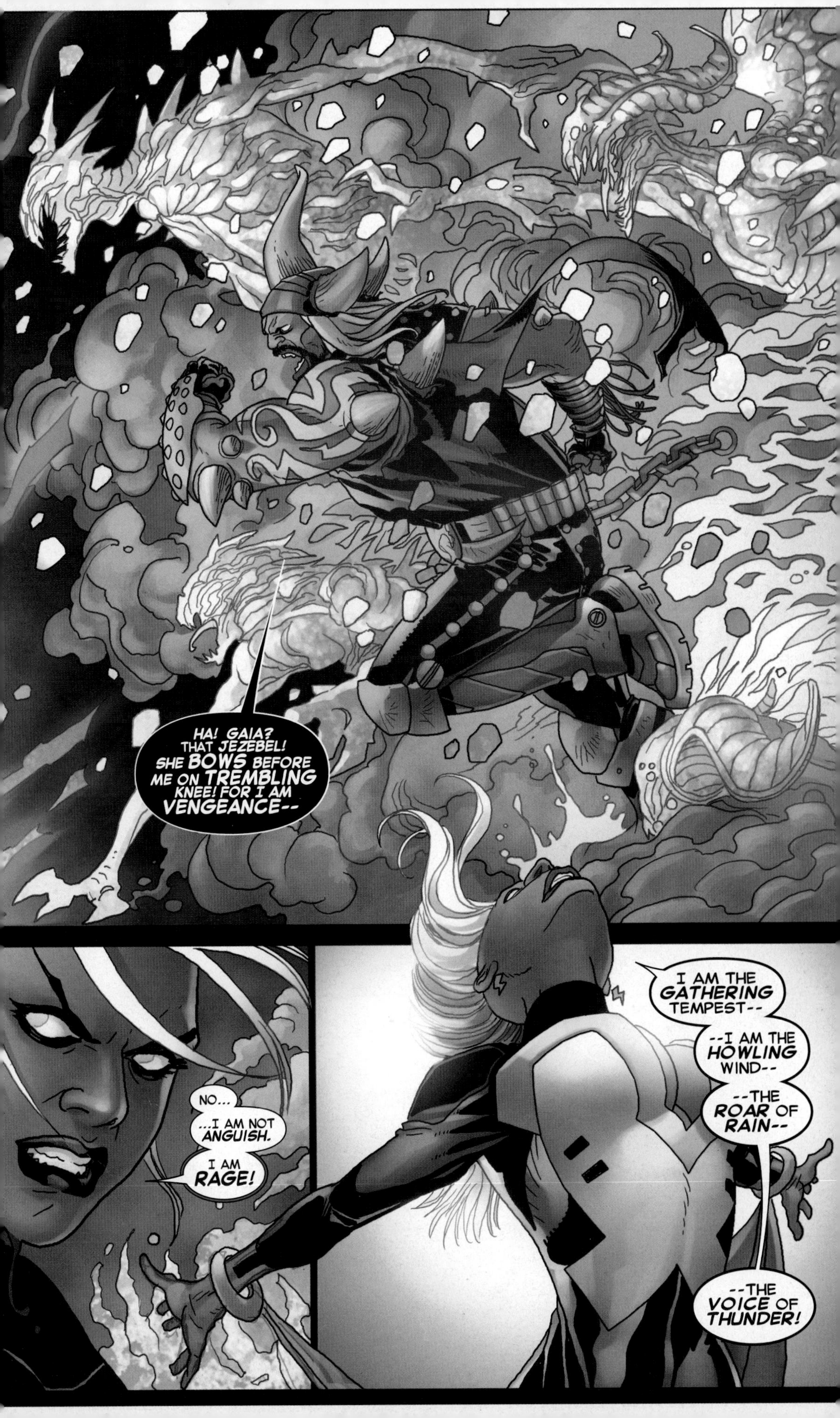
HA! GAIA? THAT JEZEBEL! SHE BOWS BEFORE ME ON TREMBLING KNEE! FOR I AM VENGEANCE--
NO...
...I AM NOT ANGUISH.
I AM RAGE!
I AM THE GATHERING TEMPEST--
--I AM THE HOWLING WIND--
--THE ROAR OF RAIN--
--THE VOICE OF THUNDER!

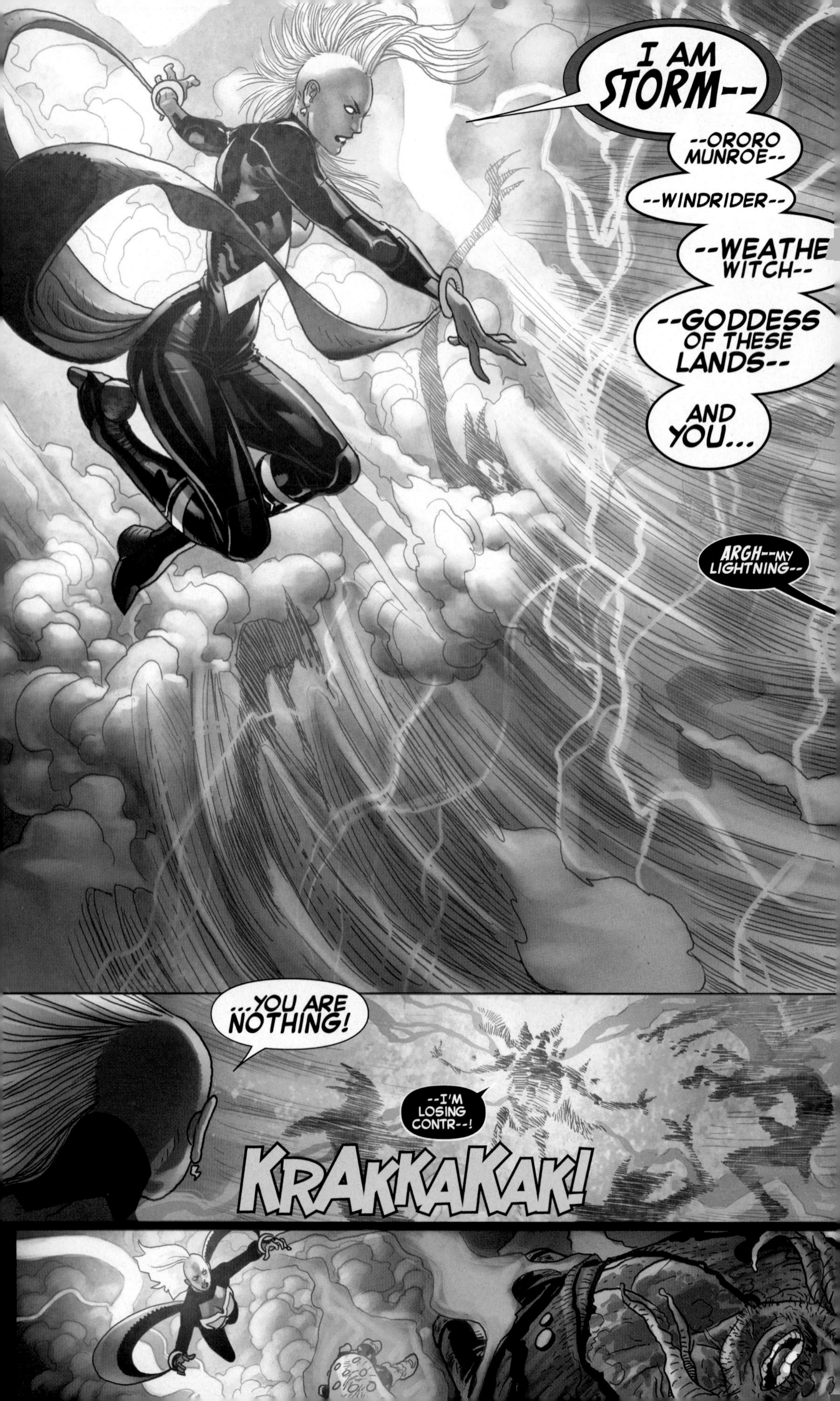
I AM STORM--
--ORORO MUNROE--
--WINDRIDER--
--WEATHE WITCH--
--GODDESS OF THESE LANDS--
AND YOU...
ARGH--MY LIGHTNING--
...YOU ARE NOTHING!
--I'M LOSING CONTR--!
KRAKKAKAK!

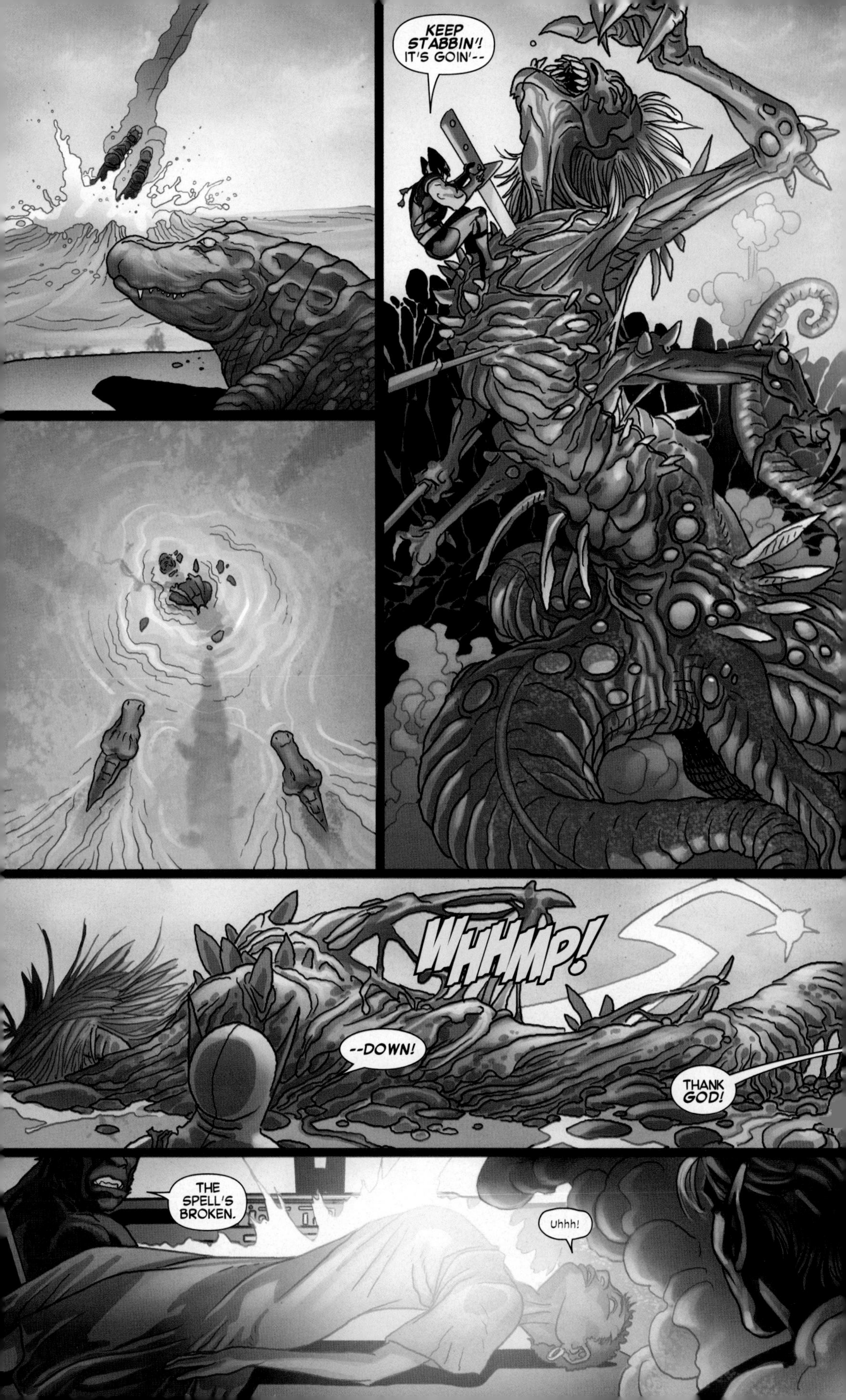
KEEP STABBIN'! IT'S GOIN'--
WHHMP!
--DOWN!
THANK GOD!
THE SPELL'S BROKEN.
Uhhh!

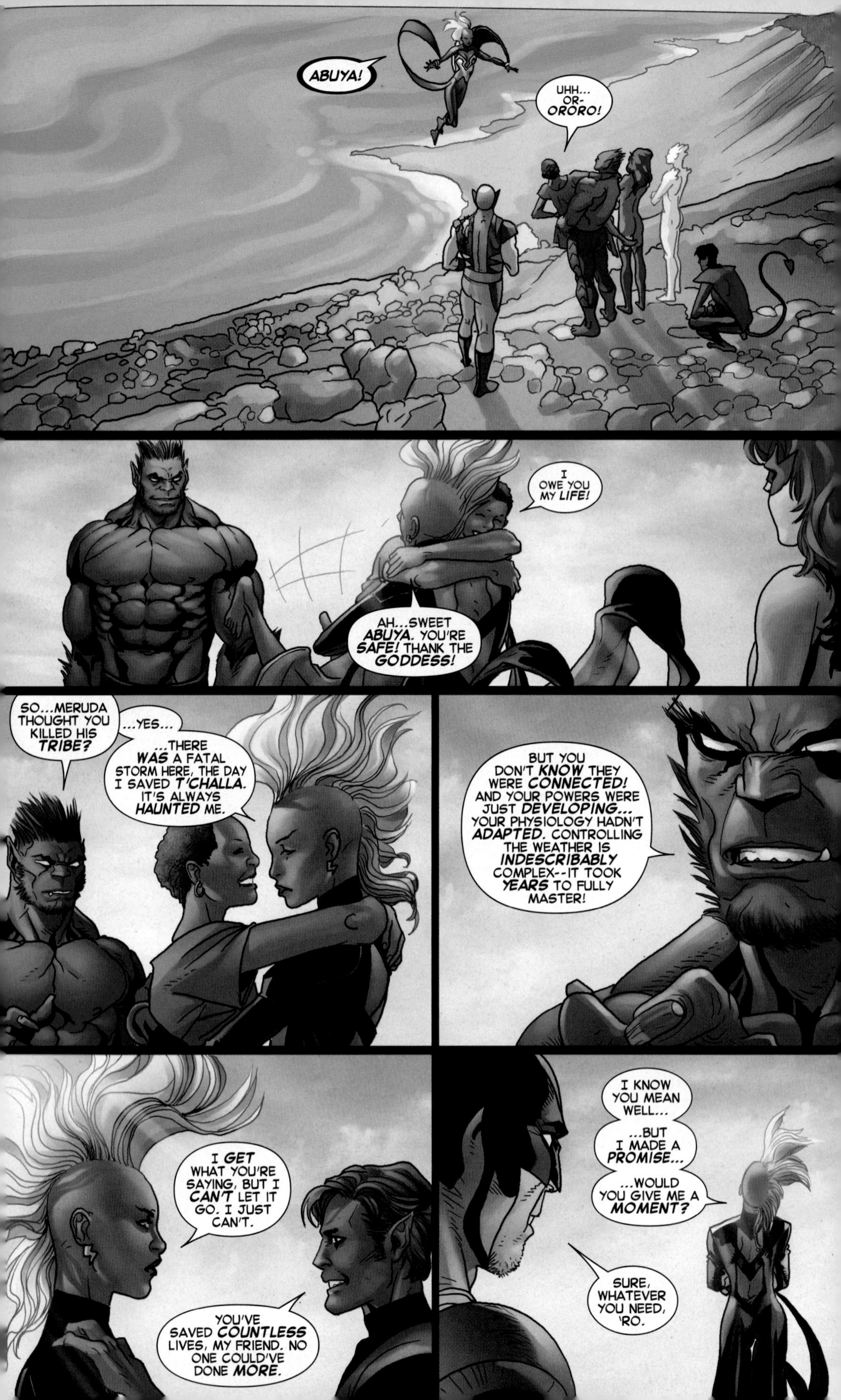
ABUYA!
UHH... OR- ORORO!
I OWE YOU MY LIFE!
AH...SWEET ABUYA. YOU'RE SAFE! THANK THE GODDESS!
SO...MERUDA THOUGHT YOU KILLED HIS TRIBE?
...YES...
...THERE WAS A FATAL STORM HERE, THE DAY I SAVED T'CHALLA. IT'S ALWAYS HAUNTED ME.
BUT YOU DON'T KNOW THEY WERE CONNECTED! AND YOUR POWERS WERE JUST DEVELOPING... YOUR PHYSIOLOGY HADN'T ADAPTED. CONTROLLING THE WEATHER IS INDESCRIBABLY COMPLEX--IT TOOK YEARS TO FULLY MASTER!
I GET WHAT YOU'RE SAYING, BUT I CAN'T LET IT GO. I JUST CAN'T.
YOU'VE SAVED COUNTLESS LIVES, MY FRIEND. NO ONE COULD'VE DONE MORE.
I KNOW YOU MEAN WELL...
...BUT I MADE A PROMISE...
...WOULD YOU GIVE ME A MOMENT?
SURE, WHATEVER YOU NEED, 'RO.

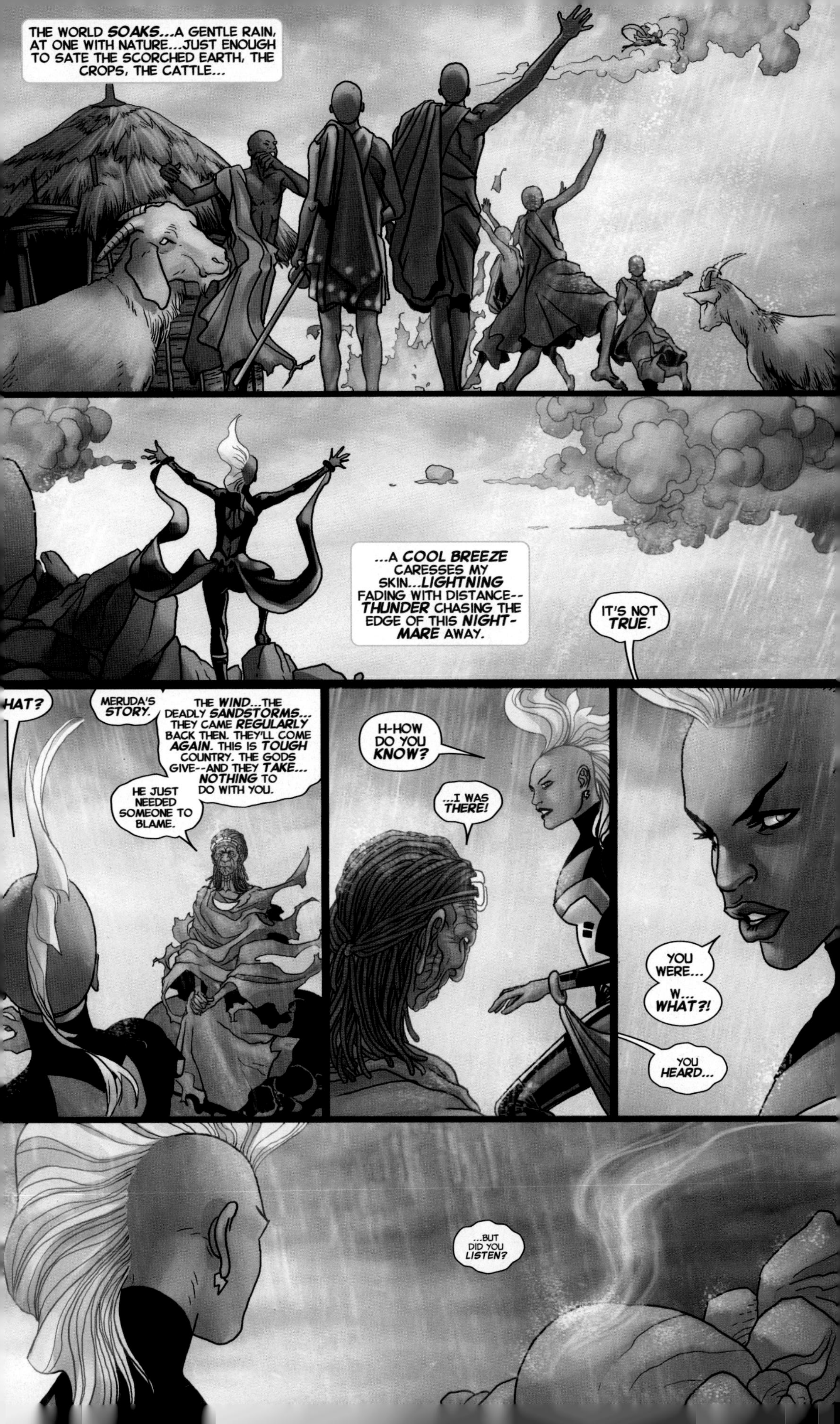
THE WORLD SOAKS...A GENTLE RAIN, AT ONE WITH NATURE...JUST ENOUGH TO SATE THE SCORCHED EARTH, THE CROPS, THE CATTLE...
...A COOL BREEZE CARESSES MY SKIN...LIGHTNING FADING WITH DISTANCE--THUNDER CHASING THE EDGE OF THIS NIGHT-MARE AWAY.
IT'S NOT TRUE.
HAT?
MERUDA'S STORY.
THE WIND...THE DEADLY SANDSTORMS... THEY CAME REGULARLY BACK THEN. THEY'LL COME AGAIN. THIS IS TOUGH COUNTRY. THE GODS GIVE--AND THEY TAKE... NOTHING TO DO WITH YOU.
HE JUST NEEDED SOMEONE TO BLAME.
H-HOW DO YOU KNOW?
...I WAS THERE!
YOU WERE...
W... WHAT?!
YOU HEARD...
...BUT DID YOU LISTEN?

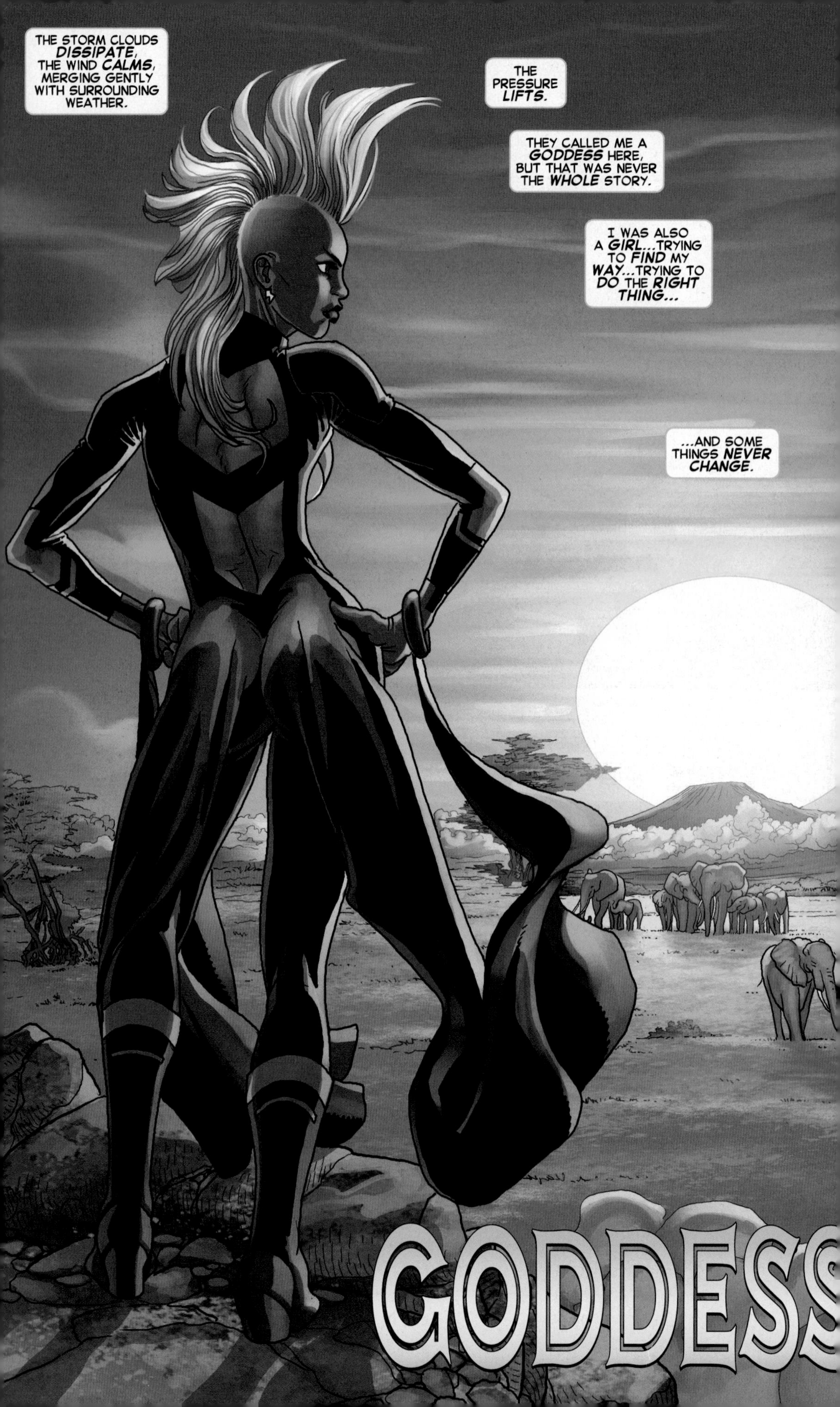
THE STORM CLOUDS DISSIPATE, THE WIND CALMS, MERGING GENTLY WITH SURROUNDING WEATHER.
THE PRESSURE LIFTS.
THEY CALLED ME A GODDESS HERE, BUT THAT WAS NEVER THE WHOLE STORY.
I WAS ALSO A GIRL...TRYING TO FIND MY WAY...TRYING TO DO THE RIGHT THING...
...AND SOME THINGS NEVER CHANGE.
GODDESS

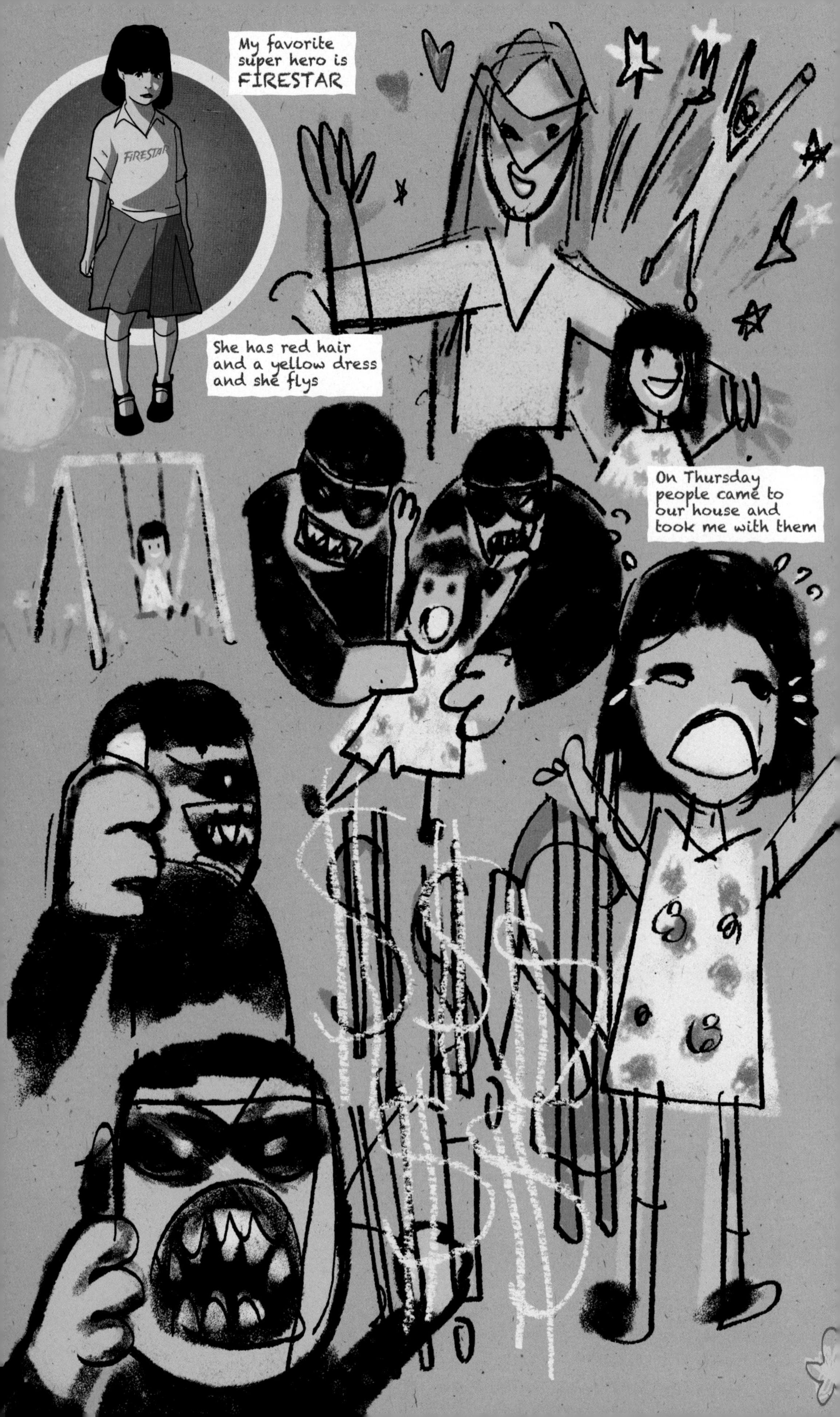
My favorite super hero is FIRESTAR
FIRESTAR
She has red hair and a yellow dress and she flys
On Thursday people came to our house and took me with them

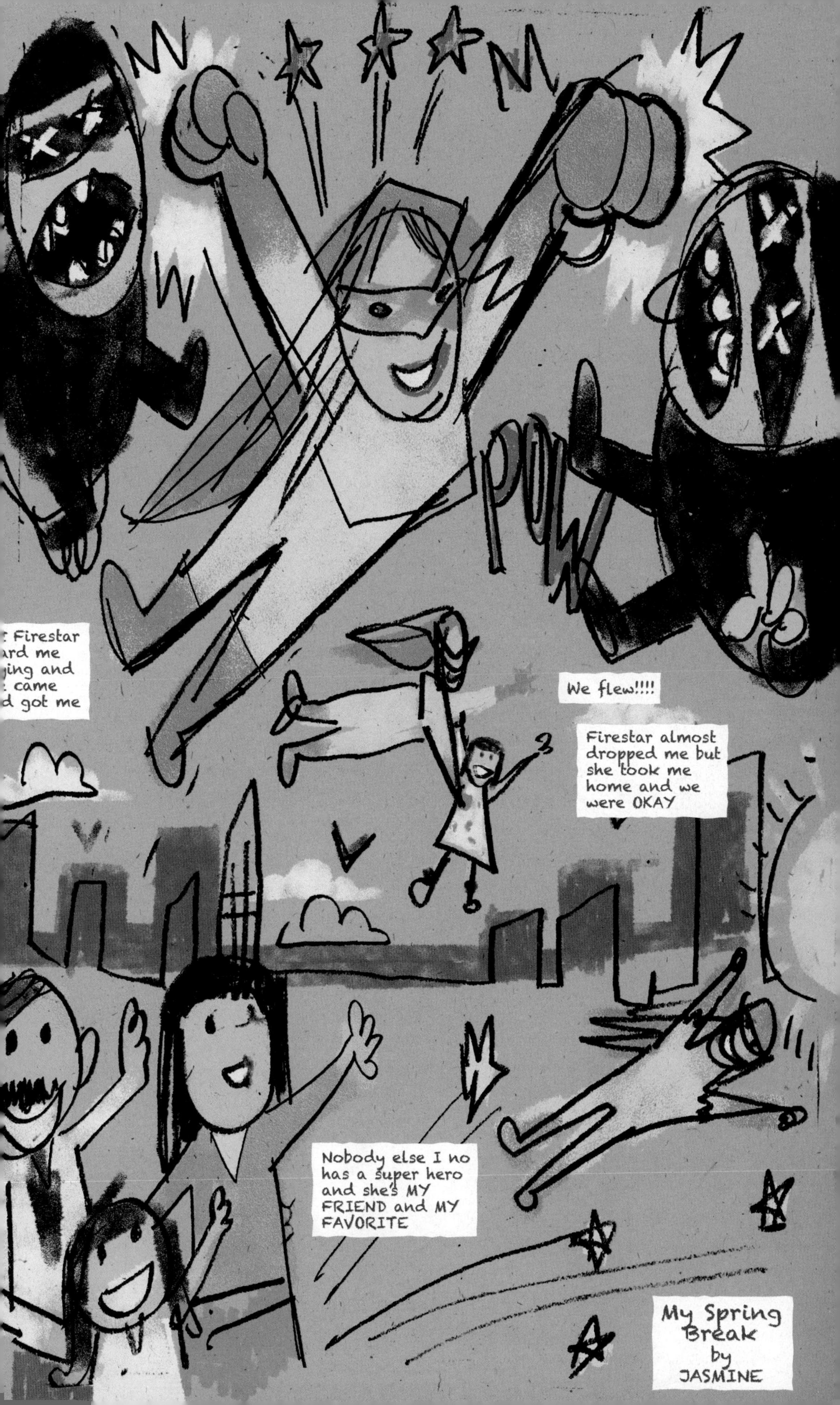

POW
Firestar
heard me
crying and
came
and got me
We flew!!!!
Firestar almost dropped me but she took me home and we were OKAY
Nobody else I no has a super hero and she's MY FRIEND and MY FAVORITE
My Spring Break by JASMINE

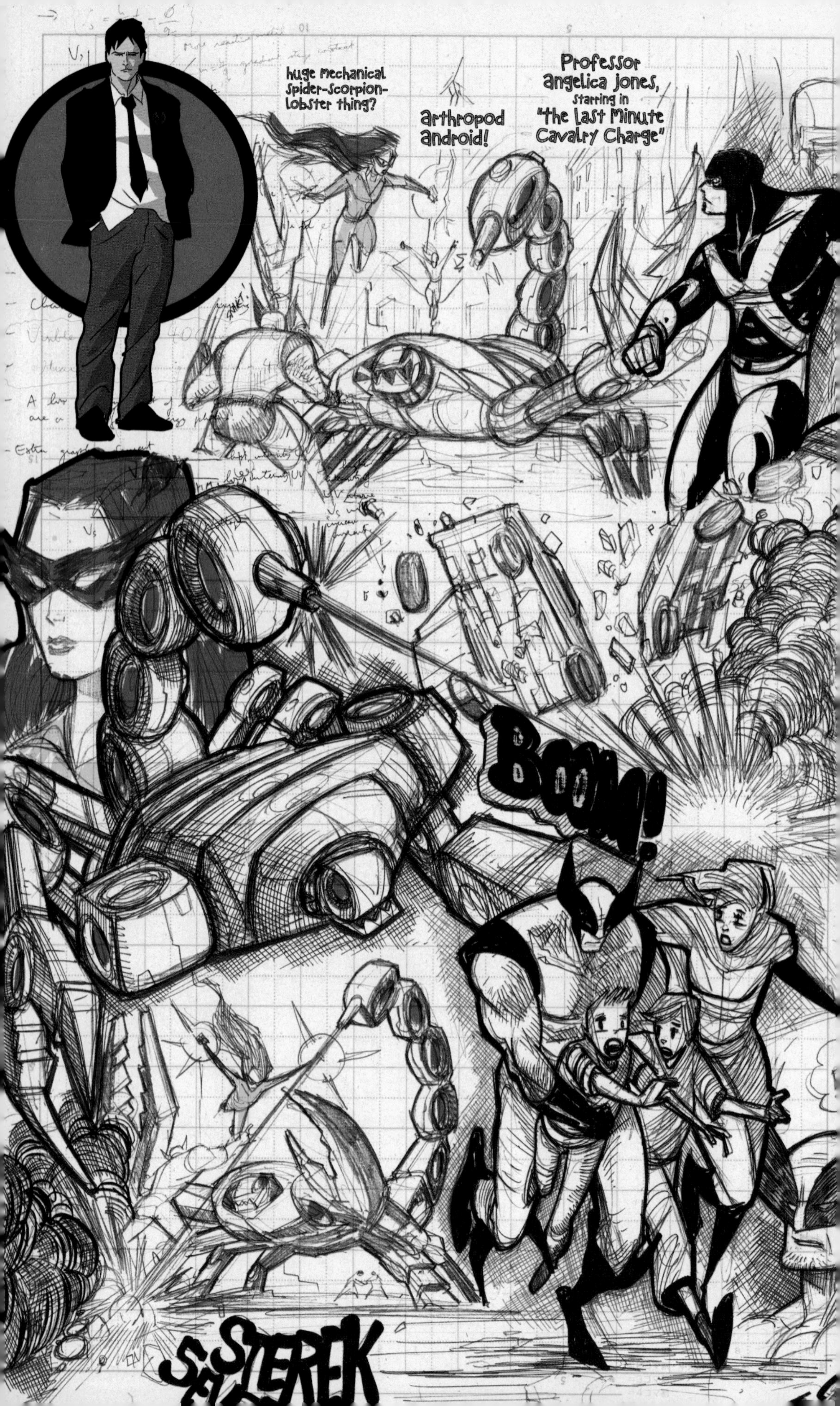

huge mechanical Spider-Scorpion-lobster thing?
arthropod android!
Professor angelica jones, starring in "the Last Minute Cavalry Charge"
BOOM!
SZEREK

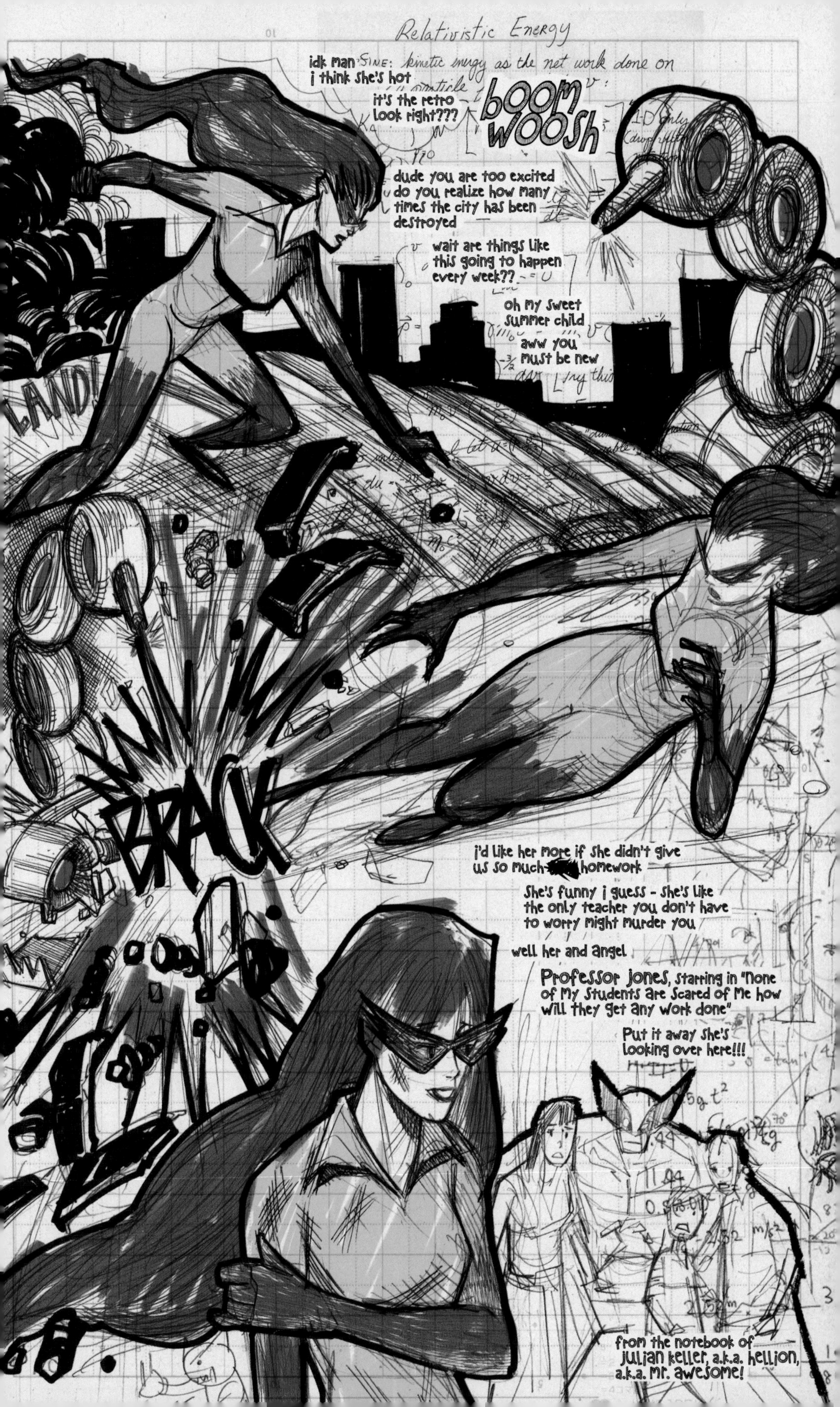
Relativistic Energy
idk man i think she's hot
it's the retro look right???
boom woosh
dude you are too excited do you realize how many times the city has been destroyed
wait are things like this going to happen every week??
oh my sweet summer child
aww you must be new
i'd like her more if she didn't give us so much [redacted] homework
she's funny i guess - she's like the only teacher you don't have to worry might murder you
well her and angel
Professor jones, starring in "None of My Students are Scared of Me how will they get any work done"
Put it away she's looking over here!!!
from the notebook of julian keller, a.k.a. hellion, a.k.a. mr. awesome!

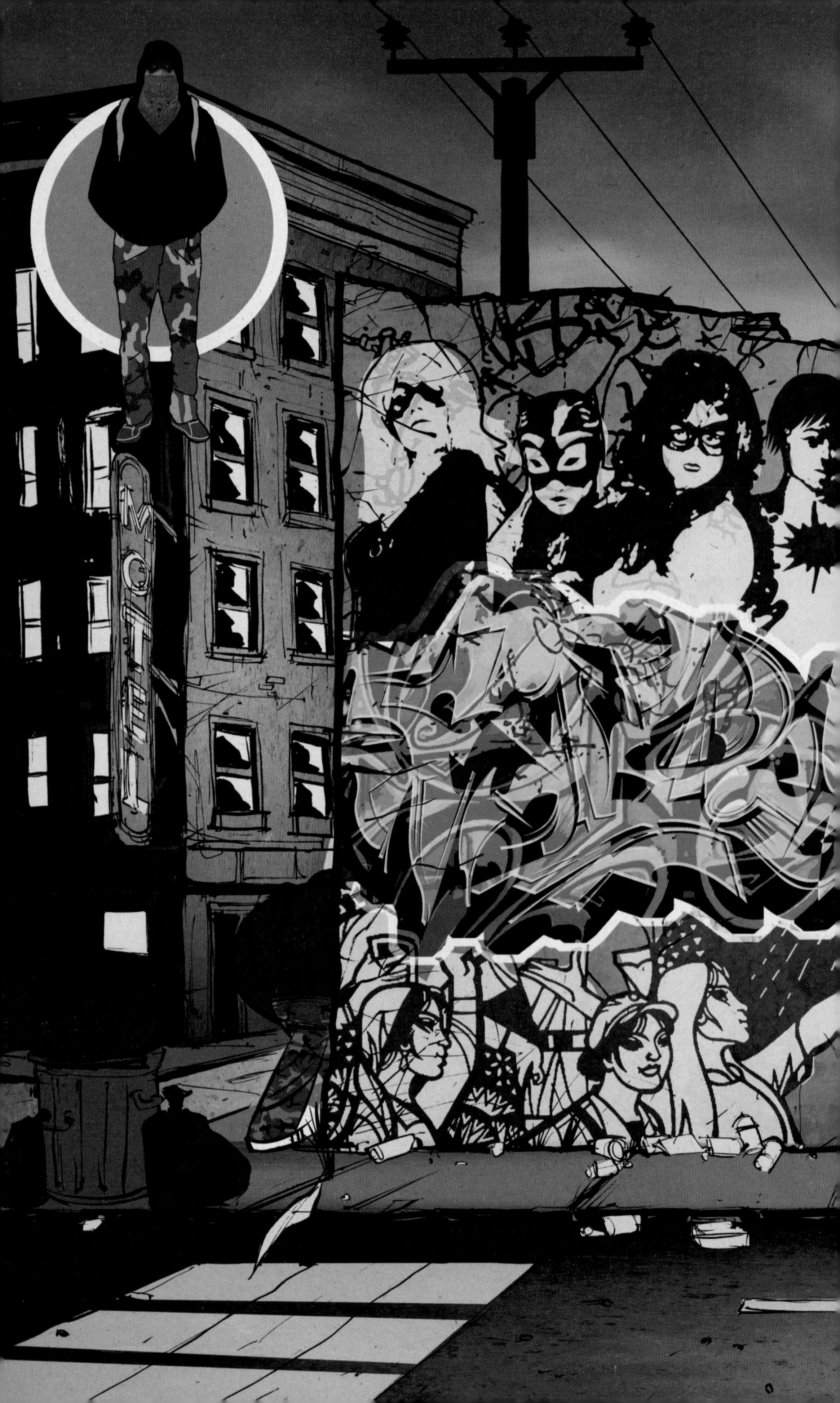
MOTEL

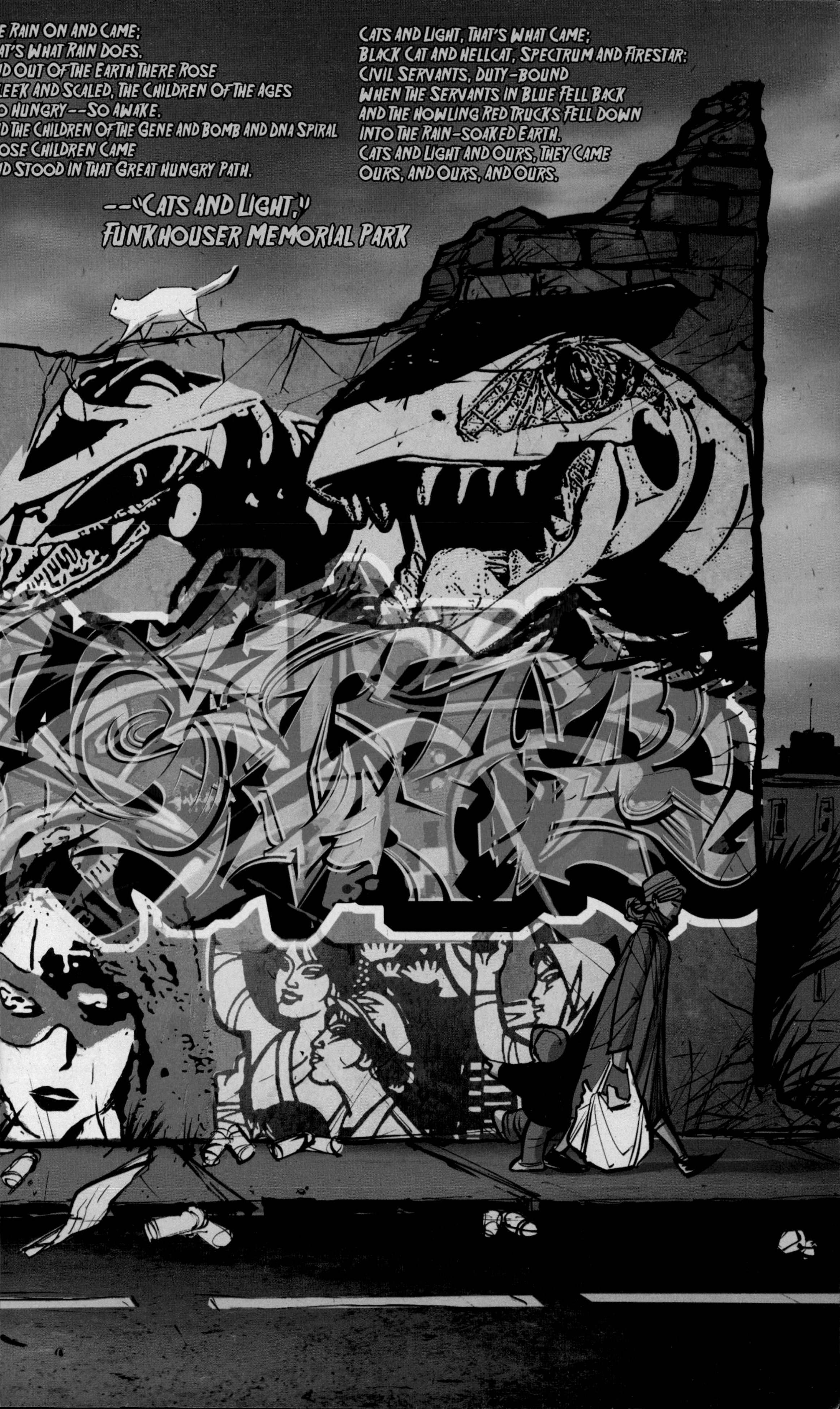
E RAIN ON AND CAME;
AT'S WHAT RAIN DOES.
D OUT OF THE EARTH THERE ROSE
LEEK AND SCALED, THE CHILDREN OF THE AGES
O HUNGRY--SO AWAKE.
D THE CHILDREN OF THE GENE AND BOMB AND DNA SPIRAL
OSE CHILDREN CAME
D STOOD IN THAT GREAT HUNGRY PATH.
CATS AND LIGHT, THAT'S WHAT CAME;
BLACK CAT AND HELLCAT, SPECTRUM AND FIRESTAR:
CIVIL SERVANTS, DUTY-BOUND
WHEN THE SERVANTS IN BLUE FELL BACK
AND THE HOWLING RED TRUCKS FELL DOWN
INTO THE RAIN-SOAKED EARTH.
CATS AND LIGHT AND OURS, THEY CAME
OURS, AND OURS, AND OURS.
--"CATS AND LIGHT,"
FUNKHOUSER MEMORIAL PARK

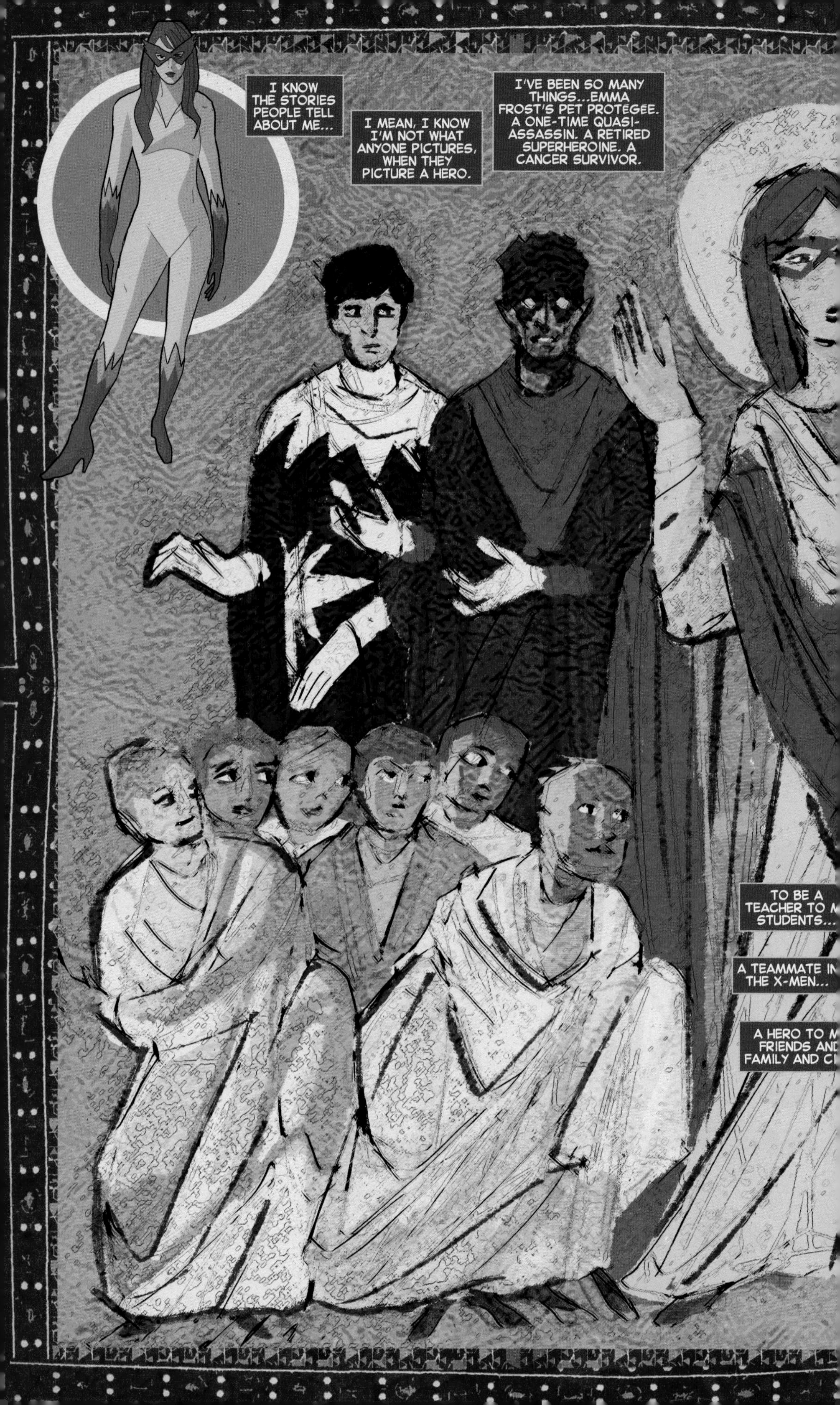
I KNOW THE STORIES PEOPLE TELL ABOUT ME...
I MEAN, I KNOW I'M NOT WHAT ANYONE PICTURES, WHEN THEY PICTURE A HERO.
I'VE BEEN SO MANY THINGS...EMMA FROST'S PET PROTEGEE. A ONE-TIME QUASI-ASSASSIN. A RETIRED SUPERHEROINE. A CANCER SURVIVOR.
TO BE A TEACHER TO M STUDENTS...
A TEAMMATE IN THE X-MEN...
A HERO TO M FRIENDS AND FAMILY AND CI

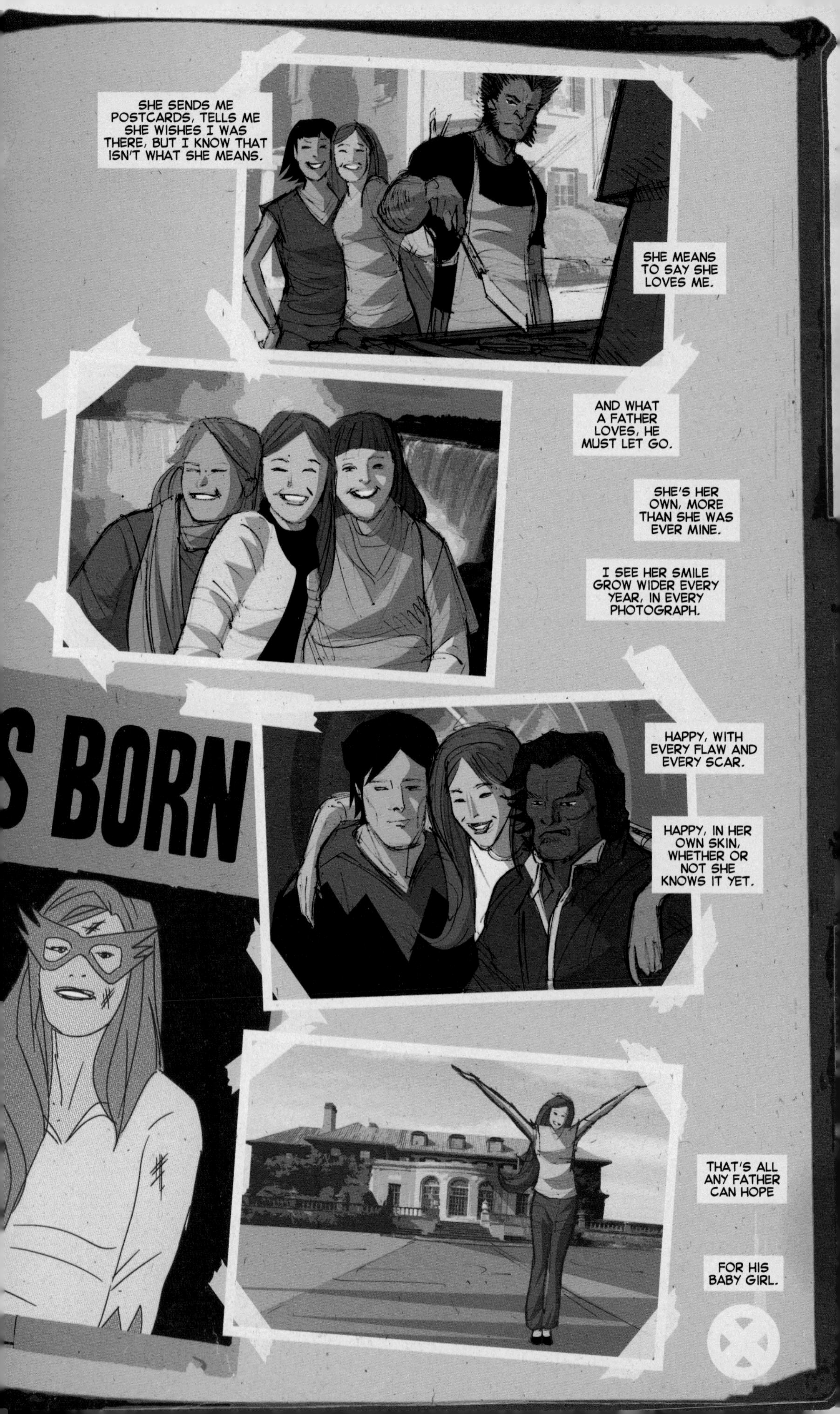
SHE SENDS ME POSTCARDS, TELLS ME SHE WISHES I WAS THERE, BUT I KNOW THAT ISN'T WHAT SHE MEANS.
SHE MEANS TO SAY SHE LOVES ME.
AND WHAT A FATHER LOVES, HE MUST LET GO.
SHE'S HER OWN, MORE THAN SHE WAS EVER MINE.
I SEE HER SMILE GROW WIDER EVERY YEAR, IN EVERY PHOTOGRAPH.
S BORN
HAPPY, WITH EVERY FLAW AND EVERY SCAR.
HAPPY, IN HER OWN SKIN, WHETHER OR NOT SHE KNOWS IT YET.
THAT'S ALL ANY FATHER CAN HOPE
FOR HIS BABY GIRL.

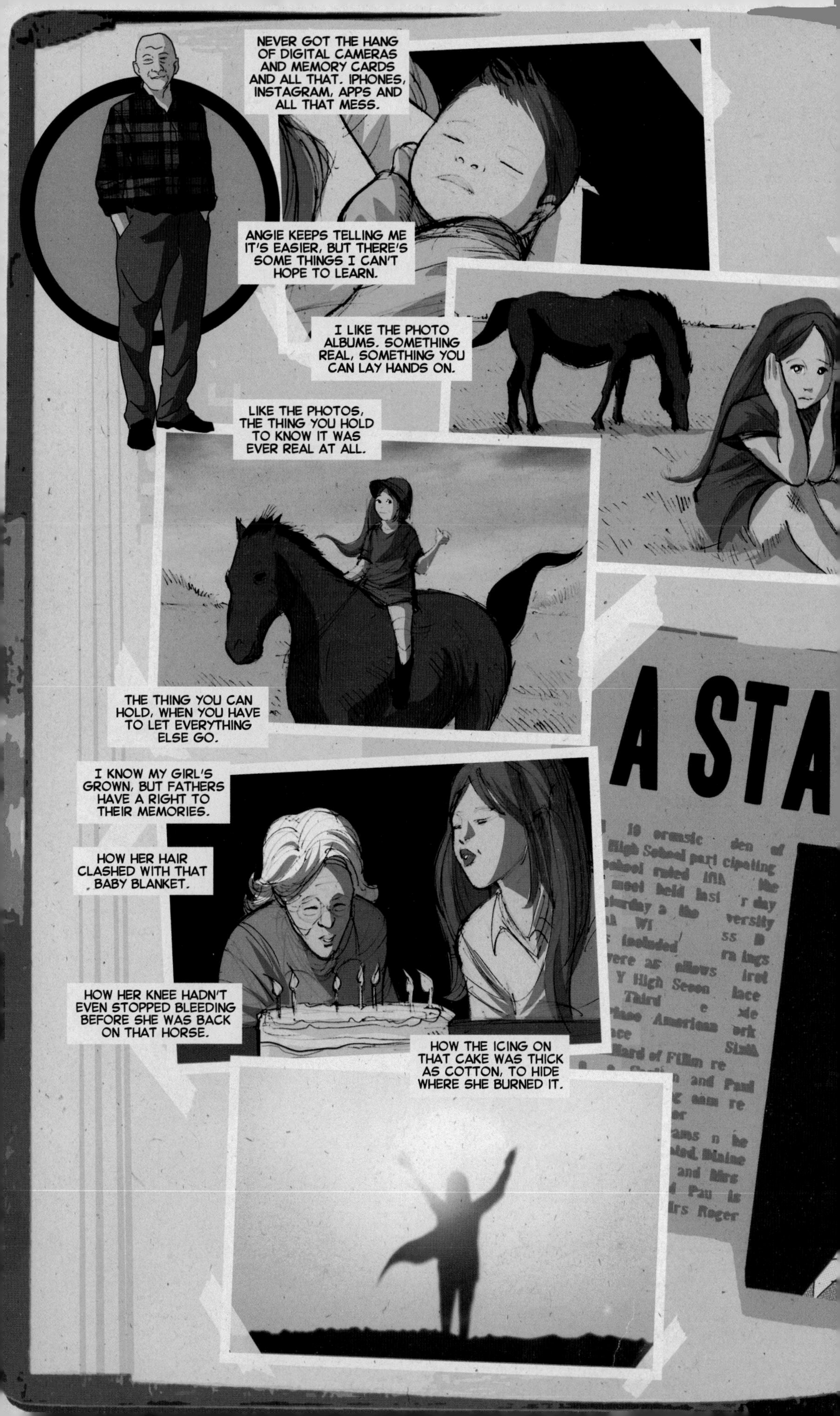
NEVER GOT THE HANG OF DIGITAL CAMERAS AND MEMORY CARDS AND ALL THAT. IPHONES, INSTAGRAM, APPS AND ALL THAT MESS.
ANGIE KEEPS TELLING ME IT'S EASIER, BUT THERE'S SOME THINGS I CAN'T HOPE TO LEARN.
I LIKE THE PHOTO ALBUMS. SOMETHING REAL, SOMETHING YOU CAN LAY HANDS ON.
LIKE THE PHOTOS, THE THING YOU HOLD TO KNOW IT WAS EVER REAL AT ALL.
THE THING YOU CAN HOLD, WHEN YOU HAVE TO LET EVERYTHING ELSE GO.
A STA
I KNOW MY GIRL'S GROWN, BUT FATHERS HAVE A RIGHT TO THEIR MEMORIES.
HOW HER HAIR CLASHED WITH THAT BABY BLANKET.
HOW HER KNEE HADN'T EVEN STOPPED BLEEDING BEFORE SHE WAS BACK ON THAT HORSE.
HOW THE ICING ON THAT CAKE WAS THICK AS COTTON, TO HIDE WHERE SHE BURNED IT.

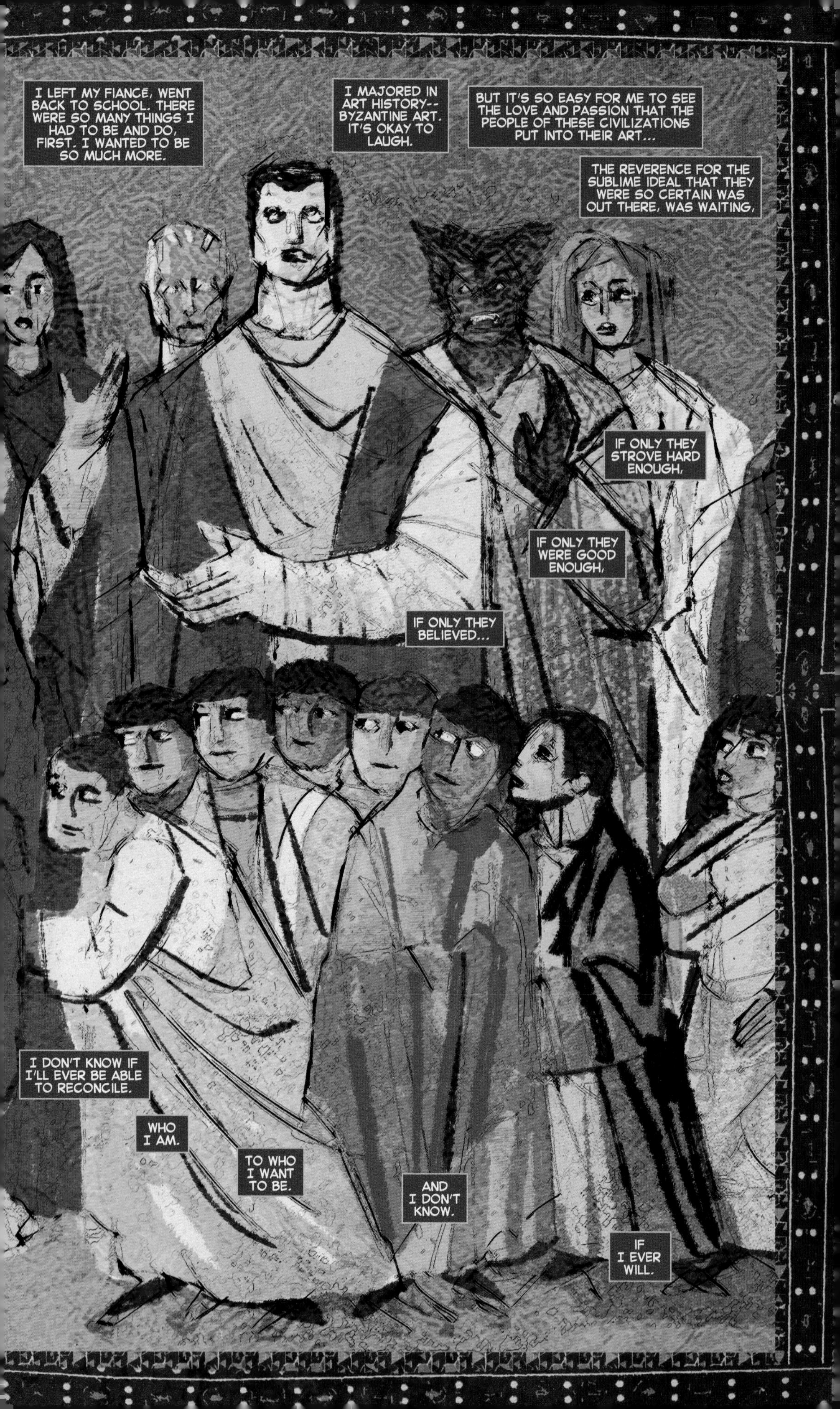
I LEFT MY FIANCÉ, WENT BACK TO SCHOOL. THERE WERE SO MANY THINGS I HAD TO BE AND DO, FIRST. I WANTED TO BE SO MUCH MORE.
I MAJORED IN ART HISTORY-- BYZANTINE ART. IT'S OKAY TO LAUGH.
BUT IT'S SO EASY FOR ME TO SEE THE LOVE AND PASSION THAT THE PEOPLE OF THESE CIVILIZATIONS PUT INTO THEIR ART...
THE REVERENCE FOR THE SUBLIME IDEAL THAT THEY WERE SO CERTAIN WAS OUT THERE, WAS WAITING,
IF ONLY THEY STROVE HARD ENOUGH,
IF ONLY THEY WERE GOOD ENOUGH,
IF ONLY THEY BELIEVED...
I DON'T KNOW IF I'LL EVER BE ABLE TO RECONCILE.
WHO I AM.
TO WHO I WANT TO BE.
AND I DON'T KNOW.
IF I EVER WILL.